HOSPITALITY
MANAGEMENT
ACCOUNTING

HOSPITALITY MANAGEMENT ACCOUNTING

FOURTH EDITION

Michael M. Coltman, MBA

VNR VAN NOSTRAND REINHOLD
New York

Library of Congress Catalog Card Number 90-40969
ISBN 0-442-00542-3

Printed in the United States of America

Van Nostrand Reinhold
115 Fifth Avenue
New York, New York 10003

Chapman & Hall
2-6 Boundary Row
London SE1 8HN, England

Thomas Nelson Australia
102 Dodds Street
South Melbourne, Victoria 3205, Australia

Nelson Canada
1120 Birchmount Road
Scarborough, Ontario M1K 5G4, Canada

16   15   14   13   12   11   10   9   8   7   6   5   4   3   2

Library of Congress Cataloging-in-Publication Data

Coltman, Michael M.
    Hospitality management accounting/Michael M. Coltman.—4th ed.
        p.   cm.
    Includes index.
    ISBN 0-442-00542-3
    1. Hotels, taverns, etc.—Accounting. 2. Food service—Accounting. 3. Managerial
accounting. I. Title.
HF5686.H75C53   1991
657′.837—dc20   90-40969
                                                                CIP

Contents

Preface to First Edition

The term *hospitality* embraces not only hotels, motels, and restaurants, but also resorts, clubs, cocktail bars, industrial and institutional feeding operations, and many similar and related businesses.

Most, if not all, of these businesses have been affected over the past several years by the worldwide growth in tourism. As governments of virtually all countries realized the economic benefits to them from tourism, they encouraged and actively promoted it. As tourism grew, so did the demand for hotel rooms, restaurants, bars, and related facilities and services.

With the growth in tourism came an expansion in the scale of hospitality industry operations. This not only occurred at the local and national level, but also at the international level since many organizations in the hospitality industry are now multinational corporations, operating around the world. With the growth in operations, resulting in increased revenue, came a growth in costs. In fact, the growth of costs has often been at a faster pace than the growth in revenue; the well-recognized inflationary trend has been a problem in the hospitality industry no less than in any other.

There are other problems in the hospitality industry. The industry has had business failures, and financing has been costly as a result of the risk and lenders' reticence to invest in the industry. Construction costs have soared, meaning that hotel room rates and restaurant menu prices have risen to the point where they frequently meet market resistance. The industry is also very labor intensive. Because of this, the productivity level, measured in average revenue per manhour worked, compares unfavorably with that of many industries. This may be inevitable due to the nature of the industry. Because of inflation the demand by employees for higher rates of pay has created a labor cost problem that the industry has not yet satisfactorily solved. Labor costs can be reduced in many industries by developing a machine to do the job. This is not easily done in the hospitality industry where human interaction is expected by guests.

For these and other reasons the industry has had to become increasingly profit and cost conscious, paying much more attention than perhaps it previously did, not only to maximizing revenue, but also minimizing costs to maintain traditional net income levels. It has had to adopt techniques of control that other industries have been using successfully for many years, and devise other controls of its own because of the industry's uniqueness. Many of these control techniques rely on an accounting, or management information, system to provide top administration with the information it needs. It is only with timely, appropriate, accurate, and meaningful information that management can act decisively to effectively run a business. Only with good information can decision making and action occur. It is with the provision of basic, meaningful information provided by the accounting system that this book is primarily concerned.

The text makes no attempt to cover the mechanics of bookkeeping. There are many other excellent books available from which the reader can learn and understand bookkeeping or basic accounting. The reader should, therefore, have some understanding of general accounting or have taken a course in basic accounting.

The book is designed and written for the student who is taking courses that are accounting oriented and related to the hospitality industry. For the student, discussion questions and problems are available at the end of each chapter. The book is also easily understood by a person presently working in the hospitality industry, or by the general reader.

The reader is also referred to the glossary at the end of the book. The glossary explains most of the technical words or terms used in accounting in the hospitality industry and which may be unfamiliar to the reader.

The chapters, are for the most part, independent of each other. They can be read or studied in sequence, but do not have to be. They can be resequenced and tailored to meet the requirements of a particular course in an educational institute.

Finally, although most of the chapters cover the chapter topics in some depth, they do not necessarily exhaust the topic covered. Many of the chapters could be expanded into an entire book of their own. The book is introductory in nature. It is hoped that the interested reader will, however, have the appetite whetted sufficiently to want to explore some of the topics in further depth on his or her own.

No book is possible without the encouragement, interest, and help of many individuals. Professor Neil R. Porta of the Hotel Administration program at the University of New Hamsphire has provided many valuable suggestions during the development of this book. His assistance is gratefully appreciated.

Preface to Fourth Edition

Another four years have gone by and the need arises again to make revisions to *Hospitality Management Accounting*. As the result of comments and suggestions from users of the book (both students and teachers), some additions have been made in this fourth edition. No material has been deleted. The following is a chapter-by-chapter summary of the changes made.

Chapter 1, Accounting Review, is unchanged. However, a new problem has been added.

Chapter 2, Understanding Financial Statements, has considerable new information inserted in the income statement section concerning the calculation of and adjustments to cost of sales, as well as new material on responsibility accounting. New material concerning balance sheet detail, presentation, and limitations has also been added to the end of the balance sheet section. Two new problems have been inserted.

Chapter 3, Analysis and Interpretation of Financial Statements, has a new section on absolute versus relative changes in comparative statement analysis. The section near the end of the chapter on operating ratios has considerable new material showing how the ratios are calculated. There are also two new problems.

Chapter 4, Ratio Analysis, has new material at the beginning of the chapter on how ratios may be expressed, how they may be compared, and who uses them. Most of the individual ratios discussed in this chapter also include new material, primarily concerned with how various users view each ratio. A new problem has also been included.

Chapter 5, Internal Control, has new sections concerning employee selection and training, product storage, and payroll control procedures. There are also two new problems.

Chapter 6, The "Bottom Up" Approach to Pricing, has considerable new material concerning traditional pricing methods at the beginning of the chapter. At the end of the section on room rates, a major new section on room rate discounting has been inserted. Also, at the end of the chapter another major new section on yield management has been included. There are also three new problems.

Chapter 7, Introduction to Food, Beverage, and Labor Cost Control, is unchanged, except for the addition of a new problem.

Chapter 8, Cost Management, has a new section on paying a fixed versus a variable lease. There is also a new problem.

Chapter 9, The CVP Approach to Decisions, has a new final section on incorporating income tax into the CVP calculations. Three new problems have also been added.

Chapter 10, Budgeting, is substantially unchanged, with some minor additions and a new section on analyzing variances in both dollar and percentage terms. There are also two new problems.

Chapter 11, Working Capital, is unchanged.

Chapter 12, Cash Management, has new sections on use of bank floats, concentration banking, accounts receivable lockboxes, and marketable securities. There is also a new end-of-chapter section on using CVP analysis with long-term cash flow. There are five new problems.

Chapter 13, The Investment Decision, is unchanged except for the addition of two new problems.

Chapter 14, Feasibility Studies—an Introduction, is unchanged except for the addition of a new problem.

Chapter 15, Financial Goals and Information Systems, has some minor additions to some sections. At the beginning of the chapter there is also a new section on mission statements. At the end of the section on goals is a new section on developing an action plan to achieve goals. At the end of the chapter is a new section on MIS system effectiveness. There are also two new problems.

Finally, an Appendix, Computers in Hospitality Management, has been added.

Once again, I would like to express my appreciation to those who have taken the time and made the effort to provide advice and suggestions for allowing the creation of an improved fourth edition of *Hospitality Management Accounting*.

1 Accounting Review

Chapter Highlights

This chapter introduces the reader to some of the more common accounting rules, such as the business entity concept, the going concern concept, the money concept, the cost principle, the periodicity concept, the matching principle, the full-disclosure principle, the consistency concept, the conservatism concept, the materiality concept, and the objectivity concept.

Depreciation is then explained and four methods of calculating depreciation are illustrated:

- Straight-line method
- Declining balance method
- Sum-of-the-years digits method
- Units of production method

The balance sheet equation is explained, as is the concept of double-entry accounting, and the rules for debiting and crediting the five basic types of accounts: assets, liabilities, owners' equity, sales, and expenses.

The remainder of the chapter takes the reader through an accounting cycle: posting to the accounts, preparing a trial balance, preparing adjusting entries to the accounts, and completing working papers so that an income statement and a balance sheet can be prepared.

Chapter Objectives

After studying this chapter the reader should be able to:

1. Define and discuss the more important accounting principles and concepts.
2. List the four methods of depreciation illustrated in the text and use the methods to solve problems.
3. Explain the balance sheet equation.
4. List the rules for debit and credit entries in accounts.
5. Post typical transactions to T-accounts.
6. Prepare period-end adjustments to accounts.
7. Complete working papers.

ACCOUNTING REVIEW

This chapter is a review of some of the basic accounting principles, conventions, and practices. It should be of particular benefit to the person who has taken an introductory accounting course.

Accounting—a dynamic information system

Accounting was developed to identify and record financial information about a business and is a common language for those interested in the business. It provides information about a company's assets and debts, owners' investment, revenue, and expenses. It permits the accountant to prepare, in addition to the basic financial statements (balance sheet and income statement), other financial reports and analyses that will facilitate the company's management in decision making and in running an efficient, effective business. Accounting is not a static art, but rather a dynamic system for providing those interested in the business with the information they need or want.

Accounting principles and concepts are broad rules that have been developed by accountants for recording and reporting on the financial statements. These rules have evolved to suit the needs of financial statement readers such as the company's management, the owners, the creditors, and government agencies. The rules make the statements more meaningful and dependable. These rules include the business entity concept, the going concern principle, the money concept, the cost principle, the periodicity concept, the matching principle, the full-disclosure principle, the consistency concept, the conservatism concept, the materiality concept, and the objectivity concept. Each of these will be discussed in turn.

BUSINESS ENTITY CONCEPT

Personal assets not part of business

Whether a company is a proprietorship, partnership, or incorporated organization, from an accounting (if not from a legal) point of view it is considered to be quite distinct and separate from its owner(s), even if the owner(s) actually work(s) in the business. Only the assets, liabilities, and other transactions of the business are entered in the accounting records. The personal assets, debts, or expenses of the owner(s) are not part of the business. A restaurant owner's living accommodation is not part of the business and should not be shown as an asset of the business. Similarly, if the restaurant owner and family are fed from food purchased by the restaurant, this is not a business expense and the failure to adjust the accounting records of the business for this fact would be a violation of the business entity concept.

GOING CONCERN CONCEPT

Balance sheet values at cost

Under normal circumstances the assumption is made that the organization is going to stay in business indefinitely, and that the cost of its assets will be recovered over time by way of profit. Under this assumption, balance sheet values (for such items as land, building, equipment) are shown at their original cost since there is no intention to sell them and therefore no need to revalue them at their true market value. One could argue that the balance sheet is therefore misleading and some companies do show such assets at their fair market value. Either way, as long as the reader of the financial statements is made aware of the fact, he or she can interpret the statements accordingly. Obviously, when an asset, such as a piece of equipment, is traded in or sold, or a business is being liquidated, market value and not original cost of the asset(s) would be used.

MONEY CONCEPT

Dollar is unit of measure

According to the money concept the assumption is made that the function of accounting is to record (1) dollars borrowed and invested, (2) how these dollars are used for purchases, and (3) revenue and expenses in dollars. In other words, money is the unit in which financial information is expressed; any other type of valuation would be purely subjective. Accounting data (the financial statements) show only financial information about a company. The statements are not intended to show all the information about a company, such as the health of the management or the staff turnover rate.

COST PRINCIPLE

True value may differ from historic cost

The assumption that money will be the medium for recording information in accounting leads to the cost principle. According to this principle, the dollar value of a transaction at the time the transaction occurs is used. However, basing dollar values on purchase price does raise some problems, as we noted when discussing the going concern concept. For example, the historical purchase price of a hotel building may not indicate the building's true value (and this true value could be either higher or lower than cost) after the hotel has been in business for a few years. Similarly, and particularly in inflationary or deflationary times, comparing income statements for different years become difficult, if not meaningless, under this stable dollar assumption. However, exceptions can be made since inventories can be valued at market price rather than at cost, and methods are available for expressing balance sheets and income statements in terms of current, rather than historic dollars.

PERIODICITY CONCEPT

Monthly financial statements

The periodicity concept states that any business should take a reading from time to time to determine how it is doing. Although an ongoing business is much like a river, that is, it cannot be completely stopped, one can look at a period in a business's life in the same way one can view a section of a river. This period is usually once a year. However, in the hotel and food service business, statements are frequently prepared on a monthly or even a weekly basis.

MATCHING PRINCIPLE

Accrual accounting matches costs with revenues

The matching principle states that transactions are recorded at the time they occur and not necessarily at the time cash is exchanged. In other words, a regular customer in a restaurant may be permitted to charge meals to an account that is sent to him or her after the end of each month. The restaurant pays cash for the food the customer eats. Under the matching principle, the sales would be shown as revenue for the month even though the cash may not be received for another month, and only the food purchases that are used up would be shown as a cost. Such matching is known as accrual accounting, as opposed to cash accounting, under which entries are made in the books only when cash is received or given out. To illustrate cash accounting, let us assume that a new restaurant had only cash sales. Assume also that it purchased for cash enough food in the first month to cover the first two months. If we prepared partial income statements on a cash basis for the first two months, this would be the result.

	Month 1	Month 2
Cash sales	$10,000	$10,000
Cash purchases	(8,000)	0
Income before other expenses	$ 2,000	$10,000

This method gives a distorted picture of the business. The combined two-month profit of $12,000 is correct, but accrual basis accounting more truly reflects the real situation, which would be a profit (before other expenses) of $6,000 in each of the two months. See the following and note the use of the term "cost of goods used."

	Month 1	Month 2
Revenue	$10,000	$10,000
Cost of goods used	(4,000)	(4,000)
Income before other expenses	$ 6,000	$ 6,000

Cash accounting for small business

This is not to suggest that cash basis accounting is never used. In many small businesses it might be appropriate to use it. For example, a motel that rents its rooms on a cash only basis and that pays cash for wages and supplies might be served well by a cash basis accounting system or a combination cash/accrual basis. However, the matching concept is used throughout this book except in cases where the cash concept is important for decision making, for example, in Chapter 12, which is on cash management (cash budgeting) and in Chapter 13, where the concept of cash flow is introduced in relation to the investment decision.

It should be noted that, since accrual basis accounting is used throughout this book, using some of the demonstrated financial analysis techniques may not be appropriate if a company uses the cash basis of accounting.

FULL-DISCLOSURE PRINCIPLE

Footnotes give further information

Even though the financial statements are primarily concerned with a period of time that is past, the full-disclosure principle states that any future events that may or will occur and that would have a material impact on the financial position of the business should be disclosed to the readers of the statements. This is frequently done by way of a foot-note.

For example, a hotel building a new wing or planning to buy another property should report this information. A motel that was facing a law-suit from a guest who broke a leg tripping over a frayed carpet edge should disclose this. Similarly, if the accounting practices on the current set of financial statements differ from past practices, the readers of the statements should be informed. This could occur, for example, if the method of depreciation was changed from one period to the next. In all cases, the effect in dollars that these future events would have on the company's business should be reported, if possible.

CONSISTENCY CONCEPT

Use same accounting basis consistently

For reasons of comparability from one accounting period to the next, consistency should be used in the preparation of financial statements. For example, switching back and forth from accrual basis to cash basis accounting would not be consistent, nor would changing inventory pricing methods from one period to the next. Readers of financial statements expect consistency unless they are advised otherwise. Therefore, if a change in practices is necessary (for example, a change in depreciation methods), then, under the full-disclosure concept, the readers should be advised of it and of the effect it may have had on the financial results of the period(s) concerned.

CONSERVATISM CONCEPT

Avoid overstating net income

It is obvious that a company should never have accounting statements that deliberately overstate revenues and understate expenses. But situations do arise where estimates are necessary, for example, in putting a value on an inventory or deciding the appropriate rate of depreciation. In such cases the conservatism concept suggests that the inventory value should be lower rather than higher (this will increase the cost of goods sold expense and thus lower profit) and that depreciation should be estimated high rather than low (again this increases the depreciation expense and lowers profit). The intention is to avoid overstating net income. However, one should not be so carried away with conservatism that the result is very misleading. For example, a piece of restaurant equipment with a five-year life could, in the interest of conservatism, be fully depreciated in its first year. This would be conservative but hardly realistic.

MATERIALITY CONCEPT

Prorate expenses realistically

In the previous paragraph it was stated that fully depreciating in year one a piece of restaurant equipment with a five-year life would be considered overly conservative, particularly if it has a material effect on the resulting net income. Let us consider the case of a motel with furnishings costing $10,000 that are depreciated fully in year one as follows:

Revenue	$100,000
Expenses	(90,000)
Income before depreciation	$ 10,000
Depreciation	(10,000)
Net income	$ 0

It would be more realistic to show depreciation of $2,000 a year, based on a five-year life for the furnishings, as follows:

Revenue	$100,000
Expenses	(90,000)
Income before depreciation	$ 10,000
Depreciation	(2,000)
Net income	$ 8,000

On the other hand, the motel might have purchased a supply of letterheads for use over the next five years. Total cost was $200. The motel could show all of this amount as an expense in the year of purchase (rather than $40 expense and $160 inventory), because the net income would not be materially affected by this complete expensing of the purchase in year one.

OBJECTIVITY CONCEPT

Transactions to be supported by documentation

This final concept states that accounting transactions should only be entered in the books if supported by objective evidence (for example, a restaurant guest check to support a sale, a payroll check in support of a wage expense, an invoice in support of a food purchase). In other words, accounting transactions should have a basis in fact. Again, however, there are exceptions. For example, in a hotel many customers do not pay their accounts for charges incurred when they check out. They have charge privileges. The unpaid accounts are known as accounts receivable and are expected to be paid at some time in the future. Not all of them will be paid. In the interest of conservatism an allowance is established to cover these future bad debts. This allowance amount has no absolute basis in fact because it relates to future events that may occur. However, the allowance can be based on previous experience regarding the percentage of accounts receivable that have not been collectible, and that supporting evidence is considered to fit the bounds of objectivity.

DEPRECIATION

In a number of the preceding principles and concepts, the term "depreciation" has been mentioned. When long-life assets (such as the building, equipment, furniture) are purchased by a hotel, motel or foodservice operation, they are recorded on the balance sheet as assets at their original cost price. If, at time of purchase, these assets were shown as expenses on the income statement, that income statement and future ones would show a distorted net income because we would not be conforming to the matching principle. In other words, what we must do is transfer to each accounting period which benefits from the use of the asset(s) a portion of the cost of the asset(s). This portion of the cost is known as

Allocates cost over life of asset

depreciation. It is shown as an expense and thus reduces net income for that period. The process is one of allocating cost and is not an attempt to put a new value on the asset at each balance sheet date. The market value of the asset is irrelevant. However, if at the end of the asset's useful life, it has a trade-in value or scrap value different from book value (cost less accumulated depreciation), then an adjustment of depreciation expense should be made at that time.

The question arises: what is the useful life of an asset? This is often a matter of opinion influenced by such factors as inadequacy, obsolescence, and economic change. In the case of a hotel building, useful life could be thirty, forty, or fifty years or more. In the case of a piece of restaurant equipment, it could be as short as a couple of years if a new and better piece of equipment became available. There are a number of methods for calculating depreciation, such as straight-line, declining balance, sum-of-the-years digits, and units of production. Each of these will be discussed and illustrated.

Straight-line Method

Equal depreciation expense each period

The *straight-line method* of depreciation is probably the simplest of all since it spreads the cost of the asset, less any estimated trade-in or scrap value, equally over each year of the life of the asset. The equation for calculating the annual amount of depreciation is:

$$\frac{\text{Cost of asset} - \text{Trade-in value}}{\text{Service life of asset in years}}$$

Let us assume the following concerning a purchase of restaurant equipment: initial cost $16,000, trade-in value $1,000 at end of five-year life. Therefore annual depreciation will be:

$$\frac{\$16,000 - \$1,000}{5 \text{ years}} = \frac{\$15,000}{5} = \$3,000 \text{ per year}$$

To obtain the monthly depreciation expense we would simply divide the annual rate by 12.

Declining Balance Method

Double straight-line rate

Under the straight-line method, with a five-year life, one-fifth (or 20 percent) of the cost of the asset less its trade-in value is the annual depreciation. Using the same facts, under the *declining balance method*, the straight-line depreciation rate of 20 percent is doubled to 40 percent; this 40 percent is multiplied by the undepreciated balance (book value) of the asset each year to obtain the depreciation expense for that year. Using this depreciation method, any trade-in or scrap value is ignored. In other words, in year one the depreciation expense is 40% × $16,000 (the cost of the asset) = $6,400. The book value of the asset is now $16,000 − $6,400 = $9,600. Year two depreciation expense is 40% × $9,600 = $3,840. If we set this information up in the form of a schedule for all five years, it would appear as follows:

Year	Annual Depreciation	Net Book Value
		$16,000
1	40% × $16,000 = $6,400	9,600
2	40% × 9,600 = 3,840	5,760
3	40% × 5,760 = 2,304	3,456
4	40% × 3,456 = 1,382	2,074
5	40% × 2,074 = 830	1,244

If the equipment were traded in at the end of five years for $1,000, an adjustment for depreciation would have to be made at that time.

Accelerated depreciation

The declining balance method of depreciation is sometimes referred to as an *accelerated method*. Note that the depreciation is high in the early years and decreases as the years go by. The reasoning behind this is that in the earlier years of the life of an asset maintenance costs are low, but they increase with age. Therefore, in theory, the sum of depreciation plus maintenance should be approximately the same each year. There are also tax advantages to using accelerated depreciation methods. Since depreciation is higher in the early years and can be claimed as an expense, the net income will be lower and thus income taxes will be reduced. Over the long run, the total tax will be the same, but by reducing income taxes in the early years, cash flow can be increased in those years. Increasing cash flow is a worthwhile objective for any company. The concept of cash flow and the time value of money will be discussed in Chapter 13.

High depreciation in early years

Note that the declining balance method of depreciation gives the highest amounts of depreciation in the earlier years. The sum-of-the-years digits method, illustrated in the next section, does not yield depreciation expense that is as high in those early years.

Sum-of-the-Years Digits Method

Another accelerated method of depreciation is the *sum-of-the-years digits method*. Using the same facts as before ($16,000 cost, $1,000 trade-in, five-year life), we must first add up the sum-of-the-years digits:

$$1 + 2 + 3 + 4 + 5 = 15$$

This number, 15, becomes the denominator of a fraction. This denominator is the same for each of the five years for which we wish to calculate the depreciation. The numerator of the fraction changes each year. In year one it is 5, in year two, 4, in year three 3, in year four 2, and in year five 1. In other words, we just reverse the order of the years to obtain the numerator. The fraction for each year is then multiplied by the cost of

Reverse order of years

the asset ($16,000) less trade-in ($1,000), or $15,000. If we prepared our depreciation in the form of a schedule for the five-year period, it would appear as follows:

Year	Depreciation		
1	5/15 × $15,000 =	$ 5,000
2	4/15 × 15,000 =	4,000
3	3/15 × 15,000 =	3,000
4	2/15 × 15,000 =	2,000
5	1/15 × 15,000 =	1,000
	Total depreciation	$15,000

Units of Production Method

The final depreciation method to be explained is the *units of production method.* The equation for calculating depreciation per unit of production is:

Units of production equation

$$\frac{\text{Cost of asset} - \text{Trade-in value}}{\text{Estimated units of production during life of asset}}$$

As an example, assume a restaurant with a delivery service purchases a delivery vehicle for $8,000. It is estimated that this vehicle will be driven for 50,000 miles before being traded in, at which time it will have a trade-in value of $800. Our cost of depreciation per unit of production will be:

$$\frac{\$8,000 - \$800}{50,000} = \frac{\$7,200}{50,000} = \$0.144 \text{ per mile}$$

Annual depreciation expense is then based on the miles driven in that year. Assuming 10,000 in year one, annual depreciation is:

$$10,000 \times \$0.144 = \$1,440$$

Subsequent years' depreciation would be calculated in the same manner.

Depreciation spread equitably

The units of production method of depreciation does have the advantage of equitably spreading total depreciation over each period of the asset's useful life. Disadvantages are that it does not easily permit calculation of each period's depreciation expense in advance (useful, for example, in budgeting, which is discussed in Chapter 10); nor is it likely to give high depreciation amounts in the early years of the asset's life which, as mentioned earlier, is useful for reducing income taxes.

THE BALANCE SHEET EQUATION

Net income part of owners' equity

In any business, a set of financial statements is prepared periodically to monitor the progress of the business. The basic documents in this set of financial statements are an income statement and a balance sheet—both of which will be discussed in some depth in the next chapter.

The income statement shows the revenues less the expenses to arrive at net income. The net income (or loss if expenses exceed revenues) is transferred to the balance sheet and becomes part of the owners' equity. If all entries for transactions have been made correctly, the balance sheet will then "balance." The balance sheet equation, as it is known, is:

$$\text{Assets} = \text{Liabilities} + \text{Owners' equity}$$

Another way of viewing this balance is to say that assets (items of value that are owned or controlled by the company) less liabilities (debts of the company, or claims on the company's assets by the creditors) equal the owners' equity. In other words, the creditors rank above the owners insofar as claims on the assets of the company are concerned.

Double-Entry Accounting

Balance sheet must always be in balance

A business transaction is an exchange of goods or services (for example, food purchases for a restaurant or the sale of rooms in a hotel). In accounting, every transaction affects two or more accounts. No transaction can affect only one account. In this way the balance sheet is always kept in balance, because every transaction causes increases and/or decreases in asset and/or liability and/or owners' equity accounts. Let us illustrate this very simply by considering what happens when the proprietor of a restaurant begins business by investing $25,000 of his own money. The balance sheet would look like this:

$$\text{Assets:} \quad \text{cash } \$25,000 = \text{Owners' equity:} \quad \$25,000$$

The restaurant owner then purchases food on credit so that he can open his restaurant: $5,000 is spent for an inventory of food. Our balance sheet now looks like this:

$$\text{Assets:} \quad \left.\begin{array}{ll}\text{cash} & \$25,000 \\ \text{inventory} & 5,000\end{array}\right\} = \left\{\begin{array}{ll}\text{Liability:} & \text{accounts payable } \$\ 5,000 \\ \text{Owners' equity:} & 25,000\end{array}\right.$$

Transactions entered in journals or in accounts

Our balance sheet still balances, since the left-hand side equals the right-hand side. However, in normal practice transactions are not recorded directly onto the balance sheet. They are entered into journals and then into accounts in a ledger, or directly into the accounts. There is one account for each type of asset, liability, owners' equity, revenue, and expense. At the end of each accounting period, only the account balances at that time are transferred to the income statement or balance sheet.

ACCOUNTS

In basic manual accounting, each account is considered to have a left-hand side and a right-hand side. The left-hand side is where debit entries are made, and the right-hand side is where credit entries are made.

Debit (Dr)	**Credit (Cr)**

Debits must always equal credits

These types of accounts are referred to as "T" accounts. In practice, account pages in ledgers are a bit more sophisticated; nevertheless, even with computer-produced financial statements, the same basic principle of debits and credits applies—when entering transactions in the accounts, the entries in the debit side of the accounts must always equal the entries in the credit side. If this is not done, at the end of the accounting period we will find that our balance sheet will not balance. At the end of each accounting period, as we close out the accounts, the difference between the debit and the credit entries in each account provides the balance figure for that account.

It is wrong to view debits as increases in the balance and credits as decreases. Debits can either increase or decrease the balance; the credits can also either increase or decrease the balance. The rules for this are illustrated in the following T accounts.

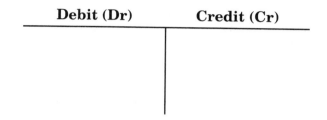

Assets		**=**	**Liabilities**		**+**	**Owners' Equity**	
Debits increase balance	Credits decrease balance		Debits decrease balance	Credits increase balance		Debits decrease balance	Credits increase balance

Since revenue (income) increases owners' equity, revenue account entries have the same effect as those for the owners' equity account, and since expenses decrease owners' equity, expense account entries are the reverse of those for revenue. This is illustrated below:

	Revenue		Expenses
Debits decrease balance	Credits increase balance	Debits increase balance	Credits decrease balance

Normal account balances

The normal account balances for each of the five types of accounts are

Account	Normal Balance
Asset	Debit
Liability	Credit
Owners' Equity	Credit
Revenue	Credit
Expense	Debit

An example of each would be

Asset:

Cash

10,000	

Liability:

Accounts Payable

	3,000

Owners' Equity:

Capital — Shares

	6,000

Revenue:

Rooms Revenue

	20,000

Expenses:

Wages

7,400	

THE ACCOUNTING CYCLE

Statements prepared at period end

As mentioned earlier, most hotels and restaurants break down their operations into monthly periods, also known as accounting periods. During each period, transactions occur, entries are made in the books to record these transactions, and at the end of the period an income statement and balance sheet are prepared. This period and sequence of events are known as the accounting cycle. Let us look at the accounting cycle (much simplified) for an investor opening a new restaurant with an initial personal investment of $55,000. If we entered this transaction in the T accounts, it would show an increase in the cash account (a debit) and an increase in the equity account (a credit).

Cash		Owners' Equity	
55,000			55,000

The owner then purchased equipment with a value of $50,000, for which she paid $25,000 cash, the balance owing by way of an account payable. The T accounts now look like this:

Cash		Owners' Equity	
55,000	25,000		55,000

Equipment		Accounts Payable	
50,000			25,000

During the first month the following transactions occurred:

Prepaid one year's rent	$12,000
Prepaid one year's insurance	3,000
Revenue (50% cash, 50% charge)	15,000
Paid cash for purchases of food	8,000
Paid cash for wages	5,000
Paid cash for other expenses	2,000

If we entered all these transactions in our ledgers, our T accounts at the end of the month would look like this:

Cash		Accounts Receivable	
55,000	25,000	7,500	
7,500	12,000		
	3,000		
	8,000		
	5,000		
	2,000		

Prepaid Rent and Insurance		Equipment	
12,000		50,000	
3,000			

Accounts Payable		Owners' Equity	
	25,000		55,000

Wages Expense		Other Expenses	
5,000		2,000	

Revenue		Purchases Expense	
	15,000	8,000	

Prepare trial balance

At this point in the cycle, before proceeding any further, it is advantageous to prepare a list of the balances in the accounts to see if the total of all the debit balances equals the total of all the credit balances. This list is known as a trial balance. In the case of some of our accounts, the balance is easy to determine. For example, in the case of accounts receivable, it is $7,500. In the case of others it has to be calculated, as shown in this cash account.

Cash

55,000	25,000
7,500	12,000
	3,000
	8,000
	5,000
	2,000
62,500	55,000
	7,500 *balance*
62,500	62,500

Debit entries add up to $62,500; credits add up to $55,000; the difference (balance) is $7,500. Although it is recorded on the credit side of the T account, it is still a debit balance since the debit entries add up to more than the credit entries. On a more conventional type of ledger account, the figures would appear as follows:

Account: Cash	Debit	Credit	Balance
January	$55,000	$25,000	
	7,500	12,000	
		3,000	
		8,000	
		5,000	
		2,000	$7,500 *Dr*

Once we have made the necessary calculations for accounts having a number of entries in them during the month, we can prepare our trial balance list as below:

Account	Debit	Credit
Cash	$ 7,500	
Accounts receivable	7,500	
Prepaid rent and insurance	15,000	
Equipment	50,000	
Accounts payable		$25,000
Owners' equity		55,000
Revenue		15,000
Purchases expense	8,000	
Wages expense	5,000	
Other expenses	2,000	
Total	$95,000	$95,000

We can see from this that our accounts do, indeed, balance. However, we cannot infer from this that everything is necessarily correct. For example, an entry might have been made in the right amount, but in the wrong account. Moreover, two correct accounts may have entries in them but in the wrong amount in both cases, or an entry may have been entirely omitted from the relevant accounts. Such errors usually show up in later stages in the accounting process and are corrected at that time by journal entry.

Month-End Adjustment

Adjustments necessary to match revenues with expenses

At the end of the accounting period, in our case a month, certain adjustments to accounts are required so that our income statement and balance sheet conform to the principle of matching revenues with expenses. Adjustments could be numerous or few, depending on the circumstances. In our case we have to make five, for cost of goods used, inventory, prepaid rent and insurance, depreciation, and wages. Each of these will be discussed.

Cost of Goods Used Adjustment and Inventory Adjustment. In any business, items that are purchased or produced for resale are not necessarily all sold during an accounting period. For example, in a restaurant there is always a minimum of food inventory on hand to take care of future business. We should not show as an expense deduction from revenue any goods still unsold. Therefore, we have to establish a new account known as cost of goods used. It is calculated as follows:

Opening food inventory + Food purchases − Closing food inventory

Normally, the first of three adjustments required would be to credit the opening inventory account balance and debit the amount to cost of goods used. But, since we had no opening inventory, we only need to make the following two adjustments, assuming the closing inventory is $3,000:

Debit cost of goods used expense $8,000
− Credit purchases expense $8,000

Purchase expense account reduced to zero balance

Note that the purchases expense account now has a zero balance.

Debit inventory asset $3,000 − Credit cost of goods used expense $3,000

Prepaid Rent and Insurance Adjustment. At the beginning of month one, the annual rent of $12,000 was paid. Since one month's rent has now been used up, we must show $1,000 on our income statement as rent expense, leaving only $11,000 as prepaid. We treat the prepaid insurance of $3,000 per year similarly. One-twelfth of this must now be shown as an expense, $250. The necessary adjustments are

Debit rent expense $1,000 — $1,000 Credit prepaid rent
Debit insurance expense $ 250 — $ 250 Credit prepaid insurance

Accumulated depreciation as a contra-account

Depreciation Adjustment. Our initial investment in equipment was $50,000. Assuming the equipment had a five-year life with no trade-in value, we are going to match this initial cost against revenue earned over a five-year period. Using straight-line depreciation, this would be $10,000 a year or $833 ($10,000 ÷ 12) a month. Also, rather than reducing the $50,000 of initial cost by entering in that account a credit of $833 a month and gradually decreasing the balance, it is common practice to set up a contra-account, known as accumulated depreciation, so that both initial cost of the asset and accumulated depreciation can appear as separate figures on the balance sheet. The entry for this would be

Debit depreciation expense $833
— Credit accumulated depreciation $833

Wages Adjustment. Unless payday happens to fall on the last day of the month, it is likely that employees may be owed wages for one or more days of work—wages that they have earned but for which they have not yet been paid. We must record this fact so that our income statement and balance sheet reflect the true situation. Assuming wages owed in the restaurant are $200 the entry would be

Debit wages expense $200 — Credit accrued wages liability $200

Adjustments posted to accounts

Adjusted Trial Balance. All adjustments are usually entered in a journal, with an explanatory note for each adjustment, and are then posted from the journal to the accounts. For example, the journal entry for our wages adjustment would look like this:

		Dr	Cr
January	Wages	200	
	Accrued wages		200
	To record wages earned but unpaid at month-end.		

At this point another trial balance should be prepared to ensure that the accounts still balance prior to preparing the income statement and the balance sheet. It is possible, and in a small business quite practical, to prepare these statements directly from the account pages in the general ledger. However, it is often helpful to use what are known as working papers.

Working Papers

Preparing working papers

Working papers can be prepared to ensure that the accounts balance before any adjustments are made (this is called the unadjusted trial balance). These working papers can then show the adjustments and serve to prepare an adjusted trial balance. This is shown in Exhibit 1.1.

After ensuring that the adjusted trial balance columns add up to the same amount, the figures from the individual accounts can be carried over into the same debit or credit columns of the income statement or the balance sheet on the working papers.

Calculation of net income on working papers

The next step is to calculate the amount of net income (net loss if debits are greater than credits) on our income statement. The net income (or loss) is the amount that is required to bring the two column figures to the same total. This net income figure is then carried from the debit column of the income statement to the credit column of the balance sheet (since net income increases owners' equity). Follow this through on Exhibit 1.2. Our balance sheet columns can now be added up and should agree. If they do not, an error has occurred and must be corrected before the income statement and balance sheet can be prepared in proper format. This proper format, and other related matters, will be discussed in the next chapter.

The Accounting Cycle Summarized

Following is a summary of the steps that have been discussed in this chapter relative to the accounting cycle which takes place during each period of an organization's life. These steps usually occur in the sequence listed.

Sequence of steps during accounting period

Journalizing

Recording transactions from source documents (such as invoices, sales checks) in a journal.

Posting

Copying (transferring) the journal entries into the accounts in the ledger.

Preparing a trial balance

Listing all the balances in the ledger accounts and ensuring total debits equal total credits.

Exhibit 1.1 Partially completed working papers for month ending January 31, _____.

Account Titles	Unadjusted Trial Balance Dr	Unadjusted Trial Balance Cr	Adjustments Dr	Adjustments Cr	Adjusted Trial Balance Dr	Adjusted Trial Balance Cr	Income Statement Dr	Income Statement Cr	Balance Sheet Dr	Balance Sheet Cr
Cash	$ 7,500				$ 7,500					
Accounts receivable	7,500				7,500					
Prepaid rent & insurance	15,000			(c) $ 1,250	13,750					
Equipment	50,000				50,000					
Accounts payable		$25,000				$25,000				
Owners' equity		55,000				55,000				
Revenue		15,000				15,000				
Purchases expense	8,000			(a) 8,000						
Wages expense	5,000		(e) $ 200		5,200					
Other expenses	2,000				2,000					
	$95,000	$95,000								
Inventory			(b) 3,000		3,000					
Cost of goods used expense			(a) 8,000	(b) 3,000	5,000					
Rent expense			(c) 1,000		1,000					
Insurance expense			(c) 250		250					
Depreciation expense			(d) 833		833					
Accumulated depreciation				(d) 833		833				
Accrued wages				(e) 200		200				
			$13,283	$13,283	$96,033	$96,033				

Adjustments
(a) Cost of goods used expense
(b) Inventory
(c) Prepaid expenses
(d) Depreciation
(e) Accrued wages

Exhibit 1.2 Completed working papers for month ending January 31, _____.

Account Titles	Unadjusted Trial Balance Dr	Cr	Adjustments Dr	Cr	Adjusted Trial Balance Dr	Cr	Income Statement Dr	Cr	Balance Sheet Dr	Cr
Cash	$ 7,500				$ 7,500				$ 7,500	
Accounts receivable	7,500				7,500				7,500	
Prepaid rent & insurance	15,000			(c) $ 1,250	13,750				13,750	
Equipment	50,000				50,000				50,000	
Accounts payable		$25,000				$25,000				$25,000
Owners' equity		55,000				55,000				55,000
Revenue		15,000				15,000		$15,000		
Purchases expense	8,000			(a) 8,000						
Wages expense	5,000		(e) $ 200		5,200		$ 5,200			
Other expenses	2,000				2,000		2,000			
	$95,000	$95,000								
Inventory			(b) 3,000		3,000				3,000	
Cost of goods used expense			(a) 8,000	(b) 3,000	5,000		5,000			
Rent expense			(c) 1,000		1,000		1,000			
Insurance expense			(c) 250		250		250			
Depreciation expense			(d) 833		833		833			
Accumulated depreciation				(d) 833		833				833
Accrued wages				(e) 200		200				200
			$13,283	$13,283	$96,033	$96,033	$14,283	$15,000	$81,750	
Net income							717			717
							$15,000	$15,000	$81,750	$81,750

Adjustments
(a) Cost of goods used expense
(b) Inventory
(c) Prepaid expenses
(d) Depreciation
(e) Accrued wages

Completing working papers	On a work sheet recording trial balance account balances, recording period-end adjustments, transferring adjusted trial balance figures to either the income statement or the balance sheet columns, calculating net income, balancing the balance sheet columns.
Preparing financial statements	Taking the working papers information and preparing an income statement and balance sheet in proper format.
Adjusting ledger accounts	Preparing adjusting journal entries from information in the adjustments column of the working papers and posting the entries to the accounts in the ledger.
Closing the accounts	Preparing any necessary journal entries to close the accounts at period-end and posting these entries to the accounts in the ledger.
Preparing a postclosing trial balance	Proving the accuracy of the adjusting and closing procedure by preparing a final trial balance.

SUMMARY

Accounting has been developed to provide financial information about a business. It is a common language having its own set of rules or assumptions, commonly called principles and concepts. These assumptions include the following:

- Business entity concept
- Going concern concept
- Money concept
- Cost principle
- Periodicity concept
- Matching principle
- Full-disclosure principle

- Consistency concept
- Conservatism concept
- Materiality concept
- Objectivity concept

It is important to have a good understanding of each of these in order to be able to interpret financial information correctly.

Depreciation is a method of writing off the cost of major assets (building, furniture, and equipment) so only a portion of the cost is shown as a deduction from income on each period's income statement. This portion of cost is called depreciation. There are various methods of depreciation such as straight-line, declining balance, sum-of-the-years digits, and units of production.

The two main documents in a set of financial statements are the income statement and the balance sheet. The net income (or loss) from the income statement is transferred at the end of each accounting period to the owners' equity section of the balance sheet. Because of the practice of double-entry bookkeeping, a balance sheet must always balance. This balance sheet equation is expressed as follows:

$$\text{Assets} = \text{Liabilities} + \text{Owners' Equity}$$

The individual accounts whose period-end balances are transferred to the income statement or balance sheet are all assumed to have two sides: the left, for debit entries, and the right, for credit entries. The rules for whether entries increase or decrease the balance for each type of account are as follows:

	Debit Entries	**Credit Entries**
Asset accounts	Increase balance	Decrease balance
Liability accounts	Decrease balance	Increase balance
Owners' equity accounts	Decrease balance	Increase balance
Revenue accounts	Decrease balance	Increase balance
Expense accounts	Increase balance	Decrease balance

At the end of each accounting cycle, when all transactions for the period have been entered into the appropriate accounts, the total of all debit balances should equal the total of all credit balances. A trial balance is often prepared to establish this. Subsequent to the initial trial balance, adjustments to the accounts are often necessary. After these adjustments are made, an adjusted trial balance should be prepared. Finally, from this adjusted trial balance, the income statement and balance sheet can be made up. To aid in this process from unadjusted trial balance through preparation of financial statements, working papers can be useful.

DISCUSSION QUESTIONS

1. In what way can a business manager use accounting information?

2. List and, in your own words, give a short description of four of the accounting principles or concepts.

3. Describe what is meant by accrual basis accounting.

4. A hotel shows office supplies (such as stationery) on its balance sheet at a $500 cost, even though to any other hotel these supplies might have a value only as scrap paper. What accounting principle or concept justifies this?

5. Describe depreciation.

6. Two methods of accelerated depreciation were described in the chapter. What are they, and what assumption justifies these methods?

7. Describe how the units of production depreciation method works. Use an example with your own figures to help with your description.

8. A restaurant has purchased a new cash register for recording revenue. With adequate maintenance the machine could last ten years. However, because of technological improvements, it is expected that a newer type of machine will be purchased in five years to replace the one just bought. For depreciation purposes, what would be the useful life of the present new machine? Why?

9. What is the balance sheet equation? Is it possible for a transaction to affect an asset account without also affecting some other asset, liability, or owners' equity account?

10. Why is the rule for debit and credit entries the same for liability and owners' equity accounts?

11. Why are period-end adjustments required prior to preparing the financial statements?

12. If the trial balance balances, under what circumstances might the individual account balances still not be correct?

PROBLEMS

1.1 A number of accounting principles and concepts (such as the matching principle) were discussed in this chapter. For each of the following situations, state which principle or concept is involved.

    a. A case of food poisoning occurred in a restaurant. The restaurant is being sued by a number of its customers, who were hospitalized. The estimated cost of the loss the restaurant is likely to suffer from this lawsuit is recorded now as an expense because of the _____ principle.

b. A hotel has traditionally depreciated its furniture and equipment using the straight-line method. This year it has used the declining-balance method without advising its financial statement readers of this change. As a result, it is violating both the _____ principle and the _____ concept.

c. A motel's normal payday for employees is every Friday. The year-end occurs on a Monday. The pay earned by employees for those three days is recorded in the motel's accounts because of the _____ principle.

d. Last year a remote fishing resort purchased a float plane to fly guests to the resort. The aircraft cost at that time was $150,000. This year, the plane is worth $160,000. However, it continues to be recorded on the books at $150,000 because of the _____ concept or the _____ principle.

e. If a restaurant operator takes home food purchased by the restaurant and uses these products to feed his family, this violates the _____ concept.

f. If a hotel estimates expenses to be higher than they actually might be, this reduces the hotel's profit and conforms to the _____ concept.

g. A hotel purchases a box of 100 pencils for use in its accounting office. At the balance sheet date, 95 of these pencils (at a total value of $4.75) are not included in inventory because of the _____ concept.

1.2 A new motel has purchased furniture at a cost of $110,000 with an eight-year life, at the end of which time it is estimated the furniture could be sold for $10,000. Under the straight-line method of depreciation, what would the annual depreciation expense be?

1.3 Using information from Problem 1.2, prepare an eight-year schedule of depreciation using the declining balance method. Round annual depreciation expense figures to the nearest dollar.

1.4 Using information from Problem 1.2, prepare an eight-year schedule of depreciation using the sum-of-the-years digits method.

1.5 A resort hotel has purchased a station wagon to transport guests and their baggage and to use for other hotel business. Original cost was $15,400. The hotel plans to trade in the station wagon when it has gone 30,000 miles. Trade-in value at that time is estimated to be $4,000. In year one 9,000 miles were traveled, in year two 11,000, and in year three 10,000. Calculate the depreciation expense for each of the three years using the units of production depreciation method.

1.6 For each of the following describe a transaction that will:
a. Increase an asset and increase owners' equity.
b. Increase an asset and increase a liability.
c. Decrease an asset and decrease a liability.

d. Increase one asset account and decrease another.

e. Decrease an asset and decrease owners' equity.

1.7 For each of the following restaurant transactions make the necessary debit and credit entries. To simplify the problem, prepare blank T accounts on a separate sheet of paper and make the entries directly to the relevant accounts. You will need blank T accounts for each of the following: Cash, Food Inventory, Beverage Inventory, Accounts Receivable, Equipment and Furniture, Accounts Payable, Bank Loan, Owners' Equity, Revenue, Food Purchase Expense, Beverage Purchase Expense, Wages Expense, Supplies Expense, Rent Expense, Interest Expense.

a. Owner invested $25,000 cash in a new restaurant.

b. Borrowed $10,000 from bank.

c. Purchased furniture and equipment for $25,000, paying $15,000 cash and owing balance.

d. Purchased food inventory, $3,000, and beverage inventory, $4,000, all on credit.

e. Paid one month rent expense, $1,200

f. Had revenue during month, $30,000—two-thirds cash and one-third charge.

g. Purchased food (food purchases) $8,000 on credit and paid cash for beverages (beverage purchases) $3,000.

h. Paid suppliers (accounts payable) who were owed money $12,000 cash.

i. Paid $1,000 on bank loan plus interest of $100.

j. Paid wages cash, $11,200.

k. Purchased supplies for cash, $3,900.

When all entries have been made, prepare a trial balance.

1.8 The following transactions occurred for a new rustic lodge owner prior to and during her first month of business:

a. Owner invested $60,000 cash.

b. Borrowed $70,000 by way of a mortgage.

c. Paid cash for land, $10,400.

d. Paid cash for building, $100,900.

e. Purchased equipment and furniture for $30,000—$10,000 cash, balance owing.

f. Purchased an inventory of linen for $6,200 on credit.

g. Room revenue during month, $6,800, all cash.

h. Revenue from vending machines, $800 cash.

i. Purchases (cash) for vending machines, $500.

j. Paid wages, $1,900 cash.

k. Purchased supplies, $800 cash.

l. Paid cash on mortgage, $300, plus interest, $600.

m. Paid $2,200 toward accounts payable.

n. Paid annual insurance, $1,200.

Enter these transactions on T accounts and transfer account balances to working papers in the unadjusted trial balance columns. Ensure a balance. Complete the adjustments column on the working papers from the following information, and then complete the rest of the working papers. Month-end adjustments are required for the following:

a. Estimated closing value of the linen inventory, $5,700.
b. Wages earned by employees but unpaid, $200.
c. One-twelfth of the prepaid insurance should be shown as an expense.
d. Interest owing, but not yet paid, on the furniture and equipment payable account is 1 percent of the balance owing at month-end.
e. Furniture and equipment depreciation, estimated five-year life, straight-line depreciation.

1.9 Joe Smart started a mobile snack food delivery service on January 1. He purchased a secondhand fully equipped truck with $8,000 cash that he had, and he put another $2,000 in the company bank account to start the business. He kept no formal accounting records during the year and now, at year-end, has asked you to calculate his net income or loss for the year. You discover that his year-end bank balance is $555 and that he has $24 of cash in the till in the delivery truck. All sales during the year have been on a cash basis. He also paid cash for all his purchases of food and beverages during the year and has a year-end inventory of these items valued at $275. Total purchases of food and beverage during the year were $12,648 according to invoices. Joe had no employees but took $1,500 a month out of the business for his own salary. His only other expenses during the year were for truck operating costs; invoices for these add up to $914. They were paid in cash at the time. Joe tells you there is still one truck repair invoice to come, for $27. It is estimated that the truck has depreciated 20 percent during the year. Calculate whether or not Joe earned a net income for the year.

1.10 Art Angel operates a tourist marina that he rents for the mid-May to mid-September season for $800 a month. He started the current season with $5,000 in the bank and paid the season's rent in advance out of this bank account. Art rents out small boats and sells snack foods to boating tourists. At the beginning of the season, he paid cash for three new boats at $500 each. The boats are estimated to have a four-year life, at the end of which time they will have a trade-in value of $100 each. Use straight-line depreciation. During the summer, invoices show he paid cash for food and beverages totaling $7,458. There is also one unpaid invoice for food for $73. There is no ending inventory of food and beverages. Boat maintenance costs during the summer were $211 cash. He also paid cash for casual labor, $254, and took $1,000 a month out of the business for his own salary. All revenue for both rentals and food and beverage was on a cash basis. Art presently has $4,697 in his bank account. He is puzzled that he has less cash now than when he started, since he is sure he made a profit. Art has no accounting background. Calculate his net income (or loss) on the season's operations.

CASE 1

This is the first part of a continuous case that will appear at the end of each chapter. It is a good idea to keep all your case solutions, notes, and other information in a separate file or binder. In some later cases you will be referred to earlier ones and having the case material all together will make them easier for you.

Charlie Driver is 23. For the past five years, since finishing high school, he has been working and saving money. He has about $20,000 in the bank and has decided to attend his local college and take courses in marketing. To help pay for his living costs and tuition fees, and to obtain some business experience, Charlie has contracted with a local mobile catering company to become an independent driver. Charlie wants to do this in a businesslike way and has given himself a company name: Charlie's Convenient Catering (or the 3C Company for short). He has opened up a bank account with $20,000 in the company's name. From this account he has purchased a secondhand fully equipped truck for $16,000.

Charlie started in business on January 1. Although he has taken no accounting courses, he realized he would have to provide an accountant, at the year end, with detailed records of all transactions during the year. At the end of the year, Charlie asked you, as a friend, to help him put together some figures. All sales during the year were on a cash basis. Unfortunately, despite the fact that Charlie carefully recorded each day's revenue in a daily diary, he cannot find that diary.

At the end of December, he had $11,110 in his bank account and $48 in change in the cash drawer in the truck. He paid cash during the year for food, beverages, and other supplies that he purchased from the catering company he was contracted to. According to invoices this totaled $25,296. He estimates year-end inventory in the truck to be $350. Charlie had no employees but took $2,000 a month out of the company for his own salary. During the year he paid operating expenses (maintenance, gas and oil, licensing) on the truck in cash. These expenses added up to $1,828. In addition there is one more unpaid repair invoice to come, for $254. The two of you decide that, since the truck has an estimated five-year life with no scrap value, depreciation should be calculated on a straight-line basis over that period.

a. Calculate the 3C Company's revenue for the year.
b. Calculate the company's net income for the year.
c. Explain why the cash in the bank is so much higher than the net income.
d. Explain why the 3C Company started out with $20,000 in the bank, has a net income for the year, yet ended up with only about $11,000 in the bank.

2 Understanding Financial Statements

Chapter Highlights

This chapter covers the two main statements making up a set of financial statements, namely the income statement and the balance sheet.

In the hospitality industry, income statements are usually prepared for each of the major operating departments. The departmental income statements include direct expenses. Direct expenses are defined, as are indirect or undistributed expenses not normally allocated to the operating departments. Undistributed expenses would normally appear on a summary income statement. Illustrations of various types of income statements are given.

Cost of sales is discussed with particular reference to how cost of food and beverages may need to be adjusted (for items such as interdepartment transfers, employee meals, and promotion items) to arrive at net food cost.

Responsibility accounting for profit and cost centers is covered.

Distribution (allocation) of indirect expenses to the departments is discussed, as is the effect that a change in the sales mix among departments would have on overall net profit.

A balance sheet is illustrated, and each classification of account that would normally appear on a balance sheet is discussed. The use of the retained earnings statement as the link between the income statement and balance sheet is demonstrated. This section also covers how the equity section of a balance sheet for a proprietorship or a partnership differs from that for an incorporated business.

The balance sheet section concludes with a discussion of the amount of detail a balance sheet will show, the way it is presented, its importance, and its limitations.

Chapter Objectives

After studying this chapter the reader should be able to:

1. Explain the main purpose of financial statements and the value of a uniform system of accounts.
2. Define and explain the difference between an income statement and a balance sheet.
3. Describe the difference between and give examples of direct and indirect or undistributed expenses.
4. Prepare income statements in proper format, calculate net food cost from given information, and discuss the concept of responsibility accounting.
5. Explain the effect that a specific change in interdepartmental revenue mix will have on overall profit.
6. List the six major classifications of accounts that could appear on a balance sheet and give examples of the types of accounts that could appear in each classification.
7. Define and calculate retained earnings.
8. Prepare a balance sheet in proper format, state the two methods of balance sheet presentation, and discuss the importance and limitations of a balance sheet.

UNDERSTANDING FINANCIAL STATEMENTS

In order to understand financial statements, it is not necessary to be able to prepare them. However, the person who is able to prepare a set of financial statements (primarily a balance sheet and an income statement) has the advantage of being able to analyze the information in greater depth.

Users of financial statements

Although there are many different users of financial statements (governments, regulatory groups, stockholders, creditors, company employees), the main emphasis in this chapter and the other chapters of this book is on their use by the internal management from the department-head level up to general management.

These management people need information. Management's function is to make decisions and plan for the future, and rational decisions can only be made with relevant information. The financial statements provide some of this information.

The Uniform System of Accounts

Most organizations in the hospitality industry (hotels, motels, resorts, restaurants, clubs) use the Uniform System of Accounts appropriate to their particular segment of the industry. The original Uniform System of Accounts for Hotels was initiated in 1925 by the Hotel Association of New York. The system was designed for classifying, organizing, and presenting financial information so that uniformity prevailed and comparison of financial data among hotels was possible.

Comparison with averages

One of the advantages of accounting uniformity is that information can be collected on a regional or national basis from similar organizations within the hospitality industry. This information can then be reproduced in the form of average figures or statistics. In this way, each individual organization can compare its results with the averages. This does not mean that the individual hotel operator, for example, should be using national hotel average results as a goal for his own organization. Average results are only a standard of comparison, and there are many reasons why the individual organization's results may differ from industry averages. But, by making the comparison, determining where differences exist, and subsequently analyzing the causes, the individual operator at least has information from which he can then decide whether or not corrective action is required within his own organization.

Income Statement and Balance Sheet

The two major statements in a set of financial statements are the income statement and the balance sheet, which will be discussed in this chapter. A third useful statement concerning the source and use of working capital will be discussed in Chapter 11. Although the income statement and the balance sheet are treated separately in this chapter, they should, in practice, be read and analyzed jointly. The relationship between the two must be kept in mind. This becomes clear when one compares the definitions of the two types of statements:

Statements to be read jointly

- The income statement shows the operating results of a business over a period of time.
- The balance sheet gives a picture of the financial position of a business at a particular point in time.

The period of time referred to for the income statement usually ends on the date of the balance sheet.

January 1   December 31

Income Statement   Balance Sheet

THE INCOME STATEMENT

The income statement can provide answers to some important questions, such as:

- What were the sales last month? How does that compare with the month before and with the same month last year?
- Did last month's sales keep pace with the increased cost of food, beverages, labor, and other expenses?
- What were the sales by department for the operating period?
- Which department is operating most effectively?
- Is there a limit to maximum potential sales? Have we reached that limit? If so, can we increase sales in the short run by increasing room rates and menu prices and/or in the long run by expanding the premises?
- What were the food and beverage cost and gross profit percentages? Did these meet our objectives?
- Were operating costs (such as for labor and supplies) in line with what they should be for the sales level achieved?
- How did the operating results for the period compare with budget forecasts?

The income statement shows the operating results of a business for a period of time (week, month, quarter, half-year, or year). The amount of detail concerning revenue and expenses to be shown on the income statement depends on the type and size of the hospitality establishment and the needs of management for more or less information.

Departmental income statements

For example, a typical hotel would prepare departmental income statements for each of its operating departments. Exhibit 2.1 illustrates one for the food department. Similar ones would be prepared for the beverage department and the rooms department. Others would be prepared for any other operating departments large enough to warrant it. Alternatively, all the other, smaller departments could be grouped together into a single income statement (this would include operating areas such as newsstands, gift shops, laundry, telephone, parking, and so on).

It should be noted that in many establishments it is not possible to

Exhibit 2.1 Sample departmental income statement.

Hotel Theoretical
Departmental Income Statement—Food Department
(for the year ending December 31, 0006)

Revenue		
Dining room	$201,600	
Coffee shop	195,900	
Banquets	261,200	
Room service	81,700	
Bar	111,200	
Total revenue		$851,600
Cost of sales		
Cost of food used	$352,500	
Less: employee meals	(30,100)	
Net food cost		322,400
Gross profit		$529,200
Departmental expenses		
Salaries and wages	$277,400	
Employee benefits	34,500	
Total payroll and related expense	$311,900	
China, glassware	7,100	
Cleaning supplies	6,400	
Decorations	2,200	
Guest supplies	6,500	
Laundry	15,500	
Licenses	3,400	
Linen	3,700	
Menus	2,000	
Miscellaneous	800	
Paper supplies	4,900	
Printing, stationery	4,700	
Silver	2,300	
Uniforms	3,100	
Utensils	1,700	
Total expenses		376,200
Departmental income (loss)		$153,000

show the food department as a separate entity from the beverage department. The reason is that, since these two departments work very closely together, they have many common costs that cannot accurately be identified as belonging to one or the other. Because of this, there is only one income statement produced for the food and beverage department. Wherever possible, it is suggested that the revenue and expenses for food be kept separate from the revenue and expenses for beverages because in this way the income statements are more meaningful. In this text, therefore, food and beverage are shown as separate operating departments, even though it is recognized that, in practice, this may not always be possible. If it is possible, the two separate sets of figures can always be added together later to give a combined food and beverage income statement for comparison with other establishments or with industry averages.

Direct expenses charged to departments

Each department's income statement will have allocated to it its share of the expenses directly attributable to it, which are the responsibility of the department head to control. These direct costs would include cost of sales (food cost, beverage cost); salaries, wages, and related payroll costs of the employees working in the department; linen, laundry, and all the various other categories of supplies required to operate the department. The resulting departmental incomes (revenue, less direct expenses) are sometimes referred to as contributory incomes, because they contribute to the indirect, undistributed expenses not charged to the operating departments. The individual departmental (contributory) incomes are added together to give a combined, total departmental income (see Exhibit 2.2). As mentioned earlier, each departmental income figure would be supported by a departmental income statement similar to Exhibit 2.1.

Undistributed operating expenses

From the total departmental income figure are deducted what are sometimes referred to as indirect expenses. Indirect expenses are broken down into two separate categories: the undistributed operating expenses and the fixed charges. Undistributed operating expenses include costs such as administrative and general, marketing, property operation and maintenance, and energy costs. Other expenses that might be included in this category in certain establishments are management fees, franchise fees, and guest entertainment. All these undistributed operating expenses are considered controllable but not by the operating department heads or managers. They are controllable by and are the responsibility of the general manager. Note that these undistributed operating expenses include the cost of salaries and wages of employees involved.

The final level of expenses, generally referred to as fixed charges, are then deducted. In this category are such expenses as property taxes, insurance, interest, and depreciation. Income tax is then deducted to arrive at the final net income.

It is this net income figure that is transferred to the statement of retained earnings and eventually appears on the balance sheet. This will be illustrated later in the chapter.

Supporting schedules detailing expenses

Each of the expenses listed in Exhibit 2.2 would have, where the size of the establishment warranted it, a separate schedule listing all the detailed costs making up the total expense. For example, the administrative and general expense schedule could show separate cost figures for such items as:

Exhibit 2.2 Sample summary income statement.

Hotel Theoretical Income Statement
(for the year ending December 31, 0006)

Departmental income (loss)		
Rooms		$ 782,900
Food		153,000
Beverage		119,100
Other income		18,600
Total departmental income		$1,073,600
Undistributed operating expenses		
Administrative and general	$238,000	
Marketing	66,900	
Property operation and maintenance	102,000	
Energy costs	71,000	477,900
Income before fixed charges		$ 595,700
Fixed charges		
Property taxes	$ 98,800	
Insurance	22,400	
Interest	82,400	
Depreciation	160,900	364,500
Income before income tax		$ 231,200
Income tax		114,700
Net income		$ 116,500

- Salary of general manager and other administrative employees
- Secretarial and general office salaries/wages
- Accountant and accounting office personnel salaries/wages
- Data processing and/or credit office employees' salaries/wages
- Postage and fax expense
- Printing and stationery expense
- Legal expense
- Bad debts and/or collection expenses
- Dues and subscriptions expense
- Travel expense

Exhibit 2.3 shows another method of income statement presentation. Accompanying this income statement should be separate departmental income statements for each operating department, similar to the one for the food department illustrated in Exhibit 2.1. Also, where necessary, the income statement should be accompanied by schedules giving more detail of the unallocated expenses.

Exhibit 2.3 Alternative summary income statement.

Hotel Theoretical Income Statement
(for the year ending December 31, 0006)

	Net Revenue	Cost of Sales	Payroll and Related Expense	Other Expenses	Income
Departmental income (loss)					
Rooms	$1,150,200		$251,400	$115,900	$ 782,900
Food	851,600	$322,400	311,900	64,300	153,000
Beverage	327,400	106,800	86,300	15,200	119,100
Other income	38,200	10,600	8,700	300	18,600
Operating department totals	$2,367,400	$439,800	$658,300	$195,700	$1,073,600
Undistributed operating expenses					
Administrative and general			$115,600	$122,400	
Marketing			35,100	31,800	
Property operation and					
maintenance			52,900	49,100	
Energy costs			15,800	55,200	
			$219,400	$258,500	477,900
Income before fixed charges					$ 595,700
Fixed charges					
Property taxes					$ 98,800
Insurance					22,400
Interest					82,400
Depreciation					160,900
					364,500
Income before income tax					$ 231,200
Income tax					114,700
Net income					$ 116,500

Cost of Sales

**Failure to
adjust for
inventory**

With reference to Exhibit 2.1, note that net food cost has been deducted
from revenue to arrive at gross profit before deducting other departmental expenses. To arrive at net food cost (and net beverage cost) some
calculations are necessary to match up food sales and beverages sales
with what it has cost in food and beverages to generate those sales. In
many restaurants (particularly small ones) food and beverage cost of
sales are simply shown on the monthly income statement according to
total purchases made that month. However, this procedure ignores the
fact that products that were in inventory at the end of the previous
month have now been used and that some of the purchases made during
the month will not have been used at the end of the current month. If
food cost (and beverage cost) are based solely on total monthly purchases,
they will not provide accurate figures and may lead to erroneous decisions about how well the food and beverage operations are doing.

As briefly discussed in Chapter 1, to calculate cost of sales correctly it
is first necessary to calculate the cost of goods (food) used. The equation
is

Opening food inventory + Food purchases − Closing food inventory

In practice, it is not necessary to calculate an opening inventory, because
it is exactly the same as the closing inventory of the previous period. It
is therefore only necessary to calculate inventory at the end of each
period.

Inventory is the value of all food in inventory in storerooms, in production areas such as kitchens, and in sales areas such as the dining room.
A physical count of each item must be taken and the count multiplied by
the cost of the item. When each item has been counted and costed, total
inventory value can be calculated. The costing of items sounds like a
simple process, and is for most items. In the case of other items, however,
the process can be more difficult. For example, what is the value of a
gallon of soup that is being prepared in a kitchen at the time inventory
is taken? In such a case, that value (because the soup has many different

**Accuracy
versus time**

ingredients in it) may have to be estimated. The accuracy of the final
inventory is, therefore, a question of the time taken to value it. There is
a trade-off between accuracy and time required. If inventory is not as
accurate as it could be, then neither food (and beverage) cost nor net
income will be accurate. Normally, however, relatively minor inventory-
taking inaccuracies tend to even out over time. Inventory figures for food
should be calculated separately from those for alcoholic beverages.

Compared to costing inventory, the cost of purchases can be calculated
relatively easily because it is the total amount of food and beverages
delivered during the month (less any products returned to suppliers for

such reasons as unacceptable quality). Invoices recorded in the purchases account during the month can readily provide this figure. In order to calculate food cost separately from beverage cost, purchase costs for these two areas must also be recorded in separate purchase accounts.

To date, we have only discussed the calculation of the cost of food used. Why is this figure called "cost of food used" rather than "net food cost," "cost of food sold," or "food cost"? In many small restaurants, cost of food used may be the same as net food cost, but in most food and beverage operations it may be necessary to adjust cost of food used before it can be accurately labeled net food cost. Some of these adjustments might be:

Adjustments to cost of sales

- Interdepartment transfers: For example, in a restaurant with a separate bar operation there might be items purchased and received in the kitchen (and recorded as food purchases) that are later transferred to the bar for use there (for example, fresh cream, eggs, or fruit used in certain cocktails). In the same way, there may be purchases received by the bar (and recorded as beverage purchases) that are later transferred to the kitchen (for example, wine used in cooking). A record of transfers should be maintained so that at the end of each month both food cost and beverage cost can be adjusted to ensure they are as accurate as possible.

- Employee meals: Most food operations allow certain employees while on duty to have meals at little or no cost. In such cases, the cost of that food has no relation to sales revenue generated in the normal course of business. Therefore, the cost of employee meals should be deducted from cost of food used. Employee meal cost is then transferred to another expense account (for example, it could be added to payroll cost as an employee benefit). Note that, if employees pay cash for meals but receive a discount from normal menu prices, this revenue should be excluded from regular food revenue (because otherwise it will distort the food cost percentage calculation) and be transferred to a separate revenue account, such as "other income."

Employee meals as benefit

- Promotion expense: Restaurants sometimes provide customers with complimentary (free) food and/or beverages. This is a beneficial practice if it is done for good customers who are likely to continue to provide the operation with business. The cost of promotional meals should be handled in the same way as the cost of employee meals. The cost should not be included in food cost of sales and/or beverage cost of sales because, again, the food and/or beverage cost will be distorted. The cost should be transferred from food cost and/or beverage cost and be recorded as advertising or promotion expense. Employees who are authorized to allow promotional items to customers should be instructed always to make out a sales check to record the item's sales value. Some restaurants for promotional purposes issue coupons that allow two meals for the price of one. In this case, the value of both meals should still be recorded on the sales check, even though the customer pays for only one meal. From sales checks, the cost of promotion meals can be calculated by using the operation's normal food cost and/or beverage cost percentage.

Responsibility Accounting

A hospitality business with several departments, each with the responsibility for controlling its own costs and with its department head accountable for the departmental profit achieved, is practicing what is known as *responsibility accounting*. Responsibility accounting is based on the principle that department heads or managers should be held accountable for their performance and the performance of the employees in their department.

Cost centers versus profit centers

Within a single organization practicing responsibility accounting, departments can be identified as either cost centers or profit centers. A cost center is one that generates no direct revenue (such as the maintenance department). In such a situation, the department manager is held responsible only for the costs incurred. A profit center is one that has costs but also generates revenue that is directly related to that department (such as the rooms department's generating revenue from guest room sales). The manager of a profit center should have some control over the revenue it can generate. In both cost and profit centers where responsibility accounting is practiced, a key question is what costs should be assigned to each center. Generally, only those costs that are directly controllable by that center's department head or manager are assigned. Common direct costs should be allocated to each center in some logical way.

Investment centers

Another form of responsibility accounting occurs in a large or chain organization with units located in several different towns or cities. Each unit in the organization is given full authority over how it operates and is held responsible for the results of its decisions. In a large organization such as this, each unit is said to be decentralized and units are sometimes referred to as investment centers. Investment centers are measured by the rate of return achieved by their general managers on the investment in that center.

In some chain organizations, products are transferred from one unit to another. For example, in a multiunit food organization, raw food ingredients might be purchased and processed in a central commissary before distribution to each individual unit. A question arises about the cost to be transferred to each unit for the partially or fully processed products. Many different pricing methods are available. It is important that an appropriate pricing method be decided so that each unit can be properly measured on its performance through responsibility accounting.

For example, the transfer price could be the commissary's cost plus a fixed percentage markup to cover its operating costs. Another method might be to base the transfer price on the market price of the products. The market price would be what the unit would have paid if it had purchased the products from an external supplier. In some cases, the market price might be reduced by a fixed percentage to reflect the commissary's lower marketing and distribution costs. Obviously, each user unit would prefer to have the transfer price as low as possible so that its costs are lower, and the commissary would prefer to have the transfer price as high as possible to enhance its performance.

Distribution of Indirect Expenses

Prorating indirect expenses among departments

One controversial issue concerning the income statement is whether or not the indirect expenses should be distributed to the departments in the same way the direct expenses are. The problem arises in selecting a rational basis on which to allocate these costs to the operating departments. Some direct expenses may also have to be prorated between two operating departments on some logical basis. For example, an employee in the food department serving food to customers may also be serving them alcoholic beverages. The food department will receive the credit for the food revenue, the beverage department for the beverage revenue. However, it would be unfair for either of these two departments to have to bear the full cost of that employee's wages. That cost should be split between the two departments, possibly prorating it on the basis of the revenue dollars. Such interdepartmental cost transfers are easily made; they are necessary in order to have a reasonably correct profit or loss for each operating department for which the appropriate department head is accountable.

Advertising expense based on revenue

Some of the normally undistributed expenses can perhaps be allocated easily and logically. For example, marketing could be distributed on a revenue ratio basis (although, if a particular advertising campaign had been made specifically for one department, and it was thought that little, if any, benefit would accrue to other departments, then the full cost of that could reasonably be charged to that one department).

With reference to Exhibit 2.3, it will be noted that the total marketing expense is $66,900. If management wished to charge (allocate) that expense to the operating departments on a revenue ratio basis, the first step is to convert each department's revenue to a percentage of total revenue as follows (percentage figures are rounded to the nearest whole number):

Department	Revenue	Percent
Rooms	$1,150,200	49%
Food	851,600	36
Beverage	327,400	14
Other	21,200	1
Total	$2,350,400	100%

The marketing cost can then be allocated as follows:

Department	Share of Cost
Rooms	$66,900 × 49% = $32,800
Food	66,900 × 36 = 24,000
Beverage	66,900 × 14 = 9,400
Other	66,900 × 1 = 700
Total	$66,900

Possible bases for allocating indirect expenses

The other indirect costs could be distributed by using the same procedure, but on a different basis. For example, total department payroll and related expense might be an appropriate basis on which to allocate the administrative and general expense. The square foot (or cubic foot) area could be used for allocating property operation and maintenance, and energy costs. Alternatively, property operation and maintenance expenses could be charged directly to the department(s) concerned at the time of invoicing. Property (real estate) taxes may similarly be charged to a specific department. Alternatively, square footage or revenue basis could be appropriate. Insurance could be charged on the basis of each department's insurable value relative to the total insurable value. Depreciation on building might be apportioned on the basis of each department's property value relative to total property value, or, if this is difficult to determine, square footage might be appropriate. Depreciation on equipment and furniture could probably easily be prorated on the basis of each department's equipment and furniture cost, or value, relative to total cost or value. Finally, with respect to interest expense, the only logical basis would be on each department's share of the asset value to total asset value at the time the obligation (mortgage, bond, debenture, loan) was incurred. If a department does not have any assets covered by the obligation, then it should bear none of the interest expense.

Consistent basis to be used

Once a method of allocating any, or all, of these indirect costs to the operating departments is selected, it should be adhered to consistently so that comparison of income statements of future periods is meaningful. However, remember that comparison with other, similar organizations' income statements may not be meaningful if that organization had not selected the same allocation basis. The resulting departmental income or loss may or may not be more revealing to the individual manager than the more traditional approach, which takes the departmental income statement to the departmental operating income (contributory income) level only. If indirect expenses are allocated, the department head should still be made responsible only for the income (or loss) before deduction of indirect expenses, since indirect expenses are not normally controllable by the department head. By allocating indirect expenses, top management will be able to determine if each department is making an income after all expenses. If any are not, it may be that the allocation of indirect costs is not fair. Alternatively, analysis of such costs may indicate ways in which the costs could be reduced to eliminate any individual departmental losses and increase overall total net income.

Advantages of indirect cost allocation

Finally, whether or not indirect expenses are allocated to the various operating departments, the resulting net income (bottom line) figure for the entire operation will not differ.

Revenue Mix Effect on Net Income

Change in revenue volume among departments

Even though the allocation of the indirect expenses to the departments does not affect the operation's total net income (because total indirect expenses are the same), there is one factor that will affect net income even though there is no change in total indirect expenses or in total revenue. That factor is a change in the revenue mix. In this particular instance, a change in the revenue mix is understood to be a change in the revenue volume of the various operating departments.

Consider Exhibit 2.4, where the contributory income percentage figures have been rounded to the nearest whole number. It can be seen that, since the rooms department has the lowest total of direct costs in relation to its revenue, its departmental income is the highest, at 68 percent of revenue. Expressed differently, this means that, for every

Exhibit 2.4 Contributory income schedule.

	Revenue	Direct Expenses	Departmental (Contributory) Income	Contributory Income Percent
Rooms	$1,150,200	$ 367,300	$ 782,900	68%
Food	851,600	698,600	153,000	18
Beverage	327,400	208,300	119,100	36
Other	21,200	19,600	1,600	9
Totals	$2,350,400	$1,293,800	$1,056,600	
Total indirect expenses			825,400	
Income before income tax			$ 231,200	

Exhibit 2.5 Contributory income schedule.

	Revenue	Direct Expenses	Departmental (Contributory) Income	Contributory Income Percent
Rooms	$1,250,200	$ 400,100	$ 850,100	68%
Food	801,600	657,300	144,300	18
Beverage	277,400	177,500	99,900	36
Other	21,200	19,600	1,600	9
Totals	$2,350,400	$1,254,500	$1,095,900	
Total indirect expenses			825,400	
Income before income tax			$ 270,500	

Contributory income percent stays constant

dollar increase in room revenue, 68 cents will be available as a contribution to the total indirect costs.

This is important if there is a change in the revenue mix. In Exhibit 2.5 there has been a change. Room revenue has been increased by $100,000 and food and beverage have each been decreased by $50,000. There is, therefore, no change in total revenue. It is assumed that the contributory income percent for each department will stay constant, despite a change in revenue volume. This may, or may not, be the case in practice. Given this assumption, Exhibit 2.5 shows that, even with no change in total revenue or total indirect expenses, because of a revenue transfer from food and beverage into the rooms department, there has been an increase in total contributory income and net income of $39,200. An awareness by management of the influence each department has on total departmental (contributory) income and thus on net income could be important for decision making. For example, it could indicate how the marketing budget should best be spent to emphasize the various departments within the organization. Alternatively, if a limited budget were available for building expansion to handle increased business, a study of each department's relative contributory income would help in deciding how to allocate the available funds.

THE BALANCE SHEET

Balance sheet equation

The balance sheet gives a picture of the financial condition of a business at a particular point in time. On the left-hand side it lists the assets or resources a company has. On the right-hand side are the liabilities (debts) of the company and the stockholders' equity. On a balance sheet

Exhibit 2.6 Sample balance sheet.

Balance Sheet
(as at December 31, 0006)

Assets		
Current assets		
Cash		
on hand	$ 8,100	
in bank	19,800	$ 27,900
Marketable securities, at cost (market value $10,500)		10,000
Accounts receivable	$ 24,600	
Less: allowance for uncollectible accounts	1,500	23,100
Inventories		
food	$ 8,200	
beverages	9,600	
supplies	2,100	19,900
Prepaid expenses		5,200
Total current assets		$ 86,100
Fixed assets		
Land, at cost		$ 161,800
Building, at cost	$1,432,800	
Less: accumulated depreciation	356,900	1,075,900
Furniture and equipment, at cost	$ 374,700	
Less: accumulated depreciation	275,300	99,400
China, glass, silver, linen and uniforms		25,600
Total fixed assets		1,362,700
Other assets		
Organization expense		5,800
Total assets		$1,454,600

Liabilities and Stockholders' Equity		
Current liabilities		
Accounts payable—trade		$ 19,200
Accrued expenses		3,500
Income tax payable		12,300
Deposits and credit balances		500
Current portion of long-term mortgage		27,200
Total current liabilities		$ 62,700
Long-term liabilities		
Mortgage on building	$840,100	
Less: current portion	27,200	812,900
Total liabilities		$ 875,600
Stockholders' equity		
Capital stock:		
authorized 5,000 common		
shares @ $100 par value; issued		
and outstanding 3,000 shares	$300,000	
Retained earnings	279,000	579,000
Total liabilities and stockholders' equity		$1,454,600

total assets always equal total liabilities plus equity. A typical balance sheet is illustrated in Exhibit 2.6.

The asset side of a balance sheet is normally broken down into three sections: current assets, fixed (or long-term) assets, and other assets.

Current Assets

Current assets defined

Current assets are cash or items that can or will be converted into cash within a short period of time, usually within one year.

Cash on Hand. Since hospitality industry organizations should deposit the entire cash receipts of the preceding day in the bank each day, the amount in this account on the balance sheet should normally be equivalent to approximately one day's cash business, plus the amount of any "floats" (changemaking funds) or "banks" kept on hand for the use of cashiers.

Excess cash to be invested

Cash in Bank. Cash kept in the bank should normally be sufficient to take care of current debts as they become due. Any excess cash should not be left idle in the bank but should be earning interest in savings accounts or be invested in short-term marketable securities.

Marketable Securities. Excess funds can be used in a number of ways. One way is to invest them in short-term securities until such time as the cash is again needed for other purposes. Usually this asset is shown at cost. If the actual market value at the balance sheet date is different from original cost, then this market value should be shown in parentheses or by a footnote.

Bad debts as a contra-account

Accounts Receivable. Accounts receivable represent rooms, food, and beverage business charged to individuals or companies for which payment has not yet been received. This account is normally offset by an amount that is considered to be uncollectible (that is, bad debts). The allowance for uncollectible accounts is often referred to as a type of "contra" account. The actual amount of the allowance is usually determined from historical records, which show the average percentage of accounts receivable that have turned out to be bad debts.

Inventories. This category includes inventories of food, beverages (alcoholic), and supplies (such as paper products, cleaning materials, and stationery). Silver, china, glassware, linen, and uniforms are not included under current assets; they are part of the fixed asset section of the balance sheet.

Prepaid Expenses. Items that might be included in the prepaid expense account are unexpired portions of prepaid insurance premiums, taxes, licenses, advertising, and similar items. Such prepaid expense items are included with current assets because, although they are not expected to be converted into cash, they have reduced the amount of cash that will have to be paid out in the near future. If any prepaid expenses are for a period of time more than one year hence, that portion should be shown under the deferred expense section of other assets (discussed later in this chapter).

Fixed Assets (Long-Term Assets)

Fixed assets (sometimes referred to as capital assets) are those of a more permanent nature, not intended to be sold, which are used in operating the business.

Land, Building, and Furniture and Equipment. These are three major and common fixed assets used in the hospitality industry. They are generally shown at their cost, or cost plus any expenditures to put the asset in condition for use (such as freight and installation charges for an item of equipment). If any part of the land or a building is not used for the ordinary purposes of the business (such as a parcel of land held for investment purposes), it should be shown separately on the balance sheet. On some balance sheets this section of the balance sheet is entitled Property, Plant, and Equipment.

Accumulated Depreciation. The cost of building, plus furniture and equipment (not land), are reduced by accumulated depreciation. Accumulated depreciation reflects the decline in value of the related asset due to wear and tear, the passage of time, changed economic conditions, or other factors. This traditional method of accounting, which shows the

net book value (cost less accumulated depreciation) of the asset, does not necessarily reflect the market value or the replacement value of the asset or assets in question.

China, Glass, Silver, Linen, and Uniforms. This amount is made up from two figures. The estimated value of items in use is added to the cost of those items still new and in storage.

Other Assets

There are other assets a company may have that do not fit into either current assets or fixed assets. Some of the more common ones are discussed here.

Deposits. If the deposit is refundable at some future time it can be considered an asset. An example of this would be a deposit with a public utility company.

Investments. Long-term investments (as opposed to short-term investments in marketable securities) in other companies or in property or plant not connected with the day-to-day running of the business (such as a separate building that is owned but is rented out to another organization) are shown as a separate category of asset.

Leasehold Costs or Leasehold Improvements. It is not uncommon for land to be leased. Where a long-term lease is paid for in advance, the unexpired portion of this cost should be shown as an asset. Similarly, if improvements are made to a leased building, these improvements are of benefit during the life of the business or the remaining life of the lease. The costs should be spread (amortized) over this life. Any unamortized cost should be shown as an asset. The term amortization is similar in concept to the term "depreciation" discussed in Chapter 1. Depreciation is generally used in conjunction with tangible assets such as buildings and furniture and equipment. Amortization is generally used with reference to intangible assets, such as goodwill or deferred expenses.

Deferred Expenses. Deferred expenses are similar to prepaid expenses (a current asset item) except that the deferred expense is of a long-term nature and is to be amortized over future years. An example of this might be the discount (prepaid interest) on a mortgage. This discount is amortized annually over the life of the mortgage. Preopening expenses (for example, for advertising, the benefit of which may be earned in future periods) would also fit into this category.

Total Assets

All of the various assets discussed, when added together, give the total assets of a company, or the total resources available to it. This information appears on the left-hand side of the balance sheet. The right-hand side is composed of two major sections: liabilities and stockholders' equity. The liabilities are further broken down into short-term and long-term. The stockholders' equity section is generally made up of capital stock and retained earnings.

Current Liabilities

Current liabilities are those debts that must be paid, or are expected to be paid, within a year.

Accounts Payable—Trade. Included here are the amounts owing to suppliers of food, beverages, and other supplies and services purchased on account or contracted for in the normal day-to-day operation of a hospitality business.

Accrued Expenses. This item includes those current debts that are not part of accounts payable. This would include unpaid wages or salaries, payroll tax and related deductions, interest owing but not yet paid, rent payable, and other similar expenses.

Income Tax Payable. This is the income tax owed to the government on the company's taxable income.

Unearned income

Deposits and Credit Balances. Money is often given in advance by prospective guests as a deposit on room reservations and banquet bookings. The accounts of guests staying in a hotel may have credit balances on them. The total of all these items should be shown as a liability because the money is due to the guest until it has been earned.

Current Portion of Long-Term Mortgage. Since, by definition, current liabilities are debts due within one year, the amount of any portion of a long-term liability payable within a year should be deducted from the long-term obligation and shown under current liabilities.

Dividends Payable. If any dividends had been declared but not yet paid at the balance sheet date, they would be recorded under current liabilities.

Long-Term Liabilities

Long-term liabilities defined

Long-term liabilities are those due beyond one year after the balance sheet date. Included in this category would be mortgages, bonds, debentures, and notes payable. If there are any long-term loans from stockholders, they also would appear in that section.

Stockholders' Equity

In general terms, the stockholder's equity section of the balance sheet can be stated to be the difference between total assets and total liabilities. It represents the equity, or the interest, of the owners in the enterprise. It comprises two main items, capital stock and retained earnings, although other items such as capital surplus may appear.

Authorized shares	**Capital Stock.** Any incorporated company is limited by law to a maximum number of shares it can issue. This limit is known as the authorized number of shares. Shares generally have a par, or stated, value, and this par value, multiplied by the number of shares actually issued up to the authorized quantity, gives the total value of capital stock. Most companies issue shares in the form of common stock. However, it is not uncommon to see balance sheets with another type of share known as
Preferred stock ranks before common	preferred stock. Preferred stock ranks ahead of common stock, up to certain limits, as far as dividends are concerned. Preferred stockholders may have special voting rights, and they rank ahead of common stockholders in the event of company liquidation.

Capital Surplus. Capital surplus or paid-in capital in excess of par value appears on some balance sheets. Some companies issue shares to stockholders at a price in excess of the par or stated value. This excess amount is recorded separately in the equity section of the balance sheet.

Retained earnings not equivalent to cash in bank	**Retained Earnings.** Retained earnings are the accumulated profits, less any losses, sustained by the business since it began, less any dividends paid out to stockholders. The retained earnings are not necessarily represented by cash in the bank at the balance sheet date because the money may have been used for other necessary purposes: expanding the volume of business, which means more cash tied up in accounts receivable and inventories, or in purchasing new equipment, refurnishing the rooms, restaurants, and other areas, or even in expanding the building. Since retained earnings are the link between the income statement and the balance sheet, details as to the change that has occurred in retained earnings from the beginning to the end of the period should be shown (see Exhibit 2.7).
Deficit defined	Alternatively, the full details, as shown in Exhibit 2.7, could be incorporated onto the balance sheet. If retained earnings are negative, that is, if accumulated losses exceed accumulated profits, this is termed a deficit.

Exhibit 2.7 Sample retained earnings statement.

Statement of Retained Earnings
(for the year ending December 31, 0006)

Retained earnings January 1, 0006	$192,500
Add: Net income for year 0006	116,500
	$309,000
Less: Dividends paid	30,000
Retained earnings December 31, 0006	$279,000

Proprietorships and Partnerships

No stock issued

In a proprietorship or partnership, no stock is issued. Therefore, the stockholders' equity section of the balance sheet is entitled simply equity. The equity information is also presented differently:

Equity

Proprietor's capital	$579,000

Details concerning the proprietor's capital, similar to those for retained earnings in an incorporated business, should be given (see Exhibit 2.8).

If, instead of a proprietorship (one owner), it were a partnership of two or more investors, the balance sheet equity section would appear as follows (assuming, in this case, only two partners):

Equity

Partner A, Capital	$289,500	
Partner B, Capital	289,500	$579,000

Details on balance sheet

Details, for each partner, would then be shown as in Exhibit 2.9.

As is the case with retained earnings, instead of showing the details concerning a proprietor or partners in a separate statement, they could be incorporated directly onto the balance sheet.

Total Liabilities and Stockholders' Equity

The total of all the liabilities and stockholders' equity, or capital, accounts should agree with the total asset accounts on the left-hand side of the balance sheet. These liability and equity, or capital, accounts show how the company's resources (assets) are currently financed.

Exhibit 2.8 Sample proprietor's capital statement.

Statement of Proprietor's Capital
(for the year ending December 31, 0006)

Investment January 1, 0006	$492,500
Add: Net income for year 0006	116,500
	$609,000
Less: Withdrawals during year	30,000
Balance December 31, 0006	$579,000

Exhibit 2.9 Sample partners' capital statement.

Statement of Partners' Capital
(for the year ending December 31, 0006)

	Partner A	Partner B
Investment January 1, 0006	$246,250	$246,250
Add: Net income for year 0006	58,250	58,250
	$304,500	$304,500
Less: Withdrawals during year	15,000	15,000
Balance December 31, 0006	$289,500	$289,500

Balance Sheet Detail

The amount of detail shown on a balance sheet depends on the amount of information desired, the operation's size and complexity, and whether it is a proprietorship, partnership, or incorporated company. For example, one business's balance sheet might show each type of cash account as a separate item, and another business's balance sheet might combine all the various cash accounts into a single figure.

Some operators want their balance sheets simplified as much as possible because this makes them easier to "read" at first glance. Where more detail about an account is needed, this might then be shown as an addendum or footnote on an adjoining page. For example, the inventories might be shown in total only on the balance sheet and be supported by a separate schedule that shows them broken down into separate figures for food, beverages, supplies, and others.

Balance Sheet Presentation

Account form versus report form

The balance sheet in Exhibit 2.6 is the way many balance sheets are presented with assets on the left, and liabilities and capital on the right. This presentation is known as the account form or method and is the one most commonly used.

Another common method is the report form. This method is vertical, rather than horizontal as in the account form. In the report form, the balance sheet is considered to have a top half and a bottom half. The top half is for the assets, and the bottom half for liabilities and owners' equity.

Importance of Balance Sheet

The balance sheet is important because it can provide information about such matters as

- A business's liquidity, or ability to pay its debts when they have to be paid.
- How much of the operation's profits have been retained in the business to help it expand and/or reduce the amount of outside money (debt) that has to be borrowed.
- The breakdown of assets into current, fixed, and other, with details about the amount of assets within each of these broad categories.
- The business's debt (liabilities) relative to owners' equity. In general, the greater the amount of debt relative to equity, the higher is the operation's financial risk.

Balance Sheet Limitations

There are some aspects of a business that the balance sheet may not disclose. For example:

Transactions at cost
- Because transactions are recorded in the value of the dollar at the time the transaction occurred, the true value of some assets on the balance sheet may not be apparent. Suppose a hotel owned the land on which the building sits and that land had been purchased several years ago. Because of inflation and demand for limited land, it is likely that the land is today worth far more than was paid for it. This may also be true of some other assets. The balance sheet normally does not show this market value.

Goodwill
- If the operation was purchased from a previous owner who had built up a successful business, and if an amount for that business above the actual market value of the purchased assets had been paid, that amount would have been recorded on the balance sheet at the time of purchase as "goodwill." Goodwill that a business has is only normally recorded at the time a business is transferred from seller to buyer. Therefore, if a business was started from scratch, and has a good location compared to its competitors, and/or a good reputation and faithful clientele, and/or a superior work force with a good morale, it is probably worth far more than the balance sheet assets show, simply because the goodwill built up is not reflected on the balance sheet.

Investment in employees
- Another value similar to goodwill that is not shown on a business's balance sheet is the investment in its employees. This investment takes the form of time and money spent on recruiting, training, evaluating, and promoting motivated individuals. Obviously, it is difficult to assign a value to these human resources, but they are, nevertheless, an asset to any hospitality business.
- Many items recorded on balance sheets are a matter of judgment or estimate. For example, what is the best depreciation method and rate

to use and what is the best of several available methods for valuing inventories? There are no absolute answers to these questions. For this reason, a balance sheet may not reflect the correct value for all assets. If the judgments or estimates used are wrong, then the balance sheet is incorrect.

- Balance sheets also reflect the financial position of a business at only one moment in time, subsequent to which the balance sheet is constantly changing. These changes will not be shown until another balance sheet is produced a month or more later. If a balance sheet showed a healthy cash position at one time, and a week later most of that cash was spent on new furniture, the balance sheet will reveal nothing about the impending use of most of the cash available.

SUMMARY

Financial statements provide information management needs for rational decision making. Most hotel and foodservice operations pattern their financial statements along the lines of one of the various types of Uniform System of Accounts available to the industry.

The two main statements in a set of financial statements are the income statement and the balance sheet. The income statement shows the operating results of a business over a period of time, ending on the balance sheet date, whereas the balance sheet gives a picture of the financial position of a business at a particular point in time.

Income statements in the hospitality industry are, wherever possible, departmentalized. In other words, each operating department has its income statement prepared showing revenue in that department less direct expenses—those expenses that are controllable by and are the responsibility of that department.

For most foodservice operations it is necessary to adjust cost of food used to arrive at the net food cost figure for an income statement. These adjustments cover such items as interdepartment transfers, employee meals, and promotion items.

Many hospitality businesses also use income statements for responsibility accounting, which is based on the principle that department heads or managers should be held accountable for their performance and the performance of the employees in their department.

The summarized departmental incomes are brought together in a general income statement and all the remaining undistributed expenses and fixed charges are deducted in order to arrive at net income. Although it is possible to distribute or allocate these undistributed expenses and fixed charges to the operating departments, the difficulty lies in finding a realistic, practical method for prorating them.

An important point to remember about an income statement for an establishment having two or more operating departments is that a given change in level of revenue in one department might have a completely different effect on net income than the same amount of change in another department. Because different departments have different contributory income percentages, one needs to be alert to possible changes in the revenue mix, and thus changes in net income potential.

The net income figure is transferred to the balance sheet by way of the statement of retained earnings, as follows:

Retained earnings at the beginning of the year
+
Net income for the year (from the income statement)
=
Retained earnings at the end of the year (to the balance sheet).

The balance sheet is composed of assets on the one side, liabilities and stockholders' equity on the other. Assets would include the following categories for most hospitality industry establishments:

Current assets:	Cash
	Accounts receivable (less allowance for bad debts)
	Marketable securities
	Inventories (food, beverage, supplies)
	Prepaid expenses
Fixed assets:	Land
	Building
	Furniture and equipment ⎫ *Less*
	China, glass, silver, ⎬ *accumulated*
	linen, and uniforms ⎭ *depreciation*
Other assets:	Deferred expenses

Under liabilities there would be:

Current liabilities:	Accounts payable
	Accrued expenses
	Income taxes payable
	Deposits and credit balances
	Current portion of mortgage payable
Long-term liabilities:	Mortgage (or other long-term debt payable)

The stockholders' equity section would include:

> *Stockholders' equity:*   Capital stock
>   Retained earnings

Note that the amount of detail that appears on a balance sheet is a matter of management decision. Balance sheets can be presented in either the account (horizontal) form or the report (vertical) form. Finally, remember that although a balance sheet has many uses, it also has a number of limitations.

DISCUSSION QUESTIONS

1. Why does the management of a hotel or foodservice operation need financial statements?
2. Of what value is a uniform system of accounts?
3. How do balance sheets and income statements differ from each other?
4. What is a departmental contributory income?
5. In a departmental organization, what is the difference between direct expenses and undistributed (or indirect) expenses?
6. State the equation for calculating cost of food used.
7. Briefly discuss three types of adjustments that are sometimes necessary to convert cost of food used to net food cost.
8. Explain the term *responsibility accounting* and differentiate a profit center from a cost center.
9. Discuss some specific types of indirect expenses and an appropriate method or methods by which to allocate them to individual operating departments.
10. Why should the change in the revenue mix among departments have any effect on net income even if there is no change in total revenue?
11. For each of the following balance sheet categories, list three accounts and briefly discuss each one:
    a. Current assets
    b. Current liabilities
    c. Fixed (long-term) assets
12. How do current assets differ from fixed assets?
13. Define retained earnings, and explain how retained earnings at the balance sheet date are calculated.

14. Why are deposits and credit balances on accounts shown as a current liability?

15. Define depreciation.

16. How is the net book value of a fixed asset determined?

17. Explain how the account form of balance sheet presentation differs from the report form.

18. Briefly discuss two limitations of a balance sheet.

PROBLEMS

2.1 Prepare a food department income statement from the following information:

Revenue	
grill room	$153,100
coffee garden	78,900
banquets	298,400
Net food cost	211,700
Employee meals expense	17,200
Salaries, wages, and related expense	174,400
China, glassware, and supplies expense	14,600
Laundry and linen expense	13,000
License expense	1,900
Printing, stationery, menus expense	4,900
Sundry expense	6,200
Other income of food department	600

2.2 Rosa's Restaurant has the following food cost information for the month of July:

Food inventory July 1	$ 2,428
Food inventory July 31	1,611
Food purchases during month	8,907
Cost of employee meals	209
Cost of promotion meals	278

Calculate Rosa's cost of food sold (net food cost) for July.

2.3 You have the following information for Stan's Steak House, a restaurant with a separate bar operation:

Food inventory January 1	$14,753
Food inventory January 31	12,811

Food purchases during month	48,798
Cost of employee meals	1,208
Cost of promotion meals	512
Transfers from kitchen to bar	107
Transfers from bar to kitchen	48

Calculate Stan's cost of food sold (net food cost) for January.

2.4 Using the food department's operating income from Problem 2.1 and the following additional information, prepare the hotel's general income statement.

Rooms department, operating income	$482,700
Beverage department, operating income	143,600
Telephone department, operating loss	25,100
Other income	40,300
Administrative and general expense	174,300
Marketing	83,600
Energy costs	62,000
Property operation and maintenance	74,900
Insurance	5,200
Property taxes	43,100
Interest	65,000
Depreciation	125,700
Income tax	50% of income before tax

2.5 A restaurant has three revenue areas with the following revenue and direct cost average monthly figures:

	Dining room	Banquet room	Service bar
Revenue	$100,000	$60,000	$40,000
Cost of sales	40,000	20,000	15,000
Wages and other direct costs	32,000	18,000	4,000

In addition, the restaurant has the following indirect expenses:

Administrative and general	$13,000
Marketing	9,000
Energy costs	6,000
Property operation and maintenance	12,000
Depreciation	12,000
Insurance	2,000

a. Prepare an income statement for the restaurant without allocating the indirect expenses to the three operating departments.

b. Prepare an income statement showing the income or loss for each department allocating the indirect expenses to the operating departments as follows:

Administrative and general, and marketing to be prorated on the basis of revenue volume. All others to be prorated on a square foot basis. The square foot areas of the three departments are as follows: dining room 2,400 sq. ft., banquet 3,000 sq. ft., service bar 600 sq. ft.

c. With reference to the results obtained in part b., explain why you would, or would not, close down any revenue area that is not making an income.

2.6 With reference to the information in Problem 2.5:

a. Calculate each department's contributory income percent.

b. If there were a switch of $14,000 in revenue from the dining room to the banquet area, would you expect the restaurant's overall net income to go up or go down? Explain your reasoning.

c. Assuming that the switch does occur and that there is no change in the undistributed (indirect) expenses, calculate the restaurant's new total income. (Note: there is no change in total revenue.)

2.7 From the following information, prepare a balance sheet listing the accounts under their appropriate classification (current assets, etc.), and making sure your statement balances.

	Debits	**Credits**
Cash	$ 4,100	
Accounts receivable	9,700	
Allowance for bad debts		$ 200
Inventories	8,200	
Prepaid expenses	1,900	
Land	80,000	
Building	712,800	
Accumulated depreciation (building)		186,400
Furniture and equipment	183,200	
Accumulated depreciation (furniture and equipment)		47,500
China and silverware	12,100	
Accounts payable		8,600
Accrued expense		2,700
Income tax payable		6,100
Current portion of long-term mortgage		13,100
Long-term mortgage		406,900
Capital stock		151,000
Retained earnings		189,500

2.8 From the following listing of accounts, prepare (and balance) a balance sheet in proper format. Balance sheet date is December 31, year 0004.

	Account Balance
Cash on hand	$ 16,400
Cash in bank	38,200
Accounts receivable	48,700
Allowance for doubtful accounts	3,400
Marketable securities (market value $20,000)	19,100
Inventories	
food	16,800
beverage	17,400
supplies	4,500
Prepaid expenses	4,100
Land	325,400
Building (at cost)	2,865,200
Accumulated depreciation, building	729,400
Furniture and equipment (at cost)	751,200
Accumulated depreciation, furniture and equipment	554,600
China, glassware, silver, etc.	50,300
Utility deposits	2,000
Organization costs	7,000
Investment in land	218,000
Deferred expenses	21,900
Accounts payable	37,100
Accrued expenses	7,900
Income tax payable	25,100
Deposits and credit balances	1,400
Dividends payable	48,200
Current portion of long-term mortgage	51,900
Mortgage payable (long-term portion)	1,621,300
Capital stock	
preferred	100,000
common	500,000
Capital surplus	21,700
Retained earnings January 1, year 0004	571,800
Net income for year 0004 (after deduction of dividends of $48,200)	132,400

2.9 (For the advanced reader or student who can prepare a set of financial statements from trial balance information.) You have the following trial balance information for the year ending December 31, 0007:

	Debit	Credit
Cash on hand and in bank	$ 71,259	
Accounts receivable	26,638	
Allowance for bad debts		$ 2,159
Inventories, January 1, 0007		
food	5,853	
beverage	8,404	
Inventory, December 31, 0007—supplies	3,210	
Prepaid expenses	4,778	
Land	90,219	
Building, at cost	910,315	
Accumulated depreciation (building) as at December 31, 0006		273,094
Furniture and equipment, at cost	304,565	
Accumulated depreciation (furniture and equipment) as at December 31, 0006		157,242
Deferred interest expense	19,563	
Goodwill	75,000	
Accounts payable		79,366
Income taxes payable		0
Dividends payable		1,500
First mortgage at 8% interest		619,850
Second mortgage at 12% interest		100,897
Common stock issued and outstanding		30,000
Retained earnings, January 1, 0007		48,930
Revenue		
rooms department		483,307
food department		499,401
beverage department		170,194
Other income		23,191
Rooms department		
payroll and related expenses	107,638	
laundry	19,732	
linen	5,333	
cleaning supplies	1,377	
guest supplies	5,710	
stationery	1,322	
sundry	3,810	
Food department		
food purchases	214,115	
laundry	17,726	
kitchen fuel	3,438	
linen	4,717	
china, glassware, etc.	8,236	
cleaning supplies	3,401	

	Debit	Credit
contract cleaning	2,395	
paper supplies	5,094	
menus and wine lists	1,342	
printing and stationery	1,133	
decorations	1,210	
licenses	2,016	
sundry	2,100	
miscellaneous income		1,432
payroll and related expense	238,899	
Beverage department		
beverage purchases	51,407	
payroll and related expense	25,568	
uniforms	290	
laundry	602	
linen	199	
glassware	319	
cleaning supplies	919	
paper supplies	1,943	
beverage lists	135	
licenses	1,930	
sundry	1,415	
miscellaneous income		1,275
Administrative and general expense	52,164	
Marketing	22,545	
Energy costs	30,536	
Property operation and maintenance	52,963	
Property taxes	26,819	
Insurance	11,336	
Mortgage interest	40,200	

The following year-end adjustments must be taken into consideration:

a. During the year 0008, $41,132 of the first mortgage principal will be paid off.

b. During the year 0008, $15,819 of the second mortgage principal will be paid off.

c. Included in the food purchases is the amount of $17,216 for cost of employee meals. Of this $17,216, $10,109 was the cost for food department staff, and the balance the cost of staff meals for the beverage department.

d. Inventories at December 31, 0007 are:

food	$6,404
beverage	7,112

e. Payroll and related expense accrued between the last payday (December 27) and December 31, 0007, is:

food department	$2,809
beverage department	1,207
rooms department	956
administration	406

f. The license fees for the food and beverage departments had both been paid on June 1, 0007 for a twelve-month period commencing on that date. An adjustment must be made to set up a prepaid license amount as at December 31, 0007 (if necessary, round the figures to the closest dollar).

g. Included in the amount listed in the trial balance under prepaid expenses is $2,415 for prepaid advertising (marketing), which should be recorded as an expense in the year 0007.

h. Of the deferred interest expense, $3,427 should also be charged to the year 0007 operations.

i. The allowance for bad debts account should be increased to an amount equal to 10 percent of the accounts receivable amount.

j. On December 15, 0007, the hotel purchased a new piece of equipment at a cost of $3,417. No invoice has yet been received for this, but record it in the accounts for the year 0007 (note that, with reference to item k. below, depreciation on this equipment may be recorded as if it had been in use for the full year).

k. Record depreciation for year 0007 at the following rates:
Building: 5 percent of net book value (cost, less accumulated depreciation as at December 31, 0006).
Furniture and fixtures: 20 percent of net book value.

l. Calculate and record income taxes at 50 percent of income before tax.

Required:

1. Income statements for each of the three operating departments (along the lines of Exhibit 2.1).
2. A summary income statement (see Exhibit 2.2).
3. A balance sheet and statement of retained earnings.

2.10 George Jarvis purchased a trailer park on January 1. It is now March 31. George has no accounting training but has kept a record of his cash receipts and cash disbursements for the three months:

	Receipts	**Disbursements**
Jarvis investment of cash for shares paid for trailer park:		$40,000
Land	$ 84,300	

	Receipts	Disbursements
Building	108,000	
Office equipment	2,600	
	$194,900	
Less: mortgage payable assumed	161,000	$33,900
Insurance		2,400
Wages		1,700
Maintenance		400
Office supplies		300
Utilities		600
Property taxes		3,000
George Jarvis salary		3,600
Rental income	16,200	
Mortgage interest expense		3,300
Principal payments made on mortgage for January and February		1,000

As Mr. Jarvis's accountant, you discover the following further information: The building has an estimated life of twenty years and straight-line depreciation is to be used. The office equipment is expected to last another five years, at which time its trade-in value is estimated at $100. The insurance was prepaid on January 1 for the entire year. The wages are for the maintenance man. He has worked and has not yet been paid for five days during the period ending March 31. He is paid $3.50 an hour and works eight hours per day. An invoice for grounds maintenance expense of $80 has not yet been paid. The utility bill for March has not yet been received. It is estimated it will amount to $200. The property taxes were paid in January for the entire year. A rental tenant has not yet paid for his space in March. He owes the trailer park $100. However, included in the $16,200 received for rental income to date is the amount for a tenant who has prepaid for the entire year. His rent is $50 a month. No interest or principal payments have been paid on the mortgage for March. Interest for March is $1,600. Principal payments for the balance of the year (including March) are $6,000.

This is an incorporated company. Using accrual basis accounting, prepare an income statement for the three months ending March 31 and a balance sheet as at March 31.

CASE 2

Charlie Driver was rather pleased with the results for the 3C Company's first year, particularly since it was operating only part time. He also discovered that he enjoyed the catering business. In fact he has decided to continue one more year with the 3C Company, finish his marketing courses, and meanwhile look for a suitable restaurant that he could operate.

Towards the end of the second year, he found what he was looking for —an 84-seat table service restaurant that had been closed for about 3 months. The present owner wishes to retire and is prepared to lease the restaurant to Charlie for five years. The first year's rent is $24,000, to be increased by 10 percent a year over the preceding year for each of the following four years. Since the restaurant's furniture and equipment are quite old and have little value, the owner agrees that Charlie can trade it in for whatever he can get toward new furniture and equipment. Charlie negotiated with a local supplier to purchase new furniture and equipment at a cost of $225,120. The furniture and equipment are estimated to have a five-year life.

Charlie realized that for tax and other reasons he should incorporate a company to operate the restaurant (even though he is going to continue with the same restaurant name) and any future endeavors he undertakes. He, therefore, incorporated a company under the name of Charles's Classic Cuisine Corporation. We shall simplify that to the 4C Company.

With cash he had saved from the 3C Company and from the sale of the truck, Charlie purchased $50,000 worth of stock in the 4C Company. Since he had established a good business record over the past two years with his local bank, he was able to borrow an additional $200,000. This amount is repayable over the next five years in monthly installments of principal and interest.

Although Charlie hired a bookkeeper, he has asked you to prepare his year-end financial statements and eventually discuss the results of the 4C Company's first year of operation with him. You have the following listing of general ledger account balances:

	Debit	Credit
Cash	$ 36,218	
Accounts receivable	17,104	
Inventory, food	6,128	
Inventory, beverage	3,207	
Prepaid expenses	2,142	
Furniture and equipment	225,120	
Accounts payable		$ 8,825

	Debit	Credit
Bank loan		$163,518
Common stock		50,000
Revenue, food		458,602
Revenue, beverage		180,509
Purchases, food	$181,110	
Purchases, beverage	38,307	
Salaries and wages	221,328	
Laundry	16,609	
Kitchen fuel	7,007	
China, glass, silver expense	13,819	
Contract cleaning	5,906	
Licenses	3,205	
Other operating expenses	4,101	
Administrative and general	15,432	
Marketing	6,917	
Energy costs	7,918	
Insurance	1,895	
Rent	24,000	
Interest	23,981	

The inventory figures in this listing of account balances are for the beginning of year one. The December 31 year-end figures are food $5,915 and beverage $2,211. Adjustments must be made for these inventories. In addition an adjustment must be made for accrued payroll of $2,215. Depreciation of furniture and equipment should be made on a straight-line basis. The amount of the bank loan principal that will have to be paid in year two is $38,260. Calculate income tax at 25 percent of income before tax.

Prepare an income statement and a balance sheet for the 4C Company for the year 0001.

3 Analysis and Interpretation of Financial Statements

Chapter Highlights

The first part of this chapter introduces the reader to the various groups of people who might be interested in analyzing a company's financial statements. However, the rest of the chapter concentrates on the types of techniques useful for internal management.

Two types of balance sheet analyses are illustrated: comparative and comparative common-size. Income statement analysis is illustrated using the same two methods. A further method of income statement analysis is explored using average check, average cost, and average income per guest.

Trend results (operating results over a period of time) are discussed, as is the use of an index trend to obtain more meaningful figures.

The implications of price and cost level changes (inflation or deflation) on the operating results of a business are covered in some detail. The reader is shown how to use a readily available index, or compile his or her own index for a specific business, and how to convert historic sales figures to current dollar amounts.

The chapter concludes with a listing of some of the other analysis tools that could be used, depending on the needs of management for more or different information, and illustrates a manager's daily report for summarizing statistical data.

Chapter Objectives

After studying this chapter the reader should be able to:

1. Explain some of the ways in which different readers of financial statements are interested in different aspects of those statements.
2. Describe comparative analysis and use it for balance sheet and income statement analysis.
3. Describe comparative common-size analysis and use it for balance sheet and income statement analysis.
4. Calculate average sale, average cost, and average income, per guest.
5. Prepare trend results.
6. Prepare an index trend.
7. Use index numbers to convert historic dollars to current dollars.
8. List and briefly describe the use of some of the various analysis techniques and tools common to the hospitality industry.

ANALYSIS AND INTERPRETATION OF FINANCIAL STATEMENTS

Analysis and interpretation of financial statements means looking at the various parts of the financial statements, relating the parts to each other and to the picture as a whole, and determining if any meaningful and useful interpretation can be made out of this analysis.

All of the various readers of financial statements (managers, owners, investors, and creditors) have an interest in analyzing and interpreting the financial statements. However, what is of interest to one may be of less interest to another. For example, managers are very concerned about the internal operating efficiency of the organization and will look for indications that things are running smoothly, that operating goals are being met, and that the various departments are being managed as profitably as possible. Stockholders, on the other hand, are more interested in the net income picture and about future earnings and dividend prospects, and in many cases would not be concerned about or be familiar with internal departmental results.

Management concerned about operating efficiency

Investors other than stockholders and creditors may be interested in the net income picture but are even more interested in the debt-paying ability of the company. A company may have good earnings but, because of a shortage of cash, may not be able to meet its debt obligations.

An exhaustive coverage of analysis and interpretation of financial statements is beyond the scope of this text. Therefore, discussion will be confined to some of the more fundamental analysis techniques that lend themselves well to the hospitality industry. Also, comment will be confined to the two major financial statements: the balance sheet and the income statement. The analysis techniques illustrated are those that would be normally used by the operation's management.

COMPARATIVE BALANCE SHEETS

Changes not always obvious

Differences in dollars and percentages

A basic set of financial statements includes a balance sheet at a specific date and an income statement for the year ending on that date. Some sets of financial statements include a balance sheet and an income statement for both the current year and the previous year. In this way the changes that have occurred between the two years can be seen. However, for the average reader of financial statements, these changes are not always obvious. It is not easy to compare mentally the differences between the two sets of figures. To aid in making comparisons it is useful to have additional information provided. Exhibit 3.1 shows balance sheets for two successive years. But the exhibit, in addition to having the asset, liability, and stockholders' equity dollar amounts alongside the various items for each year, also has two extra columns for comparative analysis—one showing the difference in dollars for each item and the other expressing this dollar difference as a percentage increase or decrease over the base year.

These latter two columns are most helpful in pinpointing large changes that have occurred, either dollar amount changes or percentage changes. Consider the cash account. The change from year 0001 to year 0002 is $12,500. This may or may not be a large change in dollar amount, depending on the size of the hotel. The change becomes more obvious when expressed in percentage terms: 54.6 percent ($12,500 divided by $22,900 and multiplied by 100). Why has the cash account more than doubled in the past year? With reference to the marketable securities account, which has declined by $13,000 (86.7 percent), it looks as if most of the securities held have been cashed in during the year. Is this conversion for a specific purpose? If not, perhaps we should use some of it to reduce accounts payable, which have gone up by $7,300 (or 38 percent).

Changes in accounts raise questions

Notice also that the amount of money tied up in inventories has gone up by $4,800. This may not be much in dollars, but it is an increase of 24.1 percent over the previous year. Has our volume of sales increased sufficiently to justify this increase in inventories? An analysis of change in inventory turnover rates might answer this question. (See Chapter 12 for a discussion of inventory turnover.)

Note that the deposits and credit balances account has gone up by 260 percent. Has there been a change in the policy concerning deposits required for future bookings or reservations, or is this change indicative of a big increase in guaranteed future business compared to a year ago?

Exhibit 3.1 Comparative balance sheets.

	Year Ending December 31 0001	Year Ending December 31 0002	Increase (+) or Decrease (−) from Year 0001 to Year 0002	
ASSETS				
Current assets				
Cash	$ 22,900	$ 35,400	+ $12,500	+ 54.6%
Accounts receivable	23,100	25,200	+ 2,100	+ 9.1
Marketable securities	15,000	2,000	− 13,000	− 86.7
Inventories	19,900	24,700	+ 4,800	+ 24.1
Prepaid expenses	5,200	4,900	− 300	− 5.8
Total current assets	$ 86,100	$ 92,200	+ $ 6,100	+ 7.1%
Fixed assets				
Land	$ 161,800	$ 161,800	Ø	Ø
Building	1,432,800	1,432,800	Ø	Ø
Furniture and equipment	374,700	415,600	+ $40,900	+ 10.9%
China, glass, etc.	25,600	28,400	+ 2,800	+ 10.9
	$1,994,900	$2,038,600	+ $43,700	+ 2.2%
Less: accumulated depreciation	(632,200)	(722,000)	+(89,800)	+(14.2)
Total fixed assets	$1,362,700	$1,316,600	− $46,100	− 3.4%
Total assets	$1,448,800	$1,408,800	− $40,000	− 2.8%
LIABILITIES AND STOCKHOLDERS' EQUITY				
Current liabilities				
Accounts payable	$ 19,200	$ 26,500	+ $ 7,300	+ 38.0%
Accrued expenses	3,500	4,100	+ 600	+ 17.1
Income taxes payable	12,300	10,900	− 1,400	− 11.4
Deposits and credit balances	500	1,800	+ 1,300	+ 260.0
Current portion of mortgage	27,200	25,100	− 2,100	− 7.7
Total current liabilities	$ 62,700	$ 68,400	+ $ 5,700	+ 9.1%
Long-term liability				
Mortgage payable	$ 812,900	$ 787,800	− $25,100	− 3.1%
Stockholders' equity				
Common shares	$ 300,000	$ 300,000	Ø	Ø
Retained earnings	273,200	252,600	− $20,600	− 7.5%
Total stockholders' equity	$ 573,200	$ 552,600	− $20,600	− 2.1%
Total liabilities and stockholders' equity	$1,448,800	$1,408,800	− $40,000	− 2.8%

Absolute versus Relative Changes

In comparative analysis, the terms "absolute" and "relative change" are sometimes used. An absolute change shows the dollar change from one period to the next. A relative change is the absolute change expressed as a percentage.

An absolute change may sometimes appear large (for example, $10,000) but when compared to its base figure (for example, $1,000,000) represents a relative change of only one percent. By the same token, a relative change may seem high (for example, 50 percent) but when compared to its base figure is quite small in absolute terms (for example, a $50 base figure increasing to $75). In terms of the total income statement, this $25 change (even though it shows a relative increase of 50 percent) is insignificant. Therefore, when analyzing comparative statements, both the absolute and the relative changes should be looked at, and only those that exceed both acceptable norms would be of concern.

Acceptable norms

For example, absolute changes of concern might be established at $10,000 and relative changes at 5 percent, and only those changes that exceeded both $10,000 and 5 percent would be investigated. In this situation, the following changes would not be investigated:

- Above $10,000 but below 5 percent.
- Above 5 percent but below $10,000.
- Below $10,000 and below 5 percent.

COMPARATIVE COMMON-SIZE BALANCE SHEETS

Another way of looking at balance sheets is to convert them to common-size statements. Exhibit 3.2 shows the balance sheets from Exhibit 3.1 converted to a common-size format. Common size means that total assets are given a value of 100 percent, and each individual asset account is then expressed as a fraction of that 100 percent. For example, the cash account in year 0001 is 1.6 percent of total assets ($22,900 divided by $1,448,800 and multiplied by 100).

Total liabilities and stockholders' equity are also given a value of 100 percent, and individual liability and equity accounts are expressed as a portion of that 100 percent. For example, accounts payable are 1.3 percent of total liabilities and stockholders' equity in year 0001 ($19,200 divided by $1,448,800 and multiplied by 100).

Advantage of comparative common-size statements

The advantage of comparative common-size statements is that they show changes in proportion of individual accounts from one period to the next. For example, the cash account in year 0001 was 1.6 percent of total assets. In year 0002 it was 2.5 percent of total assets. This change in

Exhibit 3.2 Comparative common-size balance sheets.

	Year Ending December 31		Common Size	
	0001	**0002**	**0001**	**0002**
ASSETS				
Current assets				
Cash	$ 22,900	$ 35,400	1.6%	2.5%
Accounts receivable	23,100	25,200	1.6	1.8
Marketable securities	15,000	2,000	1.0	0.1
Inventories	19,900	24,700	1.4	1.8
Prepaid expenses	5,200	4,900	0.4	0.3
Total current assets	$ 86,100	$ 92,200	6.0%	6.5%
Fixed assets				
Land	$ 161,800	$ 161,800	11.2%	11.5%
Building	1,432,800	1,432,800	98.7	101.7
Furniture & equipment	374,700	415,600	25.9	29.5
China, glass, etc.	25,600	28,400	1.8	2.0
	$1,994,900	$2,038,600	137.6%	144.7%
Less: accumulated depreciation	(632,200)	(722,000)	(43.6)	(51.2)
Total fixed assets	$1,362,700	$1,316,600	94.0%	93.5%
Total assets	$1,448,800	$1,408,800	100.0%	100.0%
LIABILITIES AND STOCKHOLDERS' EQUITY				
Current liabilities				
Accounts payable	$ 19,200	$ 26,500	1.3%	1.9%
Accrued expenses	3,500	4,100	0.2	0.3
Income taxes payable	12,300	10,900	0.8	0.8
Deposits and credit balances	500	1,800	0.1	0.1
Current portion of mortgage	27,200	25,100	1.9	1.8
Total current liabilities	$ 62,700	$ 68,400	4.3%	4.9%
Long-term liabilities				
Mortgage payable	$ 812,900	$ 787,800	56.1%	55.9%
Stockholders' equity				
Common shares	$ 300,000	$ 300,000	20.7%	21.3%
Retained earnings	273,200	252,600	18.9	17.9
Total stockholders' equity	$ 573,200	$ 552,600	39.6%	39.2%
Total liabilities and stockholders' equity	$1,448,800	$1,408,800	100.0%	100.0%

proportion would normally attract a reader's attention and raise questions. Attention might also be drawn to other accounts where large changes have occurred. The comparative, common-size technique is particularly useful when comparing two companies whose size and/or level of business is so different that other techniques of analysis are not appropriate.

Answers to questions improve effectiveness

Whether a hotel or foodservice operation uses comparative balance sheets or comparative common-size balance sheets is a matter of choice. Normally only one or the other would be wanted since both draw the attention of the reader to the relevant accounts where changes have occurred. These changes, in turn, should provoke questions, the answers to which may be helpful in running the business more effectively. Attention should be focused on the balance sheet because of the need for effective control or management of a company's assets. However, as a management technique for controlling internal day-to-day operations, comparative income statements are often more useful than comparative balance sheets.

COMPARATIVE INCOME STATEMENTS

Calculation of percentages

Exhibit 3.3 shows two annual income statements for a food department of a hotel. The statements include a column for the change in dollar amount from year 0001 to year 0002, and another column expressing this change as a percentage increase or decrease from year 0001 to year 0002. The percentage change figures are calculated by dividing the dollar change figure by the base figure in year 0001 and multiplying by 100. For example, dining room revenue has gone up 10.1 percent, calculated as follows:

$$\frac{\$20,300}{\$201,600} \times 100 = 10.1\%$$

The other percentage change figures are calculated in the same way. Note that within each revenue area, except banquets, the revenue has increased, but total revenue has gone up only 2.1 percent. The reason for this relatively small increase in total revenue is that banquet revenue was down 7.7 percent over the year. Can the reasons be determined? (Is the sales department not doing an effective job? Is there a new, competitive operation close by? Are prices too high?)

Income should increase with revenue increase

Even with the total revenue increase, small as it is, income has declined $37,100, or 24.2 percent. This is a drastic change. With revenue up, all other factors being equal, income should also be up, not down.

All other things are, obviously, not equal, because analysis of costs

Exhibit 3.3 Comparative departmental income statement—food department.

	For Year Ending December 31 0001	For Year Ending December 31 0002	Increase or Decrease from Year 0001 to 0002	
Revenue				
Dining room	$201,600	$221,900	+ $20,300	+10.1%
Coffee shop	195,900	201,700	+ 5,800	+ 3.0
Banquets	261,200	241,100	− 20,100	− 7.7
Room service	81,700	82,600	+ 900	+ 1.1
Bar	111,200	121,800	+ 10,600	+ 9.5
Total revenue	$851,600	$869,100	+$17,500	+ 2.1%
Cost of sales				
Cost of food used	$352,500	$373,700	+ $21,200	+ 6.0%
Less: employee meals	(30,100)	(32,500)	+(2,400)	+ 8.0
Net food cost	322,400	341,200	+ 18,800	+ 5.8%
Gross profit	$529,200	$527,900	−$ 1,300	− 2.5%
Departmental expenses				
Salaries and wages	$277,400	$304,500	+ $27,100	+ 9.8%
Employee benefits	34,500	37,800	+ 3,300	+ 9.6
China, glassware	7,100	7,800	+ 700	+ 9.9
Cleaning supplies	6,400	6,800	+ 400	+ 6.3
Decorations	2,200	1,800	− 400	−18.2
Guest supplies	6,500	7,000	+ 500	+ 7.7
Laundry	15,500	18,400	+ 2,900	+18.7
Licenses	3,400	3,500	+ 100	+ 2.9
Linen	3,700	4,200	+ 500	+13.5
Menus	2,000	2,500	+ 500	+25.0
Miscellaneous	800	1,100	+ 300	+37.5
Paper supplies	4,900	5,700	+ 800	+16.3
Printing, stationery	4,700	4,600	− 100	− 2.1
Silver	2,300	2,100	− 200	− 8.7
Uniforms	3,100	2,400	− 700	−22.6
Utensils	1,700	1,800	+ 100	+ 5.9
Total expenses	376,200	412,000	+ 35,800	+ 9.5%
Departmental income	$153,000	$115,900	−$37,100	−24.2%

shows that the majority of them have increased at a greater rate than the revenue increase. To select only one as an example, the laundry cost has gone up $2,900 over the year, or 18.7 percent. Are we using more linen than before? Has our supplier increased the cost to us by this percentage? Whatever the reason, corrective action can be taken once the cause is known. Each expense can be analyzed in its own way. In this particular illustration, assuming the increased costs were inevitable, perhaps the increased costs have not yet been adjusted for in menu selling prices.

COMPARATIVE COMMON-SIZE INCOME STATEMENTS

Total revenue equals 100 percent

Income statements can also be illustrated on a comparative, common-size basis. This is shown in Exhibit 3.4. On income statements, the total revenue amount is given the value of 100 percent, and all other items on the statement are expressed as a fraction of total revenue. For example, in year 0001 dining room revenue was 23.7 percent of total revenue. This is calculated as follows:

$$\frac{\$201,600}{\$851,600} \times 100 = 23.7\%$$

The other revenue area figures are calculated in the same way, using in year 0001, $851,600 as the denominator.

Expense items also use $851,600 as the denominator for year 0001. Net food cost, for example, is calculated as follows:

$$\frac{\$322,400}{\$851,600} \times 100 = 37.9\%$$

Separate food and beverage cost percentages

Note that, if this were a combined food and beverage operation, food cost should still be calculated as a percentage of food revenue and beverage cost as a percentage of beverage revenue, even if all other costs are expressed as a percentage of combined food and beverage revenue.

One way of interpreting the common-size income statement information in year 0001 is to say that, out of every $1.00 of revenue, 37.9 cents was for food, 32.6 cents was for salaries and wages, 4.0 cents for employee benefits, and 7.5 cents for all other operating expenses, leaving only 18 cents for income. In year 0002 this income was down to 13.3 cents out of every $1.00 of revenue. Comparative, common-size income statements show which items, as a proportion of revenue, have changed enough to require investigation.

Exhibit 3.4 Comparative, common-size income statement—food department.

	For Year Ending December 31		For Year Ending December 31	
	0001	0002	0001	0002
Revenue				
Dining room	$201,600	$221,900	23.7%	25.5%
Coffee shop	195,900	201,700	23.0	23.2
Banquets	261,200	241,100	30.7	27.7
Room service	81,700	82,600	9.6	9.5
Bar	111,200	121,800	13.0	14.1
Total revenue	$851,600	$869,100	100.0%	100.0%
Cost of sales				
Cost of food used	$352,500	$373,700	41.4%	43.0%
Less: employee meals	(30,100)	(32,500)	(3.5)	(3.7)
Net food cost	322,400	341,200	37.9	39.3
Gross profit	$529,200	$527,900	62.1%	60.7%
Departmental expenses				
Salaries and wages	$277,400	$304,500	32.6%	35.0%
Employee benefits	34,500	37,800	4.0	4.3
All other operating expenses	64,300	69,700	7.5	8.1
Total expenses	$376,200	$412,000	44.1	47.4
Departmental income	$153,000	$115,900	18.0%	13.3%

Food cost increase causes income decline

For example, one of the causes for the decline to 13.3 cents profit from each dollar of revenue in year 0002 is that the amount spent on food (net food cost) has risen from 37.9 cents to 39.3 cents out of each dollar of revenue. This 1.4 cent increase may seem insignificant, but if it had not occurred we would have made $12,167.00 more income, calculated as follows:

$$\$869,100 \times 1.4\% = \$12,167.00$$

Note that, in the interest of brevity in Exhibit 3.4, a number of expenses have been added together under "all other operating expenses." In year 0001 this figure is 7.5 percent of revenue, and in year 0002, 8.1 percent of revenue. This is a relatively small change and might normally be unnoticed. It is small only because many of the individual expense item increases are offset by several that decreased, thus burying the facts. In practice it would be best to detail each individual expense and express it as a percentage of revenue to have full disclosure.

Attention drawn to problems

The income statement illustrated for the food operation was both comparative (Exhibit 3.3) and comparative, common-size (Exhibit 3.4). Normally, only one or the other would be used. They each draw attention, albeit in a different way, to problem areas requiring investigation and, if necessary, corrective action.

Note again that the comparative common-size method is the more appropriate one to use when comparing two companies whose size or scale of operation is quite different.

There is one other method of comparative analysis particularly suited to the food operation, and that is to calculate and compare average revenue per guest, average cost per guest, and average income per guest information.

AVERAGE CHECK, COST, AND INCOME PER GUEST

Number of guests data required

Exhibit 3.5 illustrates average revenue (more commonly called average check or average cover), average cost, and average income information on a per guest basis. In Exhibit 3.5 a column has been added showing number of guests during the year in each of the revenue areas and in total for the entire food department. The average check per guest for each revenue area is calculated by dividing the revenue in that area by the number of guests in that area. For example, in the dining room, in year 0006 the average check is:

$$\frac{\$604,800}{35,130} = \$17.22 \text{ average check in dining room}$$

Exhibit 3.5 Comparative average check, cost, and income per guest—food department.

	Year Ending December 31, 0006			Year Ending December 31, 0007		
	Revenue	Guests	Average Check	Revenue	Guests	Average Check
Department						
Dining room	$ 604,800	35,130	$17.22	$ 665,700	36,210	$18.38
Coffee shop	587,700	71,200	8.25	605,100	78,200	7.74
Banquets	783,600	60,190	13.02	723,300	50,780	14.24
Room service	245,100	16,870	14.53	247,800	17,110	14.48
Bar	333,600	32,170	10.37	365,400	35,490	10.30
Totals	$2,554,800	215,560	$11.85	$2,607,300	217,790	$11.97

	Cost	Guests	Average Cost	Cost	Guests	Average Cost
Operating Costs						
Net food cost	$ 967,200	215,560	$ 4.49	$1,023,600	217,790	$ 4.70
Salaries and wages	832,200	same	3.86	913,500	same	4.19
Employee benefits	103,500	same	0.48	113,400	same	0.52
Other expenses	192,900	same	0.89	209,100	same	0.96
Totals	$2,095,800	215,560	$ 9.72	$2,259,600	217,790	$10.37
Income	$ 459,000	215,560	$ 2.13	$ 347,700	217,790	$ 1.60

Total average check calculation

The total average check per guest is calculated by dividing total revenue by total guests. In year 0006:

$$\frac{\$2,554,800}{215,560} = \$11.85 \text{ total average check}$$

Food cost per guest calculation

Cost and income figures are calculated by dividing the relevant cost, or income, amount by the total number of guests. For example, in year 0006, net food cost per guest is:

$$\frac{\$967,200}{215,560} = \$4.49$$

Income per guest calculation

and year 0006 income per guest is:

$$\frac{\$459,000}{215,560} = \$2.13$$

Some of the facts that come to light are that the number of guests served in all revenue areas increased, except in banquets where there was a decrease of 9,410 (60,190 less 50,780). This is a decrease of 15.6 percent (9,410 divided by 60,190, then multiplied by 100). At the same time, in the banquet area the average spending per guest increased from $13.02 to $14.24. This is an increase of $1.22 per guest, or 9.4 percent ($1.22 divided by $13.02, then multiplied by 100). The combination of higher average check (average revenue) but reduced numbers of guests meant that our banquet revenue was $60,300 lower in year 0007 than in year 0006. Is this a desirable trend? Is our banquet selling policy causing us to sell higher priced banquets but not allowing us to sell to as many customers? Has an increase in selling prices driven away a considerable amount of business?

Typical questions raised

In terms of total average revenue per guest for the food operation in year 0007, we took in 12 cents more per guest ($11.97 − $11.85), but we spent 65 cents more per guest ($10.37 − $9.72), and thus our income per guest declined 53 cents ($2.13 − $1.60). Obviously our costs per guest have risen much faster than our revenue per guest. The individual items of expense, on a per guest basis, have all increased, some more than others. They need to be investigated to see whether the trend cannot be reversed. Alternatively, sales prices may need to be increased to compensate for uncontrollable, increasing costs.

Similar approach for other departments

Although the illustration (Exhibit 3.5) was for a food operation, a beverage department could be analyzed equally as well using the same approach. Similarly, a hotel rooms department could be analyzed using number of guests or number of rooms used as the unit figure to be divided into revenue, costs, or income.

TREND RESULTS

The balance sheet and income statement illustrations discussed so far have only taken into consideration comparisons and analysis between two successive periods. Limiting an analysis to only two periods (weeks, months, or years) can be misleading if an unusual occurrence or factor distorted the results for either of the two periods. Looking at results over a greater number of periods of time can often be more useful in indicating the direction in which a business is heading. For example, the following shows trend results for a cocktail lounge for six successive months:

Distorted results

Month	Revenue	Change in Revenue	Percentage Change
1	$25,000		
2	30,000	+ $5,000	+ 20%

Month	Revenue	Change in Revenue	Percentage Change
3	$33,000	+$3,000	+10
4	35,000	+ 2,000	+ 6
5	36,000	+ 1,000	+ 3
6	36,000	0	0

Calculation of change in revenue

In the above the change in revenue dollar amount for each period is calculated by subtracting from each period's revenue the revenue of the preceding period. For example, in period 3:

$$\$33,000 - \$30,000 = \$3,000 \text{ change in revenue}$$

Calculation of percentage change

The percentage change figures are calculated by dividing each period's change in revenue dollar amounts by the revenue of the previous period and multiplying by 100. For example, in period 3:

$$\frac{\$3,000}{\$30,000} \times 100 = 10\%$$

Uses for trend information

Over a long enough period of time, trend results show the direction in which a business is going. In our particular case, the trend results indicate that, although business has been increasing over the past few periods, it now seems to have leveled off. Has the business reached its maximum potential in revenue? Trend information may be found useful in such areas as forecasting or budgeting, or in decision making. (Is it time we spent money on advertising to increase volume?)

The particular trend result illustrated above was for a specific item (revenue in a bar), but comparison of trends of related items (revenue and expenses) can be indicative of problems. For example, the cost of sales (liquor cost) figures for our lounge for the same six periods are

Period	Liquor Cost
1	$ 7,500
2	9,200
3	10,300
4	10,800
5	11,100
6	11,200

These costs could be tabulated alongside the revenue with dollar change and percentage change figures calculated for both revenue and costs following the format illustrated earlier for revenue. However, a more useful approach is to calculate for each (revenue and liquor cost) an index trend.

Index Trend

An index trend is calculated by assigning a value of 100 (or 100 percent) in period one for each item being tabulated as follows.

Period	Revenue	Liquor Cost	Revenue Index	Liquor Cost Index
1	$25,000	$ 7,500	100	100
2	30,000	9,200	120	123
3	33,000	10,300	132	137
4	35,000	10,800	140	144
5	36,000	11,100	144	148
6	36,000	11,200	144	149

**Calculation of
index number**

The index figure for each succeeding period is calculated by dividing the dollar amount for that period by the base period dollar amount and multiplying by 100. For example, in period 2 the revenue index is

$$\frac{\$30,000}{\$25,000} \times 100 = 120$$

In period 5, the liquor cost index is

$$\frac{\$11,100}{\$ 7,500} \times 100 = 148$$

Our completed index trend results show us that the liquor cost has been increasing faster than liquor revenue. Expressed another way, revenue is up 44 percent (144 − 100) and liquor cost is up 49 percent (149 − 100). This is normally an undesirable trend that needs investigation and possibly correction.

PRICE AND COST LEVEL CHANGES (INFLATION OR DEFLATION)

**Consider
implications of
price and cost
changes**

When comparing operating results, and in particular when analyzing trend figures, the reader must be aware of the effect changing dollar values have on the results. One hundred pounds of vegetables a few years ago weigh exactly the same as one hundred pounds of vegetables today; but the amount of money required to buy one hundred pounds today is probably quite different than the amount of money needed a few years ago. Prices change over time. In the same way that prices change to us, so too do the prices we charge our customers for rooms, food, beverages, and other services. When comparing income and expense items over a fairly long period of time, it is necessary to consider the implications of upward changing prices or costs (inflation), or the reverse (deflation).

Consider a restaurant with the following revenue in two successive years:

Year 1 $100,000
Year 2 $105,000

Dollars of unequal value

This is a $5,000 or 5 percent increase in volume. But if restaurant menu prices had been increased over the year by 10 percent due to inflation, then our year 2 revenue should have been at least $110,000 just to stay even with year 1 volume. In other words, when we try to compare revenue for successive periods in inflationary or deflationary times, as in this case, we are comparing unequal values. Last year's dollar does not have the same value as this year's. What a dollar would buy last year may now require $1.10. Is there a method that will allow us to convert previous period's dollars into current period dollars so trends can be analyzed more meaningfully? The answer is yes, with the use of index numbers.

Use of index to adjust revenue

The consumer price index is probably one of the most commonly used and widely understood indexes available. But many other indexes are produced by the government and other organizations. By selecting an appropriate index, conversion of previous period's dollars into current year dollars is simple. Consider the following figures showing trend results for a restaurant's revenue for the past five years.

Year	Revenue	Change in Revenue	Percentage Change
1	$420,000	0	0
2	450,000	$30,000	7.1%
3	465,000	15,000	3.3
4	485,000	20,000	4.3
5	510,000	25,000	5.2

The trend shows increasing revenue each year, generally a favorable trend. But is it reasonable to compare $420,000 of revenue in year 1 with $510,000 of revenue in year 5? By adjusting all revenue to comparable year 5 dollars, a more realistic picture of our restaurant revenue may emerge. The index used to do this would be based on restaurant revenue, and we would need to use the index numbers for the same five-year period for which we wish to adjust our restaurant revenue. Let us suppose the index numbers were as follows:

Year	Index Number
1	105
2	112
3	119
4	128
5	142

Equation for conversion to current dollars

The equation for converting past periods' (historic) dollars to current (real) dollars is as follows:

$$\text{Historic dollars} \times \frac{\text{Index number for current period}}{\text{Index number for historic period}} = \text{Current dollars}$$

The following tabulation shows the index numbers used to convert the earlier revenue figures into terms of today's current dollars.

Year	Index	Historic Revenue	×	Conversion Equation	=	Current Dollars
1	105	$420,000	×	142/105	=	$568,000
2	112	450,000	×	142/112	=	571,000
3	119	465,000	×	142/119	=	555,000
4	128	485,000	×	142/128	=	538,000
5	142	510,000	×	142/142	=	510,000

The resulting picture is quite different from the unadjusted revenue figures. In fact, in terms of current dollars, our annual revenue has generally declined from year 1 to year 5, and this would not normally be a desirable trend.

Using own inhouse index

If a restaurant revenue index were not readily available, an operator could easily compile one by converting the annual average check figure for each of a number of years to an index, giving year 1 the value of 100. This is illustrated as follows:

Year	Average Check	Index
1	$10.20	100
2	11.01	108
3	12.06	118
4	12.63	124
5	13.68	134

The index numbers for each year, other than year 1, are calculated by dividing the average check for that year by the average check for year 1 and multiplying by 100. For example, the year 3 index number is

$$\frac{\$12.06}{\$10.20} \times 100 = 118$$

Care in use of an index

A restaurant creating its own index in this way might find it much more accurate since it reflects only what has happened to prices within that restaurant. A national average restaurant index might have factors built into it that have no bearing on any one individual operation. Preferably, such an individual index should be used only if the size and nature of the operation have not changed during the period under review, otherwise the results could be misleading.

Once the index has been prepared, it can be applied using the equation already demonstrated to convert historic revenue to current dollars. A bar could use the same type of homemade index using average customer spending. For its rooms revenue, a hotel or motel could use average room rates converted to an index.

Costs can be converted in the same way, using an appropriate index for the particular cost or expense under review (for example, a wage index would probably be appropriate for adjusting labor costs). Alternatively, an individual establishment might be able to construct its own index for each individual expense, as was just demonstrated for prices, basing the indexes on a cost per guest, or cost per room occupied. In fact, complete income statements for past periods can be reconstructed by converting them in their entirety to current period, or current year, dollars.

Converting complete income statements

Such wholesale conversions would probably go beyond the needs of most hotel, or foodservice, management needs; but, whether or not such a major accounting conversion is used, the implications of price and cost level changes should not be ignored. Balance sheets are also implicated. A balance sheet showing a cash balance on hand of $100,000 in each of two successive years may seem to indicate no change in the cash position. But will $100,000 now buy as much as $100,000 a year ago? Similarly, the historic cost prices of land, buildings, and equipment on balance sheets may also be misleading. However, a complete and comprehensive discussion of inflation accounting or current dollar accounting is far beyond the scope of this book.

OTHER ANALYSIS TOOLS

Selection of appropriate tool

There are many other revenue and cost analysis techniques and tools available, apart from those already mentioned. Some of the more common ones are discussed briefly below. Caution must be exercised in their use. It is important to select the appropriate analysis tool. It is also important to remember that the information provided from the use of these techniques may only indicate that a problem exists. The solution to the problem is entirely in the hands of management.

Food and Beverage Operations

1. *Food and/or beverage cost percentage.* This is expressed as a percentage of the related revenue as illustrated and discussed earlier in the chapter with reference to Exhibit 3.4. The percentage can be compared with a standard or predetermined percentage established as a goal. Wide deviations from standard should be investigated.

Labor cost calculation

2. *Labor cost percentage.* Labor cost includes employee benefits and is expressed as a percentage of related revenue. With reference to Exhibit 3.4, in year 0001 it is

$$\frac{\$277,400 + \$34,500}{\$851,600} \times 100 = \frac{\$311,900}{\$851,600} = 36.6\%$$

and in year 0002

$$\frac{\$304,500 + \$37,800}{\$869,100} \times 100 = \frac{\$342,300}{\$869,100} = 39.4\%$$

As with food and beverage cost percentages, labor cost percentage can be compared with an established standard. Again, large differences should be investigated.

3. *Dollars of revenue per employee per meal period or per day, week, or month or number of guests served per employee per meal period or per day, week, or month.* For example, if a restaurant had revenue for a meal period of $1,200, 100 guests were served, and eight employees were on duty, the dollars of revenue per employee for that meal period would be

$$\frac{\$1,200}{8} = \$150$$

and the number of guests served per employee would be

$$\frac{100}{8} = 12.5$$

These ratios are used primarily to assess employee productivity against a standard or to determine any upward or downward trend in productivity.

Change of menu item on average check

4. *Average food and/or beverage check by meal period and by revenue area.* The method of calculating the average check was explained earlier in the chapter. The trend of this figure is important, but it can also be used to determine, for example, the effect that a change in menu item(s) may have on average customer spending.

5. *Seat turnover by meal period or by day.* Calculated by dividing total guests served during a meal period or a day by the number of seats the restaurant has. For example, if a restaurant had 40 seats and 100 guests were served during a meal period, the turnover for that meal period would be

$$\frac{100}{40} = 2.5$$

A high turnover is generally preferable to a low one, as long as the customers are receiving good service and not being rushed. The trend of turnovers should be analyzed. A declining trend may indicate a lowering of service or may indicate that high prices or low-quality food are keeping customers away.

Revenue per seat available

6. *Daily, weekly, monthly, or annual revenue dollars per seat available.* Calculated by dividing revenue for the period by the number of seats the restaurant has. For example, if a 125-seat restaurant had monthly sales of $250,000, monthly revenue per seat is

$$\frac{\$250,000}{125} = \$2,000$$

The trend of this figure can be revealing. It might also be useful to compare it with the results for similar types of establishments.

7. *Percentage of beverage revenue to food revenue.* For example, a restaurant had total monthly revenue of $85,160, of which food was $68,950 and beverages were $16,210. Beverages are 23.5 percent of food revenue, calculated as follows:

$$\frac{\$16,210}{\$68,950} \times 100 = 23.5\%$$

Since beverage revenue is generally more profitable than food revenue, sales efforts should be directed toward promoting beverage revenue (wine with meals, for example) to increase the ratio.

8. *Percentage of beverage revenue and/or food revenue to rooms revenue.* This would apply to a hotel. The calculation is similar to that in item 7 above, except that room revenue becomes the denominator and the numerator is either food revenue or beverage revenue. A change in the revenue mix among departments (such as a change in the percentages) can be important since some departments are more profitable than others. Advertising dollars are often more beneficially spent, from a cost/benefit point of view, on departments or areas with the highest profitability.

Rooms Department in a Hotel or Motel

Average room rates

1. *Average rate per room occupied.* Calculated daily by dividing rooms occupied into revenue from rooms. For example, if a hotel had total revenue for a night of $7,200 from 80 occupied rooms, its average rate per occupied room is

$$\frac{\$7,200}{80} = \$90$$

If it is to be calculated on a monthly basis, it is derived from dividing total rooms occupied during the month into total revenue for the month. The method is similar for an annual occupancy, except that annual figures are used. The trend of this figure is important. It can be influenced upward by directing sales efforts into selling higher priced rooms rather than lower priced ones, by increasing the rate of double occupancy (see the next item), or by altering other factors.

Occupancy percentages

2. *Occupancy percentage and/or double occupancy on a daily, weekly, monthly, or annual basis.* Occupancy is calculated by dividing the rooms used during a period (a night, a week) by the rooms available during that period (rooms in the establishment times days in the period) and multiplying by 100. For example, with reference to item 1 above, if this hotel had 100 rooms, occupancy for that night is

$$\frac{80}{100} \times 100 = 80\%$$

Double occupancy percentage is the percentage of rooms occupied that are occupied by more than one person. For example, if 20 of the 80 occupied rooms on that night were occupied by more than one person, the double occupancy is

$$\frac{20}{80} \times 100 = 25\%$$

Double occupancy is sometimes expressed by calculating the average number of people per room occupied (total number of guests for a period divided by total rooms occupied during that period). For example, if our 80 occupied rooms were occupied by 100 guests, the double occupancy would be

$$\frac{100}{80} = 1.25$$

Resort hotels Double occupancy is usually higher for resort hotels (catering to the family trade) than for transient hotels (catering primarily to the business person traveling alone).

Obviously, a high occupancy and a high double occupancy are both desirable because this indicates greater use of the rooms facilities, and also potentially greater usage of food and beverage facilities by guest-room occupants. Therefore, the trend of this information is important.

Note that, when an occupancy percentage is calculated for a period of time (such as a week), this does not mean that was the occupancy every night of the week. For example, a hotel could have an average occupancy of 70 percent for a week, with an occupancy of over 90 percent per night from Monday to Friday and a very low occupancy percentage at the weekend.

3. *Labor cost percentage.* This is expressed as a percentage of room revenue (in the same way as was illustrated in item 2 for food and beverage operations) and compared with an established standard.

Productivity 4. *Number of rooms cleaned per maid per day and/or dollars of room revenue*
measures *per front desk clerk per day, week, or month.* These are both productivity measures calculated in a similar way to the productivity measures illustrated in item 3 for food and beverage operations. These productivity measures can be compared against a standard or used to detect undesirable trends.

5. *Annual revenue per room available.* This figure is obtained by dividing annual revenue by rooms in the establishment. The trend of this figure is important, but it is also useful to compare it with results from similar types of hotel or motel.

6. *Undistributed cost dollars per room available per year.* Undistributed costs include such expenses as administrative and general, marketing, property operation and maintenance, and energy costs. The total cost of each for the year is divided by rooms in the establishment. Trends are again important, and comparison with similar establishments' results can be revealing.

Manager's Daily Report

Detection of trends important

Many of the operating statistics that are useful for analyzing the ongoing progress of an establishment can be calculated on a day-to-day basis. In this way the success level of the establishment can be monitored on a daily basis. Trends, favorable or unfavorable, can be detected while they are occurring, rather than too late for effective action to be taken. A sample of a manager's daily report that would be useful in a small hotel operation is illustrated in Exhibit 3.6. A food operation's operating statistics might be summarized as shown in Exhibit 3.7. Each establishment's management should decide which operating statistics are most useful for getting a daily overview and subsequently prepare a form that will allow these statistics to be summarized quickly each day.

INTERNAL AND EXTERNAL COMPARISONS

Do not ignore external trends

Up to this point only internal comparisons and trends of selected information have been emphasized. An internal change of selected information over time is probably the most meaningful method of seeking out problem areas so that any necessary corrective action can be taken. Nevertheless, external comparisons and trends should not be ignored. Many industrywide external trends are available that could be useful for comparison with internal results. However, trying to change internal results so they match external industry averages should be done with caution. Industry averages are only that—averages. An average industry figure may not be typical of any specific hotel or foodservice operation.

SUMMARY

Financial statement analysis is a matter of relating the various parts of the statements to each other and to the whole, and interpreting the results. Different viewers of financial statements have different parts they are interested in, and, possibly, also different interpretations they place on the results of their analyses.

Comparative analysis is one of the techniques used. This involves putting two balance sheets or income statements side by side, showing the differences between each pair of comparable figures in both dollars and as a percentage change, and interpreting the results.

Exhibit 3.6.   Manager's daily report.

SALES

	TODAY	MONTH TO DATE	FORECAST MONTH TO DATE	LAST MONTH TO DATE	LAST YEAR MONTH TO DATE
ROOMS					
FOOD					
BEVERAGE					
TELEPHONE/TELEGRAM					
VALET					
LAUNDRY					
OTHER					
TOTAL REVENUE					

STATISTICS

	TODAY	MONTH TO DATE	FORECAST MONTH TO DATE	LAST MONTH TO DATE	LAST YEAR MONTH TO DATE	BANK REPORT	
TOTAL ROOMS OCC.						BALANCE YESTERDAY	
COMP. & HOUSE USE						RECEIPTS	
VACANT ROOMS						DISBURSEMENTS	
TOTAL ROOMS AVAIL.						BALANCE TODAY	
AVERAGE ROOM RATE						ACCOUNTS RECEIVABLE	
% OF OCCUPANCY							
NO. OF DOUBLES						BALANCE YESTERDAY	
% OF DOUBLE OCC.						CHARGES	
% OF FOOD COST						CREDITS	
% OF BEVERAGE COST						BALANCE TODAY	

PAYROLL AND RELATED EXPENSES

	TODAY		MONTH TO DATE		FORECAST MONTH TO DATE		LAST MONTH TO DATE		LAST YEAR MONTH TO DATE	
	AMOUNT	%	AMOUNT	%	AMOUNT	%	AMOUNT	%	AMOUNT	%
ROOM										
FOOD & BEVERAGE										
OVERHEAD DEPTS.										

Date _____

Day _____

Weather _____

Exhibit 3.7. Daily report.

Day _____ Date _____ Weather _____

MEALS SERVED:	Number of Covers					Average Check	
	Breakfast	Lunch	Dinner	Total Today	Total to Date	Average Today	Check to Date
Dining Room							
Coffee Shop							
Room Service							
Banquet							
TOTAL							

Comparative, common-size statements apply the same technique of putting two sets of balance sheet or income statement figures side by side, but in this case one figure is given the value of 100 percent (total assets and total liabilities plus stockholders' equity on a balance sheet; total revenue on an income statement), and all other figures are expressed as a proportion of that 100 percent amount.

Another useful approach, for an income statement, is to express the revenue, cost, and income figures on an average per guest basis.

Trend results are similar to comparative statements, except that they show figures for several successive periods, showing the change in dollars and the percentage change from each period to the next.

A refinement of the raw trend figures is an index trend. In an index trend the base period is given the value of 100 or 100 percent. All subsequent period figures are expressed as a percentage of the base period amount.

One factor to be considered, particularly when analyzing financial results for two or more successive years, is that the figures must be interpreted with price/cost (inflation) level implications in mind. In order to convert previous periods' (historic) dollars into today's (current) dollars, appropriate index scales can be used. The equation is:

$$\text{Historic dollars} \times \frac{\text{Index number for current period}}{\text{Index number for historic period}} = \text{Current dollars}$$

Many individual analysis tools are available for food and beverage operations, and for the rooms department in a hotel/motel situation. One should select those that are appropriate for each situation. A daily report is usually prepared for recording those daily statistics that management requires.

Finally, although internal comparisons and analysis are most useful, there are a great many industrywide statistics published. For comparison with each organization's internal results, this external information should not be overlooked.

DISCUSSION QUESTIONS

1. Explain in what way a stockholder, reading a financial statement, might be interested in items different from the manager of the enterprise.
2. What is comparative balance sheet analysis?
3. Discuss absolute and relative changes with reference to comparative financial statement analysis.
4. Why are differences between two comparative statements frequently better shown in percentages rather than only in dollars?
5. What do you understand by the term comparative, common-size income statements?
6. In a food operation how is the average revenue per guest calculated?
7. Why are trend results often more meaningful than a comparison limited to two successive accounting periods?
8. How is an index trend calculated?
9. In inflationary times why is comparative analysis, and even an index trend, misleading?
10. What is the equation for converting past periods' (historic) dollars to current (real) dollars?
11. List four possible analysis tools that could be used in a food operation.
12. List and discuss the value of three possible analysis tools that could be used in a hotel operation.
13. Define a manager's daily report.

PROBLEMS

3.1 You have the following lists of assets, liabilities, and stockholders' equity for two successive years for a hotel.

Assets	Year 0004	Year 0005
Cash	$ 11,300	$ 15,400
Accounts receivable	15,600	25,200
Inventories	7,800	8,400

Assets	Year 0004	Year 0005
Prepaid expenses	3,900	4,100
Land	81,200	81,200
Building	758,100	795,300
Furniture and equipment	174,400	184,100
China, glass, linen, etc.	12,200	15,300
Accumulated depreciation	(315,500)	(335,800)

Liabilities and Stockholders' Equity

	Year 0004	Year 0005
Accounts payable	$ 9,100	$ 12,200
Accrued expenses	4,200	4,900
Income tax	12,400	15,500
Current portion of mortgage payable	13,600	11,200
Long-term 1st mortgage payable	315,900	308,400
Long-term 2nd mortgage payable	107,600	103,900
Common shares	125,200	145,200
Retained earnings	161,000	191,900

Present the information in proper form on a comparative balance sheet basis, and comment about any major differences between years 0004 and 0005 that you think are significant.

3.2 Present the information from Problem 3.1 in proper form on a comparative, common-size balance sheet basis, and comment about any significant changes from one year to the next.

3.3 You have the following statements for two successive months for a hotel's food department.

	August		September	
Revenue:				
Room service	$11,300		$ 9,000	
Dining room	75,900		63,700	
Lounge	5,500		4,100	
Coffee shop	53,400		48,700	
Banquets	66,200	$212,300	70,500	$196,000
Cost of sales		68,100		63,900
Gross profit		$144,200		$132,100
Operating costs:				
Wages and salaries	$75,800		$71,100	
Employee benefits	11,400		10,700	
Linen and laundry	3,200		3,000	
China, glass, and silver	5,300		4,900	
Supplies	4,900		4,700	
Other	9,600	110,200	8,800	103,200
Departmental income		$ 34,000		$ 28,900

Present the information in the form of comparative income statements and comment about any significant differences.

3.4 Present the information from Problem 3.3 in the form of comparative, common-size income statements and comment about any significant results.

3.5 With reference to Problem 3.3 information, the following are the customer counts in each revenue area for each of the two months.

	August	September
Room service	927	756
Dining room	4,628	3,765
Lounge	846	637
Coffee shop	9,709	8,604
Banquets	6,687	6,805

a. Prepare average revenue per guest figures for each revenue area for each month.
b. Prepare average cost per guest and average income per guest figures.
c. Comment about any significant results.

3.6 Resta's Restaurant's comparative, common-size income statements for two years show the following partial information:

	0001	0002	Differences Dollars	Differences Percentage
Revenue	$	$24,612	+$1,110	
Cost of sales	9,208			+2.5%
Gross profit				
Direct expenses	10,202		+$1,420	
Income before indirect expenses		2,403		−3.0%
Indirect expenses				
Net income				

Complete all the missing information, rounding amounts to the nearest dollar.

3.7 A company owns two restaurants in the same town. Operating results for the first three months of the current year for each of them are:

	Restaurant A	Restaurant B
Revenue	$154,300	$206,100
Cost of sales	60,200	78,900
Gross profit	$ 94,100	$127,200

	Restaurant A			Restaurant B		
Direct expenses			_diff_			
wages	$45,600	09.6	946	$70,400	34.2	
supplies	12,700	8.3		16,800	8.2	
other	4,500	2.9	62,800 40.7	6,100	3	93,300 45.3
			$ 31,300 20.3			$ 33,900 16.4
Indirect expenses						
rent	$ 6,500	42		$ 9,000	4.4	
insurance	2,000	13		3,000	1.6	
other	3,200	2.1	11,700 7.6	3,600	1.7	15,600 7.6
Net income			$ 19,600 12.7			$ 18,300 89

The owners of the company are concerned that Restaurant B has higher
revenue and a lower net income than Restaurant A. Analyze the situation using comparative common-size statements and comment about the
results.

3.8 You have the following information concerning a fast-food restaurant for
three consecutive months.

	April		May		June	
Revenue		$50,500		$56,000		$59,500
Cost of sales	$19,500		$23,000		$26,500	
Wages	12,500		14,500		16,000	
Other expenses	10,000	42,000	10,500	48,000	11,000	53,500
Income		$ 8,500		$ 8,000		$ 6,000
Customers served		20,200		24,400		29,900

Convert the consolidated income statements to common-size and use the
information, including any statistics you can develop using customers
served figures, to analyze and comment about what is happening in this
restaurant.

3.9 You have the following information about the revenue, cost of sales, and
accounts receivable for six consecutive periods for a restaurant:

Period	Revenue	Cost of Sales	Accounts Receivable
1	$201,100	$60,200	$20,800
2	226,800	72,500	25,100
3	238,900	81,400	26,900
4	248,400	84,200	28,100
5	260,700	90,600	31,300
6	265,900	93,200	33,400

For each of the three items, calculate trend percentage changes and discuss, as is indicated by the trend, whether or not the situation developing for this restaurant is desirable.

3.10 With reference to the information in Problem 3.9, calculate an index trend for each of the three items. Discuss the results.

3.11 The revenue, food cost, and guests served figures for a fast-food restaurant for the past six months are as follows:

Month	Revenue	Food Cost	Guests Served
1	$31,800	$12,200	10,200
2	32,600	12,600	10,400
3	34,300	13,400	10,300
4	33,900	13,800	10,100
5	34,700	14,500	10,400
6	36,200	14,700	10,500

For each of the six months calculate average check and average food cost figures and an index (to the nearest whole number) for each of the sets of averages. Then apply the index to the revenue and food cost results to convert them to current dollars. Round figures to the nearest 100 dollars. Comment about the results.

3.12 Assume that appropriate general index numbers for restaurant revenue and restaurant food and beverage costs (cost of sales) were as follows for the six periods referred to in Problem 3.9.

Period	Revenue Index	Food and Beverage Cost Index
1	107	121
2	114	125
3	121	131
4	130	137
5	144	144
6	147	151

Convert the historic dollars of revenue and the historic dollars of cost of sales in Problem 3.9 to real dollars, and discuss the results.

3.13 A motel had the following annual revenue and average room rate figures for the last five years. During this period there was no change in number of rooms or type of clientele.

Year	Annual Revenue	Average Room Rate
1	$654,000	$25.20
2	710,000	27.90

Year	Annual Revenue	Average Room Rate
3	746,000	29.10
4	802,000	31.40
5	830,000	32.70

Prepare an index from the average room rates, then use this index to convert the revenue figures for each year to current dollars. What comments do you have about the results?

3.14 The Colony Resort hotel has 75 guest rooms and a dining room with 40 seats. It had the following for the month of June:

- Room revenue $91,108
- 1,798 guest rooms occupied
- 3,417 guest room occupants
- Dining room food revenue $45,209
- Dining room beverage revenue $14,810
- 3,720 dining room guests
- Food cost of sales $18,904
- Beverage cost of sales $4,805
- Guest room labor cost $30,020
- Dining room labor cost $15,011

Calculate the Colony Resort's
a. Average rate per room occupied
b. Rooms occupancy percentage
c. Rooms double occupancy percentage
d. Food cost percentage
e. Beverage cost percentage
f. Rooms department labor cost percentage
g. Dining room labor cost percentage
h. Average dining room guest check
i. Average dining room daily seat turnover
j. Monthly revenue per dining room seat
k. Percentage of beverage revenue to food revenue
l. Percentage of beverage revenue to room revenue
m. Percentage of food revenue to room revenue

CASE 3

a. With reference to the financial statements you prepared for the 4C Company for the year 0001 (see Case 2), convert the income statement to common size. Use total revenue, including other income, as 100 percent. From the local restaurant association Charles has obtained the following statistical information for table service restaurants similar to his. Comment concerning how his restaurant's net income before tax compares to that of similar restaurants. Is this a valid comparison? Explain.

REVENUE—food	**70–80%**
beverage	**20–30%**
total	**100%**
COST OF SALES	35.0–44.0%
GROSS PROFIT	56.0–65.0%
EXPENSES:	
Payroll	26.0–31.0%
Employee benefits	3.0–5.0
Employee meals	1.0–2.0
Laundry, linen, uniforms	1.5–2.0
Replacements	0.5–1.0
Guest supplies	1.0–2.0
Menus and printing	0.3–0.5
Miscellaneous expense	0.3–0.5
Music and entertainment	0.5–2.0
Advertising and promotion	0.7–2.5
Utilities	2.0–4.0
Management salary	2.0–6.0
Administrative expense	3.0–6.0
Repairs and maintenance	1.0–2.0
Rent	4.5–7.0
Property taxes	0.5–1.5
Insurance	0.8–1.0
Interest	0.3–1.0
Depreciation	2.0–2.8
Franchise costs (where applicable)	3.0–8.0
TOTAL EXPENSES	51.5–62.5
NET INCOME BEFORE TAX	1.5–12.0

b. The 4C restaurant's guest count for the year was 75,428. Calculate the average food and beverage check. In your experience, does this seem reasonable for a budget-conscious family-type table service restaurant?

c. Calculate the food cost percentage, the beverage cost percentage, and the total cost of sales. How does the total cost of sales compare to the figures provided by the restaurant association for a family-style restaurant?

d. You will note that the breakdown of total revenue in the restaurant association figures for table service restaurants is 70–80 percent for food and 20–30 percent for beverage. How do Charles's figures compare with this breakdown? Given a choice, would it be better to have a higher or lower percentage of beverage revenue compared to food revenue? Explain.

4 Ratio Analysis

Chapter Highlights

The various ways of expressing a ratio and four methods of evaluating a ratio are discussed: industry averages, competitors' figures, the operation's results from a previous period, and a predetermined standard for the operation.

This chapter segregates the most common ratios used in analysis of a firm's operations into four major categories: current liquidity ratios, long-term solvency ratios, profitability ratios, and turnover ratios.

Included in current liquidity ratios are the current ratio, acid test (quick) ratio, accounts receivable as a percentage of total sales, accounts receivable turnover, and accounts receivable average collection period. Current liquidity ratios are a measure of a company's ability to pay its immediate debts.

Long-term solvency ratios, or net worth ratios, are a measure of a company's ability to meet its long-term debts. Included in this are total assets to total liabilities ratio, total liabilities to total assets ratio, total liabilities to total equity ratio, and number of times interest earned.

Profitability ratios measure management's effectiveness in its use of the assets (resources) available to it. Discussed in this category are return on assets, net return on assets, profit to sales ratio, return on stockholders' equity, and earnings per share.

The final category, on turnover ratios, includes inventory turnover, working capital turnover, and fixed asset turnover.

The chapter concludes with a discussion on leverage—the use of debt rather than equity financing to increase the return on stockholders' equity.

Chapter Objectives

After studying this chapter the reader should be able to:

1. Describe the four ways in which a ratio can be expressed.
2. List and briefly discuss the four bases on which ratios can be compared.
3. List and briefly describe the value of each of the four major categories of ratios.
4. Briefly explain and use each of the ratios illustrated.
5. Interpret the results after using each of the ratios, stating how a creditor, an owner, and the management may view it from each of their perspectives.
6. Differentiate between net income and profitability.
7. Explain how leverage works in financing.

RATIO ANALYSIS

A method of analyzing balance sheet information, in conjunction with some income statement information, is known as ratio analysis. In its simplest terms, a ratio is a comparison of two figures. A comparison can be expressed in several ways. For example, we have already seen one type of ratio comparison in the previous chapter, where common-size income statements were compared using percentages. Other percentages (such as the food cost percentage or the rooms occupancy percentage) are also ratios.

Types of ratios
Another type of ratio is a turnover. A type of turnover ratio used in restaurants is seat turnover (discussed in Chapter 3). Other types of turnover ratios are discussed in this chapter.

Another way of presenting a ratio is on a per-unit basis. For example, an occupied hotel guest room can be the unit basis, and the revenue generated overnight can be expressed as the average rate per room occupied (also discussed in Chapter 3). Some other per-unit ratios are discussed in this chapter.

Finally, a ratio can be expressed with the denominator of an equation given the value of one, and the numerator given a value to be compared to one. For example, if the numerator of an equation is $500, and the denominator $250, the ratio is

$$\frac{\$500}{\$250} = 2 \text{ to } 1 \text{ or } 2{:}1$$

The way in which a ratio is expressed depends on the particular ratio and how it best shows the relationship between the two figures to provide more useful information.

Realistic relationship

It is important to remember that when two numbers are converted to a ratio, the relationship between them must be realistic and meaningful. For example, food cost can be compared to food sales and produce realistic and meaningful information. However, if food cost is related to management salaries, this would not be a realistic comparison.

Ratio Comparisons

Ratios are used to help an establishment evaluate its financial results. A ratio by itself is simply a number, however, and has little value on its own because it does not directly show favorable or unfavorable results. For example, a restaurant's food inventory turnover of four times a month may appear good, but it needs to be compared with some standard, such as what is normal in the restaurant industry for that type of restaurant.

Comparison with standard

It is only when compared with a standard or base figure that ratios have any meaning. One of those standards is, of course, an industry average, but that type of standard is generally the least valuable of all because it generally includes all establishments of the same type and those establishments might be spread over a very broad geographic area where different operating conditions prevail in different locations. As a result, there may not be a single establishment that is just like the "average" one.

Another basis of comparison might be a comparable ratio from a direct competitor. However, how are competitors' ratios discovered? Also, if an operation's ratios differ from its competitors', which one is better? There are many reasons to explain why ratios differ among competitors.

A better method of comparing a ratio is with results from previous periods. For example, how does the rooms occupancy percentage compare with the same ratio last month or the same month last year? What is the trend of that ratio, is that trend good or bad, and how does one know whether it is good or bad? One of the problems with comparing ratios with those of prior periods is that hospitality businesses operate in a dynamic environment and comparing current ratios with previous ratios may be like comparing apples and oranges.

Best method

The best comparison is to judge each ratio against a predetermined standard for that period of time. This standard can take into consideration both internal and external factors about the operation. Internal factors might include the operation's fixed and variable costs, its operating policies, changes in its operating methods, and similar variables. External factors can include such matters as the general economic environment and what the competition is doing. Periodic standards can be determined by establishing operating plans (including ratio standards) in an annual budget broken down into monthly periods that can be adjusted for seasonal variations. Budgets should consider not only the past and the present but also expectations about the future. Because of the importance of budgeting, this topic is covered in some depth in Chapter 10.

Users of Ratios

In general, three broad groups of people are interested in ratios: the operation's management, its creditors (lenders), and its owners. Owners in an incorporated company are its stockholders. In an unincorporated business, they are the proprietor or partners.

Management
Management uses ratios primarily to monitor the operation's performance against predetermined objectives to see whether it has achieved those objectives. It uses certain ratios to measure the effectiveness of its performance as far as day-to-day operations are concerned. Many of the ratios it uses to do this are the operating ratios discussed in Chapter 3. However, a hospitality operation's management also has to achieve certain objectives that will satisfy its creditors and owners. Some of the ratios they use to do this are discussed in this chapter.

Creditors
Creditors of a business—that is, those (other than owners) who have lent the business money—are usually most interested in ratios that indicate to them how safe their loans are and to assess their risk about any future loans the business might need. Creditors also use some ratios to measure whether the business has met requirements stipulated by the lender when a loan was negotiated. For example, a lender might require an operation to maintain a minimum level of working capital at all times.

Owners
Finally, owners of a business use certain ratios to measure the risk of their investment, to assess the business's likelihood of future successful performance, and to evaluate the worth of their investment in the business.

Sometimes, members of each of these three groups do not agree on what a particular ratio means because each of them interprets it from a different perspective.

Ratio Categories

Ratio analysis will be discussed in this chapter under the following four major headings, using information from Exhibit 4.1 (comparative balance sheets for two successive year ends) and Exhibit 4.2 (income statement for the year):

- Current liquidity ratios
- Long-term solvency ratios
- Profitability ratios
- Turnover ratios

Operating ratios

Another category of ratios are operating ratios. These were discussed in Chapter 3. Note that categorizing ratios is for purposes of convenience only. For example, some people classify the working capital turnover as a current liquidity ratio, whereas in this chapter it is included among turnover ratios. What is important to understand, however, is not a ratio's category but rather its meaning and how it can be interpreted. This often requires investigating the causes that have led to a ratio's not being what was expected. Note also that individual ratios generally only tell about one aspect of a business, whereas several ratios analyzed and interpreted jointly yield a more comprehensive picture about a business than do the financial statements alone.

CURRENT LIQUIDITY RATIOS

Net income but no cash

Current liquidity ratios are indicative of a company's ability to meet its short-term debts without difficulty. A company's income statement may show a net income without the company having cash to pay its bills. This is demonstrated later in Chapter 12, which is about cash management. In particular, the reader is referred to the section on cash conservation and working capital management in that chapter. Now we will discuss some of the current liquidity ratios that are indicative of effective working capital management.

Current Ratio

The most commonly used current liquidity ratio is the current ratio. It is indicative of a company's ability to pay off its short-term debts (current liabilities) without difficulty.

Current ratio equation

$$\text{Current ratio} = \frac{\text{Current assets}}{\text{Current liabilities}}$$

$$\text{Year 0001} = \frac{\$86,100}{\$62,700} = 1.37$$

Exhibit 4.1 Comparative annual balance sheets.

	Year ending December 31	
	0001	0002
ASSETS		
Current assets		
Cash	$ 12,900	$ 25,400
Accounts receivable	43,100	45,200
Marketable securities	15,400	2,000
Inventories	9,900	14,700
Prepaid expenses	4,800	4,900
Total current assets	$ 86,100	$ 92,200
Fixed assets		
Land	$ 60,500	$ 60,500
Building	832,400	882,400
Furniture and equipment	174,900	227,900
China, glass, silver, linen	15,600	18,300
	$1,083,400	$1,189,100
Less: accumulated depreciation	(330,100)	(422,000)
Total fixed assets	$ 753,300	$ 767,100
TOTAL ASSETS	$ 839,400	$ 859,300
LIABILITIES		
Current liabilities		
Accounts payable	$ 19,200	$ 16,500
Accrued expenses	3,800	4,200
Income taxes payable	12,300	20,900
Credit balances	500	800
Current portion of mortgage	26,900	26,000
Total current liabilities	$ 62,700	$ 68,400
Long-term liability		
Mortgage payable	$ 512,800	$ 486,800
TOTAL LIABILITIES	$ 575,500	$ 555,200
STOCKHOLDERS' EQUITY		
Common shares	$ 200,000	$ 200,000
Retained earnings	63,900	104,100
TOTAL STOCKHOLDERS' EQUITY	$ 263,900	$ 304,100
TOTAL LIABILITIES AND STOCKHOLDERS' EQUITY	$ 839,400	$ 859,300

Exhibit 4.2 Condensed annual income statement (for year ending December 31, 0002).

Revenue		$1,175,200
Cost of sales		219,400
Gross profit		$ 955,800
Operating expenses		
Payroll	$319,200	
Other	201,400	520,600
		$ 435,200
Undistributed operating expenses		
Administrative and general	$ 67,900	
Marketing	20,700	
Property operation and maintenance	35,400	
Energy costs	25,100	149,100
Income before fixed charges		$ 286,100
Property taxes	$ 48,800	
Insurance	13,100	
Depreciation	91,900	153,800
Income before interest and income tax		$ 132,300
Interest		51,900
Income before income tax		$ 80,400
Income tax		40,200
Net income		$ 40,200

$$\text{Year } 0002 = \frac{\$92,200}{\$68,400} = 1.35$$

Rule of thumb

Current ratio balance

The ratio calculated for the year 0002 shows that, for every $1.00 of short-term debt (current liabilities), there is $1.35 of current assets. In general business a rule of thumb is that there should be $2.00 (or more) of current assets to each $1.00 of current liabilities. However, this rule was developed to provide a safety margin for organizations having large amounts of current assets tied up in inventories (for example, manufacturing and processing firms). The largest inventory that a hotel or motel has is its supply of guest rooms, and these are included (under building) in the fixed asset section of the balance sheet. The only current inventories that hotels, motels, and foodservice businesses have are for food, beverages, and supplies, and these generally form a relatively small part of total current assets. Hotels can safely operate with a current ratio of 1.5 or less; motels and restaurants have operated without difficulty with a current ratio of less than 1 to 1. For each individual enterprise, a balance must be struck. The balance is to work with a current asset position that neither creates short-term liquidity problems (too low a ratio) nor sacrifices profitability for safety (too high a ratio). Money tied up in working capital (current assets less current liabilities) is money that is not earning income.

Creditors want high ratio

Creditors generally prefer to see a high current ratio because it assures them that the operation will be able to meet its current payments due on loans made or credit extended. Indeed, prior to advancing a loan some lenders require that the operation maintain a minimum current ratio at all times. If this requirement is not met, the lender may then have the right to demand full repayment of any loan balance remaining.

On the other hand, owners prefer a low current ratio because a high ratio generally means that too much money is tied up in working capital and not being used as profitably as it otherwise could be. For example, a high ratio could indicate that too much money was invested in inventory or that collections on accounts receivable are not being made as quickly as they should be.

The operation's management has to try to maintain a current ratio that will satisfy both creditors and owners, something that is not always easy to achieve.

Improving ratio

It is possible, at a balance sheet date, to change the current ratio to make it look better than it really is. Exhibit 4.3 shows only the current asset and current liability section of a balance sheet. If, just prior to December 31, $15,000 of the marketable securities were cashed in and the cash were used to pay off $15,000 of accounts payable, the adjusted current asset/current liability section of the balance sheet would be as in Exhibit 4.4.

The comparable current ratios would be

$$\text{Exhibit 4.3} \quad \frac{\$86,100}{\$62,700} = 1.37$$

$$\text{Exhibit 4.4} \quad \frac{\$71,100}{\$47,700} = 1.49$$

Exhibit 4.3 Current section of balance sheet.

Current Assets		Current Liabilities	
Cash	$12,900	Accounts payable	$19,200
Accounts receivable	43,100	Accrued expenses	3,800
Marketable securities	15,400	Income taxes payable	12,300
Inventories	9,900	Credit balances	500
Prepaid expenses	4,800	Current portion of mortgage	26,900
Total	$86,100	Total	$62,700
		Working Capital $23,400	

Exhibit 4.4 Current section of balance sheet.

Current Assets		Current Liabilities	
Cash	$12,900	Accounts payable	$ 4,200
Accounts receivable	43,100	Accrued expenses	3,800
Marketable securities	400	Income taxes payable	12,300
Inventories	9,900	Credit balances	500
Prepaid expenses	4,800	Current portion of mortgage	26,900
Total	$71,100	*Total*	$47,700

Working Capital $23,400

Window dressing

The current ratio has been improved with no change in the working capital of the company. In both cases the working capital is $23,400 ($86,100 less $62,700 = $23,400 in year 0001, and $71,100 less $47,700 = $23,400 in year 0002). This manipulation is known as window dressing. If the accounts payable of $15,000 were due then, there would be no harm in paying them off in the manner illustrated. On the other hand, it may be that the company requires further short-term credit, and the potential lender will only grant this as long as the company's current ratio is higher than 1.4. In that case, reducing the payables to improve the current ratio would make good business sense.

Other methods of window dressing include contracting a new long-term loan, obtaining an additional equity contribution from owners, or selling long-term assets no longer needed to convert them into cash.

Composition of Current Assets

Breakdown of current assets

One useful method of assessing the change in liquidity of current assets is to make a comparison of their breakdown. Total current assets for a period are given a value of 100 percent, and each item of current assets is then expressed as a fraction of 100 percent. For example, in Exhibit 4.5, in year 0001 total current assets of $86,100 are 100 percent; cash is 26.6 percent ($22,900 divided by $86,100 and multiplied by 100).

Liquid assets total down

Note, in Exhibit 4.5, that cash represents 26.6% of total current assets in year 0001 and 38.4% of total current assets in year 0002. However, the three most liquid current assets (cash, accounts receivable, and marketable securities) in year 0002 now total only 67.9% (38.4% + 27.3% + 2.2%). In year 0001 these three items represented 70.8% (26.6% + 26.8% + 17.4%) of total current assets. Cash position has improved, but the total of the three most liquid assets has declined. These three most liquid assets are often referred to as quick assets.

Acid Test Ratio (Quick Ratio)

To refine the current ratio (which includes inventories that often cannot be converted quickly into cash), the quick ratio, which excludes inventories and other relatively nonliquid assets from the ratio equation, was developed.

Quick ratio equation

$$\text{Quick ratio} = \frac{\text{Cash} + \text{Accounts receivable} + \text{Marketable securities}}{\text{Current liabilities}}$$

$$= \frac{\$25,400 + \$45,200 + \$2,000}{\$68,400} = \frac{\$72,600}{\$68,400} = 1.06$$

The year 0002 quick ratio shows that there are $1.06 of quick assets for each $1.00 of current liabilities. For safety's sake, this ratio normally should not be below $1.00 to $1.00. However, the validity of this safety level is questionable for the hotel/food industry since the inventories are usually relatively low and are turned over fairly frequently (that is, they are converted into revenue and accounts receivable or cash within days, or at the most a month or so). In some industries inventories may be held for months or even years.

High inventory turnover

Because the major difference between the current ratio and the quick ratio is inventory, and because some hospitality establishments (such as a motel without a restaurant) may have little or no inventory, the current ratio and the quick ratio are often not very different.

The way that creditors, owners, and managers view and interpret the quick ratio is much the same as for the current ratio; that is, creditors like to see a high ratio, owners prefer to see a low ratio, and management tries to maintain a balance between these two viewpoints.

Exhibit 4.5 Change in liquidity of current assets.

	Year 0001		Year 0002	
Cash	$22,900	26.6%	$35,400	38.4%
Accounts receivable	23,100	26.8	25,200	27.3
Marketable securities	15,000	17.4	2,000	2.2
Inventories	19,900	23.1	24,700	26.8
Prepaid expenses	5,200	6.1	4,900	5.3
	$86,100	100.0%	$92,200	100.0%

Accounts Receivable Ratios

There are three basic approaches to analyzing accounts receivable (apart from aging the accounts, discussed in Chapter 12). These three are

- Accounts receivable as a percentage of revenue
- Accounts receivable turnover
- Accounts receivable average collection period

Relationship between cash and charge revenue

Accounts Receivable as a Percentage of Revenue. The accounts receivable at a balance sheet date are best expressed as a percentage of total annual charge revenue only. Historical percentages showing the relationship between cash and charge revenue could be applied to current year total revenue. The danger here is that the current cash/charge ratio may have changed. It would be preferable to break down current year revenue into cash and charge totals. But since revenue, when recorded, is not ordinarily broken down into cash or charge elements, the accounts receivable as a percentage of revenue figure is frequently expressed as a percentage of total revenue:

Accounts receivable as a percentage of revenue equation

$$\text{Accounts receivable as a percentage of total revenue} = \frac{\text{Average accounts receivable}}{\text{Total revenue}} \times 100$$

$$= \frac{[(\$43,100 + \$45,200) \div 2]}{\$1,175,200} \times 100$$

$$= \frac{(\$88,300 \div 2)}{\$1,175,200} \times 100$$

$$= \frac{\$44,150}{\$1,175,200} \times 100 = 3.75\%$$

Typical percentages

This tells us that, on average over the year, 3.75 percent of our total annual revenue was in the form of accounts receivable. In a drive-in, cash only restaurant this figure would obviously be 0 percent. In a private club that permits only charge transactions, with each member receiving an account after each month-end, the amount could be as high as 10 to 12 percent. The typical restaurant or hotel, with some customers paying cash, the rest charging their bills, would probably find its average accounts receivable representing some 4 to 8 percent of annual total revenue. These are industry average figures; what is more important to an individual firm is not comparison with industry averages but rather the trend of the figure within the firm.

Note that, in our illustration, average accounts receivable were calculated by adding beginning and end-of-the-year account balances and dividing by 2. In a seasonal operation with highly fluctuating sales, the average accounts receivable figure should be calculated by adding each of the monthly sales figures and dividing the total by 12.

Accounts Receivable Turnover.   The accounts receivable turnover equation is the reverse of the preceding one.

Accounts receivable turnover equation

$$\text{Accounts receivable turnover} = \frac{\text{Total revenue}}{\text{Average accounts receivable}}$$

$$= \frac{\$1,175,200}{\$44,150} = 26.62$$

Depending on the volume of charge business and the efficiency with which accounts are collected, this turnover rate could vary from ten to as high as thirty times a year. The turnover rate is not as useful by itself as it is in helping to calculate the average collection period of accounts receivable.

Accounts Receivable Average Collection Period.   The equation for calculating the accounts receivable average collection period is:

Average collection period equation

$$\text{Average collection period} = \frac{365}{\text{Turnover rate}}$$

$$= \frac{365}{26.62} = 13.7 \text{ (or 14) days}$$

The lower the collection period, the more efficient is the collection ability of the organization. Companies that extend thirty-day credit could expect to see this average as high as thirty or thirty-five days. If it were forty days or more, they might start to be concerned about having too many slow-paying guests. A change in the average collection period over time, particularly if the period is getting longer and longer, indicates a situation where collection procedures or credit policies need to be evaluated.

Another method of calculating the accounts receivable average collection period is

Alternative equation

$$\begin{array}{l}\text{Accounts receivable as a}\\\text{percentage of total revenue}\end{array} \times 365 = \text{Average collection period}$$

$$\frac{\$44,150}{\$1,175,200} \times 100 = 3.75\% \times 365 = 13.7 \text{ (or 14) days}$$

Aging schedule   If the trend of the average collection period is toward a higher number of days, preparing an aging schedule of accounts receivable may help pinpoint the problem. Preparation of such a schedule is illustrated in Chapter 12.

To reiterate, in this discussion of accounts receivable the revenue figure used was from all sales (both cash and credit). In such a case, the accounts receivable ratios must be interpreted carefully. For example, if an operation's breakdown of sales were estimated at 60 percent cash and 40 percent credit, the average collection period should only be about 40 percent of the allowable number of days. In other words, if 30-day credit is normally extended, the average collection period should be 40 percent times 30 days, or 12 days.

In general, owners and creditors prefer to see a low number of days of accounts receivable average collection period (or a high accounts receivable turnover), whereas management prefers a higher average collection period (or a low turnover) as long as it is within or close to the allowable number of days.

LONG-TERM SOLVENCY RATIOS

Debt or equity financing

Solvency ratios are sometimes referred to as net worth ratios. Net worth is defined as total tangible assets (that is, total assets excluding nontangible items such as goodwill) less total liabilities. In other words, net worth is usually the same as total stockholders' equity (assuming no intangible assets). Total assets in any business can be financed primarily by either debt (liabilities) or equity (shares and retained earnings). Solvency ratios show the balance between these two methods of financing. There are three main solvency ratios, each showing this balance in a different way. These three ratios are total assets to total liabilities ratio, total liabilities to total assets ratio, and total liabilities to total stockholders' equity ratio. We need three figures from each year's balance sheet to calculate these ratios. These figures are

	Year 0001	Year 0002
Total assets	$839,400	$859,300
Total liabilities	575,500	555,200
Total equity	263,900	304,100

Total Assets to Total Liabilities Ratio

The total assets to total liabilities ratio is

Assets to liabilities equation

$$\text{Ratio} = \frac{\text{Total assets}}{\text{Total liabilities}}$$

$$\text{Year } 0001 = \frac{\$839{,}400}{\$575{,}500} = 1.46$$

$$\text{Year } 0002 = \frac{\$859{,}300}{\$555{,}200} = 1.55$$

High ratio equals high lender security

This ratio tells us that in year 0001 there were $1.46 in assets for each $1.00 in liabilities (debt). Creditors (people to whom we owe money or with whom we have a debt) prefer to see this ratio as high as possible, that is, as high as 2:1 or more. The higher the ratio, the more security they have. They want to be assured that they will recover the full amount owed them in the event of bankruptcy or liquidation of the business. If the ratio sinks below 1:1, it could mean that if bankruptcy occurred, they might not recover the full amount owed them. In bankruptcy cases, the value of assets decreases rapidly. This is known as "asset shrinkage"; it occurs because the value of many of the productive assets declines when those assets are not employed in a going concern. In the situation illustrated, note that in year 0002 the ratio improves (from the point of view of the creditors) to 1.55:1.00.

Appreciation of assets over time

The total assets to total liabilities ratio is traditionally based on assets at their book value. If a hotel or foodservice operation includes land and building (which it owns) at book value in this calculation, the ratio could be misleading. Land and buildings frequently appreciate (increase in value) over time. Therefore, a total assets to total liabilities ratio based on book value of assets figures showing a result as low as 1:1 may not be as bad as it seems from the creditors' point of view. If assets were used at fair market or replacement value, the ratio would probably improve and then show a comfortable cushion of safety.

Total Liabilities to Total Assets Ratio

The total liabilities to total assets ratio is the reverse of the total assets to total liabilities ratio:

Liabilities to assets equation

$$\text{Ratio} = \frac{\text{Total liabilities}}{\text{Total assets}}$$

$$\text{Year } 0001 = \frac{\$575{,}500}{\$839{,}400} = 0.69$$

$$\text{Year } 0002 = \frac{\$555{,}200}{\$859{,}200} = 0.65$$

Traditional debt to equity financing ratio

The ratio tells us that in year 0001 each $1.00 of assets was financed $0.69 by debt (the balance of $0.31 was by equity). In year 0002 each $1.00 of assets was financed $0.65 by debt (and $0.35 by equity). Traditionally, the hospitality industry has been financed with between $0.60 to $0.90 of debt and $0.10 to $0.40 of equity. As debt financing reaches the higher number ($0.90 out of each $1.00), it becomes more and more difficult to raise money by debt. The risk is higher for the lender, and therefore potential lenders of money are more difficult to find. Again, this ratio is based on assets at book value. If fair market or replacement value of assets were used (assuming that this value is higher than book value), then the ratio would decline and perhaps more realistically present the true situation.

Total Liabilities to Total Equity Ratio

Sometimes known as the debt to equity ratio, the total liabilities to total equity ratio is calculated as follows:

Debt to equity equation

$$\text{Ratio} = \frac{\text{Total liabilities}}{\text{Total stockholders' equity}}$$

$$\text{Year 0001} = \frac{\$575,500}{\$263,900} = 2.18$$

$$\text{Year 0002} = \frac{\$555,200}{\$304,100} = 1.83$$

High debt to equity ratio equals high risk to lender

This ratio tells us that in year 0001 for each $1.00 the stockholders have invested, the creditors have invested $2.18. In year 0002 the comparable figures are: stockholders $1.00 and creditors $1.83. The higher the creditors' investment for each $1.00 of stockholders' investment, the higher is the risk for the creditor. In such circumstances, if a hotel or foodservice operation wished to expand, debt financing would be more difficult to obtain and interest rates would be higher.

The risk situation can perhaps be explained with some simple figures. Total assets equal total liabilities plus stockholders' equity. Assume total assets are $100,000, total liabilities are $50,000, and stockholders' equity $50,000. The debt to equity ratio will be

$$\frac{\$50,000}{\$50,000} = 1 \text{ (or \$1.00 to \$1.00)}$$

Under these circumstances total assets of $100,000 could decline by 50 percent, to $50,000, before the creditors would be running a serious risk.

Assume, with the same total assets of $100,000, total liabilities are $65,000 and stockholders' equity $35,000. The debt to equity ratio will be

$$\frac{\$65,000}{\$35,000} = 1.86 \text{ (or } \$1.86 \text{ to } \$1.00)$$

With this debt to equity ratio (higher than the earlier one, therefore riskier from the creditors' point of view), the assets could only decline 35 percent (as opposed to 50 percent) in value (from $100,000 down to $65,000) before the creditors would be facing a difficult situation.

Use of leverage   Therefore, although the creditors prefer not to have the debt to equity ratio too high, the hotel or foodservice operator often finds it more profitable to have it as high as possible. A high debt to equity ratio is known as having high leverage or trading on the equity. Using leverage will be discussed in a later section of this chapter.

Number of Times Interest Earned

Another way of looking at the margin of safety in meeting debt interest payments is to calculate the number of times per year interest is earned.

Times interest earned equation

$$\text{Times interest earned} = \frac{\text{Income before interest and income tax}}{\text{Interest expense}}$$

$$= \frac{\$132,300}{\$51,900} = 2.55 \text{ times in year 0002}$$

It is considered good if interest is earned two or more times a year.

Creditors, owners, and management all like to see this ratio as high as possible. To creditors, a high number indicates a reduction of their risk and shows that the establishment will be able to meet its regular loan interest payments when due. To owners, a high number is also desirable (particularly if the establishment has a high debt to equity ratio). Therefore, management also prefers a high ratio because it pleases each of the other two groups. Note, however, that if this ratio is extremely high it may indicate that leverage is not being maximized.

PROFITABILITY RATIOS

The main objective of most hospitality operations is to generate a profit. In a partnership or proprietorship, the profit can be withdrawn by the owners to increase their personal net worth. In an incorporated company, the profit can be paid out in dividends or be retained in the business to expand it, increase the profits further, and improve the value of the owners' equity investment in the company. Creditors of a company also like to see increases in the business's profit because the higher the profits the less is the risk to them as lenders. Therefore, one of the main tasks of management is to ensure continued profitability of the enterprise. It is with profitability ratios that management's effectiveness in achieving this is most often measured.

Profit versus profitability   Caution needs to be exercised in the use of the word "profitability." A company may have a net income on its income statement, and this net income, expressed as a percentage of revenue, may seem acceptable; however, the relationship between this net income and other items (for example, the amount of money invested by stockholders) may not be acceptable or profitable.

Return on Assets

The return on assets ratio (also known as gross return on assets) measures the effectiveness of management's use of the organization's assets. The equation is:

Return on assets equation

$$\frac{\text{Income before interest and income tax}}{\text{Total average assets}} \times 100 = \frac{\$132,300}{(\$839,400 + \$859,300) \div 2} \times 100$$

$$= \frac{\$132,300}{(\$1,698,700 \div 2)} \times 100$$

$$= \frac{\$132,300}{\$849,350} \times 100 = 15.6\%$$

Average based on monthly figures   In this illustration, total average assets are calculated by adding the beginning of year and the end of year figures and dividing by 2. If the figures fluctuated widely during the year, because of such factors as purchase and sale of long-term assets, and if monthly figures were available, the average should be calculated by adding each of the monthly figures and dividing by 12.

Interest is added back to net income (as is income tax) in the equation in order to compare the resulting percentage (in our case 15.6 percent) to the current market interest rate. For example, if, in our example, an expansion of the building were contemplated and the money were to be borrowed at a 10 percent interest rate, one could assume that the new building asset would earn a rate of return of 15.6 percent and would have no difficulty in meeting the 10 percent interest expense. This would leave the expanded part of the business 5.6 percent on assets before income tax.

Net Return on Assets

The gross return on assets calculation measures management's effectiveness in its use of assets and is also useful in assessing the likelihood of obtaining more debt financing for expansion. The net return on assets, on the other hand, evaluates the advisability of seeking equity (as opposed to debt) financing. The equation is:

Net return on assets equation

$$\frac{\text{Net income after tax}}{\text{Total average assets}} \times 100 = \frac{\$40,200}{(\$839,400 + \$859,300) \div 2} \times 100$$

$$= \frac{\$40,200}{(\$1,698,700 \div 2)} \times 100$$

$$= \frac{\$40,200}{\$849,350} \times 100 = 4.73\%$$

Since dividends are payable out of earnings after income tax, if we used equity (stockholder) financing for a building, the stockholders would not be able to anticipate a very good dividend yield. On the basis of current results, assets are only yielding a 4.7 percent return, and stockholders would probably assume that the new assets would earn the same rate of return as the old assets. This may be a poor assumption, since the old **Assets at replacement or market value** assets are at book (depreciated) value. If the calculation were made on assets at their replacement or market value, the rate could well drop below the present 4.73 percent. Under these circumstances, management would have to improve its performance considerably in order to convince stockholders to part with more money for expansion.

Net Income to Revenue Ratio

The net income to revenue ratio (also known as the profit margin) measures management's overall effectiveness in generating sales and controlling expenses. It is calculated as follows:

Net income to revenue equation

$$\text{Net income to revenue ratio} = \frac{\text{Net income after income tax}}{\text{Revenue}} \times 100$$

$$= \frac{\$40,200}{\$1,175,200} \times 100 = 3.4\%$$

This means that, out of each $1.00 of revenue, we had 3.4 cents net income. In absolute terms, this may not be very meaningful, because it does not truly reflect the profitability of the firm. Consider the following two cases:

	Case A	Case B
Revenue	$100,000	$100,000
Net income	5,000	10,000
Net income to revenue ratio	5%	10%

Effectiveness of management

With the same revenue it seems that Case B is better. In Case B, the organization is making twice as much net income, in absolute terms, as is organization A ($10,000 to $5,000). This doubling of net income is supported by the net income to revenue ratio (10% to 5%). If these were two similar firms, or two branches of the same firm, these figures would indicate the relative effectiveness of the management of each in controlling costs and generating a satisfactory level of net income. However, in order to determine the profitability of A to B, we need to relate the net income to the investment:

	Case A	Case B
Revenue	$100,000	$100,000
Net income	5,000	10,000
Net income to revenue ratio	5%	10%
Investment	$ 40,000	$ 80,000
Profitability (return on investment)	$\dfrac{\$5,000}{\$40,000} \times 100$ $= 12.5\%$	$\dfrac{\$10,000}{\$80,000} \times 100$ $= 12.5\%$

Comparable profitability

As can now be seen, despite the wide difference in net income and net income to revenue ratio, there is no difference between the two organizations as far as profitability is concerned: they are both equally good, returning 12.5 percent on the investment.

Return on Stockholders' Equity

There are many equations and definitions for return on investment. For example, should we use (1) income before income tax, (2) income before interest and income tax, or (3) net income after tax? Is the investment (1) the book value of assets, (2) the replacement or market value of the assets, (3) the total investment of debt and equity, or (4) only the stockholders' equity? Perhaps the most useful definition of return on investment is to use net income after income tax (because dividends can only be paid out of after-tax profits) and relate that net income to the stockholders' investment. It is to this group of people, the stockholders or owners, that operating management is primarily responsible. The equation for this calculation is

Return on equity equation

Return on stockholders' equity $=$

$$\frac{\text{Net income after income tax}}{\text{Average stockholders' equity}} \times 100 = \frac{\$40,200}{(\$263,900 + \$304,100) \div 2} \times 100$$

$$= \frac{\$40,200}{(\$568,000 \div 2)} \times 100$$

$$= \frac{\$40,200}{\$284,000} \times 100 = 14.2\%$$

Matter of opinion

This percentage shows the effectiveness of management's use of equity funds. How high should it be? This is a matter of personal opinion. If an investor could put money either into the bank at a 10 percent interest rate or into a hotel investment at only 8 percent with more risk involved, the bank might seem the better choice of the two.

Note that, if the business has issued both preferred and common stock, the return on stockholders' equity equation can be modified, with the numerator becoming net income less preferred dividends and the denominator becoming average common stockholders' equity. To the common stockholders, preferred stock is a form of "debt" on which a fixed dividend rate must be paid. To the extent that profits are enhanced by borrowing from preferred stockholders and the added profits exceed the fixed rate of dividends paid to preferred stockholders, the additional earnings accruing to the common stockholders will be improved.

Other Profitability Ratios

Publicly traded stocks

Other measures of profitability include annual earnings per share, dividend rate per share, and book value per share. Such ratios are of most concern to those buying and selling publicly traded stock on the open market and are of less concern to the internal management of the firm. However, management is held accountable by stockholders for producing a net income satisfactory to them. This net income is frequently measured by earnings per share. The earnings per share are important also because they tend to dictate the value of the shares in the market or indicate the desirability of purchasing stock in the company to a potential purchaser. The equation is:

Earnings per share equation

$$\text{Earnings per share} = \frac{\text{Net income after income tax}}{\text{Average number of shares outstanding}}$$

Assuming that the average number of shares outstanding (beginning of the year number plus end of the year number divided by two) was 40,000, our earnings per share would be:

$$\frac{\$40,200}{40,000} = \$1.005$$

Deduct preferred dividends

If both common and preferred stock has been issued, this equation has to be modified. The numerator will be net income (after tax) less preferred dividends. The denominator will be average number of common shares outstanding.

Note that earnings per share can be increased over time by not paying out all earnings in dividends to shareholders. By retaining some or all potential dividends and reinvesting them in expanding the business, future profits (earnings) will be increased while the number of shares outstanding is held constant.

Creditors, Owners, and Management

In general, all three groups (creditors, owners, and management) interested in financial ratios prefer to see profitability ratios high and growing rather than low and stable. Creditors will be interested in a ratio such as return on assets, particularly if it is increasing, because this indicates management's effectiveness in its use of all assets and reduces the creditors' risk.

Comparison with alternatives

On the other hand, the ratio of most interest to owners is return on their equity investment because they can easily compare this ratio with the return they might receive from alternative investments. In public companies, if equity investors are not satisfied with their return they can remove their investment by selling their shares in the stock market and purchasing shares in more "profitable" companies. If many equity investors with large shareholdings do this, it will depress the market price of the shares. In turn, this will make it more difficult for the company to raise money when needed in the future because there will be a reluctance by potential investors to buy the new shares. Stock market investors often measure the value of a share by its price earnings ratio calculated as follows:

Price earnings equation

$$\frac{\text{Market price per share}}{\text{Earnings per share}}$$

If the market price of the shares were $10.00, our price earnings ratio would be:

$$\frac{\$10.00}{\$1.005} = 9.95 \text{ times}$$

The price earnings ratio for any specific hospitality company's shares is affected by how purchasers and sellers of those shares perceive the stability and/or trend of earnings, the potential growth of earnings, and the risk of investing in those shares.

Management's task is to maintain all profitability ratios at as high a level as possible so that both creditors and owners (investors) are satisfied. Management's effectiveness in this regard will be measured by the level of that satisfaction.

TURNOVER RATIOS

Turnover ratios (sometimes known as activity ratios) are calculated to determine the activity of certain classes of assets, such as inventories, working capital, and long-term assets. The ratios express the number of times that an activity (turnover) is occurring during a certain period and can help in measuring management's effectiveness in using and controlling these assets.

Inventory Turnover Ratios

Inventory turnover ratios are discussed in some detail in the section on cash conservation and working capital management in Chapter 12. For our purpose, only the basic equation is included in this chapter:

Inventory turnover equation

$$\text{Inventory turnover} = \frac{\text{Cost of sales for the period}}{\text{Average inventory during the period}}$$

Food inventory turnover normally varies between two and four times a month. Beverage turnover varies from one-half to one time a month. An individual operator should determine, in each case, the turnover rate appropriate to that establishment (since there are major exceptions to these guidelines) and then watch for deviations from those rates.

Working Capital Turnover

The working capital turnover ratio is a measure of the effectiveness of the use of working capital. Working capital is current assets less current liabilities. Our balance sheet (Exhibit 4.1) gives us the following:

	Year 0001	**Year 0002**
Current assets	$86,100	$92,200
Current liabilities	62,700	68,400
Working capital	$23,400	$23,800

The equation for working capital turnover is

Working capital turnover equation

$$\text{Working capital turnover} = \frac{\text{Revenue}}{\text{Average working capital}}$$

$$= \frac{\$1,175,200}{(\$23,400 + \$23,800) \div 2}$$

$$= \frac{\$1,175,200}{(\$47,200 \div 2)}$$

$$= \frac{\$1,175,200}{\$23,600} = 49.8 \text{ times}$$

This ratio can vary widely, from as low as ten times per year (for a restaurant) to as high as fifty times or more a year (for a hotel).

Appropriate level of working capital

A hospitality operation should probably try to find its most appropriate level of working capital and then compare future performance with this optimum level. Too much working capital (that is, too low a turnover ratio) means ineffective use of funds. Too little working capital (indicated by too high a turnover ratio) may lead to cash difficulties if revenue begins to decline.

Note also that, all other factors being equal, the higher the working capital turnover ratio the lower will be the current ratio. This means that if an establishment has little or no credit sales and a very low level of inventory (for example, a motel doing cash-only business), it will have both a low current ratio and a high working capital turnover. Thus, with reference to the earlier section on the current ratio, creditors prefer a low working capital turnover, owners prefer a high turnover, and management tries to maintain a reasonable balance between the two extremes in order to maximize profits by reducing the amount of money tied up in current assets, while maintaining sufficient liquidity to take care of unanticipated emergencies requiring cash.

Fixed Asset Turnover

The fixed asset turnover ratio assesses the effectiveness of the use of fixed assets in generating revenue. The equation is:

Fixed asset turnover equation

$$\text{Fixed asset turnover} = \frac{\text{Revenue}}{\text{Total average fixed assets}}$$

$$= \frac{\$1,175,200}{(\$753,300 + \$767,100) \div 2}$$

$$= \frac{\$1,175,200}{(\$1,520,400 \div 2)}$$

$$= \frac{\$1,175,200}{\$760,200} = 1.55 \text{ times}$$

In the hotel industry this turnover rate could vary from as low as one-half to as high as two or more times per year. In the foodservice industry, a restaurant could find it has a turnover of four or five times a year (assuming it is in rented premises). The reason the turnover rate is lower for a hotel is that it has, relatively speaking, a much higher investment in public space (lobbies, corridors) and in guest rooms (the capacity of which cannot be changed in the short run) than does a restaurant. A restaurant can increase its fixed asset turnover rate by increasing the number of seats or, if the demand is there, serve more customers during individual meal periods.

A high fixed asset turnover ratio indicates management's effectiveness in its use of fixed assets, whereas a low ratio either indicates that management is not effective or that some of those assets should be disposed of in order to increase the ratio. All groups (creditors, owners, and management) like to see the ratio as high as possible. One of the problems with this ratio, however, is that the older the assets are (and the more accumulated depreciation there is) the lower is their net book value. This automatically tends to increase the fixed asset turnover ratio. In addition, the use of an accelerated depreciation method hastens this process. Thus, management should resist the temptation to continue to use old and inefficient fixed assets and/or to use an accelerated depreciation method only in order to have a high fixed asset turnover.

Use of fixed asset turnover ratio

One of the uses of this ratio is in evaluating new projects. If the current turnover is four in a restaurant, and a new project costing $250,000 is going to generate $750,000 in revenue, giving a turnover of only three ($750,000 divided by $250,000), the new project may not seem as profitable.

Other Analysis Techniques

The ratios discussed in this chapter are those that can be developed directly from balance sheet and income statement information. Many other operational analysis tools are available for monitoring day-to-day results. Some of them require additional information not provided by the financial statements (occupancy of rooms percentage or restaurant seat turnovers, for example). A number of these analysis techniques are listed and discussed at the end of Chapter 3.

CONCLUDING COMMENTS ON RATIO ANALYSIS

1. Financial ratios are generally produced from historical accounting information. As a result, some accounting numbers reflect historic costs rather than present values. An example is a building's cost recorded on the balance sheet at its original purchase price and offset by accumulated depreciation to produce net book value. A ratio based on total assets (such as return on assets) may show a result that is more than acceptable. If it were based on the current replacement cost of those assets, however, it would produce a much more realistic ratio that can then be compared with alternative investments. For this same reason, this type of ratio cannot be readily compared with the ratio for other hospitality companies because they may have purchased their assets at different times, at different costs, and may have used different depreciation methods.

Leasing of assets

2. Many of the guidelines or rules of thumb given in this chapter on ratio analysis have assumed ownership of all assets. If assets (particularly land and building, and furniture and equipment) are leased rather than owned, then these industry quoted guidelines must be used with caution. Indeed, rules of thumb should always be used with great care, because every organization that is part of the hospitality industry has its own unique features. This leads to the next comment.

3. Ratios are only of value when two related numbers are compared. For example, the current ratio compares current assets with current liabilities. This is a meaningful comparison. On the other hand, if current assets are compared to owner equity, this ratio has little value because there is no direct relationship between the two numbers.

Trends of ratios over time

4. Although external comparisons of ratios (that is, comparison of your ratios with industry averages or other similar hotels or food operations) are interesting, what is probably of more value is comparing the trend of your own ratios over time. If the working capital turnover ratio is constantly increasing over the years, with little change in revenue, this may be more indicative of a problem than the fact that the ratio is below the industry average.

Selectivity of ratios

5. This chapter has tried to include all the ratios that could be useful to a hospitality enterprise. There is no suggestion that a particular operator should use all of them. Selectivity is important. One should use those that are of benefit in evaluating the results of a business in relation to its objectives.

Ratios a means to an end

6. Ratios should not be an end in themselves. An objective of a company might be to have the happiest stockholders in the world. Emphasis might then be placed solely on increasing net income to the point where the stockholders will see an incredibly large return on their investment. The end result might be that, to achieve this, selling prices have been set so high, and expenses cut so low, that the business collapses.

7. Finally, ratios by themselves cure no problems but only indicate possible problems. For example, the trend of the accounts receivable ratio may show that the time that it is taking to collect the average accounts receivable is becoming longer. That is all the ratio shows. It is only management analysis of this problem to discover the causes that can correct this deteriorating situation.

LEVERAGE

Equity versus debt financing

Earlier in this chapter the concept of leverage, or trading on the equity, was introduced. To illustrate this, consider the case of a new restaurant that is to be opened at a cost of $250,000 (for furnishings, equipment, and working capital). The owners have the cash available but they are considering not using all their own money. Instead, they wish to compare their relative return on equity on the basis of using either all their own money (100 percent equity financing) or using 50 percent equity and borrowing the other 50 percent (debt financing) at a 10 percent interest rate. Regardless of which method they use, revenue will be the same, as will all operating costs. With either choice, they will have $50,000 income before interest and taxes. There is no interest expense under 100 percent equity financing. With some debt financing there will be interest to be paid. However, interest expense is tax deductible. Assuming a tax rate of 50 percent on taxable income, Exhibit 4.6 shows the comparative operating results and the return on investment (ROI) based on initial equity investment.

Increasing debt ratio

In Exhibit 4.6, not only do the owners make a better return on their initial investment under option B (15 percent versus 10 percent), but they still have $125,000 in cash they can invest in a second venture. In this case, if a 50/50 debt-to-equity ratio is more profitable than 100 percent equity financing, would not an 80/20 debt-to-equity ratio be even more

Exhibit 4.6 Effect of leverage on ROI.

	Option A	Option B
Investment required	$250,000	$250,000
Equity financing	$250,000	$125,000
Debt financing	0	$125,000 @ 10%
Income before interest and income tax	$ 50,000	$ 50,000
Interest expense	0	(12,500)
Income before income tax	$ 50,000	$ 37,500
Income tax (50%)	(25,000)	(18,750)
Net income	$ 25,000	$ 18,750
Return on equity	$\dfrac{\$\,25,000}{\$250,000} \times 100$	$\dfrac{\$\,18,750}{\$125,000} \times 100$
	$= 10\%$	$= 15\%$

profitable? In other words, what would be the return on initial investment if the owners used only $50,000 of their own money and borrowed the remaining $200,000 required at 10 percent? Exhibit 4.7 shows the result of this more highly levered situation.

Advantage of leverage

Under Option C, Exhibit 4.7, our return on initial investment has now increased to 30 percent, and we have $200,000 cash still on hand, enough for four more similar restaurant ventures. The advantages of leverage are obvious: the higher the debt-to-equity ratio, the higher will be the owners' return on equity. However, this only holds true if income (before interest) as a percentage of debt is greater than the interest rate to be

Exhibit 4.7 Effect of high leverage on ROI.

	Option C
Investment required	$250,000
Equity financing	$ 50,000
Debt financing	$200,000 @ 10%
Income before interest and income tax	$ 50,000
Interest expense	(20,000)
Income before income tax	$ 30,000
Income tax (50%)	(15,000)
Net income	$ 15,000
Return on equity	$\dfrac{\$15,000}{\$50,000} \times 100 = 30\%$

paid on the debt. For example, if the debt interest rate is 10 percent, the income-to-debt ratio must be greater than 10 percent for leverage to be profitable. With high debt (high leverage) there is a risk. If income declines, the more highly levered a company is, the sooner it will be in financial difficulty. In Option B (relatively low leverage) income before interest and income tax could decline from $50,000 to $12,500 before net income would be zero. In Option C (relatively high leverage) income before interest and income tax could decline from $50,000 to only $20,000.

SUMMARY

A number of different ways of expressing ratios (such as percentages and turnovers) were detailed in this chapter, as were four methods of evaluating a ratio: industry averages, competitors' figures, the operation's results from a previous period, and a predetermined standard for the operation. *Current liquidity ratios* measure a company's ability to meet its short-term obligations. Some of the more common measuring ratios are:

1. Current ratio $= \dfrac{\text{Current assets}}{\text{Current liabilities}}$

2. Acid test (quick) ratio $= \dfrac{\text{Cash} + \text{accounts receivable} + \text{marketable securities}}{\text{Current liabilities}}$

3. Accounts receivable as a percent of total revenue $= \dfrac{\text{Average accounts receivable}}{\text{Total revenue}} \times 100$

4. Accounts receivable turnover $= \dfrac{\text{Total revenue}}{\text{Average accounts receivable}}$

5. Accounts receivable average collection period $= \dfrac{365}{\text{Accounts receivable turnover}}$

   or, *alternatively*, $\left(\begin{array}{l}\text{Accounts receivable as a} \\ \text{percent of total revenue}\end{array}\right) \times 365$

Another useful technique is to make a comparative analysis of current assets. Total current assets are 100 percent, and each item of current asset is expressed as a proportion of 100 percent. Such an analysis can indicate a change in liquidity of current assets due to a change in the proportions.

Long-term solvency ratios, sometimes called *net worth* ratios, measure a company's ability to meet its long-term obligations. Some of the ratios are:

1. $\dfrac{\text{Total assets to total}}{\text{liabilities ratio}} = \dfrac{\text{Total assets}}{\text{Total liabilities}}$

2. $\dfrac{\text{Total liabilities to}}{\text{total assets ratio}} = \dfrac{\text{Total liabilities}}{\text{Total assets}}$

3. $\dfrac{\text{Total liabilities to}}{\text{total equity ratio}} = \dfrac{\text{Total liabilities}}{\text{Total stockholders' equity}}$

4. $\text{Times interest earned} = \dfrac{\text{Income before interest and income tax}}{\text{Interest expense}}$

Profitability ratios measure the effectiveness of management's use of the resources available to it. Some of the ratios are:

1. $\text{Return on assets} = \dfrac{\text{Income before interest and income tax}}{\text{Total average assets}} \times 100$

2. $\dfrac{\text{Net return on}}{\text{assets}} = \dfrac{\text{Net income after income tax}}{\text{Total average assets}} \times 100$

3. $\text{Net income to revenue ratio} = \dfrac{\text{Net income after income tax}}{\text{Revenue}} \times 100$

4. $\dfrac{\text{Return on stock-}}{\text{holders' equity}} = \dfrac{\text{Net income after income tax}}{\text{Average stockholders' equity}} \times 100$

5. $\text{Earnings per share} = \dfrac{\text{Net income after income tax}}{\text{Average number of shares outstanding}}$

6. $\text{Price/earnings ratio} = \dfrac{\text{Market price per share}}{\text{Earnings per share}}$

Turnover ratios include the following:

1. $\text{Inventory turnover} = \dfrac{\text{Cost of sales for the period}}{\text{Average inventory during period}}$

2. $\text{Working capital turnover} = \dfrac{\text{Revenue}}{\text{Average working capital}}$

3. $\text{Fixed asset turnover} = \dfrac{\text{Revenue}}{\text{Total average fixed assets}}$

The reader is cautioned to use ratio analysis with care and not to use rules of thumb as necessarily being the norm for all businesses. What is of most value is not how an individual operation's ratios differ from external (other businesses') results, but how the internal results are changing over time. Selection and discretion (to pick the right ratio for the right occasion) should be exercised. Ratios should not become and end in themselves. Finally, ratios cure no problems; they only point to possible problems only management action can solve.

This chapter concluded with some comments on the concept of leverage, or trading on the equity. Leverage is obtained by increasing the debt (versus equity) structure of the financing of an enterprise. The higher the debt, as long as income before the resulting interest expense is greater than the amount of interest expense, the higher will be the owners' return on equity. However, a too highly levered company may quickly be in financial trouble if income starts declining.

DISCUSSION QUESTIONS

1. Describe the four ways in which a ratio can be expressed.

2. List and briefly discuss the four bases on which a ratio can be compared.

3. Which three groups are the main users of financial ratios?

4. What is the value in calculating a current ratio? Contrast how creditors and owners view this ratio.

5. Why can a hotel, motel, or restaurant usually operate with a current ratio considerably lower than for other types of businesses such as manufacturing companies?

6. Why is too high a current ratio not good business management?

7. Explain why the calculation of an accounts receivable average collection period can be a meaningful statistic.

8. Define the term "net worth."

9. Why is a high total assets to total liabilities ratio desired by creditors?

10. Why can the book value of assets, when used in a total assets to total liabilities ratio, or, when used in a total liabilities to total assets ratio, be misleading?

11. What does the return on assets ratio measure, and of what value is it to a potential creditor?

12. How does the net return on assets ratio differ from the return on assets ratio, and why is its calculation valuable?

13. Differentiate between the terms "net income" and "profitability."

14. What does the return on stockholders' equity measure?

15. What is the equation for a firm's price earnings ratio?

16. Discuss a major limitation of the fixed asset turnover ratio.
17. Discuss the term "leverage" or "trading on the equity."

PROBLEMS

4.1 You have the following information concerning current assets and current liabilities of a restaurant for two successive years:

Current Assets	Year 0003	Year 0004
Cash	$11,500	$14,700
Accounts receivable	11,200	15,100
Marketable securities	7,500	7,500
Inventories	5,600	8,100
Prepaid expenses	2,100	2,500
Current Liabilities		
Accounts payable	$ 9,600	$13,100
Accrued expenses	4,700	6,200
Income tax payable	6,800	7,400
Deposits and credit balances	500	600
Current portion of mortgage payable	11,200	9,900

For each year calculate:
a. The working capital
b. The current ratio

Revenue for the year 0004 was $543,800. For the year 0004 calculate:
c. The accounts receivable as a percentage of revenue
d. The accounts receivable turnover
e. The accounts receivable average collection period
f. What do these calculations tell you about the restaurant?

4.2 With reference to the information in Problem 4.1, analyze the composition of current assets and current liabilities for each year on a percentage basis (in other words, express each item of current asset as a percentage of total current assets). Discuss the results.

4.3 A fire occurred in Chuck's Charbroiler restaurant overnight on December 31, 0004, and many of the accounting records were lost. However, Chuck was able to salvage some documents and obtain other information from outside sources for the year ending December 31, 0004:

- The year-end bank balance was $763, and at the time of the fire there was an estimated $1,000 in cash in the restaurant's safe.

- The inventory value was $4,915.
- Employees had been paid up to and including the night of the fire.
- Suppliers contacted indicate that in total they were owed $3,210 at December 31, 0004.
- The bank indicates that it is owed $23,000 on a long-term loan, and the current portion due in 0005 is $3,414.
- Chuck remembered that his accountant had forecast that the December 31, 0004, current ratio was 1.25 to 1.
- The balance sheet for Chuck's restaurant for the last three years shows that current assets represented 25 percent of total assets. Assume that this relationship stayed the same for December 31, 0004.

a. Calculate the total current assets.
b. Calculate the accounts receivable, assuming that the only current assets were cash, accounts receivable, and inventory.
c. Calculate the total assets.
d. Recreate Chuck's Charbroiler's balance sheet at December 31, 0004.

4.4 You have the following information from the balance sheets for two successive years for a hotel.

	Year 0002	**Year 0003**
Total assets	$411,200	$395,700
Total liabilities	302,400	315,500
Total equity	108,800	80,200

For each year calculate:
a. Total assets to total liabilities ratio
b. Total liabilities to total assets ratio
c. Total liabilities to total equity ratio
Discuss the change that has taken place from year 0002 to year 0003 from the point of view of an investor from whom the hotel wishes to borrow money for expansion.

4.5 In addition to the balance sheet information provided, the hotel in Problem 4.4 has the following income statement information for the year 0003:

Revenue	$851,800
Costs (before interest and tax)	798,900
	$ 52,900
Interest	26,100
	$ 26,800
Income tax	6,700
Net income	$ 20,100

Calculate, for year 0003:

a. Return on assets
b. Net return on assets
c. Number of times interest earned
d. Net income to revenue ratio
e. Return on stockholders' equity

Discuss the profitability of the hotel in terms of the answers you received in parts d. and e. of this problem.

4.6 You have the following information about a restaurant.

BALANCE SHEET

Assets	Dec. 31, 0007	Dec. 31, 0008
Cash	$ 6,100	$ 11,200
Accounts receivable	13,200	15,400 use ↑ op
Food inventory	14,600	13,900 source ↓ op
Prepaid expenses	3,800	4,500 use ↑ op
Land	32,000	32,000
Building	315,800	323,200 use ↑ inv.
Furniture and equipment	83,800	91,500 use ↑
Accumulated depreciation	(113,700)	(124,500)
	$355,100	$367,200

(handwritten: CA bracketing Cash through Prepaid expenses)

Liabilities and Equity

	Dec. 31, 0007	Dec. 31, 0008
Accounts payable	$ 16,700	$ 12,500
Bank loan	4,900	3,600
Income tax payable *(handwritten: wages pay)*	12,500	12,600
Accrued expenses	7,100	7,500
Current portion of mortgage	10,400	12,100
Long-term mortgage payable	192,000	180,900 ↓ use fin
Common stock	10,000	10,000
Retained earnings	101,500	128,000
	$355,100	$367,200

(handwritten: CL bracketing Accounts payable through Current portion of mortgage)

CONDENSED INCOME STATEMENT FOR YEAR ENDING DECEMBER 31, 0008

Revenue		$742,600
Cost of sales	$301,900	
Operating costs	381,200	683,100
Income before interest and income tax		$ 59,500
Interest		19,400
Income before income tax		$ 40,100
Income tax		12,600
Net income		$ 27,500

From the above information calculate:

a. The working capital for 0007 and 0008
b. The current ratio for 0007 and 0008
c. The accounts receivable as a percentage of total revenue for 0008.
d. The accounts receivable turnover for 0008
e. The accounts receivable average collection period for 0008
f. Total assets to total liabilities ratio for 0007 and 0008
g. Total liabilities to total assets ratio for 0007 and 0008
h. Total liabilities to total equity ratio for 0007 and 0008
i. Return on assets for 0008
j. Net return on assets for 0008
k. Number of times interest earned in 0008
l. Net income to revenue ratio for 0008
m. Return on stockholders' equity for 0008
n. Food inventory turnover for 0008
o. Fixed asset turnover for 0008

Assuming that the net income in year 0008 was typical of the net income per year over the past few years, and assuming that the stockholders' equity investment has remained fairly stable over the same period, discuss the profitability of the operation.

4.7 The owners of a cocktail bar have the following annual income statement information:

Annual revenue	$200,000
Cost of sales 30%	60,000
Wages	50,000
Other operating costs	20,000
Fixed charges (including depreciation)	40,000

They are contemplating refurnishing the bar at an estimated cost of $20,000, using their own funds. They anticipate that the refurnishing will bring in extra customers and that revenue will increase by 10 percent. The furnishings will have a life of five years (straight-line depreciation), with no scrap value.

To handle the extra volume of customers, more staff would have to be hired at an estimated cost of $100 per week. Other operating costs would increase by $1,800 a year. Apart from depreciation, there will be no change in fixed charges. The income tax rate is 25 percent. The owners of the bar will only go ahead if the return on their $20,000 investment is 15 percent or more in the first year.

a. Should they make the investment?
b. Assuming they had an alternative of using only $10,000 of their own money and borrowing the remainder at an interest rate of 8 percent, would the decision change?

4.8 A restaurant has the following statistical information calculated from its financial statements for the past three years:

	Year 0007	Year 0008	Year 0009
Current ratio	1.03/1	1.25/1	1.37/1
Food inventory turnover	37 times	31 times	25 times
Accounts receivable turnover	29 times	24 times	19 times
Total liabilities to total equity	2.75/1	2.3/1	1.95/1
Return on stockholders' equity	9.72%	9.51%	8.74%
Revenue	$875,400	$881,900	$879,300

Using the above information, answer each of the following questions, including an explanation of why you answered each question in this way.

a. Is the restaurant becoming more efficient in the collection of its accounts receivable?

b. Over the years has more or less money been invested in food inventory?

c. During the period, has the liquidity of the restaurant improved?

d. From the stockholders' point of view, is the profitability of the operation improving or not?

e. If the restaurant wished to expand and borrow long-term funds to do so, would it be easier for them to find a lender now than three years ago?

f. Has the restaurant been using leverage to the advantage of the stockholders over the period?

4.9 A restaurant has the following statistical information calculated from its financial statements for the past three years:

	Year 1	Year 2	Year 3
Current ratio	1.37:1	1.27:1	1.05:1
Food inventory turnover	23 times	30 times	38 times
Accounts receivable turnover	18 times	22 times	28 times
Total liabilities to equity	1.92:1	2.25:1	2.80:1
Return on stockholders' equity	8.72%	9.65%	9.87%
Revenue	$880,000	$882,500	$872,300

Using the above information, answer each of the following questions, including an explanation of why you answered each question in this way:

a. Is the restaurant becoming more efficient in the collection of its accounts receivable?

b. Over the years has more or less money been invested in inventory of food? (Assume that the food cost percentage has not changed over the three years.)

c. During the period, has the liquidity of the restaurant improved?

d. From the stockholders' point of view, is the profitability of the restaurant improving?

e. If the restaurant wished to expand and borrow long-term funds to do so, would it be easier for them to find a lender now than three years ago?

f. Has the restaurant been using leverage to the advantage of the stockholders over the period?

4.10 The owners of a catering company own a number of relatively small restaurants. Following are the average annual operating figures for one of them:

Revenue	$120,000
Cost of sales	48,000
Wages	33,600
Other expenses	24,000

The owners, because of the potential to increase revenue, are considering taking over an adjoining property on a ten-year lease. Cost of the lease would be $25,000 for the entire ten years, payable in advance. New equipment would have to be purchased at an estimated cost of $10,000 with a ten-year life and no scrap value. Additional investment in food inventory of $400 would be required.

Revenue is forecast to increase by 20 percent over present level while the food cost ratio will stay the same. Wages are expected to increase by $75 a week and other expenses by $40 week.

The owners want a minimum 15 percent return before income tax on any additional investment.

a. Should the investment be made?

b. As an alternative, the owners are considering borrowing $20,000 of the required investment at a 10 percent interest rate. Would the decision change? Support your decision with any necessary calculations.

CASE 4

With reference to the 4C Company's balance sheet and income statement for the year ending December 31, 0001, calculate each of the following:

a. Current ratio.

b. Accounts receivable average collection period. Base this on charge revenue only and assume that charge revenue is 30 percent of total revenue. Assume that the year-end accounts receivable figure is the average for the year.

c. Net return on assets (use the December 31 assets as the average).
d. Net income to total revenue ratio.
e. Return on equity.
f. Food inventory turnover.
g. Beverage inventory turnover.

Note that in order to conserve cash in the company during the first year, Charles had taken only $1,500 a month out of the company as a salary. This amount is included in the salaries and wages figure on the income statement. (Remember that Charles was able to take $2,000 a month out of the 3C Company.) Give Charles a one- or two-sentence comment about each of the ratios that you have calculated, with particular reference to whether or not the result seems satisfactory.

Since the 4C Company is presently in a very liquid cash position, prior to the year-end Charles could have had the company buy back (redeem) some of the common stock he holds. Assume that this had occurred and that $20,000 cash was used. Recalculate the ratios that would have been affected and comment about the new result compared to the previous result.

5 Internal Control

Chapter Highlights

This chapter explains the objectives of internal control and discusses some of the inputs necessary for good internal control, such as management's having an effective philosophy of control, monitoring the control systems, selecting and training employees, establishing responsibilities and preparing written control procedures, maintaining adequate records, separating record keeping and asset control, dividing the responsibility for related transactions, and using machines in control.

Control of purchases is discussed. The documents that aid in this are illustrated and explained, and the proper procedures for product storage and inventory control are outlined.

Specific controls required for cash receipts and cash disbursements, including the use of a voucher system, are also discussed. A monthly bank reconciliation, as an aspect of control of disbursements, is illustrated.

The chapter concludes with listings of various methods of loss or fraud that could occur in such areas as delivery and receipt of merchandise, cash funds, accounts payable and payroll, food and beverage sales, and in the front office of a hotel or motel.

Chapter Objectives

After studying this chapter the reader should be able to:

1. Define the purpose of internal control.
2. Briefly describe the two basic requirements for good internal control.
3. Briefly discuss some of the basic principles of good internal control, such as defining job responsibilities, separating record keeping from control of assets, and dividing responsibilities for related tasks.
4. Explain how "lapping" can be used for fraudulent purposes.
5. List and briefly discuss each of the five control documents used to control purchases.
6. List and discuss the proper procedures for product storage and inventory control.
7. Describe how a petty cash fund operates.
8. Explain briefly how control can be established over cash receipts and cash disbursements.
9. List the procedures necessary to control payroll disbursements.
10. Complete a bank reconciliation.

INTERNAL CONTROL

This book is about management accounting and management accounting systems. It is the information provided by management accounting that is used by an organization's management to make decisions. To make good decisions the information needs to be accurate. One way to help ensure the information is as accurate as possible is to have good internal control.

Internal control objectives

Internal control procedures apply to every aspect of an establishment's operations from purchases through to sales, the control of cash receipts and disbursements, and all the other assets that the establishment has. The main objective of internal control is to safeguard those assets and to provide information to indicate whether or not this is being accomplished.

In a small, owner-operated business, such as an independent restaurant or small motel, very few internal controls are required since the control is carried out by the owner who handles all the cash coming in and payments going out and, by his or her presence, ensures the smooth and efficient operation of the business.

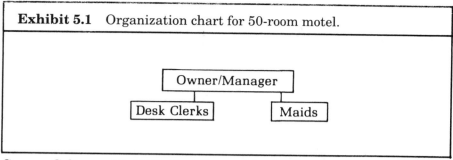

Exhibit 5.1   Organization chart for 50-room motel.

```
            ┌─────────────────┐
            │  Owner/Manager  │
            └─────────────────┘
     ┌──────────────┐   ┌──────────┐
     │  Desk Clerks │   │  Maids   │
     └──────────────┘   └──────────┘
```

Source: Coltman, M. 1989. *Cost Control for the Hospitality Industry.* New York: VNR.

Organization charts

In larger establishments, one-person control is no longer feasible. In fact, in larger organizations it is necessary to organize operations into various departments and to draw up a plan of the organization or an organization chart. Indeed, the organization chart itself is the foundation of a good internal control system since it establishes lines of communication and levels of authority and responsibility.

Organization charts for various types and sizes of hospitality establishments are illustrated in Exhibits 5.1, 5.2, 5.3, 5.4, and 5.5. As can be seen, in large establishments the organization charts show that lines of authority, responsibility, and communication become more complex. Therefore, the internal control system in a large establishment will also be more complex.

A system of internal control encompasses the following two broad requirements.

Requirements of system

1. Methods and procedures for the employees in the various job categories to follow in order to ensure that they follow management policies, achieve operational efficiency, and protect assets from waste, theft, or fraud. Assets are defined as cash, accounts receivable, inventory, equipment, buildings, and land. The types of safeguards needed include the use of safes for holding large sums of cash, use of locked storerooms for inventories of food and beverage, access restrictions to locations where cash and products are stored, and maintenance of all equipment in efficient working order.

2. Reliable forms and reports that will measure the efficiency and effectiveness of the employees and provide information usually of an accounting or financial nature, that, when analyzed, will identify problem areas. This information must be accurate and timely if it is to be useful. It must also be cost-effective; in other words, the benefits (cost savings) of an internal control system must be greater than the cost of its implementation and continuation. Information produced must also be useful. If the information is invalid and cannot be used, then effort and money have been wasted.

Internal Control   143

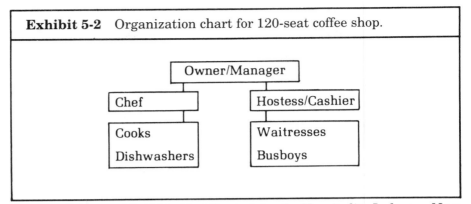

Exhibit 5-2 Organization chart for 120-seat coffee shop.

Source: Coltman, M. 1989. *Cost Control for the Hospitality Industry.* New York: VNR.

Requirements in conflict

It may seem that these two major requirements are in conflict. For example, the procedures used to store and safeguard food products and the paperwork requirements to obtain those products from storage may be so cumbersome that employees in departments (such as the dining room) that need those products do not bother to replenish depleted stocks. As a result, the operation's efficiency is reduced and sales may be lost. Alternatively, if employees complete all paperwork requirements to ensure they always have sufficient products on hand, the added labor cost may exceed potential losses of products from theft or waste.

Although in this chapter we shall be viewing internal control primarily from an accounting point of view, control is not limited to financial matters. For example, an establishment's personnel policies are part of the system of internal control. A company's policies on such matters as employee skill upgrading and education are important since they are eventually reflected in the company's financial results.

PRINCIPLES OF INTERNAL CONTROL

Some of the basic principles that provide a solid foundation for a good internal control system are discussed in the following sections.

Management Attitude

The majority of employees are honest by nature, but, because of a poor internal control system, or, worse still, complete absence of any controls, employees become dishonest because temptation is put in their way. If management does not care, why should the employees?

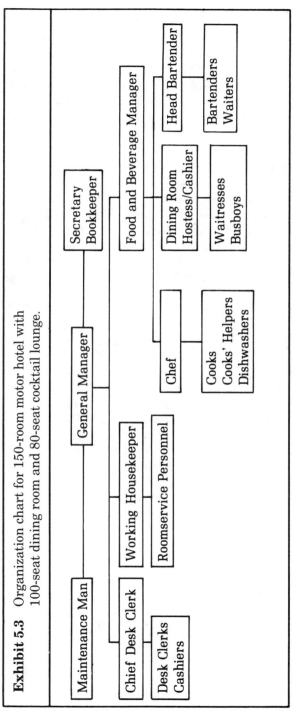

Exhibit 5.3 Organization chart for 150-room motor hotel with 100-seat dining room and 80-seat cocktail lounge.

Source: Coltman, M. 1989. *Cost Control for the Hospitality Industry.* New York: VNR.

Management supervision required	Control systems, by themselves, do not solve all problems. The implementation of a control system does not remove from management the necessity to observe constantly the effectiveness of the system by supervision. A control system does not prevent fraud or theft. The system may point out that it is happening. Also, some forms of fraud or theft may never be discovered even with an excellent control system. Collusion (two or more employees working together for dishonest purposes) may go undetected for long periods of time. The important fact to remember is that no system of control can be perfect. An effective manager will always be alert to this fact.

System Monitoring

System redundancy	Any system of control must also be monitored to ensure that it is continuing to provide the desired information. The system must therefore be flexible enough to be changed to suit different needs. If a reporting form needs to be changed, then it should be changed. If a form becomes redundant, then it should be scrapped entirely or replaced by one that is more suitable. To have employees complete forms that no one subsequently looks at is a costly exercise, and employees quickly become disillusioned when there seems to be no purpose to what they are asked to do.

Employee Selection and Training

Important aspects of effective internal control are employee competence, trustworthiness, and training. This means having a good system of screening job applicants, selecting employees, and providing employee orientation, on-the-job training, and periodic evaluation. Obviously, supervisory personnel must also be competent, with skills in maintaining the operation's standards, motivating employees they supervise, preparing staffing schedules, maintaining employee morale (to reduce the cost of employee turnover), and implementing procedures to control labor and other costs. A poor supervisor will fail to extract the full potential from employees and will thus add to the operation's cost.

Establish Responsibilities

Who does it?	One of the prerequisites for good internal control is to clearly define the responsibilities for tasks. This goes beyond designing an organization chart. For example, in the case of deliveries of food to a hotel, who will do the receiving? Will it be the chef, the storekeeper, a person whose sole function is to be receiver, or anybody who happens to be close to the receiving door when a delivery is made? Once the designated person is established, that person must be given a list of receiving procedures,

Exhibit 5.4 Organization chart for restaurant complex.

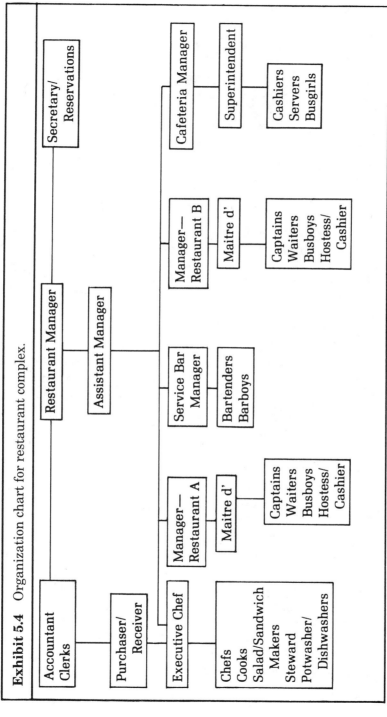

Source: Coltman, M. 1989. *Cost Control for the Hospitality Industry.* New York: VNR.

preferably in writing, so that, if errors or discrepancies arise, that person can be held accountable.

Prepare Written Procedures

Document policy and procedures

As mentioned, once procedures have been established for each area and for each job category where control is needed, these procedures should be put into writing. In this way employees will know what the policy and procedures are. Written procedures are particularly important in the hospitality industry where turnover of employees is relatively high and continuous employee training to support the system of internal control is necessary.

It is impossible in this chapter to establish procedures that will fit every possible situation in the hospitality industry because of the wide variety of types, sizes, and styles of operation. Even in two establishments of similar nature and size, the procedures for any specific control area may differ due to management policy, type of customer, layout of the establishment, or numerous other reasons. However, for illustrative purposes only, the following might be the way a written set of procedures could be prepared for the receiver in a food operation.

Typical steps in food receiving

1. Count each item that can be counted (number of cases or number of individual items).

2. Weigh each item that is delivered by weight (such as meat).

3. Check the count or weight figure against the count or weight figure on the invoice accompanying the delivery.

4. Check that the items are of the quality desired.

5. If specifications were prepared and sent to the supplier, check the quality against these specifications.

6. Spot check case goods to ensure that they are full and that all items in the case are of the same quality.

7. Check prices on invoice against prices quoted on the market quotation sheet.

8. If goods were delivered without an invoice, prepare a memorandum invoice listing name of supplier, date of delivery, count or weight of items, and, from the market quotation sheet, price of the items.

9. If goods are short-shipped or if quality is not acceptable, prepare a credit memorandum invoice listing items returned and obtaining delivery driver's signature acknowledging he has taken the items back or that they were short-shipped. Staple this credit memorandum to the original invoice.

10. Store all items in proper storage locations as soon after delivery as possible.

11. Send all invoices and credit memoranda to the accounting office so that extensions and totals can be checked and then be recorded.

As another example, the following could be a set of procedures for front office staff of a hotel or motel for the handling of credit cards.

Typical procedures for credit card verification

1. When a guest checks in, ask whether payment will be by credit card or some other method.
2. If it is to be by credit card, ask to see the card.
3. Verify that the card is one acceptable to this hotel (such as American Express, Diners Club, Carte Blance, Visa, and MasterCard).
4. If acceptable, check date on card to make sure it has not expired.
5. Copy credit card number and name as it appears on the card in the space provided on the guest's folio (account).
6. As you return the card, remind the guest to see the front office cashier before departing to verify the accuracy of the account and sign the credit card voucher for the charge.
7. Before filing folio with the cashier, check credit card number to make sure it is not on the credit card company's cancellation list. If it is, advise the front office manager of the situation.
8. Initial the credit card number on the folio to show that the card has been checked against the cancellation list and is not listed.

Credit card check out procedures

When the guest checks out:

9. Check the guest account to ensure the credit card number has been initialed.
10. If it has not been, check the cancellation list and advise the front office manager if it is listed. Do not return the card to the guest.
11. If not listed, complete the appropriate credit card company voucher, using the imprinter.
12. Have the guest sign the voucher. Check the voucher signature against the credit card signature.
13. Return the credit card to the guest with his/her copy of the voucher.

Maintain Adequate Records

Written records required

Another important consideration for good internal control is to have good written records. For example, for food deliveries there should be, at the very least, a written record on a daily order sheet of what is to be delivered, from which suppliers, and at what prices. In this way the designated receiver can check invoices (which accompany the delivered goods)

Exhibit 5.5 Organization chart for a very large hotel with full facilities.

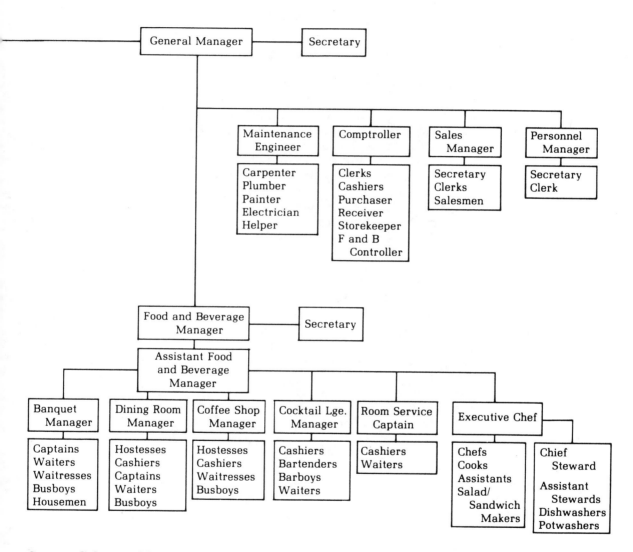

Source: Coltman, M. 1989. *Cost Control for the Hospitality Industry.* New York: VNR.

both against the actual goods and against the order form. The larger the establishment, the more written records might be necessary, such as a market quotation sheet so that some responsible person can be designated to obtain quotes from two or more suppliers before any orders are placed. Without good records employees will be less concerned about doing a good job. The forms, reports, and other records that are part of the internal control system will depend entirely on the size and type of establishment.

Separate Recordkeeping and Control of Assets

City ledger (accounts receivable) control

One of the most important principles of good internal control is to separate the functions of recording information about assets and the actual control of the assets. Consider the accounts of the guests who have left a hotel and have charged their accounts to a credit card or company. Such accounts are an asset—accounts receivable—and in some hotels are left in the front office until payment is made. These accounts are known as city ledger accounts. Checks received in payment are given to the front office cashier, who then records the payments on the accounts. These checks, along with other cash and checks received from departing guests, are turned in as part of the total remittance at the end of the cashier's shift. There is nothing wrong with this procedure as long as the cashier is honest!

Lapping

A dishonest cashier could, however, practice a procedure known as lapping. Mr. X left the hotel and his account for $175 is one of the accounts receivable. When he receives his statement at the month-end, he sends in his check for $175. The cashier does not record the payment on Mr. X's account. Instead, the check is simply put in the cash drawer and $175 in cash is removed for personal use by the cashier. The cashier's remittance at the end of the shift will balance, but Mr. X's account will still show an outstanding balance of $175. When Mr. Y, who has an account in the city ledger for $285, sends in his payment, the cashier records $175 as a payment on Mr. X's account, puts the $285 check in the cash drawer and removes a further $110 in cash for personal use. A few days later Mr. Z's payment of $350 on his city ledger account is received. The cashier records $285 on Mr. Y's account, puts the $350 check in the cash drawer and takes out $65 more in cash. This lapping of accounts will eventually snowball to the point where the cashier can no longer cover a particular account and the fraud will be discovered. However, the outstanding account may be so large that the misappropriated cash cannot be recovered from the dishonest cashier.

Procedures to prevent lapping

To aid in preventing this type of loss, the separation of cash receiving and recording on accounts should be instituted. Checks or cash received in the mail in payment for city ledger accounts could be kept in the accounting office for direct deposit to the bank. The front office cashier is simply given a list of account names and amounts received, and the appropriate accounts can be credited without the cashier handling any money. This procedure may not prevent collusion between the person in the accounting office and the cashier.

The separation of asset control and asset recording does not pertain only to cash. For example, inventories of food and beverage in a storeroom may be controlled (received and issued) by a storekeeper, but it is often a good idea to have the records of what is in the storeroom (for example, perpetual inventory cards) maintained by some other person.

Divide the Responsibility for Related Transactions

One person verifies the work of another

The reason for suggesting that the responsibility for related transactions should be separated is to have the work of one person verified by the work of another. This is not to suggest duplication of work—that would be costly—but to have two tasks that must be carried out for control reasons done by two separate employees.

Cash register possibilities of error

For example, many restaurants record items sold and their prices on hand-written sales checks. These checks, when the customers pay, are then inserted in a cash register that prints the total amount paid on the sales check and on a continuous audit tape. At the end of the shift or day the machine is cleared, that is, the total sales are printed on the audit tape and the audit tape is removed by the accounting department. The total cash turned in should agree with the total sales on the audit tape. But even if there is agreement, there is no guarantee that the audit tape figure is correct. Overrings or underrings could occur, or a sales check may have been rung up more than once, or not rung up at all, or may have been rung up without being inserted in the register.

Audit of sales checks

Because of all these possibilities, further control over sales checks is needed. First the prices, extensions, and additions of all sales checks should be verified (if time does not allow this daily, then it should be done on a spot-check basis). Then the sequence of numbers of sales checks turned in should be checked to make sure there are no missing sales checks. Finally, an adding machine listing of sales checks should be made. Assuming no errors on this adding machine listing, it will be the total on this listing against which cash turned in should be reconciled. If no errors were made by the cashier, the register audit tape will also agree with the adding machine listing.

The job of verifying sales checks for prices, extensions, and additions; of ensuring there are no missing sales checks; and of preparing the adding machine tape should be carried out by a person other than the cashier. In this way the responsibility for sales control is divided, and one person's work is verified by another. The cost of the second person's time will probably be more than recovered in increased net income as a result of reduction of losses from undiscovered errors.

Explain the Reasons

Sales check losses

Employees who carry out internal control functions should have the reasons they are asked to perform these tasks explained to them. For example, in the previous section it was suggested a second person verify the work of the cashier. The losses that can occur from servers making errors in pricing items on sales checks, in multiplying prices by quantities, and in totaling sales checks could add up to many dollars. So could losses from missing sales checks where the cash was paid by the customer, but a dishonest server or cashier kept the cash and destroyed the sales check. The importance of ensuring the minimization of these losses should be explained to the employee doing the task.

Rotate Jobs

Job rotation reduces collusion possibility

Wherever possible, jobs should be rotated. Obviously this cannot be easily done in a small establishment with few employees. In a larger operation cashiers could be moved from one department to another from time to time, or accounting office employees could have their jobs rotated every few months. Employees knowing they are not going to be doing the same job for a long length of time will be less likely to be dishonest. The possibilities of collusion are also reduced. Job rotation also has another advantage in that it prevents employees from becoming bored from constantly carrying out the same tasks. It also builds flexibility into job assignments and will give the employees a better understanding of how the various jobs relate to each other.

Use Machines

Machines aid in control

Whenever possible machines should be used. Although machines cannot prevent all possibilities of theft or fraud, they can vastly reduce these possibilities. The installation of a machine may also reduce labor cost if an employee is no longer required to perform a task manually. Such machines include front office billing/audit equipment, restaurant and bar cash registers and/or precheck machines, and mechanical or electronic drink dispensing bar equipment. For example, an electronic, preset, precheck restaurant register will eliminate many of the losses from the types of errors mentioned in an earlier section. Also, the saving in labor (because the manual verifications will no longer be required) will contribute toward the cost of the equipment.

Setting Standards and Evaluating Results

Food cost percent standard

One of the requirements of a good internal control system is not only to control the obvious visible items, such as cash or inventory, but also to have a reporting system that indicates whether or not all aspects of the business are operating properly.

For example, one of the many benchmarks used in the food industry to measure the effectiveness of the business is the food cost percentage. Management needs to know whether the food cost percentage actually achieved is close to the standard desired.

In Chapter 7 we shall see how cost control standards can be established and actual results evaluated for food, beverages, and labor.

Forms and Reports

Once procedures have been definitely established and the various employees given detailed written guidelines about how to perform tasks, standards of performance should be established and results evaluated. This will require designing forms and reports to provide information about all aspects of the business. Properly designed forms or reports will provide management with the information it needs to determine if standards are being met and to make decisions that will improve the standards, increase performance, and ultimately produce higher profits. The manager's daily report, shown earlier in Exhibit 3.6, is one type of form.

Another set of standards derives from budgets and budget reports that allow actual results to be compared with those budgeted. Budgets are discussed in Chapter 10.

System Supervision and Review

Missing sales checks

One of the management's major responsibilities in internal control is constant supervision and review of the system. This supervision and review is necessary because the system becomes obsolete as business conditions change. Also, without continuous supervision the control system can collapse. For example, one of the important control techniques in a foodservice operation is to ensure each day there are no missing, prenumbered checks on which sales are recorded. If an employee (after having served food and beverages, presented the sales check, and collected the cash) retains both the sales check and the cash and is subsequently not questioned about this, he or she will realize that the control system is not working effectively. The employee is then free to continue to hold back sales checks and pocket cash.

Internal audit

In small operations the supervision and review of the internal control system is the responsibility of the general manager. In larger establishments, with accounting departments, the supervision and review responsibility is turned over to the employees in that department. In the largest of companies internal auditing teams will be established. They will be responsible for appraising the effectiveness of the operating and accounting controls, and verifying the reliability of forms, records, reports, and other supporting documentation to ensure that internal control policies and procedures are being followed, and assets adequately safeguarded.

CONTROL OF PURCHASES

To understand the necessity for control of purchases, assume that, in a restaurant operation, every employee had the authority to buy food for resale and that there were no control procedures or forms in use. In such a situation there would be absolute confusion concerning what had been ordered and received. In addition there would be duplications, mistakes, over and short shipments, payments for items not received, and constant opportunities for dishonest employees.

In order to have control over purchasing it is necessary to divide the responsibilities among several individuals or departments. Coordination over the various purchasing tasks is achieved using five basic documents:

Five control documents

- a purchase requisition
- a purchase order
- an invoice
- a receiving report
- an invoice approval form or stamp

Each of these will be discussed.

Purchase Requisition

Centralized purchasing

In making purchases, those responsible for purchasing, whether it be employees of a purchasing department or an individual, cannot constantly be fully aware of the supply and service needs of the various operating departments. Generally, the responsibility for having an adequate supply of items in each department is delegated to each department manager. However, the department managers should not be allowed to deal directly with suppliers since control of purchasing could not then be coordinated. In order to have this control over purchases and the liabilities (accounts payable) that result, purchasing must be centralized. The purchaser, or the purchasing department, must be advised by each department manager of that department's supply requirements. This advice is made by means of a purchase requisition, prepared in triplicate. The original and duplicate are sent to the purchaser or purchasing department, the third copy is retained by the department head for later checking. A sample requisition is illustrated in Exhibit 5.6.

Purchasing department's role

The purchasing department's role is to make sure that supplies, equipment, and services are available to the operation in quantities appropriate to predetermined standards, at the right price, and at a minimum cost to meet desired standards. Generally, those responsible for purchasing have the authority to commit the establishment's funds to buying required goods or services. Sometimes a maximum dollar amount for any individual purchase may be established beyond which a higher level of authority is required before proceeding with the purchase. Those responsible for purchasing may have authority to question individual purchase requisitions with reference to the particular need or the stipulated specifications.

Purchase Order

Four copies

A purchase order is a form prepared by the purchasing department authorizing a supplier to deliver needed goods and services to the establishment. A sample purchase order is illustrated in Exhibit 5.7. Generally four copies are prepared, one for the supplier, one for the department initiating the purchase requisition (this advises them that the required items have been ordered), one remains with the purchasing department, and the fourth, with a copy of the purchase requisition attached, is sent for control purposes to the accounting department. For control purposes it is also a good idea to cross reference the purchase order number to the requisition number, and vice versa.

In many cases in the hospitality industry, particularly where it involves day-to-day food and supplies ordering, a system of purchase orders is just not practical since most orders are placed at short notice and by telephone. In such cases special procedures and forms will prevail.

Invoice

Invoices with goods

The third document in the system of purchases control is the invoice. An invoice is simply an itemized listing of the goods or services. Generally in the hospitality industry suppliers are asked to have the priced and totaled invoice accompany the shipped goods, since this aids the receiving department in the receiving process. However, for control purposes

Exhibit 5.6 A sample purchase requisition.

4964

Date _____

Department _____

Date required _____

Requested by _____

Department head checked _____

Purchasing manager approved _____

Note: Please use a separate purchase requisition
for each item or group of related items.

Description	Quantity	Purchase order number	Suggested supplier

Exhibit 5.7   A sample purchase order.

FRANKLYN HOTEL
1260 South St., Manchester
Telephone: (261)434-5734

PURCHASE ORDER
(The purchase order number must appear on all
invoices, bills of lading, or correspondence
relating to this purchase. Invoice must
accompany shipment).

653

Department _____
Purchase order date _____
To supplier:

Purchase requisition # _____
Delivery date _____

Description	Quantity	Price

Purchasing manager's signature _____

it is a good idea to have the supplier also send a copy of the invoice directly to the establishment's accounting office.

Receiving Report

The person or persons responsible for receiving should record each shipment received on a receiving report. A sample receiving report for food and beverages is illustrated in Exhibit 5.8. A report such as this should be completed on a daily basis and sent at the end of each day with accompanying invoices to the accounting office.

Invoice Approval Form or Stamp

Checking invoices

When the accounting department receives the receiving report, it can match with it a copy of the original purchase requisition, a copy of the purchase order, and the related invoice(s). All the relevant information can be compared and verified. The items on the invoice should be compared to the purchase requisition and the purchase order and to the receiving report. The invoice prices should be compared to the prices quoted and recorded on the purchase order. Finally, the invoice should be checked for arithmetical errors. If everything is in order, the accounting department can approve the invoice for payment. This can be done by stamping it or attaching a form to it. An outline of this stamp or form is illustrated in Exhibit 5.9. Initials or signatures should be put in the appropriate places to indicate that all the proper checks have been completed.

Storage

Recommended practices

The following practices should be used for product storage:

- Immediately after goods have been delivered and all receiving checks performed, they should be moved to storage areas or be sent directly to the departments that requested them. Proper storage facilities (such as refrigerated areas for perishable food products) should be used.
- Storage areas should be locked when the storekeeper is not present. Access to storerooms should be limited to the storekeeper and other authorized employees.
- Storekeepers should not maintain or have access to formal inventory records, nor should accounting department employees who maintain

Exhibit 5.8 A sample receiving report.

Daily Record of Purchases and Issues

Hotel _____

Dept. _____ Date _____ 19 ____ Day of Week _____

	Purchases			Stock to Storeroom				Bar				
1	2	3	4	5	6	7	8	9	10	11	12
Name of Item	Amount of Invoice	Direct Issues to Kitchen	Meat, Fish and Poultry	Staples	Fruits & Vegetables	Dairy Products	Liquor	Beer	Wine	Mixes Ingred	Cartage

A Today's Purchases											
B Balance Forward from Yesterday											
C Total to Date This Month											

13	14	15	16	17	18	19	20	21	22	23	24	25
					Direct Issues							
	Meat	Fish	Poultry	Fruits	Veget.	Dairy Products	Bakery Products	Staples	Coffee	Butter	Eggs	Food Cost 14 to 24
Direct Iss.												
Stores Iss.												
Total Iss.												
Fwd. Bal.												
Total M D												
I Beginning Inventory Last Month End												
J Stock to Store Room C4 to 7										5c		
K Store Room Issues E 14 to 24										21 to 25		
L (I + J=K) Balance on Hand												
M Physical Inventory												
N (L + or –M) Adjustment $												
O (N%to M) Adjustment %												
P (Sales/M) Inventory Turnover												

Exhibit 5.9 A sample invoice approval form.

Purchase order number _____

Requisition checked _____

Purchase order checked _____

Receiving report checked _____

Invoice prices checked _____

Invoice calculations checked _____

Approved for payment _____

those records have access to storeroom locations except to take inventories.

Perpetual inventory cards

- Inventory counts of stored products should be taken periodically by accounting office employees and compared to perpetual inventory cards (if used) completed by the storekeeper. A perpetual inventory card is maintained for each separate item in stock. It has recorded on it for each item quantities received in and quantities issued from the storeroom to provide a running balance of what should be in inventory.

  The best procedure for taking inventory is to make two accounting office employees responsible. One completes the actual physical count; the other compares this with the perpetual inventory card figure and then records the actual count on an inventory sheet.

- If there are any significant differences that cannot be reconciled between the inventory count and what should be in inventory according to perpetual inventory cards, the differences should be investigated to determine the cause. In this way, new procedures to help prevent future differences can be implemented.

- To aid in inventory count, preprinted inventory sheets that list items in the same order as they are located on storeroom shelves should be used.

CASH RECEIPTS

Good cash handling and control procedures are not only important to the business owner or manager but also to the employees involved because a good system will allow them to prove that they have handled their responsibilities correctly and honestly.

Proper receipt and deposit of cash

In hotels and restaurants, cash is received in payment for food, beverages, and services at any number of points. For each cash handling position (restaurants and/or bar cashiers, front office cashiers, general cashier in the accounting office) definite procedures need to be established to ensure that all cash due to the business is properly received, recorded, and deposited in the bank. The procedures vary from one operation to another because of differences in use of equipment, number of employees involved, whether or not credit is extended to customers or guests, and for numerous other possible reasons.

Cash removal precluded

In restaurants, bars, and other revenue outlets, each cash sale should be rung up on a cash register at the time of sale. Each cash register should have a locked-in tape on which is printed the amount of each sale. Those ringing up sales should not have access to this tape (another example of separation of assets and the recording thereof). The tape should be removed each day by a person from the accounting office. In the accounting office the recording of the daily sales register readings should be made by someone other than the person who collects and handles the cash. In this way, the tape forms the basis for the entry in the accounting records, and that entry can be verified against the records of the person who handles cash remittances. This precludes the possibility of the person handling the cash removing cash and changing the accounting records.

Control over cash received by mail in payment for accounts receivable was discussed earlier in this chapter. When checks are received in payment for those accounts, they should immediately be endorsed by a stamp with a statement such as "For deposit only to the ABC Hotel's account number 3459."

An important aspect to controlling losses from uncollectible accounts is to age them periodically. This should be done monthly. (Aging of accounts is discussed in Chapter 12.)

If any account receivable is to be written off as uncollectible, this should only be authorized by the general manager or a delegated responsible person who does not handle cash or have any access to recording amounts on accounts receivable. When it is apparent that someone is delinquent in paying an account, all collection efforts should be carefully documented before the final decision to write off the uncollectible amount is made.

Receipts deposited intact daily

All cash receipts should be deposited intact each day in the bank. A deposit slip stamped by the bank should be kept by the business. This is a form of receipt showing how much was deposited each day. If all cash received that day is deposited daily, no one who handles the cash will be tempted to "borrow" cash for a few days for personal use. It also ensures that no payments are made in cash on invoices (if this were allowed, a dishonest employee could make out a false invoice and collect cash for it).

Employees who handle cash (and other assets such as inventories) should be bonded. In this way losses are less likely to occur since the employee knows he or she will have to answer to the insurance company.

CASH DISBURSEMENTS

Petty cash fund
For minor disbursements that have to be handled by cash, a petty cash fund should be established. Enough cash should be put into this fund to take care of about one month's transactions. The fund should be the responsibility of one person only. Payments out of it must be supported by a receipt, voucher, or memorandum explaining the purpose of the disbursement. When the cash fund is almost used up, the supporting receipts, vouchers, and memoranda can be turned in and it will be the head cashier's authority to replenish the fund with cash up to the original amount. Receipts, vouchers, or memoranda turned in should be stamped "paid" or canceled in some similar way so that they cannot be reused.

Petty cash funds should be spot checked by accounting personnel from time to time. This spot check includes counting the cash and ensuring that the difference between that cash amount and the full petty cash fund amount is supported by authentic vouchers, memoranda, or invoices and ensuring that there are no IOUs, postdated checks, or other unacceptable items.

Payment by check
All other disbursements should be made by check and be supported by an approved invoice. All checks should be prenumbered sequentially and be used in sequence. The person who prepares checks in payment of invoices should not be the person who has authority to sign checks. Preferably, two authorized signatures should be required on checks, and invoices should be canceled in some way when paid so they cannot be paid twice. Those authorized to sign checks should not be allowed to prepare them or control the supply of unused (blank) checks. Only those who prepare (but do not sign) checks should have access to blank checks. Any checks spoiled in preparation should be voided in some way so that they cannot be reused.

It is advisable to use a check protector to print amounts on checks because this generally prevents anyone from altering the amounts.

If a mechanical check signing machine is used, the key that allows this machine to operate should be in the hands of the employee authorized to use it. If the machine keeps a sequential count of the number of checks processed through it, someone in authority should maintain a separate count of the number of blank checks used and reconcile this periodically with the machine count. Once checks have been signed (either manually or mechanically), they should not subsequently be available to the person who prepared them. They should be immediately mailed to suppliers or distributed to employees in the case of payroll checks.

Voucher system
Some larger hotels and restaurants control check disbursements by means of a voucher system. With a voucher system the procedures for control of purchases outlined earlier in this chapter are assumed to be in effect. When the invoice receives approval for payment (see Exhibit 5.9), a final document called a voucher is prepared. Vouchers are numbered

in sequence and summarize some of the information from the other documents. There is also space on the voucher for recording the date of payment and number of the check made in payment of the voucher. The supporting documents are attached to the voucher. When the voucher is to be paid, it is given to the person who prepares the checks. The person (or persons) who eventually signs the checks then knows the transaction is an authentic one since the check is accompanied by a voucher and the voucher has attached to it the purchase requisition and purchase order, the receiving report showing goods received, and the invoice, which has been checked for accuracy. There is little likelihood of fraud, unless all the documents were stolen and authorized signatures forged, or unless there is collusion.

Reduced possibility of fraud

Payroll

The procedures for cash disbursements discussed so far are intended to control purchases made externally. But since labor cost is such a high proportion of operating costs, equal care must be taken to ensure that proper control is exercised in this internal cost. In Chapter 7 we shall have a look at a system of controlling this cost with a system of labor cost standards. Suffice it to say, at this point, that payroll checks should be written on a different bank account than that used for general disbursement checks, and that the preparation and signing of payroll checks should be supported by a sound internal control system so that only properly authorized labor is paid for.

Control procedures

In addition, the following internal control procedures should be in effect for payroll:

- Only the general manager, a department head, or the personnel department (in a large hotel) should authorize the hiring or replacement of an employee and approve a salary or wage rate. The person or persons with this authority should have nothing to do with payroll check preparation.

- Procedures should be implemented for recording hours worked for hourly paid employees and reporting them to the person who prepares payroll checks. In some establishments, hours worked are recorded by time clock. Time clock cards should be approved by the employee's department head before they are forwarded to the payroll department.

- From time to time an authorized accounting office employee should spot check all payroll sheets to verify that hours worked, pay rates, and gross and net pay calculations are accurate.

- All payments for work performed should be made by check. Check usage control procedures should be the same as outlined earlier in the section on cash disbursements.

- A separate payroll bank account should be maintained with sufficient funds transferred to it each payday to cover payroll checks issued.
- Payroll check preparation and check distribution should be handled by employees independent of each other.
- Any paychecks that cannot be distributed to employees should be turned over to the chief accountant or to some other delegated person who has no responsibility for payroll check preparation. These checks should be held by that person until collected by the employees.

Bank Reconciliation

Monthly bank statement required

One control that is necessary in a good internal control system is a monthly bank reconciliation. At each month-end the bank should furnish a statement that shows each daily deposit, the amount of each check paid, and other items added to or subtracted from the bank balance. The canceled (paid) checks should accompany this statement. To ensure control the bank reconciliation should not be carried out by the person who records cash receipts or disbursements; otherwise "kiting" could occur. Kiting occurs when a check is written or drawn on bank account A without recording it as a disbursement. The check is then deposited in bank account B and the deposit is recorded. As a result the cash account is overstated (and cash can be removed) by an amount equal to the unrecorded check.

The steps in the reconciliation are:

Steps in bank reconcilation

1. To the bank statement balance add deposits made by the company and not yet recorded by the bank and subtract any outstanding checks. An outstanding check is one made out by the company but not yet paid by the bank.
2. To the company bank balance amount add any amounts added by the bank on its statement but not yet recorded by the company (for example, bank interest earned on deposits) and subtract any deductions made by the bank (such as automatic payments on loans and interest or service charges).
3. Once steps 1 and 2 have been completed, the two balances should agree. If they do not the work should be rechecked. If the figures still do not agree then errors have been made either by the bank or on the company's books. These errors should be discovered and be corrected.

To illustrate how a reconciliation is carried out, we will use the following hypothetical figures:

	Bank statement balance	$2,228
	Company bank balance	3,424
	Deposit in transit	1,448
	Outstanding checks—#3550	186
	#3726	20
	Interest earned on deposits	49
	Bank service charge	3

The reconciliation should appear as follows:

Completed reconciliation

Bank Balance	Company Balance
$2,228	$3,424
1,448	49
(186)	(3)
(20)	
$3,470	$3,470

Note that a separate reconciliation should be carried out for each type of bank account.

Cashier's Department

To reduce the possibility of fraud, the head cashier and other employees in that department should have not have the responsibility nor be allowed to

- Prepare or mail invoices or month-end statements to customers who owe the establishment money.
- Record any amounts in or have any access to accounts receivable records.
- Authorize rebates, allowances, or any other reductions to any accounts receivable.
- Write off any account as "uncollectible."
- Prepare checks or other forms of cash disbursement.
- Reconcile bank accounts.

METHODS OF THEFT OR FRAUD

The remainder of this chapter will be devoted to the ways in which theft or fraud has occurred in hospitality industry enterprises. These lists are not exhaustive. They include the more common ways in which misappropriations of assets have occurred. The lists can never be complete because, regardless of the improvements that are made to internal control systems, there is always a method of circumventing the control system, particularly if there is collusion between employees.

Collusion always difficult to control

Deliveries

There are various methods that suppliers or delivery drivers can use to defraud a hotel or restaurant when they observe that the internal control procedures for receiving are not being used.

Many ways to lose on deliveries

1. Invoicing for high-quality merchandise when poor-quality has been delivered.
2. Putting correct-quality items on the top of a box or case with subquality items underneath.
3. Opening boxes or cases, removing some of the items, resealing the boxes or cases, and charging for full ones.
4. Delivering less than the invoiced weight of meat and other such items.
5. Using padding or excess moisture in items priced by weight.
6. Putting delivered items directly into storage areas and charging for more than was actually delivered.
7. Taking back unacceptable merchandise without issuing an appropriate credit invoice.

Receiving and Inventory

The people working in and around receiving and storage areas, if these are not properly controlled, could defraud by:

Control required over receiving area and storeroom

1. Working with a delivery driver approving invoices for deliveries not actually made to the establishment.
2. Working with a supplier approving invoices for high-quality merchandise when poor-quality merchandise has been delivered.
3. Pocketing items and walking out with them at the end of the shift.
4. Using garbage cans to smuggle items out the back door.
5. Removing items from a controlled storeroom and changing inventory records to hide the fact.

Cash Funds

Under cash funds are included general reserve cash under the control of the head cashier, the petty cash fund, and banks or change funds established for front office or food and beverage cashiers for making change. Persons handling cash can cheat by:

Watch for cash removals and cover-ups

1. Removing cash and showing it as a shortage.
2. Using personal expenditure receipts and recording them as paid outs for business purposes.
3. Removing cash for personal use and covering it with an IOU or postdated check.
4. Underadding cash sheet columns and removing cash.
5. Selling combinations to safes.
6. Failing to record cash income from sundry sales, such as vending machines, empty returnable bottles, and old grease.

Accounts Payable and Payroll

The person(s) handling accounts payable and/or payroll can practice fraud by:

But don't forget noncash areas

1. Setting up a dummy company and making out checks on false invoices in the name of this company.
2. Working in collusion with a supplier and having the supplier send padded or dummy invoices directly to the accounts payable clerk.
3. Making out checks for invoices already paid.
4. Padding payroll with fictitious employees.
5. Padding gross pay amount on employee(s) checks in collusion with the employee(s).
6. Carrying employees on the payroll beyond termination date.

Food and Beverage Revenue

For good revenue control a system of sales checks and duplicates should be established (although there are exceptions, for example, a cafeteria). Even with sales checks, servers or cashiers could practice the following:

Good sales check control imperative to minimize losses

1. Obtaining food and beverages from kitchen or bar without recording items on original sales check; these items would be for personal consumption.

2. Collecting cash from customer without a sales check and not recording sale.

3. Collecting cash from customer with a sales check already presented to another customer and not recording sale.

4. Collecting cash from customer with a correct sales check, destroying check, and not recording sale.

5. Overadding sales check, collecting from customer, and then changing total of check to correct amount.

6. Purposely underadding sales check or omitting to include an item on it to influence a bigger tip.

7. Collecting cash with correct sales check and recording sales check as canceled or void.

8. Collecting cash with correct sales check and recording it as a charge, with a false signature, to a room number or credit card number.

9. Using sales checks obtained elsewhere to collect from customers and not recording the sale.

Credit cards also a vehicle for fraud

10. Not returning a customer's credit card after sale is complete, and subsequently using this stolen card to convert cash sales to charge sales using a false signature.

11. Since the customer in situation 10 will eventually discover this fact and report it to the credit card company, exchanging this stolen card after a few days with one from another customer (since customers seldom check to see if they are getting the correct card back) can prolong this fraud for a long time.

12. Collecting credit card from customer for an authentic charge transaction, but, before returning the card to the customer, running off additional blank charge vouchers with this card through the imprinter and subsequently using the vouchers to convert cash sales to charge ones.

13. Collecting cash but recording sale as a "customer walkout." One should always be alert to actual walkouts (both intentional and unintentional) in all revenue areas.

Bar Revenue

In bars where the bartender also handles cash, one needs to be even more alert to the possibilities for fraud. In particular, watch for collections of toothpicks, or matches, or coins the bartender is using to keep track of drinks sold but not recorded so that he knows how much cash to remove when the bar is closed. Watch also for:

Bar area requires some special precautions

1. Underpouring drinks (assume by one-eighth ounce on a one-ounce drink), not recording the sale, and pocketing the cash on every eighth drink sold. Using measuring devices brought in personally that are smaller than the establishment's standard ones is one way to hide this.

2. Overpouring drinks (and underpouring others to compensate) to influence a bigger tip.

3. Bringing in personally purchased bottles, selling their contents, and not recording sales.

4. Not recording sales from individual drinks until sufficient to add up to a full bottle, then recording the sale as a full-bottle sale (which usually has a lower markup) and keeping the difference in cash.

5. Selling drinks, keeping cash, and recording drinks as spilled or complimentary.

6. Diluting liquor and pocketing cash from extra sales.

7. Substituting a low-quality brand for a high-quality requested and paid for by customer, pocketing the difference in cash.

Front Office

Hotel/motel front office losses

The front office area can also be a source of extra income for dishonest employees. A dishonest desk clerk could practice fraud by:

1. Registering a late-arriving guest who is also checking out early, collecting in advance, destroying the registration card, and failing to record the revenue on a guest account or folio. This may require collusion between the desk clerk and the maid who cleans up the room.

2. Keeping cash from day-rate guests under similar circumstances to situation 1.

3. Registering the guest, collecting in advance, and subsequently canceling registration card and blank guest folio as a "did not stay." Again this may require collusion between desk clerk and maid.

4. Charging a high rate on the guest's copy of the account and recording a lower rate on the hotel's copy where the accounting system is a manual one.

5. Changing the hotel's copy of the account to a lower amount after the guest has paid and gone.

6. Making a false allowance/rebate voucher with a forged signature after a guest has paid and gone and using this voucher to authenticate a reduction of the hotel's copy of the guest folio.

7. Creating false paid outs for fictitious purchases for the hotel, or using personal expenditure receipts to justify the pay out.

8. Charging cash-paid guest accounts to fictitious companies.

9. Using credit cards from authentic charge sales to convert a cash sale to a charge sale subsequently (see situations 10, 11, and 12 under food and beverage revenue).

10. Lapping payments received on city ledger accounts (see earlier section in this chapter where this was discussed).

11. Collecting cash from a city ledger account previously considered to be a bad debt and not recording the cash credit to the account.

12. Recording the guest account as a "skip" (a guest who intentionally leaves without paying) after the guest has actually paid the account.

13. Receiving deposits for room reservations in advance of the guest's arrival and failing to set up a folio in advance with the deposit credited.

14. In collusion with the guest, not charging for an extra person in the room in order to receive a tip.

15. Selling deposit box or room keys to thieves or burglars.

16. Collecting cash from a city ledger account thought to be uncollectible, pocketing the cash, and writing the account off as a bad debt.

SUMMARY

An important aspect of any business is the safeguarding of assets; a good internal control system will accomplish this and also provide management with information on which to base business decisions. The internal control system should include methods and procedures for the employees to follow, and reliable forms and reports to provide the required information. With any internal control system, it is important to realize that the system may not prevent all forms of loss or dishonesty. For example, collusion is sometimes difficult to detect.

Once established, the control system needs to be monitored from time to time to ensure it is working well and continuing to provide valid and timely information. It is important to establish clear responsibilities for the various jobs to be performed so that a specific employee can be held accountable in the event of errors or losses. Employees who are given responsibility should also be provided with detailed written procedures about how to perform their functions.

Written records (forms or reports) should be established to help the employees carry out their jobs and to document information. A major principle of good internal control is to separate, whenever possible, recordkeeping and the actual control of the assets. For example, the person who handles cash should not be the same person who makes entries in the accounting records, otherwise it would be too easy to remove cash and alter the accounting records to hide the fact. By separating the two functions, collusion would then be required to hide theft. Similarly, wherever possible, the responsibility for related transactions should be divided so that the work of one employee will also check on the work of another. This does not mean to suggest that the work of one person should be duplicated by another person.

Employees should have their work explained to them so that they understand why they are doing specific tasks. In this way the job should have more meaning to them. Job rotation is also a good idea.

One way to reduce the possibilities of fraud is to employ machines to do certain tasks that improve internal control and may also lead to a labor cost saving.

Finally, any system of internal control requires constant supervision and review by management to guard against the system becoming obsolete.

A major area requiring a good system of internal control is purchasing. This can be accomplished using five basic documents: a purchase requisition, a purchase order, an invoice, a receiving report, and an invoice approval stamp or form.

Special procedures must be established for those handling cash, such as the cashiers at the various sales outlets, the front office cashier in a hotel, and the general cashier in the accounting office. Cash is the most liquid of assets and without complete control can disappear too easily if employees are dishonest. Employees who are handling cash should be bonded.

Precautionary procedures for the handling of checks must be instituted and a bank reconciliation should be performed once a month.

DISCUSSION QUESTIONS

1. What are the two basic requirements for an internal control system?
2. Define collusion and explain why you think it is difficult to detect.
3. Why is it necessary to define responsibility for particular jobs?
4. Explain what is meant by separating recordkeeping from control of assets.
5. Explain how lapping works.

6. What is meant by the term "division of responsibilities?"

7. List the five documents or forms used for control of purchases. Briefly explain the use of any two of these documents.

8. List and briefly discuss appropriate procedures for control over product storage and explain how perpetual inventory cards can be used in inventory control.

9. Why should all cash receipts be deposited each day intact in the bank?

10. Describe how a petty cash fund is established.

11. In paying invoices by check, how can control be established?

12. List the special procedures that are necessary for control of payroll and distribution of paychecks.

13. Why, at month-end, does a company's bank balance figure not necessarily agree with the bank statement balance prior to reconciliation?

14. List the steps in a bank reconciliation.

PROBLEMS

5.1 A motel has established a petty cash fund in the amount of $100. The fund is the responsibility of the desk clerk on duty during the day. During the month of October the following disbursements, supported by receipts or memoranda, were made from the fund. Calculate the amount of the refund check at the end of October.

October	2	$13.51	plants for lobby
	2	4.30	postage stamps
	5	15.28	cleaning supplies
	7	7.11	freight on delivery of linen
	8	1.68	office supplies
	15	11.50	postage stamps
	16	5.00	refund to guest
	20	12.00	cash wages for casual help
	22	0.48	postage due
	28	3.75	cutting new keys
	31	6.45	flowers for VIP guest

In the same establishment, the following disbursements were made out of the petty cash fund in November.

November	1	$ 3.07	office supplies
	4	14.20	flowers for lobby

7	1.30	office supplies
7	12.00	casual wages
10	0.32	postage due
13	11.50	postage stamps
14	4.60	COD parcel for owner
18	11.00	taxi cost for owner
21	3.26	collect telegram
24	4.02	freight on linen delivery
24	1.16	office supplies
29	10.50	postage stamps (note there was no receipt for this)
30	1.16	stamps

The desk clerk has added these items and requests a refund check in the amount of $88.09. A count of the cash by the manager shows there is $1.91 still in the fund plus an IOU from the clerk in the amount of $10.00. What comments do you have about the petty cash fund for the month of November?

5.2 A new bookkeeper-cashier is the only employee in the office of a restaurant complex that has a number of credit customers. She handles all cash received each day, including checks received by mail in payment of credit accounts, as well as making daily bank deposits and bookkeeping entries. She decided to practice fraud by lapping. For example, with reference to the following information, Mr. Arnold's payment received on June 2 was not applied against his account. The cashier deposited the check and removed cash from general cash receipts. Mr. Sayers's payment on June 4 was then applied to Mr. Arnold's account and the difference between the two amounts was then removed in cash. A complete listing of payments received on accounts that she lapped during the month is as follows:

Customer Name	Account Amount	Payment Received
Arnold	$ 51.40	2
Sayers	62.11	4
Carter	101.10	7
Mooney	110.90	12
Easton	141.20	14
Fossi	162.75	17
Wilson	172.83	22
Peterson	185.22	27
Levy	202.90	30

a. For each date on which a payment was received, calculate the amount of cash removed by the cashier.

b. If you were the manager of this restaurant and had discovered this going on, how would you prevent it from happening in the future?

5.3 Tavara's Tavern carries out a monthly bank reconciliation. At the beginning of July, it found the following concerning the June reconciliation: The bank balance on the bank statement was $4,810 and the bank balance according to the tavern's records was $5,112. Checks #306 in the amount of $27, #309 in the amount of $108, and #311 in the amount of $87 were still unpaid by the bank at June 30. At the end of June, the bank had added to the tavern's bank account an amount of $38 for interest earned on a separate savings account it has at the bank and had deducted $8 for a service charge. A deposit made by the tavern on June 30 in the amount of $554 did not appear on the bank's statement. Prepare Tavara's bank reconciliation for June 30.

5.4 A hotel company carries out a monthly bank reconciliation. At the beginning of November, it found the following concerning the October reconciliation: The bank balance on the bank statement was $3,506 and the bank balance according to the company records was $4,740. Checks #3581 and #3650 in the amounts of $298 and $402, respectively, were still unpaid by the bank. The bank had credited (added) to the company's bank statement an amount of $356, which the company had earned from a separate savings account it has at the bank. The bank had also debited the bank statement wrongly with a check in the amount of $20 that had not been drawn by the hotel company. There was a $4 service charge on the bank statement. The company's deposit on October 31 in the amount of $2,266 had not been recorded by the bank on the statement. Prepare the company's bank reconciliation for October.

5.5 A restaurant carries out a monthly bank reconciliation. The August 31 reconciliation showed the following: Restaurant bank balance $4,112. Bank statement balance $2,760. Deposits in transit August 30, $456 and August 31, $1,212 not yet recorded by the bank. Checks #167 for $61, #169 for $30, and #175 for $172 were still outstanding. The bank statement showed a service charge of $6 and an interest credit amount of $61. A check received by the restaurant in payment of a customer's meal in the amount of $11, and deposited in the bank on August 25, was debited back to the bank statement on August 31 with the notation that there was not sufficient money in the customer's bank account to pay the check. In verifying the bank's record of daily deposits against the restaurant's records, it is discovered that the bank statement deposit of August 11 shows $1,321 while the company records show $1,312. Further checking shows the bank statement figure is the correct one. Prepare a bank reconciliation.

5.6 The bookkeeper who has been working for more than 30 years for a small hotel is retiring. Because he was such a reliable employee he was given more and more responsibility over the years and did virtually all of the work, such as keeping all the accounting records, approving invoices for payment, preparing checks, and in the absence of the hotel's owner, signing checks that needed to be sent to suppliers. His daily duties included collecting the cash at the end of the day from the front office and restaurant, clearing the machine tapes, counting and verifying cash against tapes, depositing the cash in the bank, and making the necessary entries in the hotel's bookkeeping records. At month-end he would do the bank reconciliation. The hotel's owner realizes that she cannot hire and train someone to take over all the responsibilities of the retiring bookkeeper and that it would not be desirable for internal control purposes to do so. She knows that she will have to assume some of the retiring employee's duties. She is busy already, since, as well as generally managing the hotel she does all the ordering of food supplies for the restaurant and all the ordering and receiving of bar supplies. From an internal control point of view discuss which of the retiring bookkeeper's responsibilities the owner should take over while, at the same time, minimizing the amount of time this would require.

5.7 The owner of Charlene's restaurant believes that her food cost is higher than it should be. Charlene thinks that the problem might be in the receiving area and/or the dining area since she says she has good control over food in storage and production. She has asked you to see what you can determine. By observation, you notice that when drivers make deliveries they obtain a signature from any restaurant employee who happens to be near the receiving dock in the absence of the receiver/storekeeper. Deliveries are then left at the receiving dock until the receiver can move the goods to storage areas. Sometimes invoices are left with food containers; at other times no documentation is left and it is assumed invoices are then mailed by the supplier to Charlene's office.

In the dining area you notice that servers do not use printed sales checks to record customers' orders but simply note orders on scratch pads. They then tell cooks what they need and pick up and deliver food to customers. When the customers wish to pay, servers jot down the total amount due on the scratch pad page, present the page to the customer, collect the cash, and put it into a cash drawer. No sales are recorded in a cash register. "Used" scratch pad pages are placed in a box beside the cash drawer.

In both receiving and dining areas, outline the possible problems that present procedures create, and suggest to Charlene practices that would probably solve the problems.

5.8 A restaurant has been in operation for the past five years and has successfully increased its revenue each year. One of the reasons is that in the third year the owner began extending credit to local business people who regularly used the restaurant. They were allowed to sign their sales checks and were then sent an invoice at each month-end. The owner is concerned that this credit policy may have led to increases in losses from bad debts (uncollectible accounts receivable) that were not justified by increases in revenue. The restaurant operates at a 60 percent gross profit ratio, and other operating expenses (not including bad debts) are 50 percent of revenue. Following are the credit revenue and bad debt figures for the past five years:

Year	Credit Revenue	Bad Debts
1	$160,000	$ 960
2	180,000	900
3	240,000	3,840
4	300,000	4,500
5	360,000	5,400

In a columnar schedule for each year, record the credit revenue, cost of sales, gross profit, operating expenses, income before bad debts, bad debts, and net income. In addition, for each year, calculate the bad debts as a percentage of charge or credit revenue. Write a brief report to the owner with particular reference to control over bad debt losses and the restaurant's credit policy.

5.9 A small hotel has an outside accountant prepare an income statement after the end of each month. For the last three months the amount shown as bad debts had increased considerably over any previous month. The owner asked the accountant to verify the authenticity of all accounts receivable written off as bad debts over the last three months. The acountant discovered that a number of accounts in large amounts had in fact been paid and the persons contacted had canceled checks endorsed with the hotel's stamp to prove this. About three months ago a new hotel bookkeeper had been hired to carry out all record keeping and also act as cashier receiving and depositing the cash from the front office cashier and handling and depositing payments on accounts receivable received by mail. As the hotel's outside accountant, explain to the owner what you think has been happening and suggest how the problem can be resolved so that the same situation does not occur again.

5.10 At some of the banquets held in a hotel, the bar is operated on a cash basis. All drinks are the same price. Banquet customers buy drink tickets from a cashier at the door. The customers then present the tickets to the bartender to obtain drinks. The bartender will not serve any drink without a ticket. As each ticket is presented, it is torn in half by the bartender to prevent its reuse. Torn tickets are subsequently discarded. At the end of the function the amount of drinks sold, calculated by taking an inventory of liquor still in bottles and deducting from the opening inventory, is compared with the cash taken in by the cashier and with the number of tickets sold.

In order to cut costs the hotel is considering eliminating the cashier's position and the sale of tickets. The customers will pay the bartender directly for the drinks. From an internal control point of view, what comments do you have about this proposal?

CASE 5

The 4C Company's restaurant, with 84 seats, is not large. For this reason it does not have a large number of people on the payroll. Charles has been handling the general manager's responsibilities and has a good friend working half a day, five days a week, to take care of such matters as bank deposits, preparing accounts payable and payroll checks, and all other routine office and bookkeeping work.

Charles is not concerned about the honesty of the person, but he has learned from courses that he has taken that there is a need for any company, however small, to have some internal controls. Write a short report to Charles pointing out three specific areas where you feel controls might need to be implemented. For each of the three areas, advise Charles what might happen if a dishonest bookkeeper were hired and how internal control can be implemented to prevent dishonesty.

6 The "Bottom Up" Approach to Pricing

Chapter Highlights

This chapter introduces the reader to various pricing methods that have been used in the hospitality industry. It points out the need for both long-range and tactical pricing approaches.

The concept that net income is a type of cost and should be handled as any other cost is when determining product prices is discussed. This concept is demonstrated in calculating the required average check to cover all costs, including net income, for a restaurant. The chapter then illustrates how to determine the average check by meal period.

The subject of pricing individual menu items is discussed, as are the related difficulties. The relationship between sales mix and the average check is covered, as well as the topics of seat turnover and integrated pricing.

The chapter then moves into the area of pricing of rooms in a hotel or motel. The approach used in calculating the required average check for a restaurant is demonstrated for calculating the average room rate for a hotel or motel.

The reader is then shown how to convert an overall average room rate into an average single room rate and average double room rate. A different approach, basing the room rate on the square foot area of the room, is discussed. The relationship between room rates and rooms occupancy is covered.

Room rate discounting is discussed. The use of an equation is demonstrated to calculate the equivalent occupancy needed to hold total revenue (less marginal costs) constant if the rack rate is discounted. The use of a potential average room rate is covered and its use as a measuring device discussed. This section concludes with a section on establishing discounted room rates for various market segments.

Other pricing considerations such as an organization's objectives, elasticity of demand, cost structure, and competition are discussed.

The chapter concludes with a section on yield management, a method of matching customers' purchase patterns and their demand for guest rooms to derive more precise future occupancy forecasts with the objective of maximizing room revenue.

Chapter Objectives

After studying this chapter the reader should be able to:

1. Discuss the pros and cons of various traditional pricing methods used in the hospitality industry and differentiate between long-range and tactical pricing.

2. Explain the concept that net income is a form of cost.

3. Calculate the annual revenue required for a restaurant to cover all its forecast costs (including net income), and convert this revenue figure into an average check amount.

4. Calculate from given information a meal period average check, and explain the effect that menu item sales mix can have on an average check.

5. Discuss the variables or considerations to be kept in mind in menu item pricing, calculate seat turnover figures, and discuss integrated pricing for a restaurant.

6. Calculate the average room rate required to cover all forecast costs (including net income), convert this rate to an average single and average double rate, and calculate room rates on the basis of room size.

7. Discuss room rate discounting, calculate the occupancy figures for a discount grid, and calculate a potential average room rate and discounted rates for various market segments.

8. Discuss some of the important considerations in pricing, such as an organization's objectives, elasticity of demand, cost structure, and competition.

9. Define and discuss yield management.

THE "BOTTOM UP" APPROACH TO PRICING

Pricing theory suggests that hotel rooms and food and beverage menu items should be priced to maximize profits while offering guests value for money. The reasoning behind this theory is that it provides equity investors with a satisfactory return on their investment because products are properly priced.

The way in which products are priced will dictate, to a degree, whether or not financial goals will be achieved. If prices are too high, customers who do not believe they are obtaining value for money will stay away. If prices are too low, sales potential will not be maximized. In either event, profits will be lower than they should be.

Different methods

A number of different methods, each with its pros and cons, are used by hospitality business operators to establish prices.

Intuitive Method

The intuitive method requires no real knowledge of the business or research into costs, profits, prices, competition, and the market. The operator just assumes that the prices established are the right ones because customers are willing to pay them. This method has no advantages. Its main disadvantage is that the prices charged are unrelated to profits.

Rule-of-Thumb Method

Rule-of-thumb methods (such as that a restaurant should price its menu items at 2.5 times food cost to achieve a 40 percent cost of sales) may have had validity at one time but should not be relied on in today's highly competitive environment because they pay no attention to the marketplace (competition, value for money, and so forth).

Trial-and-Error Method

Variables affecting sales and profits

With the trial-and-error method, prices are changed up and down to see what effect they have on sales and profits. When profit is apparently maximized, prices are established at that level. However, this method ignores the fact that there are many other variables (such as general economic conditions, seasonality of demand, and competition) that affect sales and profits apart from prices, and what appears to be the optimum pricing level may later be affected by these other factors. This method can also be confusing to customers during the price-testing period.

Price-Cutting Method

Price-cutting occurs when prices are reduced below those of the competition. This can be a risky method if it ignores costs, because if variable costs are higher than prices profits will be eroded. Some restaurant operators set their food menu prices below costs on the risky assumption they will more than make up the losses by profits on alcoholic beverage sales. To use this method, the reduction in prices must be more than compensated by selling additional products. If the extra business gained is simply taken away from competitors, they will be forced also to reduce their prices and a price war may result.

High Price Method

Product differentiation

Another pricing method is to deliberately charge more than competitors and use product differentiation, emphasizing such factors as quality that many customers equate with price. If this strategy is not used carefully, however, it can encourage customers to move elsewhere when they realize that high price and high quality are not synonymous.

Competitive Method

Market price stability

Competitive pricing means matching prices to those of the competition and then differentiating in such areas as location, atmosphere, and other nonprice factors. When there is one dominant operator in the market that generally takes the lead in establishing prices, with its close competitors matching increases and decreases, this method is then referred to as the follow-the-leader method. Competitive pricing tends to ensure there is no price cutting and resulting reduction in profits. In other words, there is market price stability. This may be a useful method in the short run. However, if competitive pricing is used without knowledge of the differences that exist (in such matters as product and costs) between one establishment and another, then this method can be risky.

Markup Method

The markup method is used, for example, when a restaurant's traditional food cost percentage (as it appears on past income statements) is applied to determine the price of any new menu items offered. For example, if traditionally the restaurant has been operating at a 40 percent food cost, any new menu items offered will be priced so that they also result in a 40 percent food cost. The major problem with this method is that it assumes that 40 percent is the correct food cost for the restaurant to achieve its desired profit.

Using the Right Method

Many of the pricing methods briefly reviewed above are commonly used because operators understand them and find them easy to implement. Unfortunately, if the establishment is not operating as efficiently as it should, these methods simply tend to perpetuate the situation and sales and profits will not be maximized. Owners or managers who use these methods are not fully in control of their operations and are probably failing to use their income statements and other financial accounting information to guide them in improving their operating results.

Pricing as a tool

Pricing is a tool that can be effectively used to improve profitability. The dilemma is often a matter of finding the balance between prices and profits. In other words, prices should only be established after considering their effect on profits. For example, a restaurant can lower its prices to attract more customers, but if those prices are lowered to the point that they do not cover the costs of serving those extra customers, profits will decline rather than increase.

Long-Run or Strategic Pricing

Strategic objectives

Over the long run price is determined in the marketplace as a result of supply and demand. When prices are established to compete in that marketplace, they must be set with the establishment's overall long-term financial objectives in mind. A typical objective could be any one of the following: to maximize sales revenue, to maximize return on owners' investment, to maximize profitability, to maximize business growth (in a new operation), or to maintain or increase market share (for an established operation). A clearly thought out pricing strategy will stem from the financial objective or objectives of the business, as well as recognize that these objectives may change over the long run.

Tactical Pricing

As well as a long-run pricing strategy, a hospitality operation also needs short-run or tactical pricing policies to take advantage of situations that arise from day to day. Some of these situations might be

Typical situations

- Reacting to short-run changes in price made by competitors.
- Adjusting prices because of a new competitor.
- Knowing how large a discount to offer to accept group business while still making a profit.
- Knowing how much to increase prices to compensate for an increase in costs.

- Knowing how much price increases can be justified to compensate for renovations made to premises.
- Adjusting prices to reach a new market segment.
- Knowing how to discount prices in the off-season to attract business.
- Offering special promotional prices.

Many of the remaining chapters in this book are concerned with accounting-oriented approaches to controlling various kinds of costs in order to minimize them and thus maximize net income and return on investment. However, it is equally important to control revenue, that is to say, to control the prices that are established for the goods and services offered. Since there is a relationship between prices charged and total revenue, prices must therefore affect the general financial results such as the ability to cover all operating costs and provide a net income that yields an acceptable return on investment. Price levels also affect such matters as budgeting, working capital, cash management, and capital investment decisions—all of which will be discussed in later chapters.

Net income is also a cost

The traditional method of looking at an income statement is from the top down, that is by calculating revenue and the costs associated with that revenue in order to determine if there is a net income. A different approach might be to start with the net income that is required, calculate costs, and determine what revenue is required and what prices are to be charged in order to achieve the desired net income. This "bottom up" approach assumes that net income is a cost of doing business, which indeed it is. If a mortgage company lends money at a particular interest rate to a hotel or foodservice operation, the interest expense is considered to be a cost. The mortgage company is an investor. Another group of investors are the owners of the company (either stockholders or unincorporated individuals). They also expect interest on their investment of money and/or time, except that their interest is called net income. Therefore, net income is just another type of cost. This concept, and the bottom up approach to calculating revenue, can be useful in deciding prices.

RESTAURANT PRICING

Let us consider the following situation about a restaurant with 100 seats that wishes to determine what its average check (average customer spending) needs to be for the next year. We will use information about costs shown in Exhibit 6.1. If we put this information in the form of an income statement, without knowing what the revenue is, we would have a picture as illustrated in Exhibit 6.2.

Note that in Exhibit 6.2, since the restaurant is in an income tax bracket of 50 percent, its tax amount is the same as its net income amount. This could have been calculated as follows:

Income before income tax	$50,000
Tax 50%	25,000
After-tax net income	$25,000

In Exhibit 6.2 the total overhead costs, including net income, are $165,000, and since food, labor, and other operating costs are 80% of revenue (40% + 25% + 15%), then the overhead cost, including net income, must represent the other 20% of revenue. Therefore, the revenue level required can be calculated:

Calculation of revenue, given cost data

$$\text{If } 20\% \text{ of revenue} = \$165,000$$
$$\text{Then } 100\% \quad = \frac{\$165,000}{20\%}$$
$$= \$825,000$$

We can verify this now by preparing a traditional income statement (see Exhibit 6.3). Now that we know, assuming our cost projections to be

Exhibit 6.1 Projected restaurant costs for next year.

Net income required	present investment is $250,000 in equipment and furniture; a 10% after-tax return on investment is wanted
Income tax	50% rate
Depreciation	book value of furniture and equipment is $230,000, rate 10%
Rent	$42,000
Insurance and license	$5,400
Utilities and maintenance	$6,800
Accounting, office, and telephone	$12,200
Management salaries	$25,600
Food and labor cost	to be no more than a combined 65% of revenue
Other operating costs	to be no more than 15% of revenue

Exhibit 6.2 Projected restaurant income statement next year (incomplete).

	?	100%
Revenue		
Food cost		(40%)
Labor cost		(25%)
Other operating costs		(15%)
Management salaries	$ 25,600	
Accounting and office	12,200	
Utilities and maintenance	6,800	
Insurance and license	5,400	
Rent	42,000	
Depreciation	23,000	
Income tax	25,000	
Net income	25,000	
Total	$165,000	20%

correct, that we need $825,000 in annual revenue in order to have a 10% after-tax return on our investment next year, we can have a look at this $825,000 in relation to the individual customer.

For example, what must our average check (average customer spending) be, assuming the 100-seat restaurant is open 6 days a week ($6 \times 52 = 312$ days a year) and each seat turns over, on average, twice a day. The equation for average check is:

Calculation of average check

$$\text{Average check} = \frac{\text{Total annual revenue}}{\text{Seats} \times \text{Daily turnover} \times \text{Days open in year}}$$

$$= \frac{\$825,000}{100 \times 2 \times 312}$$

$$= \frac{\$825,000}{62,400}$$

$$= \$13.22$$

If we thought that, by giving faster service, the turnover rate could be increased to 2.5, our average check could be allowed to drop to $10.58 from $13.22, calculated as follows:

Effect of seat turnover change on average check

$$\text{Average check} = \frac{\$825,000}{100 \times 2.5 \times 312}$$

$$= \frac{\$825,000}{78,000}$$

$$= \$10.58$$

Exhibit 6.3 Restaurant income statement—next year (complete).

Revenue	$825,000
Food, labor, and other operating costs, 80%	660,000
Contribution to overhead costs and net income	$165,000
Overhead costs	115,000
Income before tax	$ 50,000
Income tax 50%	25,000
Net income	$ 25,000

Average check as a benchmark

Note that the figure of $10.58 does not tell us what every item on the menu must be priced at—only what the average customer should spend. Some will spend more, some less. Nevertheless, it gives us some idea of what the pricing structure of our menu should be with a balance of prices, some of which will be higher than the average, some lower. The average check also tells us, as the year progresses, whether or not we will achieve the net income required. If we see that our actual average spending per customer is less than required, and all other items have not changed (turnover rate, operating and other costs) then we know something must be done if we are not to have a shortfall in net income. Turnover rate must be improved, selling prices might have to be increased, costs must be decreased, or a combination of these variables might be required. The average check discussed so far is the average for all meals combined. The next section will cover the average check by meal period.

Average Check by Meal Period

Volume of revenue and turnover figures by meal period

Since most restaurants have an average check that differs by meal period (breakfast is usually the lowest, dinner the highest, and lunch somewhere in between), it might be desirable and useful to calculate what the average check needs to be by meal period rather than by day. To do this we need to know what proportion of our revenue is derived from each meal period and what our normal seat turnover is for each meal period. In an ongoing restaurant, our own historical records will provide this information. In a new venture, these figures would need to be forecast. Let us assume our restaurant is open for both lunch and dinner, and our records tell us that 40 percent of our total revenue is from luncheon trade, the other 60 percent from dinner business. Seat turnovers are 1¼ or 1.25 for lunch and ¾ or 0.75 at dinner. The equation we will use to calculate meal period average check is:

$$\frac{\text{Meal period percentage of total revenue} \times \text{Total revenue}}{\text{Seats} \times \text{Meal period turnover} \times \text{Days open}}$$

Therefore for lunch our average check will be:

$$\frac{40\% \times \$825,000}{100 \times 1.25 \times 312} = \frac{\$330,000}{39,000}$$
$$= \$8.46$$

For dinner the average check will be:

$$\frac{60\% \times \$825,000}{100 \times .75 \times 312} = \frac{\$495,000}{23,400}$$
$$= \$21.15$$

We can verify the accuracy of our average check calculation as follows:

**Checking
accuracy of
calculations**

Lunch: 100 seats × 1.25 turns × $ 8.46 average × 312 days = $329,940
Dinner: 100 seats × 0.75 turns × $21.15 average × 312 days =   494,910

Total revenue $824,850

Our original revenue total was $825,000. The difference is caused by rounding our meal period average checks to the closest cent.

Even though the illustration was for two meal periods, the same approach can be used if there are three meal periods. Also, if a restaurant is open more days for some meal periods than others (for example, five days a week for lunch and six evenings a week for dinner), the same equation can be used. The days open number will change depending on the meal period for which the average check is being calculated.

**Menus have
range of prices**

Note again that the average check by meal period is not the price of all menu items for that period. Menus generally have a range of prices.

Pricing Menu Items

**Cost
multiplication
factors**

One of the common approaches to menu pricing is to calculate, given the recipes and specific ingredient purchase costs, the standard cost (what the cost should be) for each different menu item. This cost is then multiplied by a factor obtained by dividing the overall food cost percentage desired into one hundred to get the selling price. For example, we know from Exhibit 6.2 that we wish to have an average cost of 40 percent. One hundred divided by forty = 2.5, which is our multiplication factor. To illustrate its use let us suppose we had a menu item that has been costed

Variety of markups	out to $4.00. Then $4.00 $\times$ 2.5 would give us the selling price of $10.00. However, it may not be practical to apply this multiplication factor across the board for all menu items. When developing menu selling prices one must keep in mind what market one is selling to (what the customers will bear, and what they expect to pay for certain menu items) and what competitive restaurants are charging for the same items. It becomes a bit of a juggling act, with some items having a higher markup and some lower. In other words, some will have more than a 40 percent food cost, some will have less than 40 percent. Also, it should be kept in mind that the individual food cost percentage of a menu item is not as important as the gross profit (selling price less food cost). To illustrate, compare the following two menu items.	

Item	Cost Price	Selling Price	Cost Percent	Gross Profit
1	$5.00	$10.00	50%	$5.00
2	1.00	4.00	25	3.00

High gross profit items favorable

All other factors being equal, it is more profitable to sell menu item 1, with a 50 percent food cost and a $5.00 gross profit, than menu item 2, with a low 25 percent food cost and only a $3.00 gross profit. In fact, it would be preferable if all customers chose item 1. If they did we would have more revenue since the selling price is higher. Gross profit would be greater, as would net income (assuming labor and other costs did not change). The average check would also be higher, despite a 50 percent food cost.

The sales mix

What people choose from a variety of menu selections is known as the sales mix. In menu pricing it is a good idea to keep the likely sales mix in mind since the average check, and ultimately net income, can be influenced by a change in the sales mix. To illustrate this refer to the following, which shows a sales mix for a fast-food restaurant giving an average check of $4.66.

Menu Item	Quantity Sold	Selling Price	Total Revenue
1	25	$3.00	$ 75.00
2	75	4.00	300.00
3	50	5.00	250.00
4	60	5.00	300.00
5	40	6.00	240.00
Totals	250		$1,165.00

Average check $\dfrac{\$1,165.00}{250} = \$4.66$

Changing sales mix

Let us assume that, by promotion or other means, the sales mix was changed, with twenty-five people no longer selecting menu item 2. Five will switch to menu item 1, and the other twenty will choose menu item 4. The new sales mix is shown below with a new higher average check of $4.72. The higher average check would normally result in a higher gross profit and net income, in addition to higher revenue.

Menu Item	Quantity Sold	Selling Price	Total Revenue
1	30	$3.00	$ 90.00
2	50	4.00	200.00
3	50	5.00	250.00
4	80	5.00	400.00
5	40	6.00	240.00
Totals	250		$1,180.00

$$\text{Average check } \frac{\$1,180.00}{250} = \$4.72$$

Variables make menu pricing a complex task

Because of all these variables (that different menu items must be offered with different prices and different markups, that gross profit dollars will vary from menu item to menu item, that food cost percentage by itself may not be a meaningful guide to determining selling prices, and that the sales mix must be kept in mind), menu pricing can be a complex task for management.

The comments made in this section on setting food menu selling prices are equally as valid for establishing beer, wine, and liquor prices in a beverage operation.

Integrated Pricing

In pricing food and alcoholic beverages, the manager should also keep integrated pricing in mind. This simply means that products should not be priced independently of each other. This is particularly true if the beverage operation is closely integrated with the food operation: that is, the customers eating in the dining area are the ones who provide most of the business for the beverage operation. In such cases, both food and beverage prices should complement each other to achieve profit objectives. Generally, in such a situation, the more food that is sold, the higher will beverage sales be (a concept known as derived demand) and vice versa.

Seat Turnover

Increasing seat turnovers

Earlier in this chapter it was stated that one way to offset a declining average check, or average customer spending, is to increase customer counts or seat turnover. Let us have a look at a case concerning two different restaurants, each with two hundred seats.

	Restaurant A		Restaurant B	
	Customers	Seat Turnover	Customers	Seat Turnover
Sunday	200	1.0	350	1.75
Monday	250	1.25	350	1.75
Tuesday	350	1.75	350	1.75
Wednesday	350	1.75	350	1.75
Thursday	450	2.25	350	1.75
Friday	550	2.75	450	2.25
Saturday	650	3.25	600	3.0
	2,800	14.00	2,800	14.0

Average number of customers

$$\frac{2,800}{7} = 400 \qquad\qquad \frac{2,800}{7} = 400$$

Average seat turnover

$$\frac{14}{7} = 2 \qquad\qquad \frac{14}{7} = 2$$

Weekly distribution of customers

Daily seat turnover is calculated by dividing the number of customers each day by the number of seats available (200 in this case). Average turnover for the week can be calculated by dividing total turnover for the week (14 in our case) by 7. Even though the average results in both restaurants are the same—an average of 400 customers per day, or an average seat turnover of 2 per day—the distribution of customers throughout the week is quite different. Such an analysis can be helpful in decisions concerning staffing and advertising, as well as seeing where a declining average check might be compensated for by increasing seat turnover to maintain total revenue and protect net income.

ROOM RATES

Rooms supply fixed

The approach illustrated earlier in this chapter for determining a required average restaurant check can also be used for calculating room rates. Hotel or motel rooms are, however, a different type of commodity from restaurant seats. Restaurant seats can be increased in the short run by squeezing in some extra tables to take care of high demand.

Alternatively, service can be speeded up and seat turnover increased to accommodate peak demand periods. The same cannot be done with guest rooms in a hotel or motel. Supply cannot be increased in the short run. The number of rooms is fixed. Neither can turnover be increased. Apart from selling rooms during the day for meetings or similar uses, the normal turnover rate of a room is only once per twenty-four-hour period at a maximum. One hundred single beds in a hotel can only be occupied by one hundred persons each twenty-four hours. One hundred seats in a restaurant can be occupied by one hundred, two hundred, or even three hundred persons or more, if the demand is there, during a meal period or day.

Room revenue lost forever

One other factor to be considered is that if revenue for a room on a particular night is not obtained, that revenue is gone forever. The room revenue and the cost of providing that unsold space cannot be recovered directly. This differs from food and beverages. If these items are purchased by the restaurant and not sold on a particular day, they can be stored for short periods and sold at a later date. The cost is still recoverable. The importance of having a room rate that will permit costs of providing the space to be recovered and the importance of as high a utilization of the rooms as possible is thus emphasized.

The $1 per $1,000 Method

Relationship between building cost and room rate

One of the methods developed many years ago for setting an appropriate room rate is the so-called $1 per $1,000 approach. Since the greatest cost in a hotel or motel property is the investment in building (from 60 to 70 percent of total investment), it was argued that there should be a fairly direct relationship between the cost of the building and the room rate to be charged. From this developed the rule of thumb that for each $1,000 in building cost $1 of room rate should be charged in order for the investment to be profitable. In other words, if a one-hundred-room hotel had a building cost of $4,000,000, its average cost of construction is:

$$\frac{\$4,000,000}{100} = \$40,000 \text{ per room}$$

The $1 per thousand calculation

Then, for each $1,000 of construction cost per room, there should be $1 of room rate. The average room rate would then be:

$$\frac{\$40,000}{\$\ 1,000} = 40 \times \$1 = \underline{\underline{\$40.00}}$$

Specific assumptions made

This rule of thumb worked under certain circumstances and assumptions. Some of these assumptions were that the hotel was a relatively large one (several hundred rooms), that there was sufficient rent from shops and stores in the building to pay for interest and real estate taxes, that other departments (food, beverages, and so on) were contributing income to the overall hotel operation, and that the average year-round occupancy was 70 percent. These assumptions are all quite specific. Consider the following two small hotel operations: Hotel A, which has no public facilities, and Hotel B, with more spacious lobbies and a dining room/coffee shop and banquet rooms.

	Hotel A	**Hotel B**
Building cost	$2,000,000	$2,600,000
Number of rooms	50	50
Cost per room	$40,000	$52,000
Room rate at $1 per $1,000	$40	$52

If the $1 per $1,000 rule of thumb were used, Hotel B would find itself at a distinct disadvantage to Hotel A, assuming the two properties were in the same competitive market.

The Hubbart formula

The $1 per $1,000 rule also leaves room rates tied to historical construction costs and ignores current costs, including current financing costs. The bottom up approach to room rates overcomes the pitfalls inherent in the $1 per $1,000 method. This bottom up approach to room pricing is frequently referred to as the Hubbart formula, which was developed some years ago for the American Hotel and Motel Association.

The Bottom Up Approach

The bottom up approach to room rates is quite similar to that discussed earlier with reference to determining the average check required in a restaurant. We will use the facts illustrated in Exhibit 6.4. The motel has fifty rooms. Note that the cost projections, even though based on past information from income statements, have been projected to take care of anticipated increases for next year. Our total cost of operating next year is, therefore, as in Exhibit 6.5.

Assuming the motel is going to continue to operate at a 70 percent occupancy, it will sell the following number of rooms per year.

Calculation of rooms to be sold

$$\begin{array}{c} \text{Rooms available} \times \text{Occupancy \%} \times 365 \\ 50 \qquad\qquad \times \qquad 70\% \qquad \times 365 \end{array} = \underline{\underline{12,775}}$$

Its average room rate will therefore have to be:

Calculation of required average rate

$$\frac{\text{Revenue required}}{\text{Rooms to be sold}} = \frac{\$547,500}{12,775} = \$42.86, \text{ rounded to } \$43.00$$

Exhibit 6.4 Motel cost projections next year.

Net income
  required
	10% after-tax on present investment of
	  $550,000 = $55,000

Income tax	50% rate

Depreciation	present book value of building $1,200,000 —
	  depreciation rate 5% = $60,000
	present book value of furniture and equipment
	  $150,000 — depreciation rate 20% = $30,000

Interest	present mortgage payable $750,000 @ 10% = $75,000
Property taxes and insurance	$30,000
Administrative and general	$47,000 ⎫
Marketing	$25,000 ⎬ Total $121,000
Utilities	$17,000 ⎪
Repairs and maintenance	$32,000 ⎭

Rooms department
  operating costs
	$137,000 a year for wages, linen, laundry and
	  supplies. This is based on past income statements at a 70% occupancy.

Coffee shop con- tributory income	$15,500 a year at 70% rooms occupancy

Note that this figure, $43, is only an average room rate and is not necessarily the rate for any specific room. Most large hotels have a variety of sizes and types of rooms, each type having a rate for single occupancy and a higher rate for double occupancy. Motels, even if they have only one size and type of room, have a single rate and a double rate for it.

Where there are multiple types of rooms and multiple rates, the calculated average rate can only be a guide to what the actual rate for each specific type of room will be. Size of room, decor, and view will be some of the factors to consider in arriving at a balance of rates that will be both fair and allow the resulting average rate to work out to the required figure.

Effect of double occupancy   Another factor to consider is the rate of double occupancy of rooms. A room that is occupied by two persons has a higher rate than the same room occupied by one person. The higher the proportion of double occupancies, the higher will be the resulting average rates. In our example, a safe way to assure that we achieve at least a $43 average would be to make that the minimum single rate for any room. Any rooms we then sell that have a higher single rate, or any rooms sold at the double occupancy rate, would guarantee that our average rate will end up higher

Exhibit 6.5   Motel total cost of operating next year.

Rooms department operating costs		$137,000
Total overhead costs		121,000
Property taxes and insurance		30,000
Interest		75,000
Depreciation		
building	$60,000	
furniture and equipment	30,000	90,000
Income tax		55,000
Net income required		55,000
Total costs		$563,000
Less coffee shop contributory income		(15,500)
Total net costs to be covered by revenue in rooms department		$547,500

than $43. Unfortunately, competition and customer resistance may preclude this approach.

In a simple motel situation, with only one standard type of room and all rooms having the same single or double rate, is there a method of calculating what these rates should be? The answer is yes—as long as we decide what the spread will be between the single rate and the double, and as long as we have a good idea of the double occupancy percent.

Calculating Single and Double Rates

To illustrate this we will use the information about our fifty-room motel. We know that $43 is the average rate required to cover all costs and give us the return on investment we want. Present average occupancy is 70 percent. We know from past experience that our double occupancy rate is 40 percent, and that we want a $10 difference between the single and the double rates. The double occupancy rate is calculated as follows:

Calculation of double occupancy percentage

Total number of guests during year	17,885
Less number of rooms occupied	12,775
Equals number of rooms double occupied	5,110

$$\text{Double occupancy rate} = \frac{5,110}{12,775} \times 100 = \underline{40\%}$$

A double occupancy rate of 40 percent in our operation tells us that 40 percent of all rooms sold were occupied by two people. In our motel of fifty rooms, with 70 percent occupancy rate on a typical night, we would have:

$$70\% \times 50 = 35 \text{ rooms occupied}$$

of which $\qquad 40\% \times 35 = 14$ will be double occupied

and $\qquad 35 - 14 = 21$ will be single occupied

Also, in our operation on a typical night, our total revenue will be:

Total nightly revenue $\qquad$ 35 rooms $\times$ \$43.00 average rate = $\underline{\$1,505}$

The question now is, at what rates can we sell twenty-one single rooms and fourteen double rooms (at a price \$10 higher than the singles) so that total revenue is \$1,505? Expressed arithmetically, this becomes (with \$$x$ the unknown single rate):

Calculation of average single rate

$$21\$x + 14(\$x + \$10) = \underline{\$1,505}$$

$$
\begin{aligned}
21\$x + 14\$x + \$140 &= \$1,505 \\
35\$x &= \$1,505 \\
35\$x &= \$1,365 \\
\$x &= \frac{\$1,365}{35} \\
\$x &= \underline{\$39.00}
\end{aligned}
$$

Therefore, our single rate is \$39 and our double rate is \$39 + \$10 = \$49. Let us prove the correctness of these rates.

Proof of correctness

$$
\begin{aligned}
21 \text{ singles} \times \$39.00 &= \$819.00 \\
14 \text{ doubles} \times \$49.00 &= \underline{686.00} \\
35 \text{ rooms} \times \$43.00 &= \underline{\$1,505.00}
\end{aligned}
$$

These, then, would be the rates under the given circumstances. They are the rates that, given the correctness of our assumptions about next year, we should be charging. They may not be the rates we do charge. Competition, customer resistance, or age of the property may oblige us to reduce them, in which case we will end up with a smaller return on investment than desired. On the other hand, newer establishments in the area with higher construction and operating costs and higher rates, with a customer willingness to pay them, may allow us to increase our rates above our calculated required ones. In this case we will have a higher return on investment than required.

In trying to determine appropriate room rates, influencing factors tending to decrease the average rate include

Room rate influencing factors

- Family rates
- Commercial discounts
- Travel agent commissions (unless accounted for separately)
- Convention or group rates
- Special company or government rates
- Weekly or monthly special rates

On the other hand, extra charges for three or more persons in a room would influence the average in an upward direction.

Room Rates Based on Room Size

One other possible way of determining average rates for different size rooms is to work on square foot of area basis.

Let us suppose our motel had two different sizes of rooms. Twenty-five of them are 220 square feet (including room entranceway, bathroom, and closet areas) and the other twenty-five are 180 square feet. The demand for each size of room is about equal. Total square footage available for rental is

Calculation of available square footage

$$
\begin{array}{ll}
25 \times 220 \text{ sq. ft.} = & 5,500 \\
25 \times 180 \text{ sq. ft.} = & \underline{4,500} \\
\text{Total} & \underline{\underline{10,000}}
\end{array}
$$

Even though there is a total of 10,000 square feet available, we are running at a 70 percent average occupancy. Therefore, on average, each night we are selling

$$70\% \times 10,000 = 7,000 \text{ square feet}$$

Since we must take in $1,505 a night, on average, to give us the required net income, each square foot sold should produce in revenue

Calculation of rate per square foot

$$\frac{\$1,505}{7,000} = \$0.215$$

Therefore, the average rate that should be charged for our small and large rooms is

Small room 180 sq. ft. $\times$ \$0.215 = $\underline{\underline{\$38.70}}$
Large room 220 sq. ft. $\times$ \$0.215 = $\underline{\underline{\$47.30}}$

We can check the accuracy of these figures. Since the two room sizes are in equal demand, we will sell, on average, 17.5 of each per night.

$$
\begin{array}{llll}
17.5 \text{ small} & \times \$38.70 & = & \$\ \ 677.25 \\
17.5 \text{ large} & \times \$47.30 & = & \underline{\ \ \ \ 827.75} \\
& \text{Total revenue per night} & = & \underline{\underline{\$1,505.00}}
\end{array}
$$

**Convert to
single and
double rates**

Note that these average rates for the small and the large size of room must still be converted, using the method illustrated earlier in this chapter, into single and double rates for each size.

Average Occupancy

Earlier in this chapter it was demonstrated how an analysis of restaurant seat turnover might indicate where the turnover could be increased to compensate for a declining average check. A parallel situation could exist with reference to average room rates and occupancies. Refer to the following.

	Hotel A	Hotel B
Saturday	40%	60%
Sunday	40	60
Monday	70	70
Tuesday	90	70
Wednesday	90	80
Thursday	90	80
Friday	70	70
	490%	490%
Average	$\frac{490}{7} = 70\%$	$\frac{490}{7} = 70\%$

**Analysis of
occupancy by
day of week**

Both hotels have the same average occupancies, but the analysis by day shows a different picture for each. Hotel A has very low occupancy during weekends and very high during the week. An advertising campaign directed toward bringing in weekend guests would benefit the rooms department and, no doubt, other departments in the hotel. On the other hand, Hotel B has a relatively high weekend business, and good, but not high, occupancy during the week. Its advertising should be geared not just toward weekend promotions but also toward improving midweek occupancy.

ROOM RATE DISCOUNTING

Rack rate defined

Room rate discounting is the practice of reducing prices below the rack rate. The rack rate is defined as the maximum rate that will be quoted for a room. When rates are discounted for some rooms on any night, this prevents the hotel from achieving its maximum potential average room rate and maximum potential total revenue for that night. Rooms are typically discounted for groups such as convention delegates and corporate and government travelers who are regular customers of the hotel. The discounts given are a normal cost of business to maintain occupancy levels, and the reduced room revenue is often compensated by extra profits achieved from those room guests patronizing the hotel's food and beverage facilities.

Discount Grid

In reviewing room rates and deciding on the discounts to be offered, it is useful to prepare a discount grid. This grid shows the impact of various room rate discounts on total room revenue.

Marginal costs

To prepare the grid, the marginal (variable) costs of selling each additional room must be known. Normally, marginal costs occur only in the housekeeping department because no extra costs are incurred in the reservations or front office departments to sell an extra room. Housekeeping costs include such items as employee time to clean the room, cost of linen laundering, cost of guest supplies (soap, shampoo, and similar items), and additional utility costs for lighting and heating or air-conditioning. For most hotels, marginal costs are easy to determine.

Let us assume that a 100-room hotel's marginal cost for renting each additional room were $10. The following equation can be used to calculate the equivalent occupancy needed to hold total revenue less marginal costs constant if the rack rate is discounted:

Equivalent occupancy equation

$$\text{Current occupancy} \times \frac{\text{Rack rate} - \text{Marginal cost}}{[\text{Rack rate} \times (1 - \text{discount percent})] - \text{Marginal cost}}$$

Assume that all the hotel's rooms have the same rack rate of $80 and that the hotel currently operates at a 70 percent occupancy. If rates are discounted by 10 percent, the equivalent occupancy required (using the equation) would be:

$$70\% \times \frac{\$80 - \$10}{[\$80 \times (1 - 0.10)] - \$10}$$

$$= 70\% \times \frac{\$70}{(\$80 \times 0.9) - \$10}$$

$$= 70\% \times \frac{\$70}{\$72 - \$10}$$

$$= 70\% \times \frac{\$70}{\$62}$$

$$= 70\% \times 1.13 = 79.1\%$$

Proof of calculation

This can be proved. Nightly room revenue before discounting is:

$$70\% \text{ occupancy} \times 100 \text{ rooms} \times \$80 \text{ rack rate} = \$5,600$$

and total marginal costs are:

$$70\% \text{ occupancy} \times 100 \text{ rooms} \times \$10 = \$700$$

Net revenue is therefore $5,600 − $700 = $4,900.

After discounting, nightly revenue at 79 percent occupancy will be:

$$79\% \text{ occupancy} \times 100 \text{ rooms} \times \$72 \text{ rate} = \$5,688$$

and total marginal costs will be:

$$79\% \text{ occupancy} \times 100 \text{ rooms} \times \$10 = \$790$$

Net revenue is therefore $5,688 − $790 = $4,898. In other words, net revenue (total revenue less marginal costs) is the same as before. (The small difference is due to rounding out the required occupancy level to 79 percent from 79.1 percent.)

Tabulating results

Similar calculations can be made for various occupancy levels and discount percentages and the results tabulated in a grid such as that in Exhibit 6.6. Once this has been done, the grid shows the equivalent occupancy that must be achieved to maintain room revenue (less marginal costs) at a stipulated level as discounts are increased or decreased. Thus the grid allows management to make sensible pricing decisions.

For example, the grid shows that if the hotel discounts room rates by 15 percent and its current occupancy is 70 percent, the equivalent occupancy after discounting would have to be 84.7 percent. In our 100-room hotel, this means an additional 15 rooms would have to be sold per night. If there is an advertising cost to sell 15 extra rooms this must be con-

Exhibit 6.6   Discount grid.

| Current Occupancy | New Occupancy Level Necessary to Maintain the Same Profitability if an $80 Rack Rate Is Discounted by | | | |
	5%	10%	15%	20%
70%	74.2%	79.1%	84.7%	91.0%
65	68.9	73.5	78.7	84.5
60	63.6	67.8	72.6	78.0
55	58.3	62.2	66.6	71.5
50	53.0	56.5	60.5	65.0

sidered, as would additional revenue that the additional guests might provide in the food and beverage departments. In other words, the grid should be used only as an aid in decision making and not be the only criterion.

Potential Average Room Rate

The potential average room rate is defined as the average rate that would result if all rooms occupied overnight were sold at the rack rate without a discount. This potential average rate can be used to monitor the actual average room rate.

Multiple rack rates

To this point, we have stated that the rack rate is the maximum rate that will be charged for a room. But in fact, most hotels have two or more rack rates for each room. There may be a rack rate for single occupancy, a rack rate for double occupancy, and even a rack rate for occupancy by three or more. How can a potential average room rate be determined in such a situation?

If a hotel sold all its rooms at single occupancy, its potential average rack rate would be the average rate if all rooms were single occupied. If the hotel sold all its rooms at double occupancy, its potential average rate would be the average rate if all rooms were double occupied. For most hotels, neither of these extremes is likely. For most properties on a typical night, some rooms will be single occupied and others will be double occupied. A further complication is that there may be different types of rooms whose single or double rack rates are different. Thus the potential average rate must be calculated by taking the hotel's normal sales mix into consideration.

Consider sales mix

To illustrate, assume that if all of a 100-room hotel's various rooms were each occupied by one person (single occupancy) at the maximum single-occupancy rack rate, total revenue would be $7,500. Potential minimum average rate is therefore

$$\frac{\$7,500}{100} = \$75$$

On the other hand, if all 100 rooms were double-occupied at the maximum double-occupancy rack rate, total revenue would be $8,500. Potential maximum average rate is therefore

$$\frac{\$8,500}{100} = \$85$$

(Note that if the hotel has suites or special rooms at higher rates, these can be included in the maximum potential double rate.)

Rate spread   The difference between $85 and $75 is known as the rate spread. If this hotel's percentage of double occupancy were 40 percent (that is, 40 percent of all rooms occupied are occupied by two people), the potential average room rate can be calculated as follows:

Potential average single rate + (Percentage of double occupancy
× Rate spread)

In our case, this results in a potential average room rate of

$$\$75 + (40\% \times \$10.00)$$
$$= \$75 + \$4 = \$79$$

Comparing Actual Average to Potential Average

Once the potential average room rate has been calculated, the hotel can compare its actual rate to this potential each day or each period. There may be occasions when the actual rate will be higher than the potential. This could occur when the double-occupancy rate exceeds the normal 40 percent and/or if additional charges are made for a third person in a room and/or if front desk employees are doing a good job of selling the most expensive rooms first.

Average rate ratio   In other cases, the actual average rate will be below the potential rate and can be measured by dividing it by the potential rate and converting to a percentage to arrive at the average rate ratio. For example, if the actual rate achieved during a particular week were $72, the percentage would be

$$\frac{\$72}{\$79} \times 100 = 91\%$$

This means the hotel achieved only 91 percent of its potential average rate. This could occur because the double-occupancy ratio declined below normal and/or because the front desk employees did a poor job and sold the lower priced rooms first. Alternatively, all other factors being equal, it could mean that rack rates had been discounted 9 percent on average.

Room Rates for Each Market Segment

With reference to the $79 potential average room rate calculated earlier, it is possible to calculate the room rate for each type of market (market segment) with which the hotel deals. Suppose we have the following information for each of three segments:

Information for calculations

Market segment	Annual Room Nights	Percentage	Rack Rate
Business travelers	5,110	40%	100%
Conference groups	4,471	35%	90%
Tour groups	3,194	25%	80%
	12,775	100%	

The percentage column figures show how much of total business each segment produces. For example, business travelers constitute 5,110/12,775 × 100 = 40 percent of total room nights. The rack rate column tells us the percentage of the rack rate that we are going to charge customers in that market segment. For example, business travelers are going to pay 100 percent of the rack rate (and receive no discount), whereas conference groups will be charged 90 percent of the rack rate (or receive a 10 percent discount), and tour groups 80 percent of the rack rate (or receive a 20 percent discount). What must those rates be to ensure that we continue to achieve a $79 average room rate?

New potential average rack rate

We must first calculate what the new potential average rack rate is going to be for the business travelers who receive no discount. We know that it will be higher than before because some segments are going to receive a discounted rate, and thus the new rack rate must increase to compensate for these discounts. The calculation is made by weighting the discount percentage for each market segment and, at the same time, taking into account the percentage of business that each market segment generates as follows:

$$\frac{\$79.00}{(40\% \times 100\%) + (35\% \times 90\%) + (25\% \times 80\%)}$$

Note that, in each set of parentheses in the denominator the first figure represents the portion of the business provided by that segment and the second represents the rack rate percentage for that segment. For example, in the first set of figures the business travelers provide 40 percent of the business at the full rack rate. Following through on the calculations we have

$$\frac{\$79.00}{40\% + 31.5\% + 20\%} = \frac{\$79.00}{91.5\%} = \$86.34$$

The discounted rates for the other segments are:

Conference groups $\$86.34 \times 90\% = \$77.70$
Tour groups $\$86.34 \times 80\% = \$69.07$

Proof of calculations

We can prove that these rates will generate the sales required to yield our desired potential average room rate:

Market segment	Room Nights		Average Rate		Total Sales
Business travelers	5,110	×	$86.34	=	$ 441,197
Conference groups	4,471	×	$77.70	=	347,397
Tour groups	3,194	×	$69.07	=	220,610
Totals	12,775				$1,009,204

and

$$\frac{\$1,009,204}{12,775} = \$79.00$$

OTHER PRICING CONSIDERATIONS

Simplicity ignores other factors

The method demonstrated in this chapter for determining meal selling prices and room rates to ensure an adequate return on investment has its shortcomings. So does the cost plus method discussed in conjunction with establishing food and beverage prices relative to the cost of food and beverage ingredients. Both the return on investment and cost plus methods are simple and easy to use, but, because of their simplicity, they ignore many other factors that must be taken into consideration in establishing prices. For that reason, return on investment and cost plus pricing should be used as reference points only, and should not be the only determinants in setting final prices. Some of the other considerations are discussed in the following sections.

Organization's Objectives

When prices are established they must be set with the organization's overall long-term objectives in mind. A typical objective could be any one of the following: to maximize sales revenue, to maximize return on owners' investment, to maximize profitability, to maximize business growth (in a new establishment), or to maintain or increase share of market (for an established business). A clearly conceived pricing strategy will stem from the objective or objectives of the business, as well as recognize that these objectives may change over the long run.

As well as a long-run pricing strategy, a firm also needs short-run or tactical pricing policies to take advantage of situations that arise from day to day.

Elasticity of Demand

Demand versus prices

Elasticity of demand is related to the responsiveness of demand for a product or service when prices are changed. A large change in demand resulting from a small change in prices is referred to as elastic demand. A small change in demand following a large change in prices is referred to as inelastic demand.

Perhaps the easiest way to test whether demand is elastic or inelastic is to note what happens to total revenue when prices are changed. If demand is elastic, a decline in price will result in an increase in total revenue because, even though a lower price is being received per unit, enough additional units are now being sold to more than compensate for a lower price.

Example of elastic demand

For example, assume that average banquet food check is $10 per customer and that an average of 3,000 customers per week is served. Total revenue per week is $30,000. If average food check is reduced by 5 percent to $9.50, and average weekly customer count goes up 10 percent to 3,300, total revenue will now be 3,300 × $9.50 or $31,350, which is $1,350 more than before. Demand is elastic. A generalization is that, if demand is elastic, a change in price will cause total revenue to change in the opposite direction.

If demand is inelastic, a price decline will cause total revenue to fall. The small increase in sales that occurs will not be sufficient to offset the decline in revenue per unit. Again, one can generalize and say that, if demand is inelastic, a change in price will cause total revenue to change in the same direction.

Availability of substitutes

One of the factors that influences elasticity of demand is the availability of substitutes. Generally, hospitality businesses that charge the highest prices are able to do so since there is little substitution possible. An elite hotel with little competition can charge higher room rates, since its customers expect to pay higher rates, can afford to do so, and generally would not move to a lower-priced, less luxurious hotel if room rates were increased. Demand is inelastic.

On the other hand, a restaurant that is one of many in a particular neighborhood catering to the family trade would probably lose considerable business if it raised its menu prices out of line with its competitors. Its trade is very elastic. Its price-conscious customers would simply take their business to another restaurant. Alternatively, a high-average-check restaurant will probably find less customer resistance to an increase in menu prices. In general, one can say, therefore, that the lower the income of a business's customers, the more elastic is their demand, and vice versa.

Customer habits and loyalty

Closely related to income levels are the habits of a business's customers. The more habit prone the customers are, the less likely are they to resist some upward change in prices, since customers tend to have "brand" loyalties to hotels and restaurants, just as they have with other products they buy. Enterprises that need to count on repeat business must be very conscious of the effect that price changes may have on that loyalty. Note also that the demand for a product or service tends to be more elastic as the time period under consideration increases. Even though customers are creatures of habit and do develop loyalties, those habits and loyalties can change over time.

Each separate hospitality enterprise must, therefore, be aware of the elasticity of demand of the market in which it operates and of the loyalty of its customers. In other words, it must have a market-oriented approach to pricing. This market orientation is particularly important in short-run decision making, such as offering reduced weekend and off-season room rates to help increase occupancy, or special food and beverage prices during slow periods. These reduced rates or prices are particularly appropriate where demand is highly elastic.

Cost Structure

Fixed and variable costs

The specific cost structure of a business is also a major factor influencing pricing decisions. Cost structure in this context means the breakdown of costs into fixed and variable ones. Fixed costs are those that normally do not change in the short run, such as a manager's salary or insurance expense. Variable costs are those that increase or decrease depending on sales volume. An example is food cost.

A business with high fixed costs relative to variable ones will likely have less stable profits as the volume of sales increases or decreases. In such a situation, having the right prices for the market becomes increasingly important. In the short run any price in excess of the variable cost will produce a contribution to fixed costs and net income, and the lower

Imaginative pricing possibilities

the variable costs, the wider is the range of possible prices. For example, if the variable, or marginal, costs (such as housekeeping wages, and linen and laundry expense) to sell an extra room are $10, and that room normally sells for $40, any price between $10 and $40 will contribute to fixed costs and net income. In such a situation those who establish prices have at their discretion a wide range of possibilities for imaginative marketing and pricing to bring in extra business and maximize sales and profits.

Note that this concept of variable or marginal costing is only valid in the short run. Over the long run prices must be established so that all costs (both fixed and variable) are covered in order to produce a long-run net income.

The subject of fixed and variable costs is covered in some depth in Chapter 8, Cost Management, and Chapter 9, The CVP (Cost-Volume-Profit) Approach to Decisions. In particular, in Chapter 9, the use of the break-even equation is demonstrated in conjunction with the effect a change in room rates has on volume and profits.

The Competition

A hospitality enterprise's competitive situation is also critical in pricing. Very few hospitality businesses are in a monopolistic situation (although some are, such as a restaurant operator who has the only concession at an isolated airport).

Monopolistic pricing

Where there is a monopolistic, or near monopolistic, situation, the operator has greater flexibility in determining prices and may, indeed, tend to charge more than is reasonably fair. However, in these situations the customer still has the freedom to buy or not buy a meal or drink, or to stay fewer nights in that accommodation. Also, in a monopolistic situation where high prices prevail, other new entrepreneurs are soon attracted to offer competition.

Oligopolistic pricing

In a more competitive, but not completely competitive, situation there often exists an oligopoly. In an oligopoly there tend to be one major or dominant business and several smaller, competitive businesses. In an oligopoly the dominant business is often the price leader. When the price leader's prices are raised or lowered, the prices of the other businesses are raised or lowered in tandem. An oligopolistic situation could arise in a resort area where there is one major resort hotel, surrounded by several other motels catering to a slightly lower income level of customer.

Competitive pricing

However, most hospitality enterprises are in a purely competitive situation, where the demand for the goods and services of any one establishment and highly sensitive to the prices charged. In such situations there is little difference, from a price point of view, between one establishment and the next. Where there is close competition, competitive pricing will often prevail without thought to other considerations. For example, an operator practicing competitive pricing may fail to recognize that his or her particular product or service is superior in some ways to that of competitors and could command a higher price without reducing demand.

Product differentiation

In a highly competitive situation an astute operator will look at the strengths and weaknesses of his or her own situation, as well as those of competitors. In analyzing strengths and weaknesses, operators should try to differentiate themselves and their products and services from their competitors'. The establishments that are most successful in differentiating then have more freedom in establishing their prices. This differentiation can be in such matters as ambience and atmosphere, decor, location, view and similar factors. Indeed, with differentiation, psychological pricing may be practiced. With psychological pricing the prices are established according to what the customer expects to pay for the "different" goods or services offered. The greater the differentiation, the higher prices can be set. For example, this situation prevails in fashionable restaurants and exclusive resorts, where a particular market niche has been created. At this point, a monopolistic or near monopolistic situation may again prevail.

In summary then, there is no one method of establishing prices for all hospitality enterprises. Each establishment will have somewhat different long-run pricing strategies related to its overall objectives and will adopt appropriate short-run pricing policies depending on its cost structure and market situation.

YIELD MANAGEMENT

The main goal of the rooms department in many hotels is to sell hotel rooms to increase the occupancy percentage. Management's objective is to maximize the revenue (or yield) from the rooms available. Unfortunately, many of the methods presently used to measure a hotel's marketing effort do not generate sales decisions that maximize revenue. Marketing effort has been traditionally judged in terms of either the occupancy percentage or the average room rate achieved.

Occupancy percentage misleading

The problem with occupancy percentage is that it does not show whether revenue is being maximized. For example, a hotel may be 100 percent occupied, but many of those guest room occupants may be paying less than the maximum (rack) rate for the room. In other words, managers whose performance is measured by rooms occupancy are tempted to increase occupancy at the expense of room rate.

Other managers are judged by the average room rate. Again, the average room rate can be increased by refusing to sell any rooms at less than the rack rate, turning away potential customers who are unwilling to pay this rate. Average room rate will be maximized at the expense of occupancy. Average room rate can be slightly more meaningful if it is expressed as a ratio of the maximum potential average rate, as discussed in an earlier section of this chapter, but by itself it does not provide a complete picture.

Instead of focusing on a high occupancy or a high average rate, a better measure of a manager's performance is the yield statistic. Yield is defined as

Yield statistic equation

$$\frac{\text{Actual revenue}}{\text{Potential revenue}} \times 100$$

Potential revenue is defined as the room sales that would be generated if 100 percent occupancy were achieved and each room were sold at its maximum rack rate. For example, if a hotel has 150 rooms, each of which has a maximum rack rate of $100, potential revenue is

$$150 \times \$100 = \$15,000$$

and if actual revenue on a particular night is $10,000 then yield is

$$\frac{\$10,000}{\$15,000} \times 100 = 66.7\%$$

Two factors involved

Yield thus combines two factors: the number of rooms available (inventory) and rooms pricing. Rooms inventory management is concerned with how many rooms are made available to each market segment and its demand for rooms. Pricing management is concerned with the room rate quoted to each of these market segments.

Note that there can be different combinations of room rates and occupancies that achieve the same yield percentage. For example, consider the following three situations that each show various combinations that generate the same actual revenue, and thus the same yield percentage:

Same yield percentages

Case A   100 rooms occupied × $100.00 average rate = $10,000
Case B   120 rooms occupied × $ 83.33 average rate = $10,000
Case C   140 rooms occupied × $ 71.43 average rate = $10,000

In each of these three situations, if potential revenue were $15,000 the yield will be the same: 66.7 percent. However, even though each of these situations is equal insofar as total revenue and yield percentage are concerned, they may not be equal in terms of other factors. For example, in Cases B and C there are more rooms occupied than in Case A; thus there will be additional housekeeping and energy costs. On the other hand, Cases B and C also mean more guests in the hotel who are likely to patronize and increase revenue in food and beverage areas. Further, if those additional customers are first-time guests of the hotel and leave with a favorable impression, they are likely to be repeat customers and will provide positive word-of-mouth advertising, thus increasing future revenue.

Average rate ratio defined

Finally, note that because the yield statistic is a combination of occupancy percentage and average room rate, it can be calculated by multiplying the actual occupancy percentage by the average rate ratio. The average rate ratio is the actual average rate expressed as a percentage of the average maximum potential rate. In our 150-room hotel, the maximum average potential rate is $100 ($15,000 potential maximum revenue divided by 150 rooms). In Case A, with 100 rooms occupied (66.7 percent occupancy) and an average rate ratio of 1.0 or 100 percent (because the actual average rate is the same as the maximum potential rate), the yield can be calculated as

$$66.7\% \times 1.0 = 66.7\%$$

In Case B it would be

$$\frac{120}{150} \times \frac{\$83.33}{\$100}$$

$$= 80\% \text{ occupancy} \times 0.8333 \text{ average rate ratio} = 66.7\% \text{ yield}$$

and in Case C it would be

$$\frac{140}{150} \times \frac{\$71.43}{\$100}$$

$$= 93.33\% \text{ occupancy} \times 0.7143 \text{ average rate ratio} = 66.7\% \text{ yield}$$

Integrated statistic

Even though the occupancy percentage and the average rate ratio by themselves do not provide complete information, by multiplying them together to provide the yield percentage, a single integrated statistic is produced that is much more meaningful and a more consistent measure of a hotel's performance. In order to improve this statistic, a practice known as yield management has recently been adopted by some hotels.

The objective of yield management is to maximize hotel room revenue by using basic economic principles to allocate the right type of room to the right type of guest at a price the guest is prepared to pay. The concept of maximizing revenue is not new. Indeed, hotel managers have always known that during slow periods they can increase the demand for rooms by looking at the number of reservations they already have for future periods and then reducing the prices of still-available rooms to stimulate further demand. Conversely, during high demand periods when occupancy will be at or near 100 percent, they can increase room rates, knowing that customers are prepared to pay higher rates to guarantee having a reservation. Most hotel operators have traditionally used this concept of supply and demand in their pricing.

Airline Practices

Other branches of the tourism industry also use the discounted price approach to stimulate demand. For example, the airlines have many different fares for the same aircraft seat and either directly or through a travel agency quote a price for that seat, depending on who the customer is and what he or she is prepared to pay to fly. Over the years, the airlines have developed sophisticated computer programs to help them determine how many seats on each aircraft can be allocated in advance for each type of discounted fare in order to fill all seats and maximize their revenue on each flight. This practice is known as yield management.

What makes airline yield management different from traditional hospitality industry discount pricing is that the airlines constantly update the price decision-making process. The computer systems allow discounted prices to change daily to match each day's demand from the various market segments with whom the airlines deal. In other words, airlines constantly adjust the number of seats available at any one price to maximize their revenue or yield.

Similarity of Hotels and Airlines

In many ways, hotel guest rooms are similar to aircraft seats. For example:

- There is a fixed supply in the short run. The objective is thus to use this fixed availability in the most profitable way possible to maximize revenue.

- In many cases, a known proportion of aircraft seats and hotel rooms is reserved some time ahead of their actual usage.

- A guest room not sold (just like an aircraft seat unsold) is lost revenue that can never be recovered. In other words, the inventory is extremely perishable.

- Demand for both airline seats and hotel rooms can fluctuate a great deal, particularly on a seasonal basis. However, it can also vary monthly, and even daily by day of the week. Management must know how and when each market segment makes reservations (by time of year and day of week), must have an overbooking policy for each market segment, and must know the elasticity of demand for each market segment. Computers can easily provide this information by analyzing past experience so that it can be used in forecasting. Indeed, demand forecasting is the basis of effective yield management.

Low marginal costs

- Marginal costs (the cost to sell an extra aircraft seat or hotel room) are relatively low compared to marginal revenue. For example, to sell an extra hotel room does not require any more labor in the reservations or front office area. The only additional costs are for housekeeping labor, guest room laundry and supplies expense, and energy.

- Customer characteristics (that is, the market segments with which airlines and hotels deal) are similar. These segments can be easily identified from past demand.

Price and time sensitivity

- There is a certain amount of price and time sensitivity for some market segments for both airline seats and hotel rooms. For example, vacation travelers usually reserve both airline seats and hotel rooms well ahead of travel time. These customers reserve primarily on the basis of price. Thus, to reach this market, prices must be reduced and made known to potential customers well in advance. Last-minute price reductions to fill airline seats or hotel rooms are unlikely to generate additional volume from the vacation market.

Complications for Hotels

Note, however, that the yield management practices of the airline industry become somewhat more complicated when applied to the hotel industry. For example, when a customer makes a hotel reservation, that reservation can be for one night, for one night that the guest after arriving extends for two or more nights, or for more than one night with the guest subsequently staying for a shorter period than originally reserved. This creates questions such as the following:

Problem areas

- Will a guest making a low-demand day reservation at a discounted price be allowed subsequently to extend that stay at the same price through one or more high-demand days that follow?

- In a situation where a guest inquires about a rate for a stay starting on a low-demand day but extending into high-demand days, should a high-demand price be quoted for the entire period? If so, will the potential customer decide to shop around for a better price at a competitive hotel? The yield management system must consider this type of trade-off possibility.

In addition, when guests make reservations the derived demand they provide other departments must be considered, along with the market segment that the guest is in. Guests of one market segment might be more likely to use the hotel's food and beverage areas (thus increasing revenue in those areas) than guests of another market segment. Thus, the yield management system must be programmed to consider revenue and profitability from more than the rooms department.

Effect on potential customers

Finally, airlines have many different prices for the same seat on an aircraft, and customers know that the earlier they make a reservation for a flight the lower the price is likely to be. This has not traditionally been the way hotels operate, and a hotel converting to a yield management pricing system must consider the effect this will have on its potential customers. For example, in North America the major airlines presently operate in an oligopolistic environment, and the airline customer often has little choice about using a particular airline to fly from point A to point B. Hotels, on the other hand, generally operate in a highly competitive environment, and the potential customer (except in extremely high-demand periods) can shop around for a room rate appropriate to his budget.

Elasticity of demand

Note that on a national basis and in the general market area where a hotel is located, total demand for hotel rooms is relatively inelastic. At the local level, however, demand for any particular hotel's rooms (and thus the elasticity of demand for its rooms) can be affected by its pricing decisions. It is thus important for any individual hotel's management to know what its market segments are and to determine how elastic the demand for each market segment is so that it can adjust its prices to obtain a larger share of each segment.

Implementing Yield Management

Many hotels have adopted yield management and abandoned the practice of pricing rooms according to traditional methods such as room type and season of the year. By using computers to forecast rooms demand, they have eliminated a great deal of guesswork from the room rate decision-making process. This process involves the number of rooms that should be sold at various room rates.

Wider range of rates

Currently, hotels do not generally have as wide a variety of rates as airlines. Hotels implementing yield management might find it appropriate to parallel the airlines in this regard by having a much wider range of rates than they have traditionally had in order to maximize the benefits that yield management can offer. By having more room rates, the yield management system is better able to influence demand and even length of stay to improve profits. In other words, yield management controls rooms inventory availability.

Customer education

Potential hotel customers may initially consider it unfair (because they are not used to this) to be quoted a different room rate depending on how far in advance they make a reservation. What is therefore required when yield management is implemented are a customer-education program and flexibility in the system to allow reservation department employees to use their judgment when they feel that potential customers are resisting quoted high prices.

Customer education may not be as difficult a process as it seems because, to a degree, and, depending on who they are, hotel customers are used to paying different rates for the same room. Most hotel guests know that convention delegates are quoted lower rates than transient travelers who might use the same type of room. Large corporations whose representatives stay at a particular hotel when traveling can also generally negotiate a lower rate for rooms. Vacation travelers with a group tour also have a lower room rate negotiated for them by the tour wholesaler. The last-minute walk-in guest normally pays the highest (rack) rate and has little basis for negotiating a lower rate.

Need for compromises

Clearly, yield management involves compromises. For example, the preferred situation would be to have 100 percent rooms occupancy with all rooms sold at the rack rate. For most hotels, however, this is unrealistic on a year-round basis and would likely lead to empty rooms and lost revenue because the demand for rooms at the maximum rate is not there. An alternative might be to lower all rates to ensure that there is 100 percent occupancy year round. Again, however, this will lead to lost revenue because some of the customers paying low rates would have been prepared to pay higher rates. Thus, in both of these situations yield (revenue) is not maximized. The objective of yield management is to decide what the trade-off will be between maximizing room rates and maximizing occupancy and how many rooms at rack rates and how many at discounted rates will be offered during each period to each different market segment.

Identifying Market Segments

Two major segments

In order to use yield management, management must be able to identify its major market segments (types of customer). Generally, two major market segments for hotels can be identified: the business traveler and the vacationer. However, each of these broad market segments can be broken down into subsegments. For example, the business travel segment can be subsegmented into regular business travelers, government travelers, and convention/conference delegate travelers. For each market segment or subsegment, the hotel will apply a different marketing plan in order to sell each segment an appropriate number of rooms at a price that segment is prepared to pay.

Generally, the marketing plan for the business traveler is to allocate a fixed number of rooms at the rack rate available for last-minute reservations. For the business traveler reserving in advance, the plan might be to make available a block of rooms with a small discount from the rack rate. For group business (such as conventions), a large number of rooms might be allocated and held (sometimes years in advance for large conventions) at a heavily discounted rate, and those not reserved by individual convention delegates by a stipulated period (for example, three months prior to the actual convention) will be released to other market segments. For the vacationers, the plan might be to allocate a limited number of highly discounted rooms that must be reserved well in advance and cannot be reserved at the last minute.

Different marketing plans

All these situations contain uncertainties that must be decided in advance. For example,

- How many rooms at the very lowest rate should be set aside for the budget-conscious vacation traveler? What is the likelihood of there being customers in a different market segment prepared to pay a higher rate for those rooms?
- Should the business from a small conference group that is prepared to pay only a low rate for rooms be accepted, or should the rooms be held open until later when they might be sold at higher rates to regular business travelers?

Analyzing historic data

An effective yield management system can, of course, answer this type of question for the hotel manager by analyzing historic room reservation data.

Group Sales

Yield management can be a problem in group bookings. Employees responsible for booking group sales often have their job performance measured by the volume of sales (number of room nights) that they make. The group booking department's objective is to sell rooms, and to make those sales they usually have the authority to reduce room rates. Yield management, however, may show that some low-rate group sales do not maximize revenue at certain times of the year when those rooms could be sold to transient (business) travelers at a higher rate. Thus, yield management may prevent a sales employee from making a group sale. This obviously reduces that person's incentive to sell.

Transient displacement

Another consideration is that a group booking often creates a situation where transient travelers who would otherwise stay at the hotel at higher rates are displaced. Those displaced transients will then reserve rooms at a competitor hotel. They may also be encouraged to stay at that competitor hotel on future visits. Obviously, this reduces future revenue of the hotel accepting the group booking.

It is also argued that group rooms sales should be separated from other room sales under yield management and that the group sales department's effectiveness should not be measured on number of room nights booked over a period (such as a month) but on a combination of room nights times average rate to arrive at total revenue.

Summary

Balancing supply and demand

In summary, yield management is an attempt to match customers' purchase patterns and their demand for guest rooms with future occupancy forecasts. It is a method of measuring a hotel's marketing performance. It attempts to balance the demand of each market segment the hotel deals with and the supply of rooms made available to this segment by adjusting the major variable that the hotel can most effectively control: the room rate. The yield management system should match room rates to market demand, indicate how many rooms should be held for last-minute high-rate customers, and indicate when room rates should be discounted to increase occupancy. Yield management should not be viewed as a method of forcing customers to pay the highest rate, but rather as an attempt to bring room rates into line with normal economic forces. The foundations of a good yield management system are the accuracy and availability of the information that a hotel has about its customers' historic reservation patterns.

Use in other departments

Even though the material in this section has concentrated on the rooms department of a hotel, the principles can be applied equally well to other departments. For example, most hotels have function or banquet rooms of different capacities available for group meal and/or meeting business. The banquet department can sell these rooms in various ways (for example, for meetings only, for meals only, for meetings and meals, and so forth). How these rooms are made available to different market segments, how they are priced for meetings, and how meals are priced can all affect the yield of those function rooms and indicate whether revenue is being maximized.

SUMMARY

This chapter introduces the reader to various pricing methods that have been used in the hospitality industry. It points out the need for both long-range and tactical pricing approaches. The usual way of looking at an income statement is to deduct costs from revenue and call any excess of revenue over costs net income. However, if net income is considered as a cost, it can then be budgeted for like any other cost and the required revenue that must be realized to cover all costs, including net income, can be calculated in advance each month, quarter, or year.

Once it is calculated for a restaurant, this figure permits us to calculate an average check or average customer spending. This is calculated as follows:

$$\text{Average check} = \frac{\text{Total revenue for period}}{\text{Seats} \times \text{Daily turnover} \times \text{Days open in period}}$$

The overall average check can be further broken down by meal period by using the following equation:

$$\left(\begin{array}{c} \text{Average check per} \\ \text{meal period} \end{array}\right) = \frac{\left(\begin{array}{c} \text{Meal period percentage} \\ \text{of total revenue} \end{array}\right) \times \text{Total revenue}}{\text{Seats} \times \text{Meal period turnover} \times \text{Days open}}$$

The average check is only an average, and not the price of every item on the menu. Menu pricing of individual items can be a complex problem for management. A number of factors have to be considered, including a range of menu prices to accommodate the market being catered to, the prices competitive restaurants are charging, the gross profit on different menu items, and the influence that the sales mix (what customers choose from various menu offerings) can have on the average check and on gross and net profit. The effect that seat turnovers can have on total revenue should also be considered. Increasing seat turnover can compensate for a declining average check.

The average room rate required for a hotel or motel to cover all costs, including net income, can be calculated in a way similar to the calculation of average check for a restaurant. The equation is

$$\text{Average room rate} = \frac{\text{Total revenue for period}}{\text{Rooms} \times \text{Occupancy \%} \times \text{Days in period}}$$

The average room rate is, however, only an average and not necessarily the rate for all rooms. Generally it needs to be broken down further into average rate for single rooms and average rate for double rooms.

Room rate could also be calculated on the basis of the area of the room.

Total room revenue is a combination of average room rate and actual room occupancy. Therefore, one should keep in mind the occupancy of rooms by day of the week since a declining room rate can be compensated for by increasing room occupancy, and vice versa.

In room rate discounting, an equation can be used to calculate the equivalent occupancy needed to hold total revenue less marginal costs constant if the rack rate is discounted. The equation is:

$$\text{Current occupancy} \times \frac{\text{Rack rate} - \text{Marginal rate}}{[\text{Rack rate} \times (1 - \text{Discount percentage})] - \text{Marginal cost}}$$

A potential average room rate can be compared with the actual average. Once a potential average rate has been calculated, it can be used to establish discounted room rates for various market segments.

Note that both the return on investment method and the cost plus method of establishing prices should be used primarily as reference points in establishing actual prices. There are several other considerations to be kept in mind. For example, prices must be established to meet the organization's long-run objective or objectives. In addition, factors such as the elasticity of demand, the business's cost structure (breakdown between fixed and variable costs), and the competitive environment in which it operates are all very important factors.

Most hotels measure their rooms department's effectiveness by using either occupancy percentage or average rate, both of which have shortcomings. An alternative is to use the yield statistic: a combination of occupancy percentage and average rate. The chapter concluded with a section on yield management, a method of matching customers' purchase patterns and their demand for guest rooms to derive more precise occupancy forecasts with the objective of maximizing rooms revenue.

DISCUSSION QUESTIONS

1. Discuss the pros and cons of three traditional pricing methods used by the hospitality industry.

2. Differentiate long-run from tactical pricing and list four events that might necessitate tactical pricing.

3. Explain why net income is just another cost of running a business.

4. Explain how, if revenue for a restaurant is forecast to be a certain figure, one can use this figure to determine the average customer spending or average check.

5. If a certain level of revenue is wanted in a restaurant and the seat turnover rate is expected to go down, would the average check have to go up or down to reach the desired level of revenue? Explain.

6. Define the term "sales mix" and explain what influence it can have on an average check.

7. What factors would a restaurant manager need to consider when establishing individual menu item prices?

8. Explain why you do or do not think that the food cost percentage figure is important in menu pricing.

9. Why is loss of revenue from hotel rooms not occupied more of a problem than loss of revenue from customers who did not show up in a restaurant?

10. Explain briefly how a motel's average room rate can be calculated or projected by using the bottom up approach.

11. If a hotel average room rate is projected to be $75, explain why this will not be the rate paid by every customer staying in the hotel.

12. How is a double occupancy percentage for hotel rooms calculated?

13. Of what value might it be to calculate hotel room occupancy by day of the week, or seat turnover in a restaurant by day of the week, rather than use an average weekly figure?

14. Define the terms "rack rate" and "potential average room rate."

15. A hotel's potential average single rate is $60, its rate spread is $8, and its double occupancy rate is 30 percent. Calculate its potential average room rate.

16. Define elasticity of demand and, using figures of your own choosing, show how a reduction in a hotel's average room rate, and the resulting change in total revenue, would indicate an inelastic demand situation.

17. What implications does the breakdown of a business's costs into fixed and variable ones have on the pricing decision?

18. Discuss the concept of product and/or service differentiation in a restaurant situation.

19. Explain the shortcomings of occupancy percentage and average rate in measuring a hotel's rooms department's performance.

20. Give the equation for calculating a hotel's rooms department's yield statistic.

21. Discuss the problem of group sales in a hotel using yield management.

PROBLEMS

6.1 You have the following projections about the costs in a family restaurant for next year.

Net income required	15% after income tax on the owners' present investment of $80,000, income tax rate is 25%
Depreciation	Present book value of furniture and equipment is $75,500, depreciation rate is 20%
Interest	On a loan outstanding is 8%, present amount of the loan is $35,000
Insurance	$3,000
License	$2,500
Utilities	$8,400
Maintenance	$3,600
Administration	$9,800
Management salary	$32,400
Food cost	36% of revenue
Wages	34% of revenue
Other costs	12% of revenue

a. What revenue level would the restaurant have to achieve next year in order to acquire the desired net income?

b. What would this be in terms of an average check if the restaurant were open 365 days a year, had 60 seats, and averaged two-and-a-half turnovers a day?

6.2 A twenty-five-room budget motel expects its occupancy next year to be 80 percent. The owner's present investment is $200,800. They want an aftertax return on their investment of 10 percent. Tax rate is 50 percent.

Interest on a long-term mortgage is 10 percent. Present balance outstanding is $403,200.

Depreciation is 10 percent on building (present book value is $350,100) and 20 percent on furniture and equipment (present book value is $75,200).

Other fixed charges add up to $70,900 a year.

At an occupancy of 80 percent, the motel's operating expenses (wages, supplies, laundry, and so on) are calculated to be $27,700 a year.

The motel has other income (from vending machines) of $2,600 a year.

a. To cover all expenses and produce the net income required, what should the motel's average room rate be next year?

b. Round this rate to the nearest dollar. If the motel operates at a 30 percent double occupancy ratio and has an $8 spread between its single and double rates, what will its single and double room rates be? Assume only one room size, all with the same rates.

6.3 A restaurant has 90 seats. Total annual revenue for next year is projected to be $975,000. The restaurant is open fifty-two weeks a year and is open for breakfast six days a week, for lunch six days a week, and for dinner seven days a week. Anticipated seat turnovers are as follows: breakfast two, lunch one-and-one-half, dinner one-and-one-quarter. Revenue is derived 20 percent from breakfast, 30 percent from lunch, and 50 percent from dinner. Calculate the restaurant's average check by meal period.

6.4 A dining room is keeping a record of its customer counts by meal period and by day of the week. There are 140 seats.

	Lunch	Dinner
Sunday	closed	180
Monday	160	110
Tuesday	170	112
Wednesday	175	108
Thursday	160	120
Friday	180	210
Saturday	50	250

a. For each meal period and for each day of the week calculate the seat turnover.

b. Calculate the average number of customers per day and the average seat turnover for the week for each meal period.

c. List some of the ways in which the information in parts **a** and **b** would be useful to the restaurant manager or owner.

6.5 You have gathered the following information about a hotel for the next year. The hotel has forty rooms and expects to have an occupany of 70 percent. Rooms department operating expenses (wages, supplies, laundry, and so on) are 27 percent of rooms revenue.

Administrative and general	$ 38,300
Marketing	28,900
Energy costs	35,100
Repairs and maintenance	28,800
Property taxes	17,600
Insurance	4,800
Telephone department operating loss	9,700
Operating income from food and beverage departments	103,200
There is a first mortgage to be repaid with interest of 8%, present amount owing is	601,000
There is also a second mortgage with interest at 12%, amount owing	402,000
The owners have also invested some money of their own, and expect an after-tax return of 15% on	280,000
Book value of fixed assets:	
Land	250,000
Building	1,860,000
Furniture and equipment	382,000
Depreciation rate on building is	5%

Depreciation rate on furniture and equipment is	20%
Income tax rate is	25%

    a. Calculate the hotel's average room rate for next year.

    b. What would the hotel's average rate per guest be with a 30 percent double occupancy?

    c. If the hotel did operate at a 30 percent double occupancy and management wanted a $15 spread between the single and double room rates, what would these rates be?

6.6 An owner invested $90,000 in a new family-style restaurant, of which $80,000 was for equipment and $10,000 for working cash. Estimates for the first year of business are as follows:

Menu selling prices to be established to give a markup of 150% over cost of food sold
Variable wages 28% of revenue
Fixed wages $25,800
Other variable costs 7% of revenue
Rent $16,000
Insurance $2,400
Depreciation on equipment 20%
Return on investment desired 12%
Income tax rate 25%

    The restaurant has sixty seats and is open five days a week for lunch and dinner only. Lunch revenue is expected to be 40 percent of total volume with two seat turnovers. Dinner revenue will be 60 percent of total volume with one turnover.

    Calculate the average check per meal period that will cover all costs, including the desired return on investment.

6.7 A motel has 30 rooms and expects a 70 percent occupancy next year. The owners' investment is presently $520,000, and they expect a 12 percent after-tax annual return on their investment. The motel is in a 50 percent tax bracket. The motel is carrying two mortgages: the first in the amount of $359,000 at a 10 percent interest rate, and the second in the amount of $140,000 at a 14 percent interest rate. Present book value of building is $632,000, and depreciation rate is 5 percent. Present book value of furniture and equipment is $117,000, and depreciation rate is 20 percent. Indirect expenses are $44,800. Direct expenses at a 70 percent occupancy are $59,300. The motel receives $12,000 a year income from leasing out its restaurant.

    a. Calculate the motel's required average room rate to cover all expenses and provide the owners with their desired return on investment.

b. Round this rate to the nearest dollar and then calculate the average single and double rates, assuming a 60 percent double occupancy and a $12 difference between singles and doubles.

6.8 A forty-five-room resort hotel has three sizes of rooms as follows:

15 singles at 150 sq ft.
15 doubles at 220 sq. ft.
15 suites at 380 sq. ft.

Occupancy is 80 percent. Demand for each type of room is about equal. The projected required revenue from rooms next year is $912,500. If average room rates were to be based solely on room size, what would the average room rate for each type of room be next year?

6.9 Assume that the Resolute Resort hotel currently operates at a 75 percent occupancy, that its rack rate for all rooms is $60, and that its marginal cost per room sold is $8. Calculate the Resolute's occupancy figures for a discount grid for discount percentages of 5, 10, 15, and 20 percent.

6.10 The Motley Motel's potential average room rate has been calculated to be $31.00. Assume that this motel had three market segments. Vacation travelers comprise 75 percent of the room nights and are charged 100 percent of the rack rate. Business travelers comprise 15 percent of the room nights and are charged 90 percent of the rack rate. Sports teams comprise 10 percent of the room nights and are charged 80 percent of the rack rate.

a. Calculate the room rate by market segment.
b. Prove that your calculations are correct, assuming that total annual room nights are 7,300.

6.11 The Inviting Inn has 500 available guest rooms. For a certain week next month the anticipated transient demand for rooms is

Monday	200
Tuesday	200
Wednesday	200
Thursday	200
Friday	100
Saturday	50
Sunday	50

The Inn also has committed the following number of rooms for group sales during the same week:

Monday	200
Tuesday	200

Wednesday	300
Thursday	300
Friday	100
Saturday	100
Sunday	100

The Inn has the possibility of booking another group of 100 rooms for the nights of Tuesday, Wednesday, Thursday, and Friday of that week at a discounted rate of $60 per room. The Inn's rack rate for transient guests is $80, and its marginal cost per room sold is $15.

a. Assuming the new group is booked, calculate the additional net revenue (gross revenue less marginal costs) to the Inn.

b. What factors, other than net revenue, might you consider before committing to this new group sale?

CASE 6

a. In the case at the end of Chapter 3 you calculated the average food and beverage check for the 4C Company's restaurant for year 0001. The restaurant was open for 52 weeks, 6 days a week for lunch and 5 days a week for dinner. An analysis of sales checks indicated that the average lunch turnover was 1.5 times and 1.25 times for dinner. Lunch contributes about 40 percent of total revenue and dinner 60 percent. Calculate the average lunch and the average dinner checks. Beverage revenue is about 10 percent of total revenue at lunch time and about 30 percent at dinner time. Break down your lunch and dinner average check figures into their food and beverage components. This information will be used in a later case to prepare the 4C Company's budget for year 0002.

b. Suggest to Charles a number of ways in which he could attempt to raise the average check and the total food and beverage revenue for year 0002.

c. In part b, one of the ways might be to substitute, on the food menu, items with a low selling price for items with a high selling price. Write a short report to Charles about the effect this might have on the restaurant's guests, its food cost percent, and its gross profit and net income.

7 Introduction to Food, Beverage, and Labor Cost Control

Chapter Highlights

This chapter has two main parts: control of food and beverages using a standard cost percentage approach and labor cost using a productivity standard system.

Perpetual inventory cards and requisitions are discussed from a point of view of control over food and beverage storeroom inventories. The need for establishing standard recipes and portion sizes is covered and typical recipe forms are illustrated, as is the use of these forms for calculating item costs. The reader is then referred to Chapter 6 for a discussion of establishing item selling prices. This section of the chapter concludes with an explanation and illustration of using standard menu item cost and selling prices, combined with actual quantities of each menu item sold during a period, to calculate a standard cost percent to be compared with the actual cost percent for that same period.

The chapter then moves on to labor cost control and begins by comparing procedures for food and beverage cost control with a different approach that should be used for labor control. This approach requires some preliminary steps such as job analysis, the preparation of job descriptions, and task procedures. The major element in labor cost control, the determination of labor productivity standards for each different type of job, is then covered. The use of staffing guides, volume forecasting, and staff scheduling is discussed. The chapter concludes with an explanation of the final step in labor cost control, a comparison of volume forecast and actual labor usage and an analysis of any variances.

Chapter Objectives

After studying this chapter the reader should be able to:

1. Explain how perpetual inventory cards and requisitions aid in food and beverage storeroom control.
2. Define the terms "standard recipe" and "standard portion" and discuss their roles in cost control.
3. Calculate recipe portion costs and selling prices.
4. Complete and explain the use of a standard and actual cost control form.
5. Explain how labor cost control differs from food and beverage cost control.
6. Explain job analysis, job description, and task procedures.
7. Discuss how labor productivity standards can be developed along with staffing guides.
8. Calculate volume forecasts from given information, and discuss staff scheduling and the analysis of actual labor cost from forecasts and schedules.

FOOD AND BEVERAGE COST CONTROL

Chapter 5 mentioned the need to establish standards against which actual results can be measured. In this chapter we shall see how this can be accomplished in food, beverage, and labor cost control.

To have any form of food and beverage cost control it is imperative that control over purchases be established. The system of control outlined in Chapter 5 will accomplish this. In addition, any storeroom areas where food and beverages are kept prior to being put into production should be operated with a system of perpetual inventory cards and requisitions.

Perpetual Inventory Cards

One card for each item

Each separate storage location should have its own set of perpetual inventory cards. For example, there would be a set of cards for the food storeroom and a separate set of cards for the alcoholic beverage or bar storeroom. An individual card is required for each type and size of item carried in stock. A sample card is illustrated in Exhibit 7.1. The *In* column figures are taken from the invoices delivered with the goods. The figures in the *Out* column are recorded from the requisitions (to be dis-

Exhibit 7.1   A sample perpetual inventory card.

Item _____		Supplier _____ Tel. # ____		
Minimum _____		Supplier _____ Tel. # ____		
Maximum _____		Supplier _____ Tel. # ____		

Date	In	Out	Balance	Requisition Cost Information

cussed later in this chapter) prepared and signed by persons in the department served by that particular storage location. Obviously, if all *In* and *Out* figures are properly recorded on the cards by the person in charge of the storeroom, the *Balance* column figure should agree with the actual count of the item in the storeroom. Thus the cards aid in inventory control as a double check. They are also useful for accounting purposes since the cards carry the purchase prices of the items and allow the requisitions to be costed out, thus ensuring each department is correctly charged with its share of the costs.

Cards aid in ordering

The cards also help ensure that items are not overstocked or understocked since they can show the maximum stock for each individual item and the minimum point to which that stock level can fall before reordering. Without having to count quantities of items in the storeroom, the person responsible only has to go through each of the cards once a week or however frequently it is practical to reorder, and list all items for which the *Balance* figure is at or close to the minimum point. The quantity required to bring the inventory up to par stock should then be ordered, keeping in mind possible delivery delays. Note that cards can also be designed to carry the names and telephone numbers of suppliers.

Advantages and disadvantages

The advantages of perpetual inventory cards for inventory control and the time saved in reordering are obvious. The major disadvantages are the time and cost required to keep the cards up to date. Each establishment must weigh the costs against the benefits for its own operation in order to decide whether or not to use them.

Requisitions

Whether or not perpetual inventory cards are used to control items in stock and aid in ordering, requisitions should be used in order to allow authorized people to receive items from the storeroom and to ensure that the various departments are correctly charged with their share of the costs. A sample requisition is illustrated in Exhibit 7.2.

Exhibit 7.2   A sample requisition.

Department _____ Date ___6329___

Quantity	Item description	Item cost	Total

Authorized signature _____

Original to storekeeper

Blank requisitions should only be made available, preferably in duplicate, to those authorized to sign them. The original, listing items and quantities required, is delivered to the storekeeper. Duplicates are kept by the person ordering so quantities received from the storeroom can be checked.

Costing requisitions

If perpetual inventory cards are used, they should carry the current price of the item in stock. Perpetual inventory card *Out* column figures can be recorded from the requisitions (and the *Balance* column figure adjusted) and the price of the item can be taken from the card and recorded on the requisition in the *Item Cost* column.

If perpetual inventory cards are not in use, the easiest method of recording item costs on the requisition is to simply write the price of the item, taken from the invoice at the time of delivery, on the container, case, can, bottle, or package. Alternatively, pricing machines, such as those used in supermarkets, could be used. Recording the item price on the case, container, can, bottle, or package makes it easy to transfer this price to the requisition as the requisition is completed. There is also a psychological control advantage in pricing items in this way, because each person handling them is made aware of the cost.

Departmental requisitions

Requisitions, once costed out, can then be extended and totaled so that at the end of each accounting period each department can be charged with its proper share of expenses. Issuing each department with blank requisitions of a different color will aid in departmental identification. If necessary, for control purposes, requisitions should also be numbered.

Of course, where establishments are large enough to support computerized inventory records, much of the paperwork that would otherwise be required with perpetual inventory cards and requisitions can be handled directly by the computer, including, for example, a daily printout of all items whose level has dropped to the reorder point and cost information for inventory on hand.

Establish Standard Recipes and Portion Sizes

Standard recipes must be prepared for all menu items. A standard recipe is a formula specifying the quantity of each ingredient required to produce a specific quantity and quality of a particular food item. This formula will also describe the cooking method since that can have a bearing on quality. The recipe should also include the cooking temperature, where it is appropriate, since temperature can affect the quality of the product and also the amount of shrinkage in cooking and thus the cost of the item. Recipes should be developed by each establishment according to its own standards.

Standard recipes for cost control

Standard recipes are required for all menu items, and all those employed in food preparation and service must be instructed to follow these recipes and portion sizes, not only for cost control purposes but also for consistency of size and quality from the customer's point of view. A sample standard food recipe is illustrated in Exhibit 7.3.

All recipes should indicate the portion size to be served to each customer. Portion scales should be provided in cases where they would be helpful, for example, in weighing portions of shrimp for shrimp cocktails or for slicing meat. This does not mean that every portion should be weighed, particularly if an employee is experienced. But even experienced employees should spot-check portion weights from time to time to make sure they are not deviating from the correct amount. Casserole and other cooking and serving dishes or plates that are appropriate to the portion size to be served should be used. Specific-size ladles, serving spoons, and scoops should be used for portioning such items as soups and sauces. If employees are allowed to use only their own judgment, then the portions may be random sizes, which can severely affect the food cost.

List of standard portion sizes

A list of standard portion sizes of menu items offered is a valuable control form for employees. This list can be posted in appropriate places in the establishment so that it is easy for employees to use it. A sample of such a list is illustrated in Exhibit 7.4. Those involved in food cost control should spot-check from time to time to ensure that portion sizes are being followed.

Standard cocktail recipes

Standard recipes should also be used in a bar (beverage) situation. This is relatively straightforward for the basic types of liquor served, because the recipe is simply a standard portion of liquor (measured by some type of pouring device) to which may be added ice and water or some type of soft drink or mineral water. The type of ice (such as shaved or cubed) should be included in the recipe. In the case of cocktails, the recipes will be more extensive since they must include the quantity of each of two or more ingredients and, where necessary, the garnish to be included (such as a cherry, olive, or orange slice). The food ingredients are normally considered part of beverage cost of sales. In cocktail recipes

Exhibit 7.3 A sample recipe form.

Recipe for Beef casserole   Recipe #   14
Portion size   8 oz
Quantity produced 100 portions

Ingredient	Quantity	Date: Feb.		Date:		Date:	
		Cost	Total	Cost	Total	Cost	Total
Stew beef	25 lb	2.10	52.50				
Flour	2 lb.	0.30	0.60				
Tomato paste	½ lb	1.00	0.50				
Beef stock	1 gal	0.75	0.75				
Brown stock	1 gal	0.65	0.65				
Fresh carrots	5 lb	0.35	1.75				
Fresh onions	6 lb	0.40	2.40				
Celery	3 lb	0.20	0.60				
Green peas	5 lb	0.40	2.00				
Seasonings			0.25				
Total cost			62.00				
Cost per portion			0.62				

Cooking procedure:
1. Brown meat, add flour and tomato paste and mix well.
2. Add beef and brown stocks and simmer for 1 hour.
3. Dice carrots, onions and celery and add them, with the peas, cooking until tender.
4. Add seasonings.
5. Serve in 8-oz casserole dish.

the type and quantity of ice to be used and the mixing method are quite important since they dictate to a degree the quality of the end product and the quantity of liquid that will result when the drink is poured. The size and type of glass for each different type of drink should be included with each recipe since drink appearance is important; a 2-ounce martini would not look right in a 6-ounce highball glass.

Written copies of all recipes should be kept at the bar. It is important

Exhibit 7.4 Standard portion sizes.

Effective date	February 1		
Item	**Dining room**	**Coffee shop**	**Banquet**
Tenderloin steak	8 oz.	6 oz.	5 oz.
Boneless top sirloin	8 oz.	6 oz.	6 oz.
Boneless strip loin	8 oz.	8 oz.	6 oz.

that all bartenders be familiar with all recipes since consistent quantity and quality of drinks are important for customer satisfaction. A typical drink recipe is illustrated in Exhibit 7.5.

In no case where beverage cost control is desired should any type of free pouring be allowed. To aid bartenders in measuring drink quantities, two types of measuring devices are normally used: shot glasses and jiggers. The shot glass is generally used for the basic highball drink, for example one ounce or one-and-a-half ounces, or the equivalent in metric measure. The jigger is usually of stainless steel and measures smaller quantities of ingredients (such as one-quarter or one-third ounce, or the equivalent in metric) for cocktails. Some establishments also use mechanical or electronic pouring devices. Many of the electronic pouring and measuring devices can be linked to registers that automatically record each pour as the sale of a drink to aid in revenue control.

Calculate Item Costs

Once standard recipes have been formulated for each menu item, then those menu items should be costed out. This is simply a case of multiplying the quantity of each ingredient required in that menu item by the cost of the ingredients.

If the costs of ingredients change, then portion costs should be adjusted so that one is aware when it might be necessary to adjust the selling price or, alternatively, adjust the portion size to avoid having to change menu prices. If an establishment has only a few items on its menu, then recosting portion costs to reflect changed ingredient costs is not too time consuming. If an establishment has a large number of items on its menu or is changing menu items on a cyclical basis, this problem is compounded. Some establishments have computerized their recipes so that the computer can print out portion cost changes for every menu item that has an ingredient in it whose cost has changed. Note that the recipe

Exhibit 7.5 A typical drink recipe.

BRANDY ALEXANDER		Recipe No.	25	
Ingredient	**Quantity**	**Cost**	**Cost**	**Cost**
House brandy	¾ oz	$0.15		
Creme de Cacao, dark	¾ oz.	0.18		
Cream	3 oz.	0.07		
Total cost		$0.40		
Selling price		$2.00		
Cost percent		20.0%		

Method
Shake all ingredients with small ice cubes. Pour through strainer into 5½-oz champagne glass. Sprinkle with nutmeg.

forms illustrated in Exhibits 7.3 and 7.5 have space on them for recalculating the item's cost.

Determine Selling Prices

Once costs for food and beverage items have been determined, selling prices of individual items must be established. This topic was covered in Chapter 6, and the reader is referred to the section headed "Pricing Menu Items" for a review of this material. In particular, specific reference should be made to the comments concerning the gross profit on individual items and the effect that a change in the sales mix may have. Also very important is the material in Chapter 6 under the section entitled "Other Pricing Considerations." This section stresses the importance in the pricing decision of a restaurant's objectives, as well as its elasticity of demand, cost structure, and competitive situation.

Gross profit and sales mix effect

Evaluating Results

Once cost and selling prices of individual items are known, it is a relatively simple matter to evaluate actual food and beverage cost percentages against the standard. A form, such as that illustrated in Exhibit

7.6, can be used to record information about the individual menu item cost and selling prices. The quantity sold figures are the quantities actually sold of each particular menu item during the past week. This information could be obtained by taking a tally from all the sales checks used that week. The total standard cost column is a multiplication of the menu item cost and quantity sold. The total standard revenue is a multiplication of the menu item selling price and quantity sold.

Effect of sales mix on food cost percentage

The column on the far right shows the individual standard cost percentage for each menu item. It is obtained by dividing menu item cost by menu item selling price and multiplying by 100. This information is useful when analyzing the food cost results. For example, a change in the sales mix (that is, a change in what the customers are choosing from the menu) can affect the food cost percentage. The individual menu item standard cost percent information might also be useful when deciding which items to add to or delete from a menu or to promote.

The overall standard cost percentage can be calculated using information from the total standard cost and total standard revenue columns, as illustrated in Exhibit 7.6.

Calculation of actual food cost

Finally, the actual cost percent should be calculated, as illustrated in Exhibit 7.7. The information for actual cost is taken from the accounting records and from actual physical inventories using the general equation, Beginning of the period inventory + Purchases − End of the period inventory = Cost of goods sold (actual food cost). Note that this actual food cost figure may have to be adjusted for interdepartmental transfers during the period and for employee meals. Actual revenue would normally be the same as standard revenue. A difference between the two might occur if sales prices were not recorded correctly on the sales checks or if a cashier were not recording sales correctly on the register.

Difference between actual and standard food cost

The difference between the standard and actual food cost percentages can then be recorded. A difference is to be expected since the standard is based on what the cost should be if everything goes perfectly. Such perfection seldom exists. Management must decide what difference will be tolerated before investigation is carried out to determine the cause. However, generally one would expect to see the actual percent within 0.5 on either side of standard. In other words, if the standard percent were 40.0, then the actual might be expected to fall within the range of 39.5 to 40.5 percent.

Standard and actual figures change

Exhibit 7.8 shows the completed form for the following week. Note that the figures for both the standard and actual percentages have changed. The reason for this is that different quantities of the various menu items offered have been sold, and the ratio of what has been sold among the various menu items has changed (that is, there has been a change in the sales mix). Therefore, it is to be expected that the total standard cost and revenue figures, and actual cost and revenue figures (and the related percentages) will change. But with this analysis technique, management

Exhibit 7.6 Partially completed standard vs. actual cost form—Week 1.

Menu Item	Menu Item		Quantity Sold	Total Standard Cost	Total Standard Revenue	Cost Percent
	Cost	Selling Price				
1	$4.00	$6.50	486	$ 1,944.00	$ 3,159.00	61.5%
2	2.10	6.00	1,997	4,193.70	11,982.00	35.0
3	1.25	2.75	1,810	2,262.50	4,977.50	45.5
4	1.50	5.50	939	1,408.50	5,164.50	27.3
5	0.75	2.00	602	451.50	1,204.00	37.5
TOTALS				$10,260.20	$26,487.00	

$$Standard\ Cost\ Percent = \frac{Total\ Standard\ Cost}{Total\ Standard\ Revenue} = \frac{10,260.20}{26,487.00} \times 100 = 38.7\%$$

$$Actual\ Cost\ Percent = \frac{Total\ Actual\ Cost}{Total\ Actual\ Revenue} = \frac{\underline{\qquad}}{\underline{\qquad}} \times 100 = \underline{\qquad}$$

Difference $\underline{\qquad}$

Exhibit 7.7 Completed standard vs. actual cost form—Week 1.

Menu Item	Menu Item Cost	Menu Item Selling Price	Quantity Sold	Total Standard Cost	Total Standard Revenue	Cost Percent
1	$4.00	$6.50	486	$ 1,944.00	$ 3,159.00	61.5%
2	2.10	6.00	1,997	4,193.70	11,982.00	35.0
3	1.25	2.75	1,810	2,262.50	4,977.50	45.5
4	1.50	5.50	939	1,408.50	5,164.50	27.3
5	0.75	2.00	602	451.50	1,204.00	37.5
TOTALS				$10,260.20	$26,487.00	

$$Standard\ Cost\ Percent = \frac{Total\ Standard\ Cost}{Total\ Standard\ Revenue} = \frac{10,260.20}{26,487.00} \times 100 = 38.7\%$$

$$Actual\ Cost\ Percent = \frac{Total\ Actual\ Cost}{Total\ Actual\ Revenue} = \frac{10,281.40}{26,487.00} \times 100 = 38.8\%$$

$$Difference \qquad \overline{0.1\%}$$

Exhibit 7.8 Completed standard vs. actual cost form—Week 2.

Menu Item	Menu Item		Quantity Sold	Total Standard Cost	Total Standard Revenue	Cost Percent
	Cost	Selling Price				
1	$4.00	$6.50	502	$2,008.00	$ 3,263.00	61.5%
2	2.10	6.00	1,724	3,620.40	10,344.00	35.0
3	1.25	2.75	1,828	2,285.00	5,027.00	45.5
4	1.50	5.50	759	1,138.50	4,174.50	27.3
5	0.75	2.00	742	556.50	1,484.00	37.5
TOTALS				$9,608.40	$24,292.50	

$$Standard\ Cost\ Percent = \frac{Total\ Standard\ Cost}{Total\ Standard\ Revenue} = \frac{9,608.40}{24,292.50} \times 100 = 39.6\%$$

$$Actual\ Cost\ Percent = \frac{Total\ Actual\ Cost}{Total\ Actual\ Revenue} = \frac{9,816.70}{24,292.50} \times 100 = 40.4\%$$

$$Difference \qquad \underline{0.8\%}$$

can now monitor the business in an ongoing way. Although the illustration given is for a food situation, the technique can be used equally well for alcoholic beverage sales as illustrated in Exhibit 7.9.

LABOR COST CONTROL

Fixed cost of labor

In some ways labor cost control can be more difficult and complex than control of food and beverage costs. With food and beverages, one is dealing with a tangible product that can be weighed, counted, and measured for control. This is less easy to do with labor, where the measurement is based on productivity, and productivity levels are frequently a matter of opinion. Also, as you observed in the preceding section on food and beverage cost control, costs go up or down in a linear way as revenue goes up and down. In other words, they are primarily variable costs. (The concept of variable costs will be covered in more depth in Chapters 8 and 9.)

Labor cost does not have this same variability. In fact a large proportion of labor cost is of a fixed nature. The effect of this fixed element may be hidden over time when labor cost peaks and valleys offset each other and tend to smooth out what might otherwise be a volatile cost percentage (calculated by dividing dollars of labor cost by revenue dollars and multiplying by 100). For that reason a labor cost percentage figure may not be the most useful as a standard for measuring labor cost. A labor cost based on a predetermined standard of manpower hours required, according to forecast volume of business, overcomes the cost percentage problems. The manpower standards are based on the productivity of employees.

Labor cost control objective

This part of the chapter discusses how to establish those standards and use them in labor cost planning and control. The objective of labor cost planning is to have sufficient employees on duty in each department at all times to provide the desired quality of service to the anticipated number of guests or customers, without having idle, unproductive labor that has to be paid but is generating no revenue.

Before labor cost standards can be established and implemented, some basic steps should be taken. These include job analysis and preparation of job descriptions and task procedures.

Job Analysis

Job analysis takes each type of job and questions every aspect of it. The types of questions could include any or all of the following:

Exhibit 7.9 Standard cost control—Beverage.

			Period	March 9-16	
Drink	**Drink Cost**	**Drink Selling Price**	**Quantity Sold**	**Total Standard Cost**	**Total Standard Revenue**
Scotch, house	$0.32	$1.50	1,430	$ 457.60	$2,145.00
Gin, house	0.25	1.40	1,211	302.75	1,695.40
Rum, house	0.30	1.45	854	256.20	1,238.30
			Totals	$2,436.20	$9,875.40

$$Standard\ cost\ percent = \frac{\$2,436.20}{\$9,875.40} \times 100 = 24.7\%$$

$$Actual\ cost\ percent = \frac{\$2,475.60}{\$9,875.40} \times 100 = 25.1\%$$

$$Difference \quad \underline{\underline{0.4\%}}$$

- Why is the job being done?
- Why by this category of employee?
- Why at this location?
- Why at this time?
- Can it be done during a slack period rather than at a peak period?
- Is each job step necessary?
- Why are the job steps carried out in this sequence?
- Is it necessary to have time lags between tasks?
- Are supplies moved a minimum distance without backtracking?
- Is there too much rehandling of supplies?
- Are there defined stations for location of work supplies?
- Are these stations well designed?
- Do the station locations minimize employee movement?
- Can any travel distances be shortened?
- Is one employee using a better method that other employees could adopt?

These are only some of the questions that might be posed. As a result of job analysis, inefficiencies will be observed and can be corrected. Steps may be eliminated or given to others. The time to perform the job may be shortened, or the position eliminated. It may be discovered that the job can be carried out by more efficient methods, including the use of equipment to free up employee time. The main purpose of job analysis is to review each job position, at least annually, to determine its contribution to net income and to try to increase that contribution. Job analysis also makes it easier to prepare job descriptions (to be discussed in the next section).

Job contribution to net income

The question of how productive an employee should be as a result of job analysis is often a matter of observation and judgment. This method of job analysis would generally be carried out by the department head since he/she would normally be responsible for control of the labor cost in the department and is in the best position to know the various employees' capabilities.

Job Description

Subsequent to job analysis a job description should be prepared for each category of employee. The description describes what the job entails, the steps that must be performed, and when the steps must be performed. Job descriptions should not be too detailed, but they should include sufficient information so that both employee and supervisor are sure what the job includes and not what they think it entails. A typical job description for a banquet houseperson might be:

Sample job description

1. Reports to the banquet coordinator who is supervised by the banquet manager.
2. Is responsible for setup of banquet rooms for various events such as banquets, weddings, cocktail receptions, fashion shows, and similar functions. The layout for each individual function will be provided by the banquet coordinator.
3. Is responsible for the cleanliness of the various banquet rooms both before and after each function. Cleanliness includes both general tidiness and dusting, ensuring that ashtrays and mirrors are clean and that carpets are vacuumed before each function.
4. At each month-end all lamps and banquet furniture must be cleaned.
5. At the end of the first week in each month, all upholstery is to be spot cleaned.
6. At the end of the second week in each month, all carpets must be shampooed.
7. Banquet plants must be watered when necessary.
8. The banquet storeroom must be kept clean and tidy at all times.
9. The person must have good health and be strong since frequent, heavy lifting may be necessary.
10. Since the person will have frequent contact with the public, appearance, politeness, and personality are important.
11. The person must be flexible in order to adapt to pressure situations and last-minute requests by guests.

Task Procedures

Jobs require a variety of tasks

In the hospitality industry most positions or jobs require the employee to perform a variety of different tasks. Each task requires the employee to follow definite procedures for efficiency and to reduce losses from not performing the task properly. Some procedures can be demonstrated and taught to employees. Others could be written to ensure that all employees read and follow them. We saw some examples of written procedures for food receiving and the handling of credit cards in Chapter 5.

Labor Productivity Standards

A step preliminary to the preparation of labor productivity standards involves ensuring that the establishment's quality standards are well understood. For example, the productivity of a maid measured in number of rooms cleaned in a normal shift can be easily increased by reducing the time spent cleaning each room. This would not be a good idea if it compromises room cleanliness and results in customer complaints. Similar situations would prevail in care taken in food preparation and presentation, or level of waiter or waitress service.

Value of job analysis in establishing productivity

Although productivity standards can be established based on past performance, there is no guarantee that past results were optimal. For example, based on records, the number of guests to be served by each banquet server may be established at thirty. How can we be sure that is the most productive number? It is for this reason that job analysis is helpful in determining the best number of customers that the average, reasonably good banquet server can handle. Each establishment must carry out its own analysis and determine its own standards. For any particular position, standards will vary from one establishment to another because of the layout of the property (for example, how close the kitchen is to the banquet room area), type of menu, type of clientele, and many other related factors. In some establishments the standards may be written into the union contract and may not be subject to unilateral change by either party.

After each type of position has been appropriately studied and all necessary factors have been considered, final standards should be set for each department with the close coordination of the department head.

Standard productivity units

Each standard consists of a number of units (rooms, covers, beverage sales) that an employee is expected to "produce" within a certain period. Periods for maids, cooks, bellhops, and bartenders are usually for a normal shift. For restaurant personnel, a meal standard can be established, depending on the length of the operating period of each meal. For example, a waiter might be expected to serve twenty people during lunch in the dining room, during a four-hour shift.

An allowance may be given to food waiters in dining rooms for beverage sales by converting the actual beverage sales figure into equivalent food covers. The conversion factor used depends on the types of drinks sold and the beverage price structure of each outlet. For example, in a formal dining room with a high percentage of wine sales and a high priced beverage list, the factor that will equal one food cover might be $10. In a coffee shop, it might be as low as $4 or $5, due to a lower price structure. For food preparation employees, the standard can be based on total number of covers or guests served in sales areas.

Monetary units for beverages

In bars and lounges that serve no food, the production standard is generally a monetary unit for both bartenders and servers. The reason is that the customer in an eating area has a meal, with or without drinks, and the time spent sitting there and the average spending fall within a relatively narrow range. This may not be true in a cocktail bar where one customer may occupy a seat and have five $3 drinks. The average check would be $15. Alternatively, five different customers may occupy that seat in turn and each have a $3 drink. The average check for each is $3. Thus the number of customers served in a lounge is not as realistic a standard as is revenue.

For employees such as bellhops, the standard might be expressed in number of movements: guest arrivals or departures, laundry calls, or messages delivered. For housekeeping personnel the standards can be based on rooms occcupied (rooms cleaned for maids, rooms inspected for floor supervisors). For front office personnel, standards can be based on guest movements (registrations and checkouts).

Typical standards for representative jobs in a larger hotel operation might be:

Examples of productivity units

Position	Standard	Period
Maids	16 rooms	8 hours
Bellhops	25 movements	8 hours
Coffee shop server	30–40 covers	4 hours
Dining room server	20–25 covers	4 hours
Cooks	90–100 covers	8 hours
Dishwashers	150–200 covers	8 hours
Bartenders	$750	8 hours
Floor housekeeper	90–100 rooms	8 hours
Room clerk	100 arrivals	8 hours

Once established, the standards should be reviewed from time to time and should be revised as necessary. For example, the introduction of a new piece of equipment or redesign of a restaurant could change the productivity of the affected employees.

Staffing Guides

Maximum staffing levels

After standards are established, staffing guides should be developed, department by department. Staffing guides will indicate staffing levels required for various levels of business volume. Staffing guides could be given in terms of monthly volume, but they are probably more useful if prepared on a weekly or even a daily volume basis, in situations where staff levels can be adjusted weekly or daily according to anticipated volume. When developing the guides, both minimum and maximum volume levels must be considered. The minimum level shows the minimum number of employees necessary to maintain a smooth operation. The maximum level is that point beyond which no additional staffing is allowed. For example, in a guest room situation, it makes no sense to staff beyond a 100 percent occupancy level; in a banquet situation it would be useless

Exhibit 7.10 Coffee shop staffing guide.

Volume per Week in Covers	Category A Hostess, Hours per Week	Category B Waitress, Hours per Week	Category C Bus Help, Hours per Week	Total Hours per Week
Up to 1,260	120	224	112	456 min.
1,261–1,485	120	240	112	472
1,486–1,710	120	320	112	512
5,311–5,535	160	960	240	1,360 max.

to staff beyond the largest number of guests that could be seated at any one time. Exhibits 7.10 and 7.11 show partial staffing guides for a coffee shop (weekly staffing) and a housekeeping department (daily staffing).

Revise when necessary

Just as productivity standards must be revised as conditions warrant, so too must the staffing guides be revised.

Forecasting

The next step in labor cost control is forecasting work load units (guest rooms occupied, covers served, dollars of revenue) for each department. These forecasts are developed from records and adjusted for current factors. Although for budgeting purposes many establishments forecast in months, it is recommended that, for staffing, budgeted figures be broken down to a weekly basis prior to each week of actual operations. In this way the figures can be adjusted for the most recent conditions affecting

Adjusted weekly forecasts

Exhibit 7.11 Housekeeping staffing guide.

Occupied Rooms	Number of Floor Supervisors	Number of Day Maids	Number of Night Maids	Total Employees
420	3	28	7	38
405	3	27	7	37
390	3	26	7	36
375	3	25	7	35
360	3	24	6	33

volume of business. In a hotel the weekly rooms occupancy forecast not only serves as the basis for staffing for the rooms department, but also as a basis for staffing food and beverage outlets that derive much of their business from hotel room occupants. A rooms occupancy forecast is illustrated in Exhibit 7.12.

Restaurant walk-ins

Food and beverage volume, even if dependent upon rooms occupancy, varies by area (coffee shop or dining room) and by meal period; and customers who are not guests must be included in the forecast. Restaurants not located in hotels would be dependent solely on walk-in business and that is all they would consider in their forecasts. A sample of a restaurant forecast is illustrated in Exhibit 7.13. Even though the illustrated forecasts are for weekly periods, the figures should be revised daily when possible, and the related staffing guides then used for staff scheduling. In a large hotel it is necessary to have good communication between departments in preparation of forecasts because of the business one department derives from another. After the forecasting has been carried out, staff schedules must be prepared.

Staff Scheduling

There are two basic types of staff schedules: stacked (or shift) schedules and staggered schedules. Stacked schedules are used in departments such as the front office of a hotel for employees such as clerks and cashiers. These employees normally work a full eight-hour shift regardless of volume of business. Those on the morning shift would all start at the same time and all leave at the end of the shift, when the next group of shift employees start. However, in most departments of hotels and in food establishments, staggered schedules must be used. Although staffing guides indicate the number of employees or manhours that are to be used for each level of business or revenue, they do not indicate when employees are to work. Generally, an analysis of the number of customers served or dollars of revenue earned during each hour must be made. This analysis will indicate the low-, the medium-, and the high-volume periods. Employees should be scheduled so that the maximum number are on duty during high-volume periods and the minimum number during low-volume periods, thus staggering the hours when employees are working. A staggered schedule might appear as in Exhibit 7.14. This type of schedule reduces idle time, provides for overlap of employees, recognizes variations during the day in level of sales, and can lead to reduction or elimination of overtime costs. In most cases schedules for each department are prepared in advance, week by week, showing the scheduled time of arrival and departure each day for each employee. These times would be subject to daily review prior to each day to adjust where necessary to a changed forecast. Days off also appear on the schedule. A completed individual employee schedule is illustrated in Exhibit 7.15.

Staggered schedules

Schedules prepared each week

Exhibit 7.12 Rooms occupancy forecast.

Period   April 8-14

	Sunday 8	Monday 9	Tuesday 10	Wednesday 11	Thursday 12	Friday 13	Saturday 14
Previous night's occupied rooms	311	336	332	369	394	324	329
Today's arrivals	107	98	121	120	70	65	112
Today's departures	82	102	84	95	140	60	84
Tonight's occupied rooms	336	332	369	394	324	329	357
Occupancy	75%	74%	82%	88%	72%	73%	79%
Previous night's guest count	401	439	430	490	521	408	410
Today's arrivals	168	152	194	190	112	100	178
Today's departures	130	161	134	159	225	98	130
Tonight's guest count	439	430	490	521	408	410	458

Exhibit 7.13 Restaurant volume forecast.

Department	Period June 9–15							
	Sunday 9	Monday 10	Tuesday 11	Wednesday 12	Thursday 13	Friday 14	Saturday 15	Totals
Coffee Shop								
Breakfast	150	210	285	280	290	260	190	1,665
Lunch	200	280	300	310	310	330	250	1,980
Dinner	115	180	195	195	210	210	110	1,215
Dining Room								
Lunch	—	180	200	225	180	175	225	1,185
Dinner	350	175	175	210	210	240	275	1,635

Exhibit 7.14 A sample of a staggered schedule.

Empl.	A.M.						P.M.											
	6	7	8	9	10	11	12	1	2	3	4	5	6	7	8	9	10	11	12
A																			
B																			
C																			
D																			
E																			
F																			
G																			

Labor Cost Analysis

Daily analysis preferable

Since volume forecasting and labor scheduling are carried out on a daily basis, an analysis of actual labor cost with forecast or budgeted cost can also be made daily. Daily labor cost analysis is much easier than is food or beverage cost analysis because we do not have the problem of inventories. The analysis compares, department by department, the actual hours or days used and to be paid for with the forecast hours or days for that day. In some larger operations the comparison is even made on a meal-period basis for the food department. In other establishments, knowing that there will be daily variances, the comparison is made only on a weekly, biweekly, or monthly basis. In such cases it might well be that overstaffing and understaffing on individual days will even out and only minor variances will occur overall. Because the objective is to discover all variances, analysis should preferably be carried out on a daily basis. In this way the causes of all variances can be determined and the entire process of forecasting, and thus controlling labor cost, can be made more effective.

Causes of variances

Generally, variances can be caused by one or more of the following:

1. Inappropriate staffing guidelines
2. Inaccurate forecasts
3. Poor scheduling and excessive overtime.
4. Unpredictable sales volume fluctuations

When making comparisons between forecast and actual hours, and when the comparisons are made on a man-day basis, then the hours of part-time employees must be converted to equivalent man days. If the standard man day for a full-time employee is eight hours, then equiva-

Exhibit 7.15 A sample employee schedule.

		Dining Room	Week Commencing	April 8		
Employee	Sunday	Monday	Tuesday	Wednesday	Thursday	Friday	Saturday
C. Jones	9–5	9–5	9–5	9–5	9–5	off	off
J. Hathaway	off	off	8–4	8–4	8–4	8–4	8–4
S. Heil	7–3	7–3	7–3	7–3	7–3	off	off
P. Mintz	12–8	12–8	12–8	off	off	12–8	12–8
A. Smith	7–3	7–3	off	off	7–3	7–3	7–3
C. Cohen	10–5	10–5	10–5	10–5	off	off	8–4

lent man days would be calculated by dividing total part-time hours for all such employees by eight. The actual hours figures would be taken from payroll records (time cards or sign-in/sign-out sheets) that have been approved by the department head.

Daily rate for salaried employees

Comparisons between forecast and actual figures can also be made on a dollar basis. This requires converting hours forecast and hours actually worked to dollars. In the case of employees paid by the hour, hours are simply multiplied by the related hourly rate. In the case of salaried employees, the daily rate will vary depending on the number of days in a month. For example, an employee paid $1,500 a month is assumed to be responsible for his or her department even on days off and will have a daily rate of $50 during a 30-day month and $48.39 during a 31-day month. If a salaried person has a joint departmental responsibility, then the daily rate must be split between the two or more departments involved. A sample daily labor cost summary and analysis form is illustrated in Exhibit 7.16.

SUMMARY

To have any system of food and beverage cost control, a proper system of control over purchases must first be established, using purchase requisitions, purchase orders, supplier invoices, receiving reports, and invoice approvals. Food and beverage storeroom areas should preferably be controlled with perpetual inventory cards and requisitions. Perpetual inventory cards show the movement of all goods in and out of the storeroom and provide for an inventory reconciliation with the actual count of the items in the storeroom. One card is used for each item. Requisitions prepared by the requesting department provide the authority to issue items from the storeroom and contain item cost information so that each department can be charged for its share of the costs of items used.

Standard recipes for both food and beverage items should be prepared and used in conjunction with predetermined, standard food portion sizes or drink sizes. In conjunction with the standard recipes, items can be costed to obtain the item portion cost. These costs should be updated as frequently as necessary. Standard selling prices for food and beverage items must be established. Two factors that must be kept in mind in pricing are that the gross profit on an item may be more important than its standard cost percent and that the sales mix of items (what one sells during a period of the various items offered) can affect both gross profit and net income.

Once item cost and selling prices have been determined, they can be multiplied by the actual quantity sold of each item for a week, for exam-

Exhibit 7.16 A sample labor cost summary and analysis form.

Date __April 11__

Department	Number of Employees Today		Labor Cost Today		Labor Cost To date		Labor Cost Variance	
	Budget	Actual	Budget	Actual	Budget	Actual	Today	To date
Rooms								
Front office	10	10	$ 440	$ 440	$1,320	$1,320		
Housekeeping	42	43	1,280	1,310	3,840	3,900	$+30	$+60
Service	8	8	320	320	960	930		−30
Switchboard	6	6	274	274	822	822		
Food								
Dining room	13	14	$ 456	$ 487	$1,368	$1,399	$+31	$+31
Coffee shop	7	6	245	217	735	707	−28	−28
Banquet	11	11	440	440	1,674	1,674		

ple. Thus standard cost percentage for that period can be calculated. This can then be compared with the actual cost percentage for that same period to see whether the result is satisfactory.

With labor cost control, one is dealing with a less tangible product (employee productivity) than is the case with food and beverages. Also a large portion of labor is a fixed cost, which makes the use of a labor cost percentage more difficult to interpret.

Labor cost control begins with job analysis that questions everything about each job to determine how its contribution to net income can be improved. Following job analysis is the preparation of written job descriptions and, where appropriate, task procedures.

The next step is the establishment of productivity standards for each job. Standards are expressed in units such as the number of guest rooms to be cleaned during a shift, the number of meals (guests) to be served during a meal period, or (in the front office area) the number of arrivals or departures to be handled during a shift. Once standards have been developed, they can be converted into staffing guides, job by job, and department by department.

Prior to each week, each department should prepare a volume forecast. This forecast is expressed in terms of room guest arrivals and departures each day, or number of food and beverage guests to be served by meal period each day. The forecast is used, with the staffing guide, to determine how many employees to schedule on duty each day, and for how many hours. From this, daily staff schedules are prepared for the coming week. The final step in labor cost control is a comparison of the volume forecast and actual labor usage and an analysis of any variances.

DISCUSSION QUESTIONS

1. Describe a perpetual inventory card and explain how it is used.
2. Describe a requisition and explain how it is used.
3. Define a standard recipe and list the various types of information that might appear on it for a food menu item.
4. Describe the two types of measuring devices that can be used in bar portion control.
5. Explain how total standard cost and total standard revenue are obtained for a period of time (for example, a week).
6. What is the basic equation for calculating actual cost (cost of goods sold) and what adjustments may have to be made to the basic equation?
7. Why, from one period to the next, will the forecast and actual cost percentages change?

8. In what two main ways does labor cost control differ from food and beverage cost control?

9. Explain job analysis and the purpose it serves.

10. Explain the difference between job description and task procedures.

11. Why must quality standards be considered when establishing productivity standards?

12. Differentiate between a stacked and a staggered staff schedule.

13. What are the four factors that might cause forecast and actual labor cost to differ?

PROBLEMS

7.1 The following ingredients, with their cost prices, are required for a particular menu item yielding 75 portions:

Ingredient	Cost
30 lb. boneless beef	$1.75 lb.
2 lb. flour	0.21 lb
3 lb. cooking fat	0.43 lb.
2 lb. carrots	0.18 lb.
2 lb. celery	0.24 lb.
2 lb. green peppers	0.55 lb.
½ #10 can tomato puree	1.95 can
2 gals. beef stock	0.95 gal.
10 lb. potatoes	0.14 lb.
seasonings	0.15 total

a. Calculate the portion cost for this menu item.
b. Assuming that other items to accompany this menu item (baked potato, vegetable, and side salad) were costed out to $0.43, what would the selling price have to be to yield a 30 percent food cost?

7.2 A family restaurant serves a six-ounce steak (note that this is six ounces before cooking) with potato, vegetable, and side salad. The restaurant purchases sirloins, from which it cuts the steaks, in eighteen-pound weights at a cost of $2.95 per pound. The calculated cost of the potato, vegetable, and side salad is $0.34.

a. How many individual portions can be served from each eighteen-pound sirloin?
b. What is the cost per portion including potato, vegetable, and side salad?
c. Calculate the selling price to yield a 40 percent food cost.

7.3 Items in a food storeroom are controlled with perpetual inventory cards. One card is kept for each item in the storeroom. Each card shows the date and quantity of each delivery of new items into the storeroom, and the date and quantity of items requisitioned by the various operating departments and issued from the storeroom. A running (perpetual) balance of the quantity of each item in the storeroom is recorded on the cards. All entries on the cards are made by the storekeeper. At the end of each month, a person from the accounting office takes all the cards in turn, calls out the name of the item, asks the storekeeper to count the quantity of the item on the shelf, and then compares the card balance figure with the physical count of the item given by the storekeeper. In this way a month-end inventory is taken and checked. Comment about the "looseness" of this control system.

7.4 A fast-food restaurant features only three entree items on its menu with the following cost and selling prices:

Item	Cost	Selling price
1	$1.00	$3.30
2	2.20	4.40
3	2.70	6.75

  a. For each item calculate the food cost percentage.
  b. If 50 of each item are sold each day, what will the standard food cost percentage be?
  c. If only 25 each of items one and three were sold and 100 of item two, what effect will this have on the standard cost percentage?

7.5 The sales records for a coffee shop that has only six items on its menu show the following quantities sold during the month of January. Item standard cost and selling prices are also indicated.

Item	Cost	Selling Price	Quantity Sold
1	$2.00	$6.00	654
2	1.10	4.50	2,196
3	2.25	7.00	1,110
4	1.75	5.00	990
5	2.25	5.00	295
6	2.00	7.95	259

Actual cost for the month of January was $9,201. Actual revenue for the month of January was $30,060.05.

  a. Calculate the standard cost percentage and the actual cost percentage for January. Round all dollar amounts to the nearest dollar.
  b. Compare the results. If you were the dining room manager, explain why you would or would not be satisfied with the results.

7.6 A fast-food restaurant uses a standard cost approach to aid in controlling its food cost. The following are the standard cost and sales prices, and quantities sold, of each of the five items featured on the menu during a particular week:

Item	Standard Cost	Sales Price	Quantity Sold
1	$1.80	$3.95	$260
2	2.10	4.95	411
3	4.20	8.95	174
4	3.05	6.95	319
5	1.40	3.95	522

Total actual cost for the week was $3,804.10 and total actual revenue $8,873.40.

a. Calculate actual and standard food cost percentages and comment on the results.

b. The following week, with no change in menu or standard cost and selling prices, there was a change in the sales mix. Although quantities sold of items two, three, and five were virtually the same, many more of item four and many less of item one were sold. As a result of this, would you expect the overall standard cost percentage to increase or decrease? Explain your answer.

7.7 Danielle, the owner of Danielle's Diner, is concerned about the financial statement she has received from her accountant. The amount recorded for "food cost" ($29,708) yields a food cost percentage that is higher than Danielle thinks it should be for the month of March, when sales were $75,806. The beverage cost in the bar operation appears to be in order. She has asked you to review the restaurant's accounts and see what you can discover about the food cost. You find the following:

Food inventory beginning of the month	$ 8,763
Food inventory end of the month	7,421
Food purchases during the month	28,166
Employee meals cost	748
Promotion meals cost	321
Transfers of food items to the bar	103
Cooking wine transferred from the bar to the kitchen	79

Calculate Danielle's correct amount for cost of food sold (net food cost) and comment.

7.8 A cocktail lounge sells only a limited variety of types of drinks. Its individual drink standard cost and selling prices are as follows. The quantity sold during the week ending March 14 is shown for each type of drink.

Drink	Cost	Selling Price	Quantity Sold
Gin	$0.60	$2.50	680
Rye	0.64	2.60	556
Scotch	0.74	2.80	720
Bourbon	0.70	2.70	905
Rum	0.58	2.60	380
Manhattan	0.80	3.00	1,058
Martini	0.70	3.00	1,382

Actual beverage cost for the week ending March 14 was $4,025.00. Actual beverage revenue for the week ending March 14 was $15,911.65.

a. Calculate the standard cost percentage and the actual cost perentage for the week ending March 14. Round all dollar amounts to the nearest dollar.

b. For the week ending March 21, because of a special purchase, the cost per drink for scotch dropped to $0.70. There was no change in the selling price. Quantities sold during the week of March 21 were: gin, 657; rye, 608; scotch, 708; bourbon, 963; rum, 425; manhattan, 1,158; martini, 1,299. Actual beverage cost for the week ending March 21 was $4,237.00. Actual beverage revenue for the week ending March 21 was $16,283.30. Recalculate the standard cost percentage and the actual cost percentage for the week ending March 21 and explain why the percentages would change from the week ending March 14.

c. Would you as the lounge manager be satisfied with the results for each of the two weeks? Explain your answer in each case.

7.9 The restaurant of a resort hotel depends solely on its room guests for all its customers. There are 180 rooms in the resort. Rooms occupancy figures for next week are forecast to be

Monday	80%
Tuesday	80
Wednesday	84
Thursday	84
Friday	90
Saturday	90
Sunday	85

Round the figures for number of rooms occupied to the nearest whole number. There are, on average, four people per occupied room per night. From past experience, management knows that 90 percent of the people occupying rooms eat breakfast in the restaurant, 70 percent eat lunch, and 80 percent eat dinner (some units have their own kitchens). Calculate the restaurant's forecast volume, in terms of number of covers, for each meal period for each day next week.

7.10 A hotel's rooms department has forecast the following for next week.

	Guest Arrivals	Guest Departures
Sunday	190	159
Monday	100	98
Tuesday	168	206
Wednesday	152	161
Thursday	194	134
Friday	112	225
Saturday	178	130 302

The Saturday night guest count for this week is 302. The hotel's restaurant is using this information to prepare its volume forecast for next week. On Saturday and Sunday, it knows from past experience, 75 percent of the previous night's guests eat breakfast in the restaurant, 50 percent eat lunch, and 60 percent eat dinner. For the other five days of the week, the figures are: breakfast 60 percent, lunch 20 percent, and dinner 40 percent. In all cases, round figures to the nearest whole number. In addition, the restaurant usually has the following count of walk-ins for each day of the week.

	Breakfast	Lunch	Dinner
Sunday	15	25	50
Monday	25	40	30
Tuesday	25	40	30
Wednesday	25	40	30
Thursday	25	50	40
Friday	25	60	55
Saturday	15	25	75

For each meal period for each day next week, prepare the restaurant's volume forecast in terms of numbers of covers to be served.

7.11 The volume forecast of covers to be served in a restaurant on Monday is as follows, with guest counts rounded to the nearest ten.

6–7 A.M.	60
7–8	80
8–9	60
9–10	40
10–11	40
11–12	80
12–1 P.M.	80
1–2	20
2–3	20

3–4	20
4–5	40
5–6	60
6–7	60
7–8	100
8–9	80
9–10	20

The productivity standard for this restaurant is one waiter for each twenty covers. For Monday, prepare a schedule for waiters, using Exhibit 7.14 in this chapter as a guide. Assume that the standard shift for a waiter is eight hours. As far as is practical, each waiter working should have an eight-hour shift. Part-time waiters can be used, but the minimum shift cannot be less than four hours.

CASE 7

From his experience in the mobile catering company, Charles had learned the value of standard cost control. In that business he purchased most of his food items preportioned and wrapped. Portion sizes were always the same. Food cost was easy to control since, each day, an inventory count of each item he carried, plus the quantity purchased of that item that day, less the quantity still in inventory at the day's end, gave him a figure that, when multiplied by the selling price of the item, produced the standard sales revenue that he should have. When this was done for all food items, he could then compare his total standard food revenue each day with the actual revenue to make sure there were no differences. In this situation he was in complete control of the entire operation.

In the 4C Company's restaurant, because food dishes are produced in the restaurant's own kitchen, it is not feasible to operate and control costs and revenue as with the 3C Company. The restaurant basically operates with eight main entree items on its menu, with three soups and four desserts. These are changed seasonally. Coffee is free if an entree is ordered; otherwise there is a charge. Explain as briefly as possible to Charles the steps that could be implemented to have a system of standard food cost and revenue control. What about the problem that some people have free coffee while others pay, and the fact that customers have to pay for items such as milk and soft drinks?

8 Cost Management

Chapter Highlights

The chapter begins by discussing some of the various types of cost that a business may have. The list includes direct costs, indirect costs, controllable costs, joint costs, discretionary costs, relevant costs, sunk costs, opportunity costs, fixed costs, variable costs, semifixed or semivariable costs, and standard costs.

A method of allocating indirect costs to departments and the difficulties this may create are illustrated.

The chapter then demonstrates how to use relevant costs to help decide which piece of equipment to buy.

How a knowledge of fixed and variable costs can be used in a business decision (for example, to accept or not accept a banquet booking) is explained. The use of fixed and variable costs is illustrated in three additional problems: closing or not closing during the off-season, deciding which business to buy, and paying a fixed or a variable rent for leased premises.

Having illustrated how useful an awareness of fixed and variable costs can be, the chapter then demonstrates how to separate semifixed or semivariable costs into their fixed and variable elements.

Chapter Objectives

After studying this chapter the reader should be able to:

1. Briefly define and give examples of some of the major types of cost such as direct and indirect costs, fixed and variable costs, and discretionary costs.

2. Prorate indirect costs to revenue departments and make decisions based on the results.

3. Use relevant costs to help determine which piece of equipment to buy.

4. Use a knowledge about fixed and variable costs for a variety of different business decisions, such as to close or not during the off season.

5. Define the term "high operating leverage" and explain its advantages and disadvantages.

6. Explain and use each of the following three methods to separate semifixed or semivariable costs into their fixed and variable elements: maximum/minimum calculation, multipoint graph, and regression analysis.

COST MANAGEMENT

Most of the revenue in a hotel or foodservice enterprise is eaten up by costs: as much as 90 cents or more of each revenue dollar may be used to pay for costs. Therefore, cost management is important. Budgeting costs and cost analysis is one way to control (manage) costs to improve net income. Another way to improve net income is to cut costs, without regard to the consequences. The latter course of action may not always be wise. Perhaps a better way is to look at each cost (expense) and see how it contributes toward net income. If advertising (a cost) leads to higher net income than would be the case if we did not advertise, then it would not pay to cut the advertising expense.

Understand type of cost

One of the ways to better manage costs is to understand that there are many types of cost. If one can recognize the type of cost that is being considered, then better decisions can be made. Some of the most common types of cost are defined in the following sections.

TYPES OF COST

Direct Cost. A direct cost is one that is the responsibility of a particular department or department manager. Most direct costs will go up or down, to a greater or lesser degree, as revenue goes up and down. For this reason they are considered to be controllable by, and thus the responsibility of, the department to which they are charged. Examples of this type of cost are food, beverages, wages and salaries, operating supplies and services, linen and laundry.

Responsibility for indirect costs

Indirect Cost. An indirect cost is one that cannot easily be identified with a particular department or area, and thus cannot be charged to any specific department. General building maintenance could only be charged to various departments (such as rooms, food, or beverage) with difficulty. Even if this difficulty could be overcome, it must still be recognized that indirect costs cannot normally be made the responsibility of an operating department manager. Indirect costs are frequently referred to as undistributed costs.

Controllable Cost. The mistake is often made of calling direct costs controllable costs and indirect costs noncontrollable costs. It is true that direct costs are generally more easily controlled then indirect costs, but all costs, in the long run, are controllable by someone.

Joint Cost. A joint cost is one that is shared by, and thus the responsibility of, two or more departments or areas. A dining room waiter who serves both food and beverage is an example. His labor is a joint cost, and should be charged (in proportion to revenue, or by some other appropriate method) partly to the food department, and the remainder to the beverage department. Most indirect costs are also joint costs. The problem is to find a rational basis for separating the cost and charging part of it to each department.

Difficulty of allocation

Discretionary Cost. This is a cost that may or may not be incurred at the sole discretion of a particular person, usually the general manager. Nonemergency maintenance is an example of a discretionary cost. The building exterior could be painted this year, or the painting could be postponed until next year. Either way revenue should not be affected. The general manager has the choice, thus it is a discretionary cost.

Relevant Cost. A relevant cost is one that affects a decision. For example, a restaurant is considering replacing its mechanical sales register with an electronic one. The relevant costs would be the cost of the new register (less any trade-in of the old one), the cost of training employees on the new equipment, and any change in maintenance and material supply costs on the new machine. As long as no change is necessary in number of servers required, the restaurant's labor cost would not be a relevant one. It would make no difference to the decision.

No effect on future decisions

Sunk Cost. A sunk cost is a cost already incurred and about which nothing can be done. It cannot affect any future decisions. For example, if the same restaurant had spent $250 for an employee to study the relative merits of using mechanical or electronic registers, the $250 is a sunk cost. It cannot make any difference to the decision.

Opportunity Cost. An opportunity cost is the cost of not doing something! An organization can invest its surplus cash in marketable securities at 10 percent, or leave the money in the bank at 6 percent. If it buys marketable securities, its opportunity cost is 6 percent. Another way to look at it is to say that it is making 10 percent on the investment, less the opportunity cost of 6 percent; therefore, the net gain is a 4 percent interest rate.

Fixed Cost. Fixed costs are those that over the short run (a year or less) do not vary with revenue. Examples are management salaries, fire insurance expense, rent paid on a square foot basis, the comitted cost of an advertising campaign. Over the long run all these costs can, of course, change. But in the short run they would normally change, if at all, only by a specific top management decision.

Linearity of variable costs

Variable Cost. A variable cost is one that varies on a linear basis with sales or revenue. Very few costs are strictly linear, but two that are (with only a slight possibility that they will not always fit this strict definition) are the costs of food and beverages. The more food and beverages sold, the more have to be purchased. If sales are zero, then purchases will also be zero.

Semifixed or Semivariable Cost. Most costs do not fit neatly into the fixed or the variable category. Most have an element of fixed expense and an element of variable—and then not always variable directly to sales on a straight-line basis. Such costs would include payroll, maintenance, utilities, and most of the direct operating costs. In order to make some useful decisions, it is advantageous to break down these semifixed or semivariable costs into their two elements: fixed or variable. Ways of doing this will be discussed later in this chapter.

Standard costs differ in each establishment

Standard Cost. A standard cost is what the cost should be for a given volume or level of sales. We saw some uses of such standards in Chapter 7. Other uses would be in budgeting (see Chapter 9), in pricing decisions, and in expansion planning. Standard costs need to be developed individually by each establishment since there are many factors that influence standard costs and that differ from one establishment to another.

Let us look at some of the ways in which an analysis of the type(s) of cost(s) with which we are dealing would help make a better decision.

ALLOCATING INDIRECT COSTS TO REVENUE AREAS

One of the difficulties in allocating indirect costs to sales outlets is in determining the correct basis on which to apportion the cost to each department. Some of the methods that could be used are discussed in Chapter 2. If an allocation of indirect costs is made on an incorrect basis, then wrong decisions could be made. If the correct allocation is made then, presumably, the wrong decisions would not be made.

Consider the following restaurant complex that has two main sales outlets, a dining room and a snack bar. Revenue and direct costs for each sales area and indirect costs for the entire operation are shown below for a typical month with an average monthly net income for the total operation of $8,000.

	Dining Room	Snack Bar	Total
Revenue	$70,000	$30,000	$100,000
Direct costs	50,000	26,000	76,000
Operating income	$20,000	$ 4,000	$ 24,000
Indirect costs			16,000
Net income			$ 8,000

Indirect costs pro rata to revenue

Management feels that the indirect costs should be charged to each of the two operating departments, and that the $16,000 total indirect cost should be prorated and allocated according to revenue. In other words, 70 percent allocated to the dining room and 30 percent to the snack bar. The following is the new monthly income statement.

	Dining Room	Snack Bar	Total
Revenue	$70,000	$30,000	$100,000
Direct costs	50,000	26,000	76,000
Operating income	$20,000	$ 4,000	$ 24,000
Indirect costs	11,200	4,800	16,000
Net income (loss)	$ 8,800	($ 800)	$ 8,000

This shows that, by distributing indirect costs on a basis of revenue, the snack bar is losing $800 a month. Management of the restaurant complex has an opportunity to lease out the snack bar, as is, for $500 a month rent. The new operator will pay for his own indirect costs (such as administration, advertising, utilities, maintenance). This seems to be a good offer. A $500 profit appears better than an $800 loss. After a few months the dining room monthly income statement is as follows:

Revenue	$70,000
Direct costs	50,000
Operating income	$20,000
Indirect costs	12,900
Income before rent	$ 7,100
Rent income	500
Net income	$ 7,600

Wrong allocation basis

The above figures indicate that the dining room's net income including rent is only $7,600. Earlier it was calculated to have been $8,800 without any rent income. Overall net income is now worse than it was before ($7,600 versus $8,000). Obviously, the mistake was made in allocating indirect costs to the dining room and the snack bar on the basis of revenue, and then making a decision based on this allocation. A more careful assessment of indirect costs should have been made, and allocation made on a more logical basis. If this had been done (with the information we now have about the dining room's indirect costs) the real situation would have been as follows, which shows that both sales departments were, in fact, making a net income.

	Dining Room	**Snack Bar**	**Total**
Revenue	$70,000	$30,000	$100,000
Direct costs	50,000	26,000	76,000
Operating income	$20,000	$ 4,000	$ 24,000
Indirect costs	12,900	3,100	16,000
Net income	$ 7,100	$ 900	$ 8,000

This shows that renting out the snack bar, which is making $900 a month profit, for $500 a month would not be profitable. To look at it another way, the $500 is the opportunity cost of not renting out, but since it is less than the $900 we are presently making we can comfortably ignore it.

WHICH PIECE OF EQUIPMENT TO BUY?

Choosing among alternatives

One of the ongoing decisions all managers face is that of choosing between alternatives. Which items to offer on a menu, which employee to hire, how to spend the advertising budget? One area of such decision making where a knowledge of costs is helpful is that of selecting a piece of equipment. The following might be a typical situation.

A motel owner has asked his public accountant to research the front office guest accounting equipment available and to recommend the two best pieces of equipment on the market. A decision will then be made by the motel owner about which of the two to use. The accountant's fee for this research was $500. The accountant, in her report, produced the following information.

	Equipment A	Equipment B
Initial cost, including installation	$10,000	$ 8,000
Economic life	10 years	10 years
Scrap value at end of economic life	0	0
Initial training cost	$ 500	$ 1,000
Annual maintenance	$ 400	$ 300
Annual cost of forms	$ 750	$ 850
Annual wage cost	$22,500	$22,500

Note that the $500 fee is a sunk cost: it has to be paid regardless of the decision, and, indeed, would have to be paid if a decision to buy neither piece of equipment were made.

Determine relevant information

In order to make a decision, the motel owner must sort out the relevant information, which is as follows for year one.

	Equipment A	Equipment B
Depreciation	$1,000	$ 800
Initial training cost	500	1,000
Annual maintenance	400	300
Annual cost of forms	750	850
Total for year one	$2,650	$2,950

Note that the initial cost of the equipment is not relevant, but the annual depreciation is. Staff wage cost is also irrelevant, since it is the same in both cases.

The relevant cost information shows that in year 1 equipment A is cheaper than equipment B by $300. However, this saving is in year 1 only. Perhaps the motel owner should look ahead to see what the relevant costs are over the full economic life of the equipment. The following shows the information concerning these costs for each of the years 2 to 10.

	Equipment A	Equipment B
Depreciation	$1,000	$ 800
Annual maintenance	400	300
Annual cost of forms	750	850
Total annual cost	$2,150	$1,950

Total cost for years 2 to 10	9 × $2,150 = $19,350	9 × $1,950 = $17,550

Training cost a sunk cost

Note that, in the above calculations, the training cost of year 1 is now a sunk cost; it is no longer relevant.

To finalize the decision, the motel manager must then add the total cost for years 2 to 10 to the cost for year 1.

	Equipment A	Equipment B
Year 1 cost	$ 2,650	$ 2,950
Years 2 to 10 total cost	19,350	17,550
Total cost	$22,000	$20,500

Factors other than costs

This shows that, despite year 1, the total 10 year cost is less for Equipment B. Certain assumptions have been made: that one can forecast costs for 10 years, and that the costs as originally estimated are accurate. In the final decision, costs may not be the only factor to be considered. A more comprehensive look at the investment decision situation will be taken in Chapter 13.

CAN WE SELL BELOW COST?

The obvious answer to the question would be, Not unless you want to go broke. But before we can intelligently answer that question, we should first ask, Which cost? If the answer is, Below total cost but above variable cost, then yes, indeed, we can sell below total cost under certain circumstances.

Calculation of daily fixed cost

Consider the case of a catering company that rents its premises for $80,000 a year and has other fixed costs (including management salaries, insurance, furniture and equipment depreciation) of $66,000 a year. This is a total fixed cost of $146,000 or:

$$\frac{\$146{,}000}{365} = \$400 \text{ a day}$$

The catering company in its hall can only handle one function a day, and operates a variable cost (for food, wages for preparation and service staff, and supplies) of 60 percent of revenue. It has been approached by an organization that wishes to have a lunch for only 60 people at a price of $10 per person. Normally the catering company would not handle a group as small as this, but on this occasion it does not see any likelihood of having the hall used by any other organization. If it handles the function, its income statement for that day will be as follows:

Revenue 60 people × $10.00	$600
Variable costs 60% × $600	(360)
Fixed costs	(400)
Net loss	($160)

Reduction of loss

The net loss of $160 does not look good, but what is the loss if we do not accept the function? It will be $400, because the fixed costs for that day will still have to be met. But, by selling below total cost of $760 ($400 fixed plus $360 variable) our loss is less than it would otherwise be.

In the short run, as long as sales revenue is greater than variable cost, it pays to accept business, because the excess of revenue over variable cost will contribute to (help pay for) the fixed costs, which are there in any case. We can rearrange our income statement to illustrate this concept of contribution margin as follows:

Revenue	$600
Variable costs	(360)
Contribution margin	$240
Fixed costs	(400)
Net loss	($160)

SHOULD WE CLOSE DURING THE OFF-SEASON

The same reasoning as in the previous case can be applied to a seasonal operation to answer the question of staying open or closing during the off-season. Consider the case of a motel that has the income statement shown below:

Revenue	$130,000
Expenses	(110,000)
Net income	$ 20,000

Off-season loss

The owner decided to make an analysis of his revenue and costs by the month, and found that for ten months he was making money and for two months he was losing money. His variable costs were 20 percent of revenue; his total fixed costs were $84,000, or $7,000 a month. The following summarizes his findings:

	10 months	2 months	Total
Revenue	$125,000	$ 5,000	$130,000
Variable costs	$ 25,000	$ 1,000	$ 26,000
Fixed costs	70,000	14,000	84,000
Total costs	$ 95,000	$15,000	$110,000
Net income	$ 30,000	($10,000)	$ 20,000

His analysis seemed to indicate to him he should close to eliminate the $10,000 loss during the two-month loss period. But, if he does, the fixed costs for the two months ($14,000) will have to be paid out of the ten months' net income, and $30,000 (10 months' net income) less two months' fixed costs of $14,000 will reduce his annual net income to $16,000 from its present $20,000. If he does not want a reduction in annual net income he should not close.

Close-down and start-up costs

In such a situation there might be other factors that need to be considered and that would reinforce the decision to stay open. For example, there could be sizable additional close-down and start-up costs that would have to be included in the calculation of the cost of closing.

Also, would key employees return after an extended vacation? Is there a large enough pool of skilled labor available and willing to work on a seasonal basis only? Would there be recurring training time (and costs) at the start of each new season? These are some of the types of questions that would have to be answered before any final decision to close was made.

WHICH BUSINESS TO BUY?

Just as a business manager has to make choices between alternatives on a day-to-day basis, so too does an entrepreneur going into business or expanding an existing business frequently have to choose between alternatives. Let us look at one such situation.

A restaurant chain is eager to expand. It has an opportunity to take over one of two similar existing restaurants. The two restaurants are close to each other, they have the same type of clientele and size of operation, and the asking price is the same for each. They are also similar

Exhibit 8.1 Statements showing differences in cost structure.

	Restaurant A		Restaurant B	
Revenue	$1,000,000	100.0%	$1,000,000	100.0%
Variable costs	$ 500,000	50.0%	$ 300,000	30.0%
Fixed costs	400,000	40.0%	600,000	60.0%
Total costs	$ 900,000	90.0%	$ 900,000	90.0%
Net income	$ 100,000	10.0%	$ 100,000	10.0%

in that each is presently taking in $1,000,000 in revenue a year, and each has a net income of $100,000 a year. With only this information it is difficult to make a decision as to which would be the more profitable investment. But a cost analysis as shown in Exhibit 8.1 reveals differences.

Different cost structures

Although the revenue and net income are the same for each restaurant, the structure of their costs is different, and this will affect the decision about which one could be more profitable. The restaurant chain that wishes to take over either A or B is optimistic about the future. It feels that, without any change in fixed costs, it can increase annual revenue by 10 percent. What effect will this have on the net income of A and B? Net income will not increase for each restaurant by the same amount. Restaurant A's variable cost is 50 percent. This means that, out of each dollar of additional revenue, it will have variable expenses of $0.50 and a net income of $0.50 (fixed costs do not increase). Restaurant B has variable costs of 30 percent, or $0.30 out of each revenue dollar, leaving a net income of $0.70 from each dollar of extra revenue (again, fixed costs do not change).

Assuming a 10 percent increase in revenue and no new fixed costs, the income statements of the two restaurants have been recalculated in Exhibit 8.2. Note that Restaurant A's net income has gone up by $50,000

Exhibit 8.2 Effect of increased revenue on costs and net income.

	Restaurant A		Restaurant B	
Revenue	$1,100,000	100.0%	$1,100,000	100.0%
Variable costs	$ 550,000	50.0%	$ 330,000	30.0%
Fixed costs	400,000	36.4%	600,000	54.5%
Total costs	$ 950,000	86.4%	$ 930,000	84.5%
Net income	$ 150,000	13.6%	$ 170,000	15.5%

Exhibit 8.3   Effect of decreased revenue on costs and net income.

	Restaurant A		Restaurant B	
Revenue	$900,000	100.0%	$900,000	100.0%
Variable costs	$450,000	50.0%	$270,000	30.0%
Fixed costs	400,000	44.4%	600,000	66.7%
Total costs	$850,000	94.4%	$870,000	96.7%
Net income	$ 50,000	5.6%	$ 30,000	3.3%

High operating leverage

Break-even revenue level

(to $150,000), but Restaurant B's has gone up by $70,000 (to $170,000). In this situation Restaurant B would be the better investment.

A company that has high fixed costs relative to variable costs is said to have high operating leverage. From a net income point of view it will do better in times of rising revenue than will a company with low operating leverage (low fixed costs relative to variable costs). A company with low fixed costs, however, will be better off when revenue starts to decline. Exhibit 8.3 illustrates this, under the assumptions that our two restaurants are going to have a decline in revenue of 10 percent from the present $1,000,000 level and that there will be no change in fixed costs. Exhibit 8.3 shows that, with declining revenue, Restaurant A's net income will be higher than Restaurant B's.

In fact, if revenue declines far enough, Restaurant B will be in financial difficulty long before Restaurant A. If the break-even point were calculated (the break-even point is that level of revenue at which there will be neither net income nor loss), Restaurant A's revenue could go down to $800,000, while Restaurant B would be in difficulty at $857,000. This is illustrated in Exhibit 8.4.

One could determine the break-even level of revenue by trial and error, but there is a formula for quickly calculating this level. The formula, and a more in-depth discussion of fixed and variable costs and how an aware-

Exhibit 8.4   Break-even revenue level depends on cost structure.

	Restaurant A		Restaurant B	
Revenue	$800,000	100.0%	$857,000	100.0%
Variable costs	$400,000	50.0%	$257,000	30.0%
Fixed costs	400,000	50.0%	600,000	70.0%
Total costs	$800,000	100.0%	$857,000	100.0%
Net income	0	0	0	0

ness of this structure can be of great value in many types of business decisions, is covered in Chapter 9.

PAYING A FIXED OR A VARIABLE LEASE

Another situation where fixed and variable cost knowledge can be very useful is in comparing the alternative of a fixed lease cost versus a variable lease based on a percentage of sales. For example, consider the case of a restaurant that has an opportunity to pay a fixed rent for its premises of $5,000 a month ($60,000 a year) or a variable rent of 6 percent of its revenue. Before making the decision, the restaurant's management needs to determine first the break-even point of sales at which the fixed rental payment for a year would be identical to the variable rent. The equation for this is:

Break-even equation

$$\text{Annual break-even revenue} = \frac{\text{Fixed lease cost}}{\text{Variable lease percentage}}$$

and inserting the figures we can determine the revenue level as follows:

$$\frac{\$60,000}{0.06} = \$1,000,000$$

In other words, at $1,000,000 of sales it makes no difference whether the restaurant paid a fixed rent of $60,000 or a variable rent of 6 percent of sales. At this level of sales, management would be indifferent. For this reason the break-even revenue point is sometimes referred to as the indifference point.

If management expected revenue to exceed $1,000,000, it would select a fixed rental arrangement. If revenue were expected to be below $1,000,000, it would be better off selecting the percentage of sales arrangement.

HOW TO SEPARATE COSTS INTO FIXED AND VARIABLE ELEMENTS

Once costs have been categorized into fixed or variable elements, valuable information is then available for use in decision making. Some costs are easy to identify as definitely fixed or definitely variable. The semifixed or semivariable types must be broken down into the two separate elements.

A number of different methods are available for breaking down these semicosts into fixed and variable, some more sophisticated (and thus usually more accurate) than others. Three will be discussed.

1. Maximum/minimum calculation
2. Multipoint graph
3. Regression analysis

To set the stage, we will use the income statement of the Model Motel for a year's period (see Exhibit 8.5). The Model Motel is a no-frills, budget seventy-unit operation without food or beverage facilities. It operates at a 60 percent occupancy and, as a result of good cost controls, is able to keep its average room rate down to $20.00. Last year it sold a total of 15,300 rooms ($306,000 total income divided by $20.00).

**Previous
accounting
records useful**

The first step is to list the expenses by category (fixed, variable, semivariable). The owner's or manager's past experience about the costs of the Model Motel, or the past year's accounting records, will be helpful in this listing. The figures in the fixed column (see Exhibit 8.6) are those that do not change during the year with a change in volume (number of rooms sold). In other words, even though a fixed cost may change from year to year (for example, insurance rates do change, the amount to be spent on advertising can be increased or decreased at management's discretion), such changes are not directly caused by the number of guests

Exhibit 8.5   Income statement without cost breakdown.

Revenue		$306,000
Expenses		
Employee wages	$120,800	
Management salary	20,000	
Laundry, linen, and guest		
supplies	38,700	
Advertising	7,500	
Maintenance	17,300	
Utilities	18,100	
Office/Telephone	4,000	
Insurance	4,600	
Interest	8,300	
Property taxes	20,100	
Depreciation	35,000	
Total expenses		294,400
Net income		$ 11,600

Exhibit 8.6 Costs allocated as fixed, variable, and semi-variable.

	Fixed	Variable	Semi
Employee wages			$120,800
Management salary	$20,000		
Laundry, linen, and guest supplies		$38,700	
Advertising	7,500		
Maintenance			17,300
Utilities			18,100
Office/Telephone			4,000
Insurance	4,600		
Interest	8,300		
Property taxes	20,100		
Depreciation	35,000		

Monthly analysis adequate

accommodated. The items in the variable column are the costs that are the direct result of guests using the facilities (if there are no customers, there will be no cost for laundry, linen, and guest supplies). The higher the occupancy, the higher will be this cost. The figures in the semi column are those we must analyze into their fixed and variable components.

To demonstrate the three methods of breakdown of a semi cost, we will use the wage amount of $120,800. Since much of the wage cost is related to number of rooms sold, we need a month-by-month breakdown of the revenue for each month and the related wage cost for each month. (This information could be broken down by week, but there should be sufficient accuracy for all practical purposes with a monthly analysis.) The sales and labor cost breakdown is given in Exhibit 8.7. Note that the sales column figures are in numbers of units sold. This column could have been expressed in dollars of revenue without it affecting our results (as long as the average room rate of $20.00 had been relatively consistent during the year).

Maximum/Minimum Method

Three steps required

With reference to Exhibit 8.7, note that the month of January has the word minimum alongside it. In January, units sold and wage cost were at their lowest for the year. In contrast, August was the maximum month. There are three steps in the maximum/minimum method:

Step 1: Deduct the minimum from the maximum figures.

How to Separate Costs into Fixed and Variable Elements   275

Exhibit 8.7 Analysis of units sold and wages by month.

	Units (Rooms) Sold	Wage Cost
January (minimum)	500	$ 7,200
February	1,000	7,900
March	1,300	9,900
April	1,200	10,800
May	1,400	12,200
June	1,500	12,100
July	2,100	13,100
August (maximum)	2,100	13,200
September	1,500	11,800
October	1,000	7,600
November	1,000	7,400
December	700	7,600
Totals	15,300	$120,800

	Units (Rooms) Sold	Wage Cost
August (maximum)	2,100	$13,200
January (minimum)	500	7,200
Differences	1,600	$ 6,000

Step 2: Divide wage difference by units sold difference.

$$\frac{\$6,000}{1,600} = \$3.75$$

which is the variable cost per unit sold.

Calculation of fixed cost amount

Step 3: Use the answer to Step 2 to calculate the fixed cost element.

Total wages for August	$13,200
Variable cost, 2,100 units sold × $3.75 a unit =	7,875
Fixed cost	$ 5,325

Instead of units sold, dollars of revenue could equally well have been used, as follows:

	Units Sold	Average Rate	Total Revenue	Wage Cost
August (maximum)	2,100 ×	$20.00 =	$42,000	$13,200
January (minimum)	500 ×	20.00 =	10,000	7,200
Differences			$32,000	$ 6,000

Step 2: $\dfrac{\$6,000}{\$32,000} = \$0.1875$

which is the variable cost per dollar of revenue.

Step 3:	Total wages for August	$13,200
	Variable cost $42,000 revenue × $0.1875 =	7,875
	Fixed cost	$ 5,325

Use minimum or maximum month

Also, in Step 3 we could have used the minimum sales month (instead of the maximum) to calculate our fixed cost, and still obtain the same result:

Step 3:	Total wages for January	$7,200
	Variable cost, 500 units sold × $3.75 a unit =	1,875
	Fixed cost	$5,325

The calculated fixed cost is $5,325 a month or

$$12 \times \$5,325 = \$63,900 \text{ a year}$$

Breakdown of total cost

With reference to Exhibit 8.6, we can now separate our total annual wage cost into its fixed and variable elements:

Total annual wages	$120,800
Fixed cost	63,900
Variable cost	$ 56,900

The calculation of the monthly fixed cost figure has been illustrated by arithmetical means. The maximum/minimum figures could equally as well have been plotted on a graph, as illustrated in Exhibit 8.8, and the fixed cost read off where the dotted line intersects the vertical axis. If the graph is accurately drawn, the same monthly figure of approximately $5,300 is obtained.

How to Separate Costs into Fixed and Variable Elements   277

Possible distortions

The maximum/minimum method is quick and simple. It uses only two sets of figures. Unfortunately, either one or both of these sets of figures may not be typical of the relationship between sales and costs for the year (for example, a one-time bonus may have been paid during one of the months selected). Other, perhaps less dramatic, distortions may be built into the figures.

These distortions can be eliminated, as long as one is aware of them, by adjusting the raw figures. Alternatively, standard costs (rather than actual costs) could be used for the minimum and for the maximum sales months.

Another way to improve the maximum/minimum method and remove possible distortions in individual month figures is to plot the cost and sales figures for each of the twelve months (or however many periods there are involved) on a graph.

Multipoint Graph

Dependent and independent variables

Exhibit 8.9 illustrates a multipoint graph for our sales in units and our wage cost for each of the twelve months. Sales and costs were taken from Exhibit 8.7. The graph illustrated is for two variables, sales and wages. In this case wages are given the name dependent variable and are plotted on the vertical axis. Wages are dependent on sales: they vary with sales. Sales, therefore, are the independent variable. The independent variable

Exhibit 8.8

Exhibit 8.9

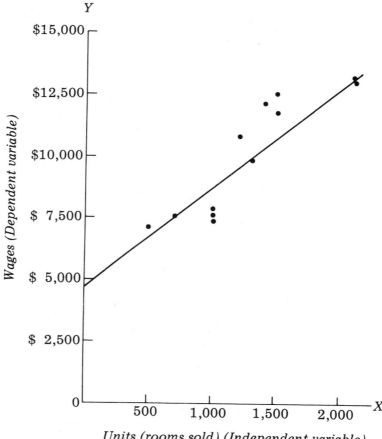

Units (rooms sold) (Independent variable)

is plotted on the horizontal axis. After plotting each of the twelve points, we have what is known as a scatter graph: a series of points scattered around a line that has been drawn through them. A straight line must be drawn. There is no limit to how many straight lines could be drawn through the points. The line we want is the one that, to our eye, seems to fit best. Each individual doing this exercise would probably view the line in a slightly different position, but most people with a reasonably good eye would come up with a line that, for all practical purposes, is close enough. The line should be drawn so that it is continued to the left until it intersects the vertical axis (the dependent variable). The intersect point reading is our fixed cost (wages in this case). Note that, in Exhibit 8.9, our fixed cost reading is $4,500 (approximately). This is the monthly cost. Converted to annual cost it is

Fixed cost on vertical axis

How to Separate Costs into Fixed and Variable Elements 279

$$\$4,500 \times 12 = \$54,000$$

Our total annual wage cost would then be broken down into

Fixed $54,000
Variable $66,800 ($120,800 less $54,000)

Line of best fit

Note that, in drawing graphs for the purpose discussed, the point where the vertical and horizontal axes meet should be given a reading of zero. The figures along each axis should then be plotted to scale from zero.

The straight line on a scatter graph can be drawn by eye, and for most purposes will give us a fixed cost reading that is good enough. However, the question arises whether there is one best line that can be drawn that is the most accurate. The answer is yes. The method used to determine it is known as regression analysis.

Regression Analysis

Different equations

With regression analysis there is no need to draw a graph, plot points, and draw a line through them. The objective in drawing the line is to find out where the line intersects the vertical axis so we can read, at that intersection point, what the fixed costs are. Once we know the fixed costs, we can then easily calculate the variable costs (total costs − fixed costs = variable costs). From regression analysis, a number of equations have been developed for different purposes. One of the equations allows us to calculate the fixed costs directly, without a graph.

Before the equation is used, we have to take the units (rooms) sold and the wage cost information from Exhibit 8.7 and develop it a little further, as has been done in Exhibit 8.10. In Exhibit 8.10 the units (rooms) sold column has been given the symbol X (X is for the independent variable). The wage cost column (the dependent variable) has been given the symbol Y. Two new columns have been added: XY (which is X multiplied by Y) and X^2 (which is X multiplied by X). The equation is

Equation for fixed costs

$$\text{Fixed costs} = \frac{(\Sigma Y)(\Sigma X^2) - (\Sigma X)(\Sigma XY)}{n(\Sigma X^2) - (\Sigma X)^2}$$

Two new symbols have been introduced in this equation: Σ means the sum of, or the column total figure and n is the number of periods, in our case 12 (months).

Replacing the symbols in the above equation by the column totals from Exhibit 8.10 we have

Exhibit 8.10   Illustration of calculation of regression analysis data.

Month	Units (Rooms) Sold X	Wage Cost Y	XY (X × Y)	X² (X × X)
1	500	$ 7,200	$ 3,600,000	250,000
2	1,000	7,900	7,900,000	1,000,000
3	1,300	9,900	12,870,000	1,690,000
4	1,200	10,800	12,960,000	1,440,000
5	1,400	12,200	17,080,000	1,960,000
6	1,500	12,100	18,150,000	2,250,000
7	2,100	13,100	27,510,000	4,410,000
8	2,100	13,200	27,720,000	4,410,000
9	1,500	11,800	17,700,000	2,250,000
10	1,000	7,600	7,600,000	1,000,000
11	1,000	7,400	7,400,000	1,000,000
12	700	7,600	5,320,000	490,000
Totals	15,300	$120,800	$165,810,000	22,150,000

$$\text{Fixed costs} = \frac{\$120,800(22,150,000) - (15,300)(\$165,810,000)}{12(22,150,000) - (15,300)(15,300)}$$

$$= \frac{\$2,675,720,000,000 - \$2,536,893,000,000}{265,800,000 - 234,090,000}$$

$$= \frac{\$138,827,000,000}{31,710,000}$$

$$= \underline{\$4,378.02 \text{ a month}}$$

Total annual fixed cost

Our answer could be rounded to $4,400 a month, which gives us a total annual fixed cost of

$$\$4,400 \times 12 = \$52,800$$

Comparison of Results

Let us compare the results of our fixed/variable breakdown of the Model Motel's annual wage cost using each of the three methods described. The results are tabulated as follows:

How to Separate Costs into Fixed and Variable Elements   281

	Fixed	Variable	Total
Maximum/minimum	$63,900	$56,900	$120,800
Multipoint graph	54,000	66,800	120,800
Regression analysis	52,800	68,000	120,800

In practice only one of the three methods would be used. We know that regression analysis is the most accurate; however, because it requires time to perform the necessary arithmetic, it should probably only be used by those who are mathematically adept or as a spot check on the results of either of the other two methods. Alternatively, the figures can be fed into a programmed calculator that will carry out all the necessary calculations.

Graph can give good results

Multipoint graph results are fairly close to the regression analysis figures, which seems to imply that, if the graph is well drawn, we should have results accurate enough for all practical purposes. The maximum/minimum results are about 20 percent different from what regression analysis tells us the most correct result should be. Therefore this method should be used with caution and only if the two periods selected are typical of all periods, which might be difficult to determine.

Once a method has been selected, it should be applied consistently to all semivariable expenses. With reference to our Model Motel's cost figures in Exhibit 8.6, so far we have analyzed the semivariable wage cost. We need to analyze similarly the three other semivariable costs: maintenance, utilities, and office/telephone. Let us assume we have done so; our completed cost analysis gives us the fixed and variable costs shown in Exhibit 8.11.

Alternative Method

As an alternative to separating semivariable costs by individual expense, the situation can be simplified by first adding together all semivariable costs, then applying one of the three methods outlined in this section to separate only the total into its fixed and variable elements. This considerably reduces the time and effort involved. On the other hand, it might reduce the accuracy of the results. In many cases, however, this reduced accuracy might still be satisfactory for decisions.

Reduced time and profit

In Chapter 9 we shall see how we can use this cost breakdown information for decision making concerning many aspects of our motel operation. Even though a motel situation has been used, the same type of analysis can be carried out equally well for a restaurant or a department in a hotel. Regarding hotel departments, the difficulty may be in allocating the overhead costs in an equitable manner to the individual departments.

Exhibit 8.11 Final cost allocation by fixed or variable.

	Fixed	Variable
Employee wages	$ 52,800	$ 68,000
Management salary	20,000	
Laundry, linen, and guest supplies		38,700
Advertising	7,500	
Maintenance	15,400	1,900
Utilities	14,200	3,900
Office	3,500	500
Insurance	4,600	
Interest	8,300	
Property taxes	20,100	
Depreciation	35,000	
Totals	$181,400	$113,000

SUMMARY

One way of increasing net income in a business is to increase revenue. Another way is to control costs. In order to do this, one must understand that there are different types of costs.

A direct cost is one that is the responsibility of, and controllable by, a department head or department manager. An indirect cost, sometimes called an overhead cost, is not normally charged to an individual department. If such costs are broken down by department and shown on the departmental income statement, the resulting departmental profit or loss figure must be interpreted with great care.

All costs are controllable costs whether they are direct or indirect ones; it is only the level of responsibility for control of a cost that changes.

A joint cost is one that is shared by two or more departments, or by the organization as a whole. A joint cost could be a direct one (such as wages), or an indirect one (such as building maintenance). A discretionary cost is one that can be incurred only at the discretion of a particular person, generally the manager. A relevant cost is one that needs to be considered when making a specific decision. If a cost makes no difference to the decision, then it is not relevant.

A sunk cost is an example of a cost that is not relevant to certain decisions. The initial expenditure on a piece of equipment bought five years ago and now to be traded in is a sunk cost insofar as the decision to buy a new machine today is concerned.

An opportunity cost is the income forgone by not doing something. A motel could run its own restaurant at a profit, or lease it out. If it runs it itself, the loss of rent income is an opportunity cost. However, the motel owner would happily endure this opportunity cost if net income from running the operation were greater than any potential rent income.

A standard cost is what a cost should be for a given level of revenue or volume of business.

The final three types of cost discussed in this chapter were fixed costs, variable costs, and semifixed or semivariable costs. Fixed costs are costs that do not change in the short run regardless of the volume of sales (the general manger's annual salary is an example). Variable costs are those that do vary in the short run and do so in direct proportion to sales (food and liquor costs are two good examples of variable costs). Most costs, however, do not fall neatly into either the fixed or the variable category; they are the semifixed or semivariable category. In order to make useful decisions concerning fixed and variable costs and their effect on net income at various levels of sales, the semitype costs must be analyzed into their fixed and variable elements. Three methods were used to illustrate how this can be done.

1. The maximum/minimum method, which, although quick and easy to use, may give misleading results if the maximum and minimum sales periods selected are not truly representative of all periods.

2. The multipoint graph eliminates the possible problem built into the maximum/minimum method. The graph is subject to some element of personal judgment, but in most cases will give results that are close enough for most decision making purposes.

3. Regression analysis, which is the most accurate method, involves quite a number of calculations and can probably best be used as a spot check on the results of using one of the other two methods.

DISCUSSION QUESTIONS

1. Differentiate between a direct cost and an indirect cost.

2. Define discretionary cost and give two examples (other than those given in the text) of such a cost.

3. Differentiate between a fixed cost and a variable cost and give an example of each.

4. Why are some costs known as semifixed or semivariable?

5. Why might it not be wise to allocate an indirect cost to various departments on the basis of each department's revenue to total revenue?

6. What do you think might be the relevant costs to be considered in deciding which one of a number of different vacuum cleaner models to buy for housekeeping purposes?

7. Explain why you think it sometimes makes sense to sell below cost.

8. Define the term high operating leverage and explain why, in times of increasing revenue, it is more profitable to have high rather than low operating leverage.

9. With figures of your own choosing, illustrate how the maximum/minimum calculation method can be used to separate the fixed and variable elements of a cost.

10. Explain why the maximum/minimum method may not be a good one to use to separate the fixed and variable portions of a cost.

11. Give a brief explanation of how to prepare a graph when using the multipoint graph method for separating the fixed and variable elements of a cost.

PROBLEMS

8.1 You are planning to purchase a new electronic register and have to make a choice among the following three models.

	Model I	Model 2	Model 3
Cash cost *Rel*	$ 5,000	$ 5,500	$ 5,300
Estimated life	5 years	5 years	5 years
Trade-in value at end of life *Rel*	$ 1,000	$ 1,200	$ 800
Cash from sale of old machine N	$ 200	$ 200	$ 200
Installation of new machine *R*	$ 75	$ 100	$ 100
Initial training cost in year 1 on *R* new machine	$ 350	$ 300	$ 250
Annual maintenance contract *R*	$ 300	$ 275	$ 200
Annual cost of supplies N	$ 200	$ 200	$ 200
Annual wage cost of employees N operating machine	$32,000	$32,000	$32,000

Strictly on the basis of lowest cash cost over the five-year period, which model would be the best investment? (Note: in your calculations ignore any costs that are not relevant.)

8.2 The fixed cost of the banqueting department of a hotel is $400 a day. A customer has selected a menu for 100 persons that would have a food cost of $6.00 a person, a variable wage cost of $1.75 per person, and other variable costs of $0.25 per person.

a. Calculate the total cost per person if this banquet were booked.

b. What should be the total selling price (revenue) and the price per person if a 20 percent net income on revenue is wanted?

c. The customer does not want to pay more than $11.25 per person for this function. She is a good customer and has booked many functions in the banquet room in the past, and is expected to do so in the future. The function is for three days from now. There is no likelihood you will be able to book the room for any other function. Explain why you would, or would not, accept the $11.25 per person price.

(Note: assume that the hotel has only one banquet room.)

8.3 You have the following annual information about a restaurant complex comprising three departments.

	Dining Room	Coffee Shop	Lounge	Total
Revenue	$184,800	$135,600	$152,900	$473,300
Direct costs	154,600	129,000	127,600	411,200
	$ 30,200	$ 6,600	$ 25,300	$ 62,100
Indirect costs				52,000
Net income				$ 10,100

The owner is thinking that, to get a better picture of how each department is doing, the indirect costs should be allocated to each department prorated according to area compared to total area. Square footage is as follows:

Dining room	1,200 sq. ft.
Coffee shop	840
Lounge	960

a. Allocate the indirect costs as indicated and advise the owner whether or not he should accept an offer from a souvenir store operator who is willing to take over the coffee shop space for a rental of $8,000 a year.

b. Before making a final choice, the operator of the restaurant decides to carry out more analysis about his indirect costs and what would happen to them if he rented out the coffee shop space. The information is

	Present Cost	Cost if Coffee Shop Rented
Administrative and general	$14,100	$13,400
Advertising and promotion	9,800	9,200

	Present Cost	Cost if Coffee Shop Rented
Utilities	4,500	4,300
Repairs and maintenance	4,200	3,900
Insurance	3,600	3,300
Interest	5,400	5,400
Depreciation	10,400	7,100

One other factor to be considered is that, if the coffee shop is not operated, lounge revenue will decline by $13,600 a year and lounge direct costs will go down by $10,200. Dining room revenue and direct costs will not be affected. Should the owner accept the offer to rent out the coffee shop?

8.4 You have the following income statements for each of the four quarters of a restaurant operation.

	Quarter 1	Quarter 2	Quarter 3	Quarter 4
Revenue	$34,200	$44,800	$37,200	$20,300
Cost of sales	12,800	16,900	14,700	8,400
Gross profit	$21,400	$27,900	$22,500	$11,900
Expenses:				
Wages	$ 9,800	$11,600	$10,200	$ 7,400
Supplies	1,600	1,900	1,700	900
Advertising	600	800	700	400
Utilities	2,500	2,900	2,600	1,900
Maintenance	300	400	300	200
Insurance	500	500	500	500
Interest	600	600	600	600
Depreciation	400	400	400	400
Rent	3,000	3,000	3,000	3,000
Total expenses	$19,300	$22,100	$20,000	$15,300
Net income (loss)	$ 2,100	$ 5,800	$ 2,500	($ 3,400)

The owner is contemplating closing down the restaurant in Quarter 4 in order to eliminate the loss and take three months vacation. The owner has asked for your help and, after analysis of the expenses allocated to Quarter 4, you determine the following:

- *Wages.* $3,000 is a fixed cost of key personnel who would be kept on the payroll even if the operation were closed for three months.
- *Supplies.* Cost varies directly with revenue, none fixed.
- *Advertising.* Half of the cost is fixed, the rest is variable.

- *Utilities.* Even if closed for three months, the restaurant will still require some heating; this is expected to cost $100 a month.
- *Maintenance.* Some maintenance work could be done during the closed period; estimated cost $100.
- *Insurance.* There would be a $200 reduction in the insurance cost if closed for three months.
- *Interest.* Will still have to be paid, even if closed.
- *Depreciation.* With less customer traffic and reduced wear and tear on equipment there would be a 75 percent reduction in this expense.
- *Rent.* This expense is an annual contract for $12,000 that must be paid regardless of whether the restaurant is open or closed.

What advice would you give the owner?

8.5 A company owns three motels in a ski resort area. Although there is some business during the summer months, the company finds it very difficult to staff the three operations during this period and is contemplating closing one of the three motels. The revenue and breakdown of costs during this period are as follows:

	Motel A	Motel B	Motel C
Revenue	$265,000	$325,000	$425,000
Variable costs	160,000	150,000	135,000
Fixed costs	110,000	167,000	260,000

a. Assuming one of the motels must be closed and that its closing will have no effect on the revenue of the other two, explain which motel should be closed and why.

b. Would your answer be the same if, with revenue as shown above, the costs were broken down as follows:

	Motel A	Motel B	Motel C
Variable costs	$100,000	$167,000	$250,000
Fixed costs	110,000	113,000	112,000

8.6 An entrepreneur is contemplating purchasing one of two similar, competitive motels and has asked for your advice. Present revenue of each motel is $450,000 per year. Jack's motel has annual variable costs of 50 percent of revenue and fixed costs of $200,000; Jock's motel has annual variable costs of 60 percent of revenue and fixed costs of $155,000. The entrepreneur thinks that, if he purchased Jack's motel, he could save $10,000 a year on interest expense (a fixed cost). Alternatively, if he purchased Jock's motel, he could improve staff scheduling to the point that the wage saving would reduce total variable cost to 55 percent. In the case of either purchase, he thinks that revenue can be increased by 20 percent a year. Calculate the present net income of each motel, then, given the above assumptions, advise the entrepreneur which one he should buy, including any cautionary comments.

8.7 Stella's Steak House has been operating for the past ten years, and Stella has to negotiate her lease on the premises for the next five years. Her options are to pay a fixed monthly rent of $2,500 or pay a variable monthly rent of 6 percent of her sales. Over the next five years she anticipates her sales to average $550,000 per year.

    a. What is Stella's indifference point on an annual sales basis?
    b. Which option should she choose? Explain.

8.8 A hotel wishes to analyze its electricity cost in its rooms department in terms of fixed and variable elements. Monthly income statements show that during its busiest and slowest months cost and rooms occupied information is as follows:

	Cost	Rooms Occupied
Busiest	$2,600	2,400
Slowest	2,000	1,200

Use the maximum/minimum method to calculate
    a. The variable cost per room occupied.
    b. The total variable cost for the busiest and for the slowest month.
    c. The total fixed cost per month.

8.9 You have the following information from the records of a restaurant.

	Revenue	Wages
January	$11,100	$5,500
February	13,100	5,900
March	14,900	6,100
April	19,100	7,100
May	22,000	9,000
June	24,200	9,600
July	26,300	9,700
August	27,000	9,900
September	23,900	8,500
October	20,100	7,600
November	18,200	8,000
December	16,000	7,100

    a. Use the maximum/minimum method to calculate total fixed cost and total variable cost for a year.

b. Plot the information on a graph and compare the results with the results arrived at in part **a**.

8.10 Take the information concerning sales and wages in Problem 8.9 and use regression analysis to calculate total fixed cost and total variable cost for a year. Compare the results with the results obtained in both parts of Problem 8.9 and comment about the three sets of figures.

8.11 A restaurant has the following twelve-month record of revenue and wages:

	Revenue	Wages
January	$24,900	$11,300
February	24,200	11,100
March	25,600	11,200
April	24,200	11,400
May	34,000	13,200
June	46,200	18,600
July	53,300	21,600 _19 200 high_
August	44,000	16,100
September	34,200	15,100
October	30,400	12,800
November	28,200	11,200
December	27,000 _23 800_	13,000 _10 900 Low_

Included in the July wages is a lump sum retroactive wage increase of $2,400, which would not normally be part of the July wage cost. Also, in December, the restaurant catered to a special Christmas function that brought in $3,200 in revenue and cost the restaurant an additional $900 in wages. The December wage figure also included $1,200 in Christmas bonuses to the staff. Use the maximum/minimum method to calculate the restaurant's fixed wage cost.

CASE 8

Charles is thinking of spending $3,000 more next year on advertising (part of marketing expense). Because of his marketing courses he feels he can design appealing advertisements to be placed in local newspapers and aimed at the business luncheon trade. He estimates that if the ads are placed they will bring in fifteen more people at lunch each day.

The average check for the additional lunch guests would be the same as that calculated in Case 6. Use a fifty-two-week year. Assume that the food and beverage total cost of sales percentage will be the same as in year 0001. (This percentage was calculated in Case 3.)

To serve the extra guests a new employee will have to be hired at lunch for four hours. Hourly rate of pay including fringe benefits (a free meal while on duty, vacation pay, and so on) will be $5.42 an hour. The following variable expenses will remain at the same percentage to revenue as they were in year 0001 (see Case 3):

- Laundry
- China, glass, etc.
- Other operating expenses

All other expenses are assumed to be fixed and unaffected by the increased volume of business.

Prepare calculations to show whether or not the $3,000 should be spent. Refer to the income statement for the 4C Company's restaurant for year 0001.

9 The CVP Approach to Decisions

Chapter Highlights

This chapter begins by asking some of the questions that cost-volume-profit (CVP) analysis can help a business answer. Before demonstrating the technique, however, the assumptions and limitations inherent in the CVP approach are listed.

A graphical explanation and presentation of CVP is then given, showing how the break-even level of sales or revenue can be determined and how the level of profit (income) for a particular volume of sales can be arrived at.

The CVP equation (which eliminates the need for a graph) is given. The equation is used to determine the break-even level of sales, the sales required to give a stipulated profit, the additional sales needed to cover a new fixed cost, the additional sales required to cover a changed variable cost, or multiple changes in costs. These answers can be obtained in dollar amounts or in units sold (such as rooms sold or guests served).

The equation can also be used to determine the effect that a change in selling prices will have on operating results, to determine additional volume required to cover a loss, or to analyze a new investment.

The chapter illustrates how the equation can be used to handle various situations concerning joint costs in multidepartment establishments and concludes with a section on incorporating income tax into the CVP calculations.

Chapter Objectives

After studying this chapter the reader should be able to:

1. Briefly discuss some of the assumptions and limitations inherent in CVP analysis.
2. Prepare and use a graph, given information about sales and fixed and variable costs.
3. State the CVP equation for determining sales levels in dollars.
4. State the CVP equation for determining sales levels in units.
5. Use either of the two equations as an aid in making a variety of different business decisions.
6. Explain the term "contribution margin."
7. Use CVP analysis to solve problems concerning joint fixed costs in a multi-department establishment.
8. Incorporate tax considerations into CVP analysis.

THE CVP APPROACH TO DECISIONS

A great many questions are asked in the management of a hotel or foodservice operation. Questions such as:

- What will my income be at a certain level of sales or revenue?
- What is the extra sales revenue I need to cover the cost of expansion and still give me the profit I want?
- What effect will a change of price have on my profit?
- By how much must sales be increased to cover the cost of a wage increase and still give me the net income to revenue ratio I want?

These and many similar types of questions cannot be answered simply from the traditional income statement. However, the cost-volume-profit (CVP) approach breaks down income statement costs into those that are variable and those that are fixed, and then uses this information for rational decision making. However, before the CVP decision-making technique is used, the assumptions and limitations built into it must be clearly understood.

ASSUMPTIONS AND LIMITATIONS

The following are the assumptions and limitations built into CVP analysis:

Breakdown of costs into fixed and variable

1. It assumes that the costs associated with the present level of sales or revenue can be fairly accurately broken down into their fixed and variable elements.

2. It assumes that fixed costs will remain fixed during the period affected by the decision being made.

3. It assumes that variable costs vary directly (in a linear fashion) with sales or revenue during the period affected by the decision being made.

4. It is limited to individual situations or departments. Caution should be exercised when using it for decisions concerning an entire operation, such as a hotel, where a number of departments contribute to overall income. In such cases the problem is one of revenue mix (see the discussion and Exhibits 2.4 and 2.5 in Chapter 2).

5. It is limited to situations where economic and other conditions can be assumed to stay relatively stable. In highly inflationary times, for example, when it is difficult to predict sale and/or cost prices more than a few weeks ahead, it would be dangerous to use CVP analysis for decisions concerning the next year.

Analysis only guide to final decision

6. Finally, CVP analysis is only a guide to decision making. The accounting/mathematical CVP approach might indicate a decision in a certain direction, but other factors (such as employee relations, customer goodwill, social or environmental impact) may dictate a decision that contradicts the CVP analysis.

In this chapter, for the most part, we shall use the information developed in Chapter 8 concerning the Model Motel's sales and fixed and variable costs. The information we need is summarized in Exhibit 9.1.

Contribution margin and fixed costs

In CVP analysis the income statement is sometimes presented in the form of a contribution statement. The income statement information from Exhibit 9.1 is converted as follows to a contribution statement.

Revenue	$306,000
Variable costs	113,000
Contribution to fixed costs	$193,000
Fixed costs	181,400
Income (before tax)	$ 11,600

Exhibit 9.1 Information required for CVP analysis.

Revenue (15,300 units @ $20 average rate)		$306,000
Variable costs	$113,000	
Fixed costs	181,400	294,400
Income (before tax)		$ 11,600

Other information

a. 70 units available

b. occupancy % $= \dfrac{15,300}{70 \times 365} \times 100 = 60\%$

c. average occupancy $= 60\% \times 70$ units $= 42$ units per night

d. variable cost per unit used $= \dfrac{\$113,000}{15,300} = \$7.39$

e. variable cost as % of revenue $= \$\dfrac{113,000}{306,000} \times 100 = 37\%$

Details of the variable and fixed costs, listing them expense by expense, would normally be shown, either directly on the statement or on a supporting schedule. The contribution to the fixed costs figure is commonly referred to as the contribution margin. This will be discussed later in this chapter. If the income statement were for a large hotel with a number of departments, revenue and variable costs would be shown for each department with a combined figure of contribution margin from which total hotel fixed costs are then deducted to arrive at net income. An example is illustrated (in abbreviated form without detailing costs) later in this chapter in Exhibit 9.8.

GRAPHICAL PRESENTATIONS

One of the ways of using CVP analysis is with a graphical presentation of the data. There are three steps required in the preparation of a graph (sometimes known as a break-even chart). To prepare a chart, units or dollars of sales are shown on the horizontal axis, and dollars of sales and costs on the vertical axis.

Steps in graph presentation

Step 1: Draw the fixed cost line (using the data from Exhibit 9.1, $181,400) from a point on the vertical axis representing $181,400. The fixed cost line is a straight line parallel to the horizontal axis. See Exhibit 9.2.

Exhibit 9.2

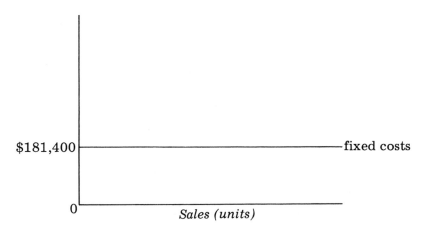

Step 2: Draw the total cost line (using the data from Exhibit 9.1, $294,400). To do this, plot a point on the graph opposite $294,400 on the vertical axis and 15,300 units on the horizontal axis. Connect this point with a straight line to the point on the vertical axis where the fixed cost line intersects ($181,400). See Exhibit 9.3.

Step 3: Draw the sales line (using the data from Exhibit 9.1, $306,000 or 15,300 units). Plot a point on the graph that is opposite $306,000 on the vertical axis and 15,300 units on the horizontal axis. Connect this point with a straight line to the intersect point of the two axes (that is, 0). See Exhibit 9.4.

Exhibit 9.3

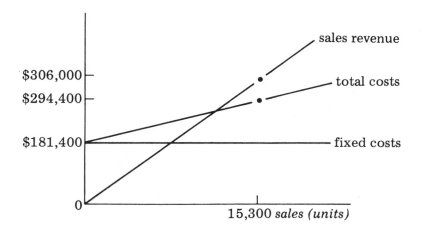

Exhibit 9.4

In Exhibit 9.4, we now have our completed break-even chart. Since Exhibits 9.2, 9.3, and 9.4 are for illustrative purposes only, they have not been drawn to scale. The completed chart, drawn to scale, is shown in Exhibit 9.5. This completed chart allows us to easily read certain information. For example, at what level of sales will the motel make neither a profit nor a loss (its break-even point)? On the chart, the break-even point is where the sales revenue line intersects with the total cost line. In Exhibit 9.5, a dotted line has been drawn from this point to the vertical axis and the sales level can be read off to be $288,000. Alternatively, the dotted line can be drawn down to the horizontal axis and the break-even number of units can be read as 14,400 (14,400 × $20 average rate = $288,000). That this is indeed the break-even level of sales can be easily verified.

Questions to be answered

Break-even sales level

Break-even revenue	$288,000
Variable expenses − 37% of sales (see Exhibit 9.1)	$106,600
Fixed expenses	181,400
Total costs	$288,000
Income	nil

If sales drop below $288,000, the Model Motel will begin losing money.

In Exhibit 9.6 a new graph has been drawn to answer the question: By how much will my income increase if I can increase sales of units to 17,500 a year? A dotted line has been drawn from 17,500 units to intersect the total cost and the sales revenue lines. Dotted lines have then been drawn horizontally to the left from these two intersect points to meet

Exhibit 9.5

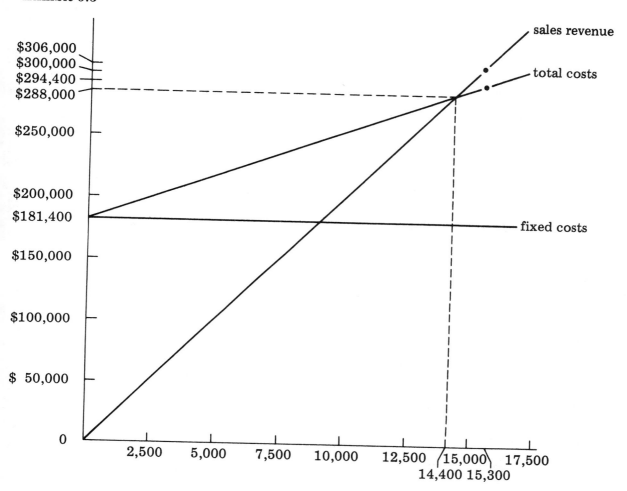

with the vertical axis. Where the two horizontal dotted lines meet with the vertical axis will give us our readings of total sales revenue and total costs. The difference is our income.

Confirmation of income amount

Revenue (17,500 units at $20) =	$350,000
Total costs	(311,000)
Net income	$ 39,000

Questions like this can be answered once a graph has been prepared. However, if a cost item changes (that is, if fixed costs change, or if the relationship between variable costs and sales or revenue changes) or if sale prices (room rates) change, then the lines must be redrawn on the

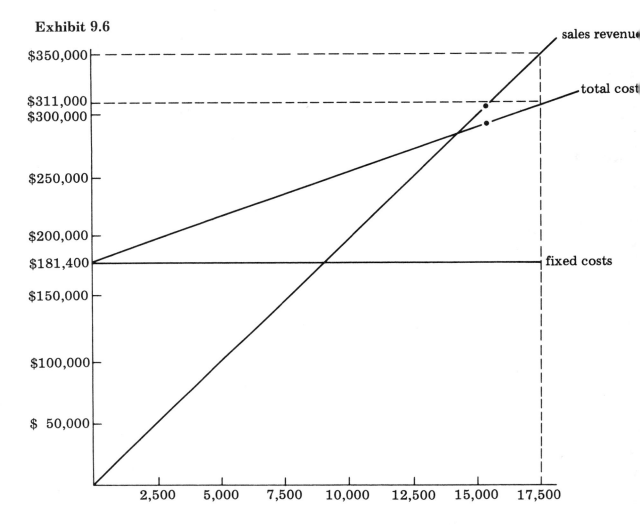

Exhibit 9.6

graph (which can become rather messy) or a new graph must be pre-pared, which is time consuming. Questions that need to be answered concerning changing costs or sales can be answered more quickly by using a formula (equation) that is much more flexible than a graph.

How to handle other income

Before moving on to the equation, a comment needs to be made. It concerns what to do with any fixed income an operation might have. For example, assume our Model Motel had a coffee shop that it leased out for $10,000 a year. The $10,000 should not be included with regular revenue because it is a fixed item. The easiest solution is to show it as a reduction of fixed expenses. In other words, our fixed expenses would be reduced from $181,400 to $171,400 and would be shown at this amount on the graph, or would be included at this amount in our equation.

THE CVP FORMULA

The CVP formula is simple and easy to use. The equation is

$$\text{Sales or revenue level} = \frac{\text{Fixed costs } + \text{ Profit (income) desired}}{100\% - \text{Variable costs as \% of revenue}}$$

Let us use this equation first to solve two questions, the answers to which we already have from our graphs.

At What Level of Revenue Will We Break Even?

Suppose we want to know the level of revenue at which we will make neither a profit nor a loss, the break-even point. The solution is

Illustration of CVP formula

$$\text{Revenue level} = \frac{\$181,400+0}{100\%-37\%} \quad \text{or} \quad \frac{\$181,400+0}{1-.37}$$

$$= \frac{\$181,400}{63\%} \quad \text{or} \quad \frac{\$181,400}{.63}$$

$$= \$287,937, \text{ rounded to } \underline{\$288,000}$$

In the equation, the variable cost as a percent of revenue (37 percent) had already been calculated in Exhibit 9.1. Also, one can use either percentage or decimal figures in the denominator (as illustrated); the answer will be the same. Note also that the formula gives an exact answer that has been rounded and thus agrees with the amount already read from our graph in Exhibit 9.5. It is difficult to get a very exact figure from a graph. However, an exact figure serves no real purpose. Our breakdown of fixed and variable costs is not necessarily exact. Therefore, in circumstances such as we have for the Model Motel, a solution to the closest $1,000 would be acceptable.

Solution not necessarily exact

At What Level of Revenue Will We Make $39,000 Profit?

The level of revenue at which we will make a profit of $39,000 is already known from the graph illustrated in Exhibit 9.6. It is $350,000. Let us confirm this with the equation.

$$\text{Revenue level} = \frac{\$181,400 + \$39,000}{100\% - 37\%}$$

$$= \frac{\$220,400}{63\%}$$

$$= \$349,841, \text{ rounded to } \underline{\$350,000}$$

How Much Must Revenue Increase to Cover a New Fixed Cost?

Higher revenue equals higher variable costs

Normally, if fixed costs increase and no change is made in selling prices, then profits could be expected to decline by the amount of the additional fixed cost. We could then ask the question: By how much must revenue increase to compensate for a fixed cost increase and not have a reduction in profit? A simple answer is that revenue has to go up by the same amount as the fixed cost increases. But this is not correct, because to increase revenue (with no increase in selling prices) we have to sell more units; if we sell more units, our variable costs (such as wages and guest supplies) are going to increase. By trial and error we could arrive at a solution, but our equation will solve this kind of question for us quickly.

$$\text{Revenue level} = \frac{\text{Old fixed cost + New fixed cost + Profit desired}}{100\% - \text{Variable }\%}$$

Suppose we wish to spend $5,000 more on advertising a year. How much more in sales revenue must we have (assuming no room rate change) to maintain our present $11,600 profit?

$$\text{Revenue level} = \frac{\$181,400 + \$5,000 + \$11,600}{100\% - 37\%}$$

$$= \frac{\$198,000}{63\%}$$

$$= \$314,286, \text{ rounded to } \underline{\$314,300}$$

We can easily prove the correctness of our result (as we can with any solution to a problem using this formula) by the following:

Proof of correctness of result

Revenue	$314,300
Variable costs 37% × $314,300	$116,300
Fixed costs	186,400
Total costs	$302,700
Profit (income)	$ 11,600

The solution to the problem tells us that revenue must be at the $314,300 level: an increase of $8,300 over the previous revenue level of $306,000. If we wish to know how many additional rooms this is, we simply divide the increase by our average room rate:

$$\frac{\$8,300}{\$20} = 415 \text{ rooms a year}$$

This is just a little over one more room a night. We can then assess this against the $5,000 to be spent. If we anticipate that we will generate more than 415 additional room sales a year, we will not only pay for our advertising fixed cost and cover our increased variable costs, but we will also increase our profit above its present level.

Solution in dollars or units

In the problem just discussed, we worked out the solution in dollars, then converted this to units to be sold. We could have worked out the solution directly in units (rooms) with a short-cut method, which will be demonstrated later in this chapter.

What Additional Revenue Do I Need to Cover a Change in Variable Cost?

Fixed cost changes are easy to handle with our basic equation. Variable cost changes require a little extra arithmetic but are no more difficult to handle. Our variable expenses have been calculated to be 37 percent of revenue. This was arrived at as follows:

Calculation of variable cost percentage

$$\text{Variable cost \%} = \frac{\text{Total variable costs}}{\text{Revenue}} \times 100$$

$$= \frac{\$113,000}{\$306,000} \times 100$$

$$= 36.928 \text{ or } \underline{37\%}$$

Our variable cost percentage could equally well have been calculated as follows:

$$\text{Variable cost \%} = \frac{\text{Variable cost \$ per unit}}{\text{Average sale \$ per unit}} \times 100$$

Variable cost per unit is $7.39 (see Exhibit 9.1) and average sale per unit (average room rate) is $20.

$$\text{Variable cost \%} = \frac{\$\ 7.39}{\$20.00} \times 100 = 36.95\% \text{ or } \underline{37\%}$$

Included in the $7.39 variable cost per unit is the cost of the wages of a maid to clean the unit. Suppose the hourly wage rate for maids (including all benefits) is $4.00 an hour, and a maid takes one-half hour to clean a room. Therefore, two dollars of the $7.39 variable cost per room sold is for wages and benefits. Let us assume a 20 percent increase in maids' wages; our wage cost per unit will now be:

$$\$2.00 + (20\% \times \$2.00) = \$2.00 + \$0.40 = \underline{\$2.40}$$

Alternatively, we could say that our variable cost per unit is going to go up by $0.40 and will now be:

$$\$7.39 + \$0.40 = \underline{\$7.79}$$

But, if our variable cost per unit is now $7.79 and there is no change in the average room rate, our variable cost percentage will no longer be the same as before. It will be:

$$\frac{\$\ 7.79}{\$20.00} = 38.95 \quad \text{or} \quad \underline{39\%}$$

We can now use this to answer the question: What must my new level of revenue be if my fixed costs do not change, my profit must not drop, but my maids' wages are going to increase by 20 percent?

$$\text{Revenue level} = \frac{\text{Fixed costs} + \text{Profit}}{100\% - \text{Variable }\%}$$

$$= \frac{\$181,400 + \$11,600}{100\% - 39\%}$$

$$= \frac{\$193,000}{61\%}$$

$$= \$316,390 \text{ or } \underline{\$316,400}$$

Again, let us see if this answer is correct.

Revenue	$316,400
Variable costs 39% × $316,400	$123,400
Fixed costs	181,400
Total costs	$304,800
Profit (income)	$ 11,600

What About Multiple Changes?

So far, only single changes have been considered. Multiple changes can be handled in the same way with no difficulties. For example, let us assume we are going to spend $5,000 more on advertising, that our maids are to get a 20 percent wage increase and, in addition, we now want our profit to be $20,000 rather than $11,600. What must our revenue level be? Combining all these changes into one equation we have:

Combined changes

$$\text{Revenue level} = \frac{\$181,400 + \$5,000 + \$20,000}{100\% - 39\%}$$

$$= \frac{\$206,400}{61\%}$$

$$= \$338,361 \text{ or } \underline{\$338,400}$$

And the proof is:

New revenue level verified

Revenue	$338,400
Variable costs 39% × $338,400	$132,000
Fixed costs	186,400
Total costs	$318,400
Profit (income)	$ 20,000

How Can We Convert the Revenue Level Directly into Units?

In the equation used so far the denominator has been

$$100\% - \text{Variable costs as a \% of revenue}$$

The resulting net figure in the denominator is referred to as the contribution margin. In other words, if revenue is 100 percent and variable costs are 39 percent, then 61 percent of revenue is available as the contribution toward fixed costs and profit. The 61 percent figure is the contribution margin.

Contribution margin in dollars

   The contribution margin can be expressed as a dollar amount, rather than as a percentage figure. For example, the Model Motel's average room rate (average sale per room) is $20 and the variable costs (assuming an increase in maids' wages) total $7.79 per room; therefore, the contribution margin is $12.21. In fact, our general equation for the sales level (either revenue or units) can be simplified to:

$$\text{Sales level} = \frac{\text{Fixed costs} + \text{Profit desired}}{\text{Contribution margin}}$$

If we use this equation and express our contribution margin in percentages (which we have been doing), then our sales level will be expressed in revenue dollars. If we use the equation and express the contribution margin in dollars, we shall have a sales level expressed in units. Let us test this using information from the problem in the preceding section.

Sales level result in units

$$\text{Sales level (in units)} = \frac{\$181,400 + \$5,000 + \$20,000}{\$20.00 - \$7.79}$$

$$= \frac{\$206,400}{\$12.21}$$

$$= \underline{\underline{16,904}} \text{ units (rooms)}$$

The reason we might want the solution in units is that in the case of a motel or hotel it might be useful to have the sales level required converted to an occupancy percentage, and this can be quickly calculated if we know the sales level in units.

From Exhibit 9.1 we know that our present occupancy level for the 70 room Model Motel is 60 percent. This is calculated by dividing units used by units available, or:

$$\frac{15,300}{70 \times 365} \times 100 = \underline{\underline{60\%}}$$

To cover our changed fixed and variable costs we are now going to have to sell 16,904 units a year, which is an occupancy of:

New occupancy percentage required

$$\frac{16,904}{70 \times 365} \times 100 = \underline{\underline{66 + \%}}$$

If We Change Room Rates How Will This Affect Units Sold?

The contribution margin expressed in dollars is also used in answering questions concerning a change in selling prices. For example, assuming fixed costs are $186,400, profit required is $20,000, variable costs are $7.79 per room used, what will our occupancy have to be to offset a 10 percent reduction in selling prices? In other words, our new average rate will be $18.00 instead of $20.

Effect of change in rates

$$\text{Sales level (in units)} = \frac{\$186{,}400 \ + \$20{,}000}{\$18.00 \ - \ \$7.79}$$

$$= \frac{\$206{,}400}{\$10.21}$$

$$= \underline{20{,}216} \text{ units}$$

Occupancy will therefore have to be:

$$\frac{20{,}216}{70 \times 365} \times 100 \ = \ \underline{\underline{79+\%}}$$

In other words, to compensate for a 10 percent cut in selling prices, our occupancy will have to jump from 66+ percent to 79+ percent. Expressed another way, we could say that we are going to have to sell nine more rooms per night on average (13% × 70 rooms available) to pay for a decrease in average rate of 10 percent.

We could have arrived at the same result using the contribution margin expressed in percentages. In fact, it is sometimes necessary to do it this way when we have sales figures or results that cannot be converted to a unit basis. The equation in this case is a little lengthier:

Equation for contribution margin in percentage

$$\text{Sales level} = \frac{\text{Fixed cost} \ + \ \text{Profit desired}}{100\% \ - \ \left(\dfrac{\text{Present variable cost}}{100\% \ \pm \ \text{Proposed percentage change in prices}} \right)}$$

We will use the same figures we have been using: fixed cost is $186,400, profit desired $20,000, present variable cost 39 percent, and a proposed rate decrease of 10 percent. Substituting in the equation we have:

Illustration of use of equation

$$\text{Sales level} = \frac{\$186{,}400 \ + \ \$20{,}000}{100\% \ - \ \left(\dfrac{39\%}{100\% \ - \ 10\%} \right)}$$

$$= \frac{\$206{,}400}{100\% \ - \ \left(\dfrac{39\%}{90\%} \right)}$$

$$= \frac{\$206{,}400}{100\% \ - \ 43.3\%}$$

$$= \frac{\$206{,}400}{56.7\%}$$

$$= \underline{\$364{,}020}$$

In terms of number of units to be sold, this is:

$$\frac{\$364{,}020}{\$18 \text{ (new rate)}} = \underline{\underline{20{,}223}}$$

This answer of 20,223 differs slightly from the answer obtained by using the earlier method (20,216), but the difference is caused solely by some slight rounding out of certain figures in our calculations.

How Does the Equation Work if We Have a Loss?

So far we have looked at the CVP equation in break-even or profitable situations only. It can also be used to answer questions concerning a loss position. For example, suppose the Model Motel were in the following situation:

Revenue	$272,100	(13,605 units)
Variable costs 37% × $272,100	$100,700	($7.40/unit)
Fixed costs	181,400	
Total costs	$282,100	
Loss	($ 10,000)	

Elimination of loss

The question is, how much do we have to do in extra sales to eliminate the loss? The answer is to divide the amount of the loss by the contribution margin (using percentage figures if we want the answer in dollars or using dollar figures if we want the answer in units).

$$\text{Extra sales required} = \frac{\$10{,}000}{100\% - 37\%} \quad \text{or} \quad \frac{\$10{,}000}{\$20.00 - \$7.40}$$

$$= \frac{\$10{,}000}{63\%} \quad \text{or} \quad \frac{\$10{,}000}{\$12.60}$$

$$= \underline{\underline{\$15{,}873}} \text{ (or 794 units at \$20)}$$

Eliminate loss and give profit

If we wanted to calculate the additional volume required to eliminate the loss and give a profit of $15,000, the numerator becomes the amount of the loss plus the profit desired.

$$\text{Sales level required} = \frac{\$10,000 + \$15,000}{100\% - 37\%} \quad \text{or} \quad \frac{\$10,000 + \$15,000}{\$20.00 - \$7.40}$$

$$= \frac{\$25,000}{63\%} \quad \text{or} \quad \frac{\$25,000}{\$12.60}$$

$$= \underline{\$39,683} \text{ (or 1,984 units at \$20)}$$

Is our answer the correct one? This can be tested (rounding the additional revenue required to $39,700).

<table>
<tr><td rowspan="10">Proof of correctness</td><td>Previous revenue level</td><td>$272,100</td></tr>
<tr><td>Additional revenue required</td><td>39,700</td></tr>
<tr><td>Total revenue</td><td>$311,800</td></tr>
<tr><td>Variable costs 37% × $311,800</td><td>$115,400</td></tr>
<tr><td>Fixed costs</td><td>181,400</td></tr>
<tr><td>Total costs</td><td>$296,800</td></tr>
<tr><td>Profit (income)</td><td>$ 15,000</td></tr>
</table>

What About a New Investment?

Estimation of costs

The CVP equation has been used so far to illustrate how historical information from accounting records can be used to make decisions about the future. CVP analysis is equally as valid when we have no past accounting information to help us. In such a case the fixed and variable costs have to be estimated in the best possible way. Suppose our Model Motel were considering renting the adjacent premises and converting them to a fifty-seat coffee shop to better serve the needs of its motel customers. The owner of the motel and the accountant have developed the cost projections shown in Exhibit 9.7. With this information we can answer the question, What must the minimum sales be to earn the return on investment desired? This can be answered by using the basic CVP equation.

$$\text{Sales level} = \frac{\text{Fixed expenses} + \text{Return on investment (profit)}}{100\% - \text{variable cost \%}}$$

$$= \frac{\$42,800 + \$15,100}{100\% - 55\%}$$

$$= \frac{\$57,900}{45\%}$$

$$= \underline{\$128,667}, \text{ or approximately } \$129,000$$

Exhibit 9.7   Investment and cost data for proposed coffee shop.

Investment required for remodeling and for equipment and furniture, table settings, inventories, and other pre-opening items	$100,500
Annual fixed costs are estimated to be	
Rent	$ 7,500
Depreciation of furniture and equipment	5,200
Basic labor cost for supervision, food preparation, and service	24,200
Insurance, telephone, utilities, advertising	5,900
Total	$ 42,800
Variable operating costs will be kept to these levels relative to revenue	
Food cost	35%
Labor cost	15%
Other items	5%
Total	55%
Return on investment required (15% on initial investment of $100,500) =	$ 15,100

Feasibility of sales volume forecast

Assuming the estimates of costs are reasonably accurate, the owner of the Model Motel would have to decide whether the projected required revenue of $129,000 could be attained from motel customers and other potential customers in the area. If the volume could be reached, then the new venture would be profitable.

Once in business with the new restaurant, decisions about the restaurant can then be made using CVP analysis in the same way as was demonstrated for the motel operation. Restaurant sales can also be handled on a unit basis. In this case the unit is the customer and the average check is the measure of the amount of sale per unit, or customer. For example, at a restaurant sales level of $129,000 and with a $6.00 average check, the number of units (customers) is:

$$\frac{\$129,000}{\$6.00} = 21,500$$

What About the Problem of Joint Costs?

Costs shared by departments

In the problems handled to date, the fixed costs have been identified with a single operation (a motel) or department (the restaurant) and this identification has been easy. What happens in the case of joint costs, for example, a restaurant that has a food department and beverage department? Some of the costs involved will be joint costs shared by the entire operation. In such a case, as long as the variable costs can be identified for each department, CVP analysis can still be useful. The fixed costs and the fixed portion of semifixed costs can still be handled in a joint manner.

Different effect on profits

Let us consider the restaurant situation in Exhibit 9.8. Because each of the two departments has a different percentage of variable costs, and therefore a different percent of contribution margin, a given revenue increase for one department will affect profit in a way different from the same given revenue increase in the other. Consider a $15,000 sales increase in each of the two departments in Exhibit 9.8. Assuming no fixed cost change, the effect on profit will be as follows:

	Food Department	Beverage Department
Revenue increase	$15,000	$15,000
Variable costs	7,500 (50%)	6,000 (40%)
Increase in profit	$ 7,500	$ 9,000

The problem of which department the additional revenue is to come from if a revenue increase is desired is one of revenue mix. The problem does not, however, prevent us from using our CVP analysis.

Different ways to increase revenue

Let us suppose the restaurant wanted a $5,000 increase in profits, with no change in the fixed costs or in the variable cost percentages. Under these circumstances, there are three ways to obtain the extra profit: an increase in food revenue only, an increase in beverage revenue only, and (what is more likely to happen in practice) a combined increase in food and beverage revenue.

Exhibit 9.8 Operation with joint fixed costs.

	Food Department		Beverage Department	
Revenue	$150,000	100%	$50,000	100%
Variable costs	75,000	50%	20,000	40%
Contribution margin	$ 75,000	50%	$30,000	60%
Total contribution margin		$105,000 ($75,000 + $30,000)		
Fixed costs		85,000		
Profit (income)		$ 20,000		

Increase in Food Revenue Only. In the case of increasing food revenue only, the solution is arrived at with the basic CVP equation:

$$\text{Food revenue} = \frac{\text{Profit required}}{100\% - \text{Variable food \% to food revenue}}$$

$$= \frac{\text{Profit required}}{\text{Food contribution margin \%}}$$

$$= \frac{\$5,000}{50\%}$$

$$= \underline{\underline{\$10,000}}$$

Substitution of contribution margin

Increase in Beverage Revenue Only. The approach is exactly the same as for a food revenue increase only, except that we substitute the beverage contribution margin percentage for the food contribution margin percentage.

$$\text{Beverage revenue} = \frac{\$5,000}{60\%}$$

$$= \underline{\underline{\$8,333}}$$

Combined Increase in Food and Beverage Revenue. Since food revenue increases have a different effect on profit than beverage revenue increases, to calculate how much we need in combined total revenue, we have to specify the anticipated ratio of food revenue to total revenue and the ratio of beverage revenue to total revenue. Let us suppose that any revenue increases will be in the ratio of 75 percent food and 25 percent beverage. Our equation for solving this type of revenue mix problem is:

$$\left(\begin{array}{c}\text{Combined revenue} \\ \text{required}\end{array}\right) = \frac{\text{Profit}}{\begin{array}{c}(\text{Food revenue to total revenue percentage} \times \text{Food contribution margin}) \\ + (\text{Beverage revenue to total revenue percentage} \\ \times \text{Beverage contribution margin})\end{array}}$$

$$= \frac{\$5,000}{(75\% \times 50\%) + (25\% \times 60\%)}$$

$$= \frac{\$5,000}{37\frac{1}{2}\% + 15\%}$$

$$= \frac{\$5,000}{52\frac{1}{2}\%}$$

$$= \underline{\underline{\$9,524}}$$

	Weighted contribution margin

It should be noted that the 52½% contribution margin in this illustration is a weighted figure. It is weighted by the revenue mix. We can easily check the accuracy of the answer obtained.

	Food		**Beverage**	
Revenue	75% × $9,524 = $7,143		25% × $9,524 = $2,381	
Variable costs	50% × $7,143 =	3,572	40% × $2,381 =	952
Contribution to profit		$3,571		$1,429

Combined profit (income) $3,571 + $1,429 = $5,000

Compound Changes.   Compound changes can be made with no difficulty. With reference to Exhibit 9.8, let us ask the following question: What would the total revenue level be if we wanted a profit of $25,000, if fixed costs increased to $87,000, and if the revenue ratio changed to 70 percent for food and 30 percent for beverage? There is no change in the contribution margin percentages. The solution is:

Illustration of multiple changes

$$\text{Total revenue} = \frac{\$87,000 + \$25,000}{(70\% \times 50\%) + (30\% \times 60\%)}$$

$$= \frac{\$112,000}{(35\% + 18\%)}$$

$$= \frac{\$112,000}{53\%}$$

$$= \$211,320 \text{ or } \underline{\$211,300}$$

To confirm whether this is the correct answer, we can prepare a new income statement for the restaurant as in Exhibit 9.9.

Exhibit 9.9.   Income statement proving correctness of calculations.

	Food Department		**Beverage Department**	
Revenue	70% × $211,300 = $147,900		30% × $211,300 = $63,400	
Variable costs	50% × $147,900 =	73,950	40% × $ 63,400 =	25,350
Contribution margin		$ 73,950		$38,050
Total contribution margin	$112,000 ($73,950 + $38,050)			
Fixed costs	87,000			
Profit	$ 25,000			

INCOME TAXES

To this point in the discussion of CVP analysis, the effect of income taxes has been ignored. Obviously, at the break-even level of sales there are no tax implications because there is no profit. Also, with a proprietorship or partnership the organization pays no income taxes. Any profits are deemed to be paid out to the owner(s), who then pay income tax on those profits at personal tax rates.

An incorporated company that has a taxable net income must, however, consider the tax implications when using CVP for decisions. Unfortunately, income tax is neither a fixed cost nor a variable cost dependent on sales. Taxes vary with income before tax and thus require special treatment in CVP analysis. This requires adjusting the CVP equation, substituting the term "profit desired" for "profit before tax."

Consider the figures used earlier in this chapter where the motel's net income desired was $39,000 and the sales required to achieve this were calculated to be $350,000. Assume now that the motel is in a 45 percent tax bracket. What sales are required to achieve a $39,000 after-tax profit? The $39,000 can be converted to a before-tax figure as follows:

Before tax equation

$$\text{Profit before tax} = \frac{\text{After-tax profit}}{1 - \text{Tax rate}}$$

and substituting our figures:

$$= \frac{\$39,000}{1 - 0.45}$$

$$= \frac{\$39,000}{0.55}$$

$$= \$70,909 \text{ (rounded to } \$71,000)$$

This can be proved:

Proof of calculations

Before-tax profit	$71,000
Income tax 45%	32,000
After-tax profit	$39,000

Thus, if the motel with fixed costs of $181,400 and variable costs of 37 percent of revenue wanted a before-tax profit of $71,000, the sales would have to be:

$$\frac{\$181,400 + \$71,000}{1 - 0.37} = \frac{\$252,400}{0.63} = \$400,600 \text{ (rounded)}$$

This can be proved as follows:

Revenue	$400,600
Variable costs 37% × $400,600	$148,200
Fixed costs	181,400
Total costs	$329,600
Profit before tax	$ 71,000

CONCLUDING COMMENTS

Refer to assumptions and limitations

We have seen only a few of the ways in which the CVP approach and the CVP equations can provide useful information for decision making. However, the mathematical answers arrived at are only as accurate as the cost breakdowns used and the forecasts about changing costs and sales levels. The results of CVP analysis are not guaranteed because uncertainty about the future can never be eliminated. However, uncertainty is reduced using CVP analysis. Without it, decisions made might be nothing more than guesses. Finally, the reader is cautioned to refer again to the assumptions and limitations about CVP analysis listed at the beginning of this chapter.

SUMMARY

CVP analysis is a method of using knowledge about the level of fixed and variable costs in a business to help in making certain business decisions. The CVP approach must only be used with full knowledge about the assumptions and limitations inherent in it.

Information about sales, costs, and profits can be presented in a graphical form. Graphs are easy to prepare, and the information wanted can be read quickly. Graphs, however, are not too flexible when a variety of possible changes are to be introduced. In such cases an arithmetical approach using the CVP formula is much handier. The basic equation is

$$\frac{\text{Sales level}}{\text{(in dollars)}} = \frac{\text{Fixed costs} + \text{Profit desired}}{100\% - \text{Variable costs as a \% of revenue}}$$

If we wanted a sales level expressed in number of units (for example, number of rooms or number of customers) the equation is

$$\text{Sales level (in units)} = \frac{\text{Fixed costs} + \text{Profit desired}}{\underset{\text{(in dollars)}}{\text{Selling price per unit}} - \underset{\text{(in dollars)}}{\text{Variable costs per unit}}}$$

In both the above equations, the denominator is termed the "contribution margin." Depending on whether the sales level is wanted in dollars or units, the general CVP formula can be abbreviated to

$$\text{Sales level} = \frac{\text{Fixed costs} + \text{Profit desired}}{\text{Contribution margin}}$$

With the CVP equation any of the variables (fixed costs, profit, variable costs) can be changed individually, or they can all be changed together, and the required sales level can be calculated. A special equation is required if unit selling prices are to be changed and variable costs are to be expressed as a percentage of revenue. It is

$$\text{Sales level} = \frac{\text{Fixed cost} + \text{Profit desired}}{100\% - \left(\dfrac{\text{Present variable cost } \%}{100\% \pm \text{Proposed percentage change in price}} \right)}$$

The CVP formula can also be used where there are two or more departments (even if they have joint fixed costs) as long as the variable costs can be identified for each department, and thus a contribution margin percentage calculated for each department. The equation is

$$\text{Sales level} = \frac{\text{Fixed costs} + \text{Profit desired}}{\begin{pmatrix} \text{Department } A \text{ percentage of} \\ \text{total revenue} \times \text{Department} \\ A \text{ contribution margin} \\ \text{percentage} \end{pmatrix} + \begin{pmatrix} \text{Department } B \text{ percentage of} \\ \text{total revenue} \times \text{Department} \\ B \text{ contribution margin} \\ \text{percentage} \end{pmatrix}}$$

Although the equation shown is for two departments, it can be extended for as many departments as an establishment may have.

Finally, the CVP analysis equation can be amended to take income tax rates into consideration. The equation for converting an after-tax profit to a before-tax profit is:

$$\frac{\text{After-tax profit}}{1 - \text{Tax rate}}$$

DISCUSSION QUESTIONS

1. Discuss two of the assumptions built into CVP analysis.

2. Discuss two of the limitations built into CVP analysis.

3. Give a brief explanation of how to prepare a break-even graph or chart to be used in CVP analysis.

4. If one has used a break-even graph to determine the break-even level of revenue, how can one arithmetically test that the level selected is correct?

5. In an ongoing business, why is a graph not necessarily the best technique to use in CVP analysis?

6. What is the equation for calculating a particular revenue level in dollars using CVP analysis?

7. What is the equation for calculating a sales level in units using CVP analysis?

8. Define the term "contribution margin."

9. If an enterprise is operating at a loss and wishes to know the sales level it would have to achieve in order to make a specific profit, how can sales level be calculated?

10. In studying the feasibility of a new operation, how can CVP analysis be used to determine the volume of sales required to give a desired return on investment?

11. A restaurant has a food department and a beverage department. Total revenue is made up of 80 percent food and 20 percent beverages. Food variable costs are 35 percent, beverage variable costs are 33 percent. What is the restaurant's combined contribution margin?

12. State the equation for converting an after-tax profit figure to a before-tax profit amount.

PROBLEMS

9.1 A restaurant has the following average monthly figures:

Revenue	$500,000 (average guest spending $10.00)
Variable costs	260,000
Fixed costs	160,000

a. Prepare a chart or graph to illustrate this information.
b. From the chart, what is the break-even level of revenue?

c. If revenue were $440,000, what would be the restaurant's profit?

d. Assuming that $440,000 was the restaurant's level of revenue, how many fewer customers per month would be served than at a level of $500,000 (assume average check stays at $10)? Can this decrease in numbers of guests be read directly from the chart?

9.2 A restaurant is planned that will require an investment of $150,000 in equipment by the owner.

> Variable costs will be:
> food, 40% of revenue
> wages, 25% of revenue
> other items, 10% of revenue
> Fixed costs will be:

management salary and other wages	$22,000
insurance	2,500
advertising and utilities	3,700
rent	12,000
equipment depreciation	20%

a. What is the break-even level of revenue for the restaurant?

b. What level of revenue will it have to achieve if the owner wants a 10 percent return on his investment?

9.3 The owner of a cocktail bar is presently doing $500,000 a year in sales. Liquor cost is 40 percent and other variable costs at this level of revenue total $150,000. Fixed costs are $120,000, including the owner's salary.

a. What is the present annual profit?

b. The owner wishes to take $10,000 more a year out of the business (that is, increase her salary). By how much will revenue have to increase to give this added salary and maintain the present profit level? (Assume that any revenue increase will be from serving more customers, rather than by increasing selling prices.)

c. Rather than increase her revenue by serving more customers, the owner decides to raise present prices by 5 percent. If she could do this without losing any present customers and without paying any more for liquor than she is doing now, or increasing other variable costs, what will the bar's profit be (assume she is going to take out the extra $10,000 a year in salary)?

d. With the new pricing structure as indicated in part **c**, how much could revenue decrease before the bar started making less than $30,000 profit per year?

9.4 A motel has seventy rooms it usually rents out in the following proportions:

> 40% singles at $48.00/night
> 40% doubles at $60.00/night
> 20% triples at $72.00/night

Fixed costs of the motel are $345,000 annually. Variable costs are $15.00 per room occupied.

a. Calculate the motel's break-even level of occupancy.

b. Calculate the occupancy that will give the owner a profit of $60,000 a year.

c. Calculate the occupancy required to give a $60,000 profit if the average rate were decreased by 20 percent.

d. Calculate the occupancy required to give a $60,000 profit assuming the average rate is going to be increased by 10 percent, that variable costs per unit sold will be $16.20, and that $30,000 per year is to be spent on advertising.

9.5 A ninety-room motel has a present average room rate of $65.60. Its fixed costs are $300,000 a year and its variable costs total $476,000 at an average occupancy of 70 percent.

a. What is the motel's occupancy break-even level?

b. What level of revenue is required to give a profit of $100,000 a year?

c. If average room rate is increased by $8.00, and $100,000 a year were desired as a profit, how many fewer rooms per night would need to be sold than is the case in part **b**?

d. Wage rates for maids are to be increased by $4.00/hr. It takes a maid half an hour to clean a room. Other cost increases are going to cause an increase of $1.00 in the variable cost per room occupied. Fixed wages and other fixed costs are expected to go up by $4,000 a month. To compensate for the increase in room rate to $73.60 (see part **c**), $30,000 more per year is to be spent on advertising to bring in more guests. The owners want their profit to be increased by 20 percent over the present $100,000 per year. What level of revenue is required? What is that in terms of an occupancy percentage?

9.6 The Relax Inn's rooms department has annual sales of $600,000 and variable costs of $180,000. The Inn's food department has annual sales of $200,000 and variable costs of $180,000. The Inn's fixed costs are $220,000. (Ignore income tax.)

a. Calculate the Inn's break-even point, assuming that the ratio of rooms sales to food sales remains constant at any level of total sales.

b. The owners want to increase their restaurant revenue. To do this they plan to spend $1,000 (a fixed cost) on brochures to be displayed in the guest rooms. What level of incremental food sales must be achieved to cover the brochure cost? (Assume that room sales stay constant.)

c. If the Inn's owners wished to increase their net income by $40,000 by increasing their rooms occupancy rate, what increase in room sales is required? (Assume that there will be no effect on food sales.)

9.7 A motel has a rooms department and a dining room. Annual revenue and cost figures are

	Rooms	**Food**
Revenue	$440,000	$110,000
Variable costs	132,000	66,000

Total fixed costs of the operation are $335,000.

a. What will be the increase in profit if there is a $20,000 increase in revenue only in the rooms department?

b. What will be the increase in profit if there is a $20,000 increase in revenue only in the food department?

c. If we want to double the present profit, by how much would room revenue only have to increase? (What would the additional room revenue have to be?)

d. If we want to double the present profit, by how much would food revenue only have to increase?

e. If we want to double the present profit with a combined increase in revenue from both departments, what would this combined increase be? (Assume revenue ratios stay as at present.)

f. What would total revenue have to be to give us all of the following:

  i. A doubling of present profit.

  ii. $5,000 more spent on advertising.

  iii. The revenue ratio to change from its present 80%:20% (rooms:food) to 75%:25%.

  iv. Food variable costs to be decreased to 50 percent.

9.8 A neighborhood restaurant open for lunch only has only five items on its food menu. A history of the total revenue of food and beverage shows the following:

Item	Item Sales as Percentage of Total Revenue
Food 1	16%
Food 2	20
Food 3	22
Food 4	14
Food 5	8
Beverage	20

Food item selling prices and variable costs are as follows:

Item	Selling Price	Variable Cost
Food 1	$7.50	$3.90
Food 2	6.30	3.78
Food 3	5.50	2.75
Food 4	4.40	1.54
Food 5	4.80	3.36

Total variable cost on beverage revenue averages 55 percent. The restaurant has fixed costs of $273,000 a year and wants a profit of $25,000 a year.

a. What level of revenue will give the desired profit?

b. Because of relatively low sales of food item 5 and its relatively high variable cost percentage, the management is considering removing this item from the menu. It is felt that customers who formerly favored this item would then be split evenly over the remaining four items. Management also believes that by improved cost control, the beverage variable cost percentage can be reduced to 52 percent. Given these circumstances, what level of revenue will now show a $25,000 profit?

c. Assuming that the level of revenue remained as in the answer to part **a**, but all the changes stated in part **b** were made, what would be the restaurant's profit?

9.9 An owner has $100,000 to invest in a new restaurant: $80,000 of it for furniture and equipment and the balance for working capital (such as cash on hand and inventory). Estimates for the first year of business are that food cost will be 35 percent, variable wage cost 30 percent, and other variable costs 15 percent of total annual revenue. Other cost estimates are:

Management and supervisory salaries	$24,600
Rent	16,000
Insurance	2,400
Depreciation on furniture and equipment	20%

The owner wants a 20 percent before tax return on his initial investment. As an alternative, the owner is considering borrowing $30,000 from the bank at a 10 percent interest rate, instead of using all his own money for the investment, and, instead of buying the equipment outright, he would rent $20,000 of it at a rental cost of $5,000 a year (the rent amount would be an operating expense). For each alternative (that is, using all his own money, or borrowing some and renting equipment), calculate the required annual revenue that will give him the desired profit.

9.10 The Riviera Resort hotel has total annual revenue of $1,000,000, variable costs of $350,000, and fixed costs of $570,000. The fixed costs include $80,000 a year for land rent.

a. Calculate the hotel's break-even point.

b. If the hotel's owners had an equity investment in the business of $1,000,000, what level of sales is needed to give them a 12 percent return (before tax) on their investment?

c. In a renegotiation of the land lease, the land owner has offered the resort's management an alternative to the fixed lease amount presently being paid. The alternative is 10 percent of the resort's contribution margin.

    i. If management accepts this proposal, what would be the resort's new break-even point?

    ii. Should management accept this proposal if they expect next year's total revenue to be $1,200,000?

    iii. Should management accept this proposal if they expect next year's total revenue to be $1,400,000?

    iv. Calculate the indifference point.

9.11 A hotel management company operates a leased hotel with present revenue of $2,000,000 a year, variable costs of $800,000, and fixed costs of $1,100,000. The lease contract calls for the company to pay an annual rental of 5 percent of revenue plus a fixed amount of $80,000. The owners of the building wish to renegotiate the lease contract for next year and are asking for a flat 10 percent of revenue and no fixed amount, or, alternatively, 7 percent of revenue plus a fixed amount of $30,000. The hotel company anticipates revenue will increase by 10 percent next year.

    a. Under each alternative, state whether or not the hotel company would be wise to sign the lease. Support your statement with any necessary calculations.

    b. Calculate the percentage rate at which rent, based solely on a percentage of revenue for next year, would be equivalent to 5 percent of next year's revenue plus $80,000.

9.12 The Swiss Inn restaurant has annual fixed costs of $86,000, variable costs of 70 percent of sales, and a tax rate of 25 percent. The restaurant's owner wants an after-tax profit next year of $30,000.

    a. What sales level must the Swiss Inn achieve to provide this?

    b. Prove your answer.

CASE 9

An analysis of the 4C Company's restaurant costs for the year 0001 revealed the following:

- **Food and beverage.** Directly variable with total revenue.
- **Salary and wages.** $156,400 fixed, the remainder directly variable with total revenue.
- **Laundry.** Directly variable with total revenue.
- **Kitchen fuel.** $3,800 fixed, the remainder directly variable with total revenue.
- **China, glass, etc.** Directly variable with total revenue.

- **Contract cleaning.** Fixed.
- **Licenses.** Fixed.
- **Other operating expenses.** Directly variable with total revenue.
- **Administrative and general.** Fixed.
- **Marketing.** Fixed.
- **Energy costs.** $3,100 fixed, the remainder directly variable with total revenue.
- **Insurance.** Fixed.
- **Rent.** Fixed.
- **Interest.** Fixed.
- **Depreciation.** Fixed.

a. Refer to the income statements in Cases 2 and 3 and calculate the restaurant's total variable cost as a percentage of total revenue.
b. Calculate the restaurant's total fixed cost.
c. Calculate the restaurant's break-even level of revenue and express it in terms of number of guests.
d. In year 0001 the restaurant's income before income tax is 3 percent of total revenue. How many extra guests would it require to raise this figure to 5 percent?

10 Budgeting

Chapter Highlights

This chapter begins by defining budgeting and its purposes and then describes various kinds of budgets such as capital, operating, department, master, fixed, and flexible.

The responsibility for budget preparation is discussed. The advantages and disadvantages of budgeting are covered.

The reader is then taken through the five-step cycle of the budgeting process:

- Establishing attainable goals or objectives.
- Planning to achieve these goals or objectives.
- Comparing actual results with those planned and analyzing the differences (variances).
- As a result of step three, taking any corrective action if required.
- Improving the effectiveness of budgeting.

The steps in the preparation of a departmental income budget are then detailed (since it is from these budgets that most of the other kinds of budgets are derived). Budgeting in a new operation, which has no information from the past on which to base budgets, is then discussed.

Zero-based budgeting (ZBB) is covered with reference to its value in controlling some types of undistributed cost. The two major aspects of ZBB (decision unit analysis and ranking) are discussed in some detail.

The chapter concludes with a section on variance analysis.

Chapter Objectives

After studying this chapter the reader should be able to:

1. Explain the concept of budgeting.
2. Define the three purposes of budgeting.
3. Describe some of the types of budgets, such as departmental, capital, fixed, and flexible.
4. Briefly discuss some of the advantages and disadvantages of budgeting.
5. List and briefly discuss each of the five steps in the budget cycle.
6. Briefly explain some of the limiting factors to be kept in mind when budgeting.
7. Define the term "derived demand."
8. Explain what information is required to determine budgeted revenue in a restaurant operation, and budgeted revenue in the rooms department of a hotel or motel.
9. Prepare budgeted (pro forma) income statements given appropriate information about estimated revenue and costs.
10. Discuss ZBB with reference to decision units and the ranking process.
11. Briefly discuss the pros and cons of ZBB.
12. Use variance analysis to compare budgeted figures with actual results.

BUDGETING

Forecasts up to five years

Budgeting is planning. In order to make meaningful decisions about the future, a manager must look ahead. One way to look ahead is to prepare budgets or forecasts. A forecast may be very simple. For a restaurant owner/operator the budget may be no more than looking ahead to tomorrow, estimating how many customers will eat in the restaurant, and purchasing food and supplies to accommodate this need. On the other hand, in a large organization a budget may entail forecasts up to five years (such as for furniture and equipment purchases), as well as requiring day-to-day budgets (such as staff scheduling). Budgets are not necessarily always expressed in monetary terms. They could involve numbers of customers to be served, number of rooms to be occupied, number of employees required, or some other unit as opposed to dollars.

The main purposes of budgeting can be summarized as follows:

1. To provide organized estimates of future revenues, expenses, manpower requirements, or equipment needs, broken down by time period and department.
2. To provide a coordinated management policy both long-term and short-term, expressed primarily in accounting terms.
3. To provide a method of control so that actual results can be evaluated against budget plans and adjustment, if necessary, can be made.

KINDS OF BUDGETS

There are a number of different kinds or types of budgets. The following are some of these:

Policies for long-term plans

Long-term versus Short-term Budgets. Budgets can generally be considered to be either long-term or short-term. A long-term or strategic budget would be anywhere from one year to five years ahead. Such a budget concerns the major plans for the organization (expansion, creation of a new market, financing, and other related matters). From such long-term plans evolve the policies concerning the day-to-day operations of the business, and thus the short-term budgets.

Short-term budgets could be for a day, a week, a quarter, or a year, or for any period less than a year. Such budgets involve middle management in using its resources to meet the objectives of the long-term plans.

Capital Budget. A capital budget relates to items that appear on the balance sheet. A three-month budget for a restaurant is a capital budget. A five-year replacement schedule for hotel room furnishings is also a capital budget.

Budget for ongoing revenue and expenses

Operating Budget. An operating budget concerns the ongoing projections of revenue and expense items that affect the income statement. For example, a forecast of revenue for a restaurant for a month is an operating budget. Similarly, in a multidepartment hotel the forecast of total payroll expense for the year is an operating budget.

Periodic departmental budgets

Department Budget. A department budget would only be of concern to a restaurant complex (with, for example, dining room, bar, and banquet areas) where departmental income statements are prepared, or to a hotel that has a number of departments. A department budget would, therefore, be for a specific department, and show the forecast revenue less operating expenses for that department. Alternatively, if a department does not directly generate any revenue (for example, the maintenance department of a hotel), a department budget could be prepared showing anticipated expenses in detail for a period of time. Generally such department budgets are prepared annually, broken down month by month.

Master Budget. A master budget is the most comprehensive of all budgets. Generally a master budget is prepared for a year's period and includes a balance sheet for a year hence, and all the departmental income and expense statements for the next year's period.

Difficulty with fixed budget

Fixed versus Flexible Budgets. A fixed budget is one that is based on a certain level of activity or revenue. Expense estimates are based on this level of sales. No attempt is made to introduce greater or lesser levels of sales revenue, and thus different expense amounts in the budget. The disadvantage of such a budget is that, if the actual sales level differs from budgeted sales level, because there is no plan covering this possibility, expenses can only then be adjusted in the short run by guesswork. For example, suppose the rooms department budget in a hotel is based on an average year-round rooms occupancy of 70 percent. Operating costs (such as payroll, supplies, linen, and laundry) are based on this level of occupancy. If actual occupancy dropped to 60 percent because of unforeseen economic conditions, it might be difficult for the rooms department manager to know, in the short run, what the new payroll level should be, and similarly with the other expenses.

On the other hand, a flexible (or variable) budget is prepared based on several levels of activity. In our rooms department, revenue could be forecast for 60 percent, 70 percent, and 80 percent occupancy levels (or as many levels as are appropriate). As the actual year progresses it can be determined at which level the operation is going to fit best, and the appropriate expense levels will have already been determined for this

Management prepared for adjustment

level. In other words adjustment is easier. The question could be raised, using the rooms department example, whether it is truly flexible (variable) budgeting, or whether it is three (or more, if more occupancy levels are used) fixed budgets at three different occupancy levels. The question is valid, but the practical result is that management is prepared to adjust to the actual situation when adjustment is required.

Even with flexible budgeting it is possible for a particular expense to remain fixed. For example, a budget might be prepared for a restaurant based on a number of levels of revenue. Expenses are calculated based on each different revenue level. However, advertising expense might be left the same (that is, fixed) regardless of the actual level of revenue. In other words, regardless of the volume of sales, a definite, fixed amount is budgeted to be spent on this expense. A really flexible budget would show expenses that are truly variable with revenue as a percentage of that revenue, and fixed costs as a dollar amount.

BUDGET PREPARATION

Involve department heads

In a small, owner-operated restaurant or motel, the owner would prepare the budget. If it were a formal budget, the help of an accountant might be useful. If the budget were an informal one, there might be no written supporting figures. The owner might just have a mental plan about where he or she wants to go and operate from day to day to achieve the objective, or come as close to it as possible.

In a larger organization, a great many individuals might be involved in budget preparation. In such organizations budgets are prepared from the bottom up. At the very least, the department heads or managers must be involved. If their subsequent performance is to be evaluated on the plans included in the budget, then they should be involved in preparing their own departmental budgets. They in turn might well discuss the budget figures with employees in their own departments.

Above the department heads would be a budget committee. Department managers might be members of this committee. Such a committee is required for overall coordination of the budget to ensure that the final budget package is meaningful. For example, the rooms occupancy of a hotel determines, to a great extent, the breakfast revenue for the food department. The budget committee must ensure that the food breakfast sales are not based on an occupancy that differs from the rooms department figure.

Final budget submission

The formal preparation of the budget is a function of the accounting department. The organization's comptroller would probably be a member of the budget committee, and his or her task is to prepare final budget information for submission to the general manager for approval.

The worst form of budget preparation is to have budgets imposed from the top down through the accounting department to the operating and other departments. Coordination might be present, but the cooperation of the employees where the activity takes place will be minimal.

When Are Budgets Prepared?

Long-range budgets for up to five years forward are generally prepared annually by top-level management. They may or may not involve department managers. Each year such budgets are revised for the next period (up to five years) forward. For coordination the budget committee would be involved.

Revising monthly budgets

Short-term budgets are prepared annually, for the most part, with monthly projections. Each month, budgets for the remaining months of the year should be revised to adjust for any changed circumstances. Department managers should be involved in such revisions, as should the budget committee for overall coordination.

Weekly or daily short-range budgets are usually handled internally by the department heads or other supervisory staff. For example, the house-keeper would arrange the maid staffing schedule (which affects the pay-roll budget) on a daily basis based on the anticipated rooms occupancy.

ADVANTAGES AND DISADVANTAGES OF BUDGETING

A number of advantages accrue to an organization that uses a budget planning process.

1. Since the budgeting process involves department heads and possibly other staff within the department, it encourages their participation and thus improves communication and motivation. The operating personnel can better identify with the plans or objectives of the organization.

Alternative courses of action

2. In preparing the budget, those involved are required to consider alternative courses of action. For example, should the advertising budget be spent to promote the organization as a whole, or would better results be obtained if emphasis were placed more on a particular department rather than another? At the department level a restaurant manager might need to consider increasing the number of customers to be served per meal period per waiter (increased productivity per waiter) against the possible effects of slower service, reduced seat turnover, and perhaps lower total revenue.

3. Budgets outline in advance the revenues to be achieved and the cost involved in achieving these revenues. After each budget period the actual results can be compared with the budget. In other words, a standard for comparison is predetermined, and subsequent self-evaluation by all those involved in the operation is possible.

Adjustment of level of activity

4. In the case of flexible budgets, the organization as a whole and each department within it are prepared for adjustment to any level of activity between minimum and maximum sales, assuming that the departments have been involved in developing their budgets within these sales levels.

5. Budgeting forces those involved to be forward-looking. This is not to suggest that what happened in the past is not important and not to be considered in budget preparation; but from now on only future revenue and future costs are important to future plans and profits. For example, do our menu item selling prices need to be changed to take care of anticipated future increases in food, labor, and other operating costs?

6. Budgeting requires those involved to consider both internal and external factors. Internal factors include such matters as seating ca-

pacity, seat turnover, and menu prices in a restaurant and rooms available, rooms occupancy, and room rates in a hotel. External factors include such matters as the competition, the local economic environment in which the business operates, and the general inflation rate trend.

Obviously, just as there are advantages to budgeting, so too are there disadvantages. Some of these are

1. The time and cost to prepare budgets can be considerable. Usually, the larger the organization the larger is the amount of time, and thus the cost, of preparing budgets.

Unpredictability of future
2. Budgets are based on unknown factors (as well as some known factors) that can have a big bearing on what does actually happen. (It could be argued that this is not a disadvantage since it forces those involved to look ahead and prepare for the unknown.)

3. Budget preparation may require that confidential information be included in the budget.

Spending "surplus" funds
4. The "spending to the budget" approach can be a problem. If an expense budget is overestimated, there can be a tendency to find ways to spend the money still in the budget as the end of the budget period arrives. This tendency can be provoked by a desire to demonstrate that the budget forecast was correct to begin with and to protect the budget from being cut for the next period.

However, despite these "disadvantages," in most cases the advantages far outweigh the disadvantages.

THE BUDGET CYCLE

The budget cycle is a five-part process that can be summarized as follows:

1. Establishing attainable goals or objectives.
2. Planning to achieve these goals or objectives.
3. Comparing actual results with those planned and analyzing the differences (variances).
4. As a result of step three, taking corrective action if required.
5. Improving the effectiveness of budgeting.

Each of these five steps will be discussed in turn.

1. *Establishing Attainable Goals or Objectives.* In setting goals what would be the most desirable situation must be tempered with realism. In other words, if there are any factors present that limit revenue to a certain maximum level, these factors must be considered. An obvious example is that a hotel cannot achieve more than a 100 percent room occupancy. In the short run, room revenue (if a hotel were full every night) can only be increased by increasing room rates. But since very few hotels do run at 100 percent occupancy year-round, it would be unwise, desirable as it might be, to use 100 percent as the budgeted occupancy on an annual basis.

Similarly, a restaurant is limited to a specific number of seats. If it is running at capacity, revenue can only be increased, again in the short run, by increasing meal prices or increasing seat turnover (seat occupancy). But, again, there is a limit to increasing meal prices (customer resistance and competition often dictate upper pricing levels), and if seat turnover is increased by giving customers rushed service the end result may be declining sales.

**Training and
supervision**

Other limiting factors are a lack of skilled labor or skilled supervisory personnel. Increased productivity (serving more customers per waiter) would be desirable and would decrease our payroll cost per customer, but well-trained employees, or employees who could be trained, are often not available. Similarly, supervisory personnel who could train others are not always available.

Shortage of capital could limit expansion plans. If financing is not available to add guest rooms or expand dining areas, it would be a useless exercise to include expansion in our long-term budget.

Management's policy concerning the market in which the organization will operate may limit budgets. For example, a coffee shop department head may propose that catering to bus tour groups would help increase revenue. On the other hand, the general manager may feel that catering to such large transient groups is too disruptive to the regular clientele.

Another limiting factor might be in the area of increasing costs. An operation might find that it is restricted in its ability to pass on increasing costs by way of higher prices to its customers.

**Supply and
demand**

Finally, customer demand and competition must always be kept in mind when budgeting. In the short run there is usually only so much business to go around. Adding more rooms to a hotel does not automatically increase the demand for rooms in the area. It takes time for demand to catch up with supply, and new hotels or an additional block of rooms to an existing hotel will usually operate at a lower occupancy than normal until demand increases. A new restaurant or additional facilities to an existing restaurant must compete for its share of business.

2. *Planning to Achieve Goals or Objectives.* Once objectives have been determined, plans must be laid to achieve them. At the departmental level, a restaurant manager must staff with employees skilled enough to handle the anticipated volume of business. A chef or purchaser must purchase food in the quantities required to take care of anticipated demand, and of a quality that meets the required standards expected by the customers and allows the food operation to match as closely as possible its budgeted food cost. Over the long term, a budget expansion of facilities might require top management to make plans for financing and seek the best terms for repayment to achieve the budgeted additional profit required from expansion.

Importance of comparison of results

3. *Comparing Actual Results with Those Planned and Analyzing the Differences.* This is probably the most important and advantageous step in the budget cycle. Comparing actual results with the budget allows one to ask questions such as:

a. Our actual dining room revenue for the month of April was $30,000 instead of the budgeted $33,000. Was the $3,000 difference caused by a reduction in number of customers? If so, is there an explanation (for example, are higher prices keeping customers away or did a competitive restaurant open nearby)? Is the $3,000 difference a result of reduced seat turnover (is service slowing down)? Are customers spending less (a reduced average check, or customer spending, because of belt tightening by the customer)?

b. Yesterday the housekeeper brought in two more maids than were required to handle the actual number of rooms occupied. Is there a communication problem between the front office and the housekeeper? Did the front office fail to notify the housekeeper of reservation cancellations, or did the housekeeper err in calculating the number of maids actually required?

c. The annual cocktail lounge departmental income was greater than the previous year, but still fell short of budgeted income. Did the revenue increase reach budgeted level? Or did costs increase over the year more than in proportion to revenue? If so, which costs? Was there a change in what we sold (change in the sales mix); in other words, are we now selling less profitable items (such as more beer and wine than liquor) in proportion to total revenue?

Variances may indicate problems

These are just a few examples of the types of questions that can be asked, and for which answers should be sought, in analyzing differences between budgeted performance and actual performance. Analysis of such differences will be commented upon further in a later section of this chapter on variance analysis. It should be noted that the variances themselves do not offer solutions to possible problems. They only point out the fact that problems may exist.

**Action to take
care of causes
of variance**

4. *Taking Corrective Action if Required.* Step three in the budget process points to differences and possible causes of the differences. The next step in the budget cycle necessitates taking corrective action if required. The cause of a difference could be the result of a circumstance that no one could foresee or predict (for example, weather, a sudden change in economic conditions, or a fire in part of the premises). On the other hand, a difference could be caused by the fact that selling prices were not increased sufficiently to compensate for an inflationary rate of cost increases; or that the budgeted forecast in occupancy of guest rooms was not sufficiently reduced to compensate for the construction of a new, nearby hotel; or that staff were not as productive in number of customers served or rooms cleaned as they should have been according to predetermined standards. Whatever the reason, it should be corrected if it can be so that future budgets can more realistically predict planned operations. The fact that there are variances between budget and actual figures should not be an argument in favor of not budgeting. For, without a budget, the fact that the operation is not running as effectively as it should and could be would not even be apparent. If the variance were a favorable one (for example, guest room occupancy was higher than budgeted), the cause should also be determined because that information could help in making future budgets more accurate.

5. *Improving the Effectiveness of Budgeting.* This is the final step in the five-step budget cycle. All those involved in budgeting should be made aware of the constant need to improve the budgeting process. The information provided from past budgeting cycles and particularly the information provided from analyzing variances between actual and budgeted figures will be helpful. By improving accuracy in budgeting, the effectiveness of the entire organization is increased.

DEPARTMENTAL BUDGETS

The starting point in any complete budgeting process is the departmental income statement. The rest of the budgeting process hinges on the results of these operating departments. For example, a budgeted balance sheet cannot be made up without reference to the income statements; a cash budget cannot be prepared without knowledge of departmental revenue and expenses; long-term budgets for equipment and furniture replacement, for dividend payments, or for future financing arrangements cannot be prepared without a budget showing what income (or funds) is (are) going to be generated from the internal operation.

Budgeted income statements

The departmental budgets are probably the most difficult to prepare. However, once this has been done, the preparation of the rest of any budgets required is a relatively straightforward process. This chapter will, therefore, only deal with income statement budgets since they are the prime concern of day-to-day management of a hotel or restaurant. In summary, the procedure is as follows:

1. Estimate revenue levels by department.
2. Deduct estimated direct operating expenses for each department.
3. Combine estimated departmental operating incomes and deduct estimated undistributed expenses to arrive at net income.

Further explanation about each of these three procedures follows:

Annual comparisons too infrequent

*1. **Estimate Revenue Levels by Department.*** Even though departmental income statements are prepared for a year at a time, they should be prepared initially month by month (with revisions, if necessary, during the budget year in question). Monthly income statements are necessary so that comparisons with actual results can be made each month. If comparison between budget and actual were only made on a yearly basis, any required corrective action might already be eleven months too late. The following should be considered in monthly revenue projections.

a. past actual revenue figures and trends
b. current anticipated trends
c. economic factors
d. competitive factors
e. limiting factors

Information about how top management views these trends and factors must be communicated to those who prepare departmental budgets. This information must also be put into language that the department managers understand, that is, in specific numeric terms rather than in vague, general language. For example, if an anticipated competitor is due to open nearby during the budget period, top management must state in specific percentage terms how that may impact the operation's sales.

For example, the dining room revenue for the past three years for the month of January was:

0001	$30,000
0002	35,000
0003	37,000

It is now December in year 0003 and we are finalizing our budget for year 0004, commencing with January. The increase in volume for year 0002 over 0001 was about 17 percent ($5,000 divided by $30,000). Year 0003 increase over year 0002 was approximately 6 percent. These increases were caused entirely by increases in number of customers. The size of the restaurant has not changed and no change in size will occur in year 0004. Because a new restaurant is opening a block away we do not anticipate our customer count to increase in January, but neither do we expect to lose any of our current customers. Because of economic trends we are going to be forced to meet rising costs by increasing our menu prices by 10 percent commencing in January 0004. Our budgeted revenue for January 0004 therefore would be:

Calculation of budgeted revenue

$$\$37,000 + (10\% \times \$37,000) = \$40,700$$

The same type of reasoning would be applied for each of the eleven other months of year 0004, and for each of the other operating departments. One other factor that in some situations might need to be considered in revenue projections is that of derived demand. In other words, what happens in one department may have an effect on what happens to the revenue of another. An example of this might be a cocktail bar that generates revenue from customers in the bar area as well as from customers in the dining room where drinks are served from the adjacent bar.

Interdependence of departments

In budgeting the bar total revenue, the revenue would have to be broken down into revenue within the lounge area and revenue derived from dining room customers. Similarly, in a hotel the occupancy of the guest rooms will affect the revenue in the food and beverage areas. The interdependence of departments must, therefore, be kept in mind in the budgeting process.

2. Deduct Direct Operating Expenses for Each Department.

Since most departmental direct operating costs are specifically related to revenue levels, once the revenue has been calculated, the major part of the budget has been accomplished. Historic accounting records will generally show that each direct expense varies within very narrow limits as a percentage of revenue. The appropriate percentage of expense to revenue can therefore be applied to the budgeted revenue in order to calculate the dollar amount of the expense. For example, if laundry expense for the rooms department of a hotel varies between $4\frac{1}{2}$ to $5\frac{1}{2}$ percent of revenue, and revenue in the rooms department for a particular month is expected to be $100,000, then the laundry expense for that same month would be:

Direct expenses as percentage of revenue

$$5\% \times \$100,000 = \$5,000$$

The same is true for all other direct expenses for which cost to revenue percentages are obvious.

In certain cases, however, the problem may not be as simple because there may not be as direct a relationship between cost and revenue. A good example of this is labor, where much of the cost is fixed and does not vary as revenue goes up or down. In a restaurant the wages of the restaurant manager, the cashier, and the host are generally fixed. Such people receive a fixed salary regardless of volume of business. Only the wages of servers and bus help can be varied in the short run. In such cases, a month by month staffing schedule must be prepared listing the number of variable staff of each category required for the budgeted revenue level, calculating the total variable cost, and adding this to the fixed cost element to arrive at total labor cost for that month. It is true that this requires some detailed calculations, but without it the budget might not otherwise be as accurate as it could be for effective budgetary control.

Preparation of staffing schedules

Staffing schedules for each department for various levels of sales could be developed. These schedules would be based on past experience and the standards of performance required by the establishment. Then when sales levels are forecast the appropriate number of man-hours or staff required for each type of job can be read directly from the staffing schedule. The number of hours of staffing required or number of employees can then be multiplied by the appropriate rates of pay for each job category. A typical such staffing schedule is illustrated in Exhibit 10.1.

Alternatively, if labor (and other costs) have been broken down for use with CVP analysis (see Chapter 9) into their fixed and variable elements then this information is already available for use in budgeting.

3. Combine Departmental Operating Incomes and Deduct Undistributed Expenses to arrive at Net Income. The depart-

Deduction of unallocated expenses

mental operating incomes budgeted for in steps one and two can now be added together. At this point certain undistributed expenses must be calculated and deducted. These expenses are not distributed to the de-

Exhibit 10.1 Staffing schedule—coffee shop.

Monthly Volume in Covers	Waitress Hours	Bus Help Hours
Up to 5,500	970	485
5,500 to 6,500	1,040	485
6,500 to 7,500	1,210	485
21,500 to 22,500	3,890	990
Over 22,500	4,160	1,040

partments because an appropriate allocation is difficult to arrive at. Nor are they, for the most part, controllable by or the responsibility of the department managers.

These unallocated expenses (including fixed charges) usually include:

• Administrative and general
• Marketing
• Property operation and maintenance
• Energy costs
• Property or municipal taxes
• Rent
• Insurance
• Interest
• Depreciation
• Income taxes

Discretionary expenses

Since these expenses are usually primarily fixed, they vary little with revenue; historic records will generally indicate the narrow dollar range within which they vary.

Sometimes these expenses will vary at the discretion of the general manager. For example, it may be decided that a special extra allocation will be added to the advertising and promotion budget during the coming year, or that a particular item of expensive maintenance can be deferred for a year. In such cases the adjustment to the budget figures can be made at the general manager's level. Usually these undistributed expenses are calculated initially on an annual basis (unlike departmental revenue and direct operating expenses, which are initially calculated monthly). If an overall pro forma (projected or budgeted) income statement, including undistributed expenses, is to be prepared monthly, then the simplest method is to divide each undistributed expense by twelve

Exhibit 10.2 Undistributed costs allocated on time basis.

	Quarter 1	Quarter 2	Quarter 3	Quarter 4	Annual Total
Revenue	$300,000	$600,000	$800,000	$300,000	$2,000,000
Direct operating expenses	(250,000)	(450,000)	(550,000)	(250,000)	(1,500,000)
Operating income	$ 50,000	$150,000	$250,000	$ 50,000	$ 500,000
Undistributed costs	(75,000)	(75,000)	(75,000)	(75,000)	(300,000)
Net income (loss)	($ 25,000)	$ 75,000	$175,000	($ 25,000)	$ 200,000

Exhibit 10.3 Calculation of undistributed cost breakdown by sales volume.

Quarter	Revenue	Percent to Total Revenue	Share of Undistributed Costs
1	$ 300,000	15%	15% × $300,000 = $ 45,000
2	600,000	30	30 × $300,000 = 90,000
3	800,000	40	40 × $300,000 = 120,000
4	300,000	15	15 × $300,000 = 45,000
Totals	$2,000,000	100%	$300,000

and show one-twelfth of the expense for each month of the year. A three-month budget would show one-fourth of the total annual expense. (Note that it is only the undistributed expenses that are handled in this way. Revenue and allocated direct expenses should be calculated correctly month by month to take care of monthly or seasonal variations.)

Unallocated expenses as a ratio of revenue

For example, Exhibit 10.2 shows how the undistributed costs could be allocated in a budget prepared on a quarterly basis. Exhibit 10.2 also indicates a budgeted loss in two of the quarters. It is argued that such budgeted losses are misleading, because the quarters with low revenue are unfairly burdened with undistributed costs. A fairer way to distribute such costs would be in ratio to budgeted revenue. Such a distribution would be calculated as in Exhibit 10.3.

The revised budget, prepared on the new allocation of undistributed expenses to the various quarters, would be as in Exhibit 10.4. The method illustrated in Exhibit 10.4 may, as it does in our case, ensure that no period has a budgeted loss. Over the year, however, there is no change in total net income.

Exhibit 10.4 Allocation of undistributed costs on sales volume basis.

	Quarter 1	Quarter 2	Quarter 3	Quarter 4	Annual Total
Revenue	$300,000	$600,000	$800,000	$300,000	$2,000,000
Direct operating expenses	(250,000)	(450,000)	(550,000)	(250,000)	(1,500,000)
Operating income	$ 50,000	$150,000	$250,000	$ 50,000	$ 500,000
Undistributed costs	(45,000)	(90,000)	(120,000)	(45,000)	(300,000)
Net income	$ 5,000	$ 60,000	$130,000	$ 5,000	$ 200,000

BUDGETING IN A NEW OPERATION

New hotels and restaurants will find it more difficult to budget in their early years because they have no internal historic information to serve as a base. If a feasibility study had been prepared prior to opening, it could serve as a base for budgeting. Alternatively, forecasts must be based on a combination of known facts and industry or market averages for the type and size of operation. For example, a restaurant could use the following equation for calculating its breakfast revenue:

Forecasting meal period revenue

$$\begin{array}{c}\text{Number} \\ \text{of} \\ \text{seats}\end{array} \times \begin{array}{c}\text{Seat} \\ \text{turnover} \\ \text{rate}\end{array} \times \begin{array}{c}\text{Average} \\ \text{check}\end{array} \times \begin{array}{c}\text{Days} \\ \text{open in} \\ \text{month}\end{array} = \begin{array}{c}\text{Breakfast} \\ \text{total} \\ \text{monthly} \\ \text{revenue}\end{array}$$

This same equation could be used for the luncheon period, for the dinner period, and even separately for coffee breaks. Meal periods should be separated because seat turnover rates and average check figures can vary considerably from period to period. The number of seats and days open in the month figures in the above equation are known facts. The seat turnover rates and average check figures can be obtained by reference to published information or from observation at competitive restaurants.

Once monthly revenue figures have been calculated for each meal period they can be added together to give total revenue. Direct operating expenses can then be deducted applying industry average percentage figures for each expense to the calculated budgeted revenue.

In a rooms department a similar type of equation would be:

Forecasting room revenue

$$\begin{array}{c}\text{Forecast} \\ \text{occupancy} \\ \text{percentage}\end{array} \times \begin{array}{c}\text{Average} \\ \text{room} \\ \text{rate}\end{array} \times \begin{array}{c}\text{Number} \\ \text{of rooms} \\ \text{available}\end{array} \times \begin{array}{c}\text{Days} \\ \text{in} \\ \text{month}\end{array} = \begin{array}{c}\text{Total} \\ \text{revenue for} \\ \text{month}\end{array}$$

Again, direct operating expenses can then be budgeted for using industry percentages for the type of hotel. Note that, to arrive at the average room rate to be used in the above equation, one must consider the rooms sales mix: that is, the rates for different rooms and for different market segments and for discounted rates for weekends and off-seasons. The reader is referred to Chapter 6 for a comprehensive discussion of room rate pricing.

Beverage figures are a little more difficult to calculate. There are some industry guidelines in that a coffee shop serving beer and wine generates alcoholic beverage revenue approximating 5 to 15 percent of food revenue. In a dining room the alcoholic beverage revenue (beer, wine, and liquor) approximates 25 to 30 percent of food revenue. For example, a dining room with $100,000 a month of food revenue could expect to have about $25,000 to $30,000 of total liquor revenue. These are only approximate figures, but they may be the only ones that can be used until the operation can refer to its own accounting records.

Refer to historic records

As for beverage figures in a cocktail lounge, there is no simple equation. An average check figure (such as average spending figure per customer) can be misleading. For example, one customer can occupy a seat and spend $3 on five drinks; average spending for that customer is $15. On the other hand, five different customers could occupy the same seat and each spend $3 over the same period of time: average spending, $3. Therefore, the equation used for calculating food revenue may be difficult to apply in a bar setting. One alternative is to use the current industry average revenue per seat per year in a cocktail bar.

Forecasting lounge revenue

$$\begin{array}{c}\text{Average annual} \\ \text{revenue} \\ \text{per seat}\end{array} \times \begin{array}{c}\text{Number} \\ \text{of} \\ \text{seats}\end{array} = \begin{array}{c}\text{Total} \\ \text{annual} \\ \text{revenue}\end{array}$$

To convert to a monthly basis for budget purposes, this figure can then be divided by twelve and added to the already calculated beverage revenue by month generated from the food departments. Direct operating expenses can then be allocated by using industry average percentage guidelines.

Although these equations do not cover all possible approaches they should give the reader some idea of the methods that can be used when budgeting for a new operation.

Break down past revenue into elements

However, the equations illustrated are not limited to a new operation. They could also be used in an ongoing organization. For example, instead of applying an estimated percentage of revenue increase to last year's figure for the current year's budget, it might be better to break down last year's revenue figure into its various equation elements and adjust each of them individually (where necessary) to develop the new budget amount. For example, last year rooms revenue was $100,200 for June. This year we expect a 5 percent increase, therefore budgeted revenue will be:

$$\$100,200 \times (5\% \times \$100,200) = \$105,210$$

A more comprehensive approach would be to analyze last year's figure in the following way:

	Actual occupancy × percent	Average room rate	Number × of rooms × available	Days in = month	Total revenue for month
	83.5% ×	$40.00 ×	100 ×	30 =	$100,200

Apply current year trends

We can then apply the budget year trends and information to last year's detailed figures. In the budget period, because of a new hotel in the area, we expect a slight drop in occupancy down to 80 percent. This will be compensated for by an increase in our average room rates of 12 percent. Our budgeted revenue is therefore:

	Budgeted occupancy × percent	Budgeted average room rate	Number × of rooms × available	Days in month	Budgeted = monthly revenue
	80.0% ×	$44.80 ×	100 ×	30 =	$107,520

This approach to budgeting might require a little more work but will probably give budgeted figures that are more accurate and can be analyzed more meaningfully than would otherwise be the case.

SUMMARY OF RESULTS

Variances require explanation

As each period goes by (day, week, month, quarter), budgeted figures should be compared with actual figures. This can best be done by summarizing the figures on a report by department or by type of cost. For example, one of the major and most difficult costs to control in a hotel or food operation is labor, and an ongoing comparison of actual with budgeted labor cost is useful in controlling this cost. An illustration of a type of report summarizing payroll costs is shown in Exhibit 10.5. The variances each day would require explanation.

Variances

In analyzing variances, it may be useful to calculate percentage variances. Percentage variances are calculated by dividing the dollar variance by the budgeted figure for that item. For example, if the budgeted figure were $100, and the variance $10, the percentage variance would be

$$\frac{\$10}{\$100} \times 100 = 10\%$$

Exhibit 10.5 Sample payroll costs summary and analysis.   *Date: September 3*

Department	Number of Employees Today Budget	Actual	Labor Cost Today Budget	Actual	Labor Cost to Date Budget	Actual	Labor Cost Variance Today	To Date
Rooms								
Front office	10	10	$ 440	$ 440	$1,320	$1,320		
Housekeeping	42	43	1,280	1,310	3,840	3,900	$+30	$+60
Service	8	8	320	320	960	930		−30
Switchboard	6	6	274	274	822	822		
Food								
Dining room	13	14	$ 456	$ 487	$1,368	$1,399	$+31	$+31
Coffee shop	7	6	245	217	735	707	−28	−28
Banquet	11	11	440	440	1,674	1,674		
Beverage								

Significance test

It is unlikely that any revenue or controllable expense item will not have a variance because, even with comprehensive information available during the budgeting process, budgeted figures are still estimates. The variances to be analyzed are those that show significant differences from budgeted amounts. What is important in this significance test is the amount of the variance in both dollar and percentage terms, and not just in one of them. If only one is used, it might not provide information that the other provides. For example, using dollar differences alone ignores the base or budgeted figure, and the dollar difference may not be significant when compared to the base figure. To illustrate, if the dollar difference in revenue is $5,000 (which seems significant) and the budgeted revenue is $5,000,000 the percentage variance is

$$\frac{\$5,000}{\$5,000,000} \times 100 = 0.001\%$$

Effective budgeting

This percentage variance is quite insignificant. In other words, if the actual amount can be this close to the budget in percentage terms, this would indicate remarkably effective budgeting. But this is not disclosed if only the dollar difference is considered.

Similarly, considering the percentage difference alone may not be useful. For example, if a particular expense for this same property were budgeted at $500, and the actual expense were $550, the variance of $50 represents 10 percent of the budget figure. Ten percent seems a large variance but is insignificant when the dollar figure is also considered. In other words, a variance of $50 is insignificant in a business with revenue of $5,000,000, and investigating it would not be worth anybody's time.

What is significant as a dollar and percentage variance depends entirely on the type and size of establishment. Those responsible for budgets need to establish in advance the variances allowed in both dollar figures and percentages for each revenue and expense item. At the end of each budget period, only those variances that exceed what is allowed in both dollar and percentage terms will be further analyzed and investigated.

ZERO-BASED BUDGETING

Most costs (food, beverage, labor, supplies, and others) are usually linked to revenue levels in a fairly direct way. That is why they are generally referred to as direct costs and budgeting for them is relatively easy.

Undistributed expenses

However, there is one category of expenses in the hospitality industry that is not related as directly to revenue levels. These indirect expenses, more commonly referred to as undistributed expenses, include:

- Administrative and general
- Marketing
- Property operation and maintenance
- Energy costs

These undistributed costs are not normally charged to the operating departments but are kept separate. There are also other fixed costs that an operation may have, such as property taxes, insurance, interest, and rent, that are also not charged to the operating departments. However, the level of these costs is usually imposed from outside the operation. Since they are not subject to day-to-day control, or even to monthly or annual control, they shall not be of concern here.

Incremental budgeting

Traditionally, the four undistributed costs listed above have been budgeted for, and presumably "controlled," by incremental budgeting. With incremental budgeting, the assumption is made that the level of the last period's cost was correct. For the new period's budget or control period, one only needs to adjust last period's figure upward, or downward, to take care of current conditions. Management monitors only the changes to the budgeted amounts. Whether last period's total cost was justified is not an issue. The amount of cost is just assumed to have been essential to the company's objectives. It is also frequently assumed that, even with no management guidance, the department heads responsible for controlling the undistributed costs are practicing effective cost/benefit analysis, that they are keeping costs in line and preventing overspending. No doubt many of the expenses incurred in this category do meet these criteria. But it is likely that the reverse is also true in many establishments that use incremental budgeting.

A technique that might be used by hospitality industry enterprises to control these undistributed expenses is zero-based budgeting (ZBB). As its name implies, with ZBB, no expenses can be budgeted for or incurred unless they are justified in advance. Normally, most establishments prepare budgets for undistributed expenses once a year. ZBB basically requires that each department head rejustify, in advance, the entire annual budget from a zero base. ZBB has little value in direct cost budgeting, since the use of other controls (such as those outlined in Chapter 7 for food, beverage, and labor) should ensure that they are not out of line for any given revenue level. But ZBB, properly implemented for undistributed expenses, can not only control these indirect costs, but may lead to cost reduction from previous levels. The main reason for this is that it puts previously unjustified expenses on the same basis as requests for increases to the budget, increases that must also be justified.

Justifying entire budget

Decision Units

One of the key elements in successful implementation of ZBB is the decision unit. The number of decision units will vary with the size of each establishment. For example, a small operation with only one employee in its marketing department would probably have only one decision unit for marketing expenses. A larger organization might have several decision units for marketing. These units might be labeled sales, advertising, merchandising, public relations, and research. A very large organization might further break down these units into decision units covering different activities. For example, advertising might be broken down into a print decision unit and a radio and television decision unit.

Examples of decision units

Each separate decision unit should contain no more than one or two employees and related costs. Each decision unit should be about the same size insofar as total cost for that unit is concerned. In this way, when all budget requests and justifications are finalized, the general manager can more easily evaluate each of them and rank each of them against all the other units that are, so to speak, competing for the same limited resource dollars.

Once decision units have been established, the next step is for each department head to prepare an analysis of each separate unit that is his or her responsibility. This analysis is carried out each year prior to the start of the new budget period. A properly designed form should be used so that each department head will present the data in a standard format. For each decision unit the department head will document the following:

Standard format required

1. The Unit's Objective. Each decision unit's objective must obviously relate to the organization's overall objectives. For example, the objective of a hotel marketing department's print-advertising decision unit might read as follows:

> To seek out the most appropriate magazines, journals, newspapers, and other periodicals that can be used for advertising in the most effective way at the lowest cost in order to increase the number of guests using the hotel's facilities.

2. The Unit's Present Activities. This would include the number of employees, their positions, a description of how the work is presently carried out, and the resources used. For example, a resource used by the print-advertising decision unit might be an external advertising agency.

Measuring activities

The total cost of present activities would be included in this section. Also included would be a statement of how the unit's activities are measured. For example, this might be the number of guests using the hotel's facilities versus column inches or cost of print advertising.

3. Justification for Continuation of Unit's Activities. In the case of our print-advertising unit, this might include a statement to the effect that it would be advantageous for the unit to continue because the employees involved are familiar with the marketing strategy of the hotel, with the various operating departments and their special features, and know what special attractions to promote in the advertisements. The explanation should also include a statement of the disadvantages that would accrue should the decision unit's activities be discontinued.

4. A List of Alternative Ways of Carrying Out the Activities. In the example of the print-advertising decision unit, the alternatives might include taking over some of the work presently given to the advertising agency, having the agency take over more of the unit's activities, having more of the work centralized in the head office (assuming the hotel is one of a chain), doing more head office work at the local level, or combining the print decision unit's activities with those of the radio and television advertising unit. The list should not be overly long, but it should include as many alternatives as would be practical that differ from present activities.

Example of alternatives

Included with the list would be the advantages and disadvantages of each alternative, and, for each alternative, an estimate of the total annual cost.

5. Selection of Recommended Alternative. The department head responsible must then recommend the alternative that he or she would select for each unit. One alternative would be to stay with the present activities rather than make a change. The selection is based on a consideration of the pros, cons, practicality, and cost of each alternative.

6. *Budget Required.* The department head's final responsibility is to state the funding required for each decision unit for the next budget based on the alternative recommended. This request starts out with a base, or minimum level. This minimum level may be established at a level below which the unit's activities would no longer exist or be worthwhile. Alternatively, the level may be arbitrarily determined by the general manager at, say, 60 percent of the present budget. Whatever the minimum level established, each activity above that level is to be shown as an incremental cost. These incremental activities may or may not be subsequently approved.

Ranking Process

Once the decision unit activities have been documented as outlined, it is then the general manager's turn to begin the review process. In order to determine how much money will be spent, and in what areas or departments, the manager must rank all activities in order of importance to the organization. Once this order is established, the activities would be accepted up to the total predetermined budget for all activities.

Ranking difficulty

The major difficulty in ranking is to determine the order of priority for all the operation's activities under review. In a small organization, with the aid of a committee, if necessary, this might not be too difficult. Alternatively, each department head might be asked to rank all activities that come within his or her authority. This procedure can then continue through successive levels of midmanagement until they reach the general manager.

Another approach might be for the general manager to approve automatically, say, the first 50 or 60 percent of all activities ranked within each department. The next 10 or 20 percent might then be ranked by midmanagement and also be automatically approved. Top management might, subsequently, review all these rankings, then rank the remainder and decide how many of them will be funded along with any proposed new programs not proposed or adopted at lower levels.

Confidence in budget

The completed ranking process and approved expenditures constitute the new budgets for those areas or departments. This information can then be incorporated into the regular budget process. Theoretically, as a result of ZBB, the activities of that part of the organization have been examined, evaluated, modified, discontinued, or continued as before. This should produce the most effective possible budget. At the least, it should produce a budget that one can have more confidence in than one produced solely on an incremental basis.

Advantages of ZBB

Some of the advantages of ZBB are that it:

1. Concentrates on the dollar cost of each department's activities and budget and not on broad percentage increases.
2. Can reallocate funds to the departments or areas providing the greatest benefit to the organization.
3. Provides a quality of information about the organization (because all activities are documented in detail) that would otherwise not be available.
4. Involves all levels of management and supervision in the budgeting process and encourages these employees to become familiar with activities that might not normally be under their control.
5. Obliges managers to identify inefficient or obsolete functions within their areas of responsibility.
6. Can identify areas of overlap or duplication.

Disadvantages of ZBB

Some of the possible disadvantages of ZBB are that it:

1. Implies that the budgeting method presently in use is not adequate. This may or may not be true.
2. Requires a great deal more time, effort, paperwork, and cost than traditional budgeting methods.
3. May be unfair to some department heads who, even though they may be very cost-effective in managing their departments, are not as capable as others in documentation and defense of their budgets. They might thus find themselves outranked by other more vocal, but less cost-effective, department heads.

VARIANCE ANALYSIS

Once a comparison has been made between budget figures and actual results, it is useful to analyze any difference for each revenue and expense item. Let us consider the following situation.

Banquet Revenue, Month of March

Budget	Actual	Difference	
$50,000	$47,250	$2,750	(unfavorable)

The difference is unfavorable because our total revenue was less than anticipated. If we analyze the budget and actual figures, we might get the following additional information.

Analysis of budget and actual figures

Budget 5,000 guests × $10.00 average check = $50,000
Actual 4,500 guests × $10.50 average check = 47,250
Variance $ 2,750

This variance amount is actually composed of two separate figures: a price variance and a quantity (number of guests) variance. These are calculated as follows:

Price Variance. The price variance is $0.50 per customer more than budgeted. This is considered to be favorable.

4,500 guests × $0.50 = $2,250 (favorable)

Quantity Variance. The quantity variance is 500 guests, each of whom did not spend the $10.00 we had budgeted for. This would be unfavorable.

500 guests × $10.000 = $5,000 (unfavorable)

If we combine these results, our total variance is made up of

Combining variances

Price variance	$2,250	(favorable)
Quantity variance	5,000	(unfavorable)
Total variance	$2,750	(unfavorable)

We now have information that tells us the major reason for our difference between budget and actual is a reduction in revenue of $5,000 (due to fewer customers served). This has been partly compensated for by $2,250 resulting from the average banquet customer having a more expensive meal. This tells us that our banquet sales department is probably doing an effective job in selling higher priced menus to banquet groups, but is failing to bring in as many banquets or guests as anticipated.

Costs can be analyzed in the same way. Let us examine the following situation for a rooms department in a hotel.

Laundry Expense, Month of June

Budget	Actual	Difference	
$6,000	$6,510	$510	(unfavorable)

Cost higher than budgeted

The difference is unfavorable because we spent more than we budgeted for. With the following additional information we can analyze this variance.

Budget 3,000 rooms sold at $2.00 per room = $6,000
Actual 3,100 rooms sold at $2.10 per room = 6,510
Variance $ 510

The $510 total variance is made up of two items: a cost variance and a quantity variance.

Cost Variance. The cost variance is $0.10 over budget for each room sold. This is an unfavorable trend.

3,100 rooms × $0.10 = $310.00 (unfavorable)

Quantity Variance. The quantity variance is 100 rooms over budget, at a budgeted cost of $2.00 per room. From a cost point of view, this is considered to be unfavorable.

100 rooms × $2.00 = $200.00 (unfavorable)

If we combine these results our total variance is therefore made up of:

Combining variances

Cost variance	$310.00	(unfavorable)
Quantity variance	200.00	(unfavorable)
Total variance	$510.00	(unfavorable)

Increased costs covered by additional revenue

This tells us that, although our total variance was $510, or 8.5 percent over budget ($510 divided by $6,000 × 100), only $310 is of concern to us. The remaining $200 was inevitable. If we sell more rooms, as we did, we would obviously have to pay the extra $200 for laundry. Even though this is considered unfavorable as a cost increase, we would not worry about it since it would be more than offset by the extra revenue obtained from selling the extra rooms. Whether or not the other $310 overspending is serious would depend on the cause. The cause could be a supplier cost increase that we may, or may not, be able to do something about; or it could be that we actually sold more twin rooms than budgeted for (which would mean more sheets to be laundered and therefore cause our average laundry cost per room occupied to go up). In the latter case, the additional cost would be more than offset by the extra charge made for double occupancy of a room.

Let us have a look at another example:

Coffee Shop Variable Wages, Month of May

Budget 4,350 hours at $4.00/hr. = $17,400
Actual 4,100 hours at $4.10/hr. = 16,810
Variance $ 590 (favorable)

Cost variable: 4,100 hours × $0.10/hr. = $ 410 (unfavorable)
Quantity variance: 250 hours × $4.00/hr. = 1,000 (favorable)
Variance: $ 590

Note that the net variance is a $590 favorable amount. Variance analysis shows that there was a $1,000 saving on labor due to a reduced number of hours paid for (perhaps as a result of less business than budgeted for). However, the saving was reduced by $410 because the actual average hourly rate was higher than budgeted for. Was there an increase in the hourly rate paid or because of poor scheduling was there unanticipated overtime (which would tend to increase the average hourly rate paid)? This would need to be verified.

Information helps identify causes

Therefore, as can be seen, variance analysis can provide additional information that is of help in identifying causes of differences between actual and budgeted figures.

SUMMARY

Budgeting is part of the planning process. It can involve decisions concerning the day-to-day management of an operation or involve plans for as far ahead as five years.

There are various types of budgets such as capital, operating, departmental, master, and fixed or flexible.

The purposes of budgeting are

1. To provide estimates of future revenues and expenses.
2. To provide short- and long-term coordinated management policy.
3. To provide a control by comparing actual results with budgeted plans, and to take corrective action if necessary.

In a small operation, budgets can be prepared by an individual, or by a committee in a large organization. In all cases, whether for a day, a year, or some other time period, budgets should be prepared in advance of the start of the period.

Some of the advantages of budgets are:

1. They involve participation of employees in the planning process, thus improving motivation and communication.
2. They necessitate, in budget preparation, consideration of alternative courses of action.
3. They allow a goal, a standard of performance, to be established, with subsequent comparison of actual results with that standard.
4. Flexible budgets permit quick adaptation to unforeseen, changed conditions.
5. They require those involved to be forward-looking, rather than looking only at past events.

The budgeting cycle has five parts:

1. Establishing attainable goals (remember the limiting factors).
2. Planning to achieve these goals.
3. Analyzing differences between planned and actual results.
4. Taking any necessary corrective action.
5. Improving the effectiveness of budgeting.

The starting point in budgeting is to predetermine revenue levels. In a large organization this forecast would be done by department. In forecasting, one must consider past actual revenue and trends, current anticipated trends, and the economic, competitive, and limiting factors.

Once revenue has been forecast, direct operating expenses can be calculated based on anticipated revenue, and, finally, undistributed expenses can be deducted to arrive at the net income for the operation. Once the departmental and general income statement budgets have been prepared, other required budgets (such as balance sheets and capital budgets) can be made up, if required.

If there is no historic accounting information available, which would be the case in a new venture. then the forecasting of revenue and expenses is more difficult. Quite a bit more educated estimating is required.

Zero-based budgeting (ZBB) is a method of controlling certain types of undistributed cost that cannot be related directly to volume or revenue levels. With ZBB each category of cost is broken down into decision units that are then analyzed. The analysis is prepared by the department head responsible for the cost. After each decision unit is analyzed, all decision units are ranked by management and the final budget is allocated according to this ranking.

Variance analysis is a useful technique for isolating the causes of differences between budgeted and actual figures. These differences are broken down into price and quantity variances (when analyzing revenue figures) or cost and quantity variances (when analyzing expense figures).

DISCUSSION QUESTIONS

1. How would you explain the concept of budgeting?
2. What are some of the purposes of budgeting?
3. List and discuss three advantages of budgeting.
4. Explain the difference between long- and short-term budgeting.
5. Give an example of
   a. A hotel departmental budget.
   b. A capital budget for a restaurant.
6. Explain the difference between a fixed and a flexible budget.
7. Two of the steps in the budgeting cycle are
   a. Establishing attainable goals.
   b. Planning to achieve these goals.
   What are the other three steps?
8. Discuss three possible limiting factors to consider in preparing a budget for a hotel or restaurant.
9. A cocktail lounge had revenue in May of $40,000. Budgeted revenue was $42,000. List three possible questions that could be asked, the answers to which might explain the $2,000 difference.
10. In projecting revenue for the coffee shop breakfast period in a hotel, what factors need to be considered?
11. What is derived demand?
12. List the four items that must be multiplied by each other to forecast total annual food revenue for the dinner period of a restaurant.
13. What is a pro forma income statement?
14. List three types of cost that are controllable with ZBB.
15. Give an example of a decision unit in a hotel's accounting office, and write a one-sentence objective for that decision unit.
16. Briefly describe the ranking process under ZBB.
17. Give two advantages and two disadvantages of ZBB.

PROBLEMS

10.1 A motel has thirty units. During the month of June its average room rate is expected to be $45.00 and its room occupancy 75 percent. In July the owner is planning to raise rates by 10 percent, and occupancy is expected to be 80 percent. In August no further room rate raises are contemplated, but occupancy is expected to be up to 90 percent. For each of the three months of June, July, and August calculate the budgeted rooms revenue.

10.2 You are the manager of the eighty-room Motorway Motel and are preparing next year's budget from the following information:

- Annual occupancy: 70 percent
- Average room rate: $44.00
- Variable costs per room occupied: $8.00
- Annual fixed costs: $220,000

Prepare the Motorway Motel's budget for next year. Assume a 365-day year.

10.3 A dining room has seventy-five seats and is open for lunch and dinner only six days a week (closed Sundays). During the month of August management has forecast the following:

	Seat Turnover	Average Food Check
Lunch	1½	$10.50
Dinner	2	15.20

Beverage revenue usually averages 15 percent of luncheon food revenue and 30 percent of dinner food revenue. This particular August has four Sundays. Calculate budgeted total revenue of food and beverage for the month.

10.4 A hotel coffee shop has 130 seats and is open seven days a week for all three meal periods. During the month of January it anticipates the following seat turnovers and average food checks.

	Turnover	Average Check
Breakfast	1½	$ 4.00
Lunch	1¾	7.50
Dinner	1¼	12.50

Calculate the coffee shop's budgeted revenue for January.

10.5 The manager of Buffy's Buffet is preparing next year's budget. She wants to produce a flexible budget for three different annual revenue levels—$800,000, $900,000, and $1,000,000—and has the following information to help in preparing these budgets:

- Food cost: 40 percent of sales
- Variable labor expense: 25 percent of sales
- Fixed labor cost: $60,000
- Other variable costs: 12 percent of sales
- Other fixed costs: $120,000
- Income tax rate: 30 percent on income before tax

From this information, prepare Buffy's three budgets and comment about the results of each with particular reference to how higher sales affect net income.

10.6 A resort hotel that has a dining room that has no business from street trade is dependent solely on the occupancy of its rooms for its revenue. It has 150 rooms. During the month of June it expects an 80 percent occupancy of those rooms. Because the resort caters to the family trade, there are on average three people per occupied room per night. From past experience, management knows that 95 percent of the people occupying rooms eat breakfast, 25 percent eat lunch, and 75 percent eat dinner in the hotel's dining room (some of the units have kitchen facilities, which is why some of the resort's guests do not use the dining room). The dining room is open seven days a week for all three meals. Its average meal prices are

Breakfast	$ 4.50
Lunch	7.50
Dinner	12.60

Calculate the budgeted dining room revenue for the month of June.

10.7 A 120-seat family restaurant is open Monday to Saturday (inclusive) for both lunch and dinner. On Sundays and other holidays (which total sixty days during the year), it is open for dinner only. During the coming year it anticipates the following:

	Seat Turnover	Average Food Check
Weekday lunch	1½	$ 5.50
Weekday dinner	1¼	10.70
Sunday/Holiday dinner	2	11.00

In addition, it has a small private party room and estimates food revenue from this to be $144,000 next year. Beverage revenue is 12 percent of luncheon food revenue and 25 percent of weekday dinner food revenue (there is no beverage revenue on Sundays and holidays). In addition, beverage revenue is generated in the private party room and averages 40 percent of total food revenue in that area. Food cost averages 37 percent of total food revenue, and beverage cost averages 33 percent of total beverage revenue. Fixed wages (from salaried personnel) are estimated to be $284,000. The balance of total wage cost is a variable cost that averages 15 percent of total restaurant revenue. Employee benefits (such as meals and vacation pay) total 12 percent of total wage cost (that is, the total of both the fixed and variable wages).

Other operating costs are expressed as percentages of total revenue from all food and beverage sales:

Cost	Percentage
China, glass, silver, linen	1.7
Laundry	1.5
Supplies	3.2
Menus and beverage lists	0.8
Advertising	2.0
Repairs and maintenance	1.5
Miscellaneous operating expense	1.0

In addition, there are certain overhead costs as follows:

Administration and general	$24,000
Licenses	15,000
Rent	90,000
Equipment depreciation	73,400

From the preceding information, prepare the restaurant's budgeted income statement for next year. (For purposes of this problem, ignore income tax. Also, in this problem, round figures to the nearest whole dollar where necessary.)

10.8 A restaurant's average monthly income statement is as follows:

Revenue		
Food	$40,000	
Beverage	10,000	$50,000
Cost of Sales:		
Food (45% of food revenue)	$18,000	
Beverage (30% of beverage revenue)	3,000	21,000
Gross profit		$29,000
Operating expenses:		
Wages	$13,600	
Operating supplies	4,000	
Administration and general	2,600	

Advertising and promotion	1,800	
Repairs and maintenance	900	
Energy costs	1,300	
Depreciation	700	
Interest	600	25,500
Income before income tax		$ 3,500

The owner is considering two possible alternatives for the coming year:

1. By improved purchasing and reducing portions, cutting the food cost from 45 percent to 40 percent of food revenue. There would be no other changes.

2. Cutting the food cost from 45 percent to 40 percent and spending an additional $2,000 a month on advertising. It is estimated that the advertising would bring in extra customers and increase the volume of both food and beverage revenue by 20 percent over present levels. The extra customers would also incur extra costs over present levels as follows:

Wages	$2,000
Supplies	800
Administration	200
Repairs	300
Energy costs	100

Prepare budgeted average monthly income statements for both alternatives 1 and 2, and advise the owner which alternative you consider best, with reasons.

10.9 a. Budgeted liquor sales at a banquet were 1,500 drinks at $3.15 each. Actual sales were 1,550 drinks at $2.85 each. Analyze the information for price and volume variances.

b. Banquet food sales for a month were estimated to be 20,000 covers (customers) at $10.80 each. Actual sales were 21,000 at $11.25. Analyze this for price and volume variances.

c. Budgeted banquet food cost for a week was 1,000 covers at $3.00 each. Actual cost was 980 covers at $3.10. Analyze this for cost and volume variances.

d. A snack bar budgets the following: 12,000 customers, average check $5.45, average cost per customer $2.05. Actual results showed: 12,800 customers, average check $5.27, average cost $2.01. Analyze total revenue for price and volume variances; analyze total cost for cost and volume variances.

e. At a convention buffet 450 customers are expected. It is estimated that a waitress will be required for each thirty anticipated guests (for serving beverages). Basic wage rate is $5.50/hr., and a minimum of four hours must be paid each waitress. No overtime is anticipated, but it may occur. Calculate the budgeted payroll cost for this function.

After the event, payroll records indicate that a total of sixty-four hours work were actually paid for at a total labor cost of $371.20. Analyze the total payroll for cost and volume variances.

10.10 An 80-room budget motel forecasts its average room rate to be $22.00 for next year at a 75 percent occupancy. The rooms department has a fixed wage cost of $85,725. The variable wage cost for housekeeping is $4.50 an hour, and it takes half an hour to clean a room. Fringe benefits are 15 percent of total wages. Linen, laundry, supplies, and other direct costs are $2.50 per occupied room per day. The motel also has a 50-seat limited menu snack bar. Breakfast revenue is derived solely from customers staying overnight in the motel. On average, one-third of occupied rooms are occupied by two persons and, on average, 80 percent of overnight guests eat breakfast. Average breakfast check is $2.00. Luncheon seat turnover is 1 with an average check of $3.50. Dinner turnover is 0.8 with an average check of $5.50. The snack bar is open 365 days a year for all three meals. Direct operating costs for the snack bar are 75 percent of total snack bar revenue. Indirect costs for the motel are estimated at $289,400 for next year.

a. Calculate the budgeted net income of the motel for next year.

b. Assume that at the end of next year actual revenue was from 21,700 rooms occupied at an average rate of $22.10, and that actual housekeeping wages (before fringe benefits) were $49,910. Analyze room revenue for quantity and price variance, and housekeeping wages for quantity and cost variances, assuming half an hour to clean each room actually sold.

10.11 You have been asked to help prepare the operating budget for a proposed new 100-room motel, with a 65-seat coffee shop, 75-seat dining room, and 90-seat cocktail lounge. The operating budget for the first year will be based on the following information:

Rooms Department

Occupancy 60 percent. Average room rate $63. Wages for bellmen, front office employees, and other fixed wage personnel attached to the rooms department have been calculated to be $326,900. In addition, for every fifteen rooms occupied each day one maid will be required for an eight-hour shift at a rate of $6 an hour. Staff fringe benefits will be 12 percent of total wages. Linen and laundry cost will be 6 percent of total rooms revenue. Supplies and other items will be 3 percent of total rooms revenue.

Food Department

Dining Room. Open 6 days a week 52 weeks a year for lunch and dinner only. Lunch seat turnover 1½, average check (food only) $7. Dinner seat turnover 1, average check (food only) $14.

Coffee Shop. Open seven days a week for all meal periods. Breakfast seat turnover 1, average food check $5.50. Lunch seat turnover 1½, average food check $8. Dinner seat turnover ¾, average food check $13. Coffee breaks 6 seat turnovers, average check $1.

Cocktail Lounge. Food orders served in the lounge are estimated to be about 20 a day at an average check of $5.50 (note the lounge is closed on Sundays and certain holidays and is therefore open only for 310 days during the year).

Total payroll cost (including fringe benefits) in the food department will be 45 percent of total food revenue. Other costs (also as a percentage of total food revenue) are:

Food cost	35%
Laundry and linen	2
Supplies	5
Other items	2

Beverage Department (open 310 days a year only)

Each seat in the cocktail lounge is expected to generate $5,250 per year. In addition, the lounge will be credited with any alcoholic beverages served in the coffee shop and dining room. In the coffee shop beverage revenue is estimated to be 15 percent of combined lunch and dinner food revenue, and in the dining room 25 percent of combined lunch and dinner food revenue. Operating costs in the beverage department are:

Liquor cost 32 percent of total beverage revenue
Payroll (including benefits) 25 percent of total beverage revenue
Supplies and other operating costs 5 percent of total beverage revenue

From the preceding information prepare income statements for the first year of operation for each of the three departments. Then combine the departmental operating incomes into one figure and deduct the following undistributed costs to arrive at budgeted income (before depreciation, interest, and income tax).

Administrative and general	$156,800
Marketing	147,600
Energy costs	58,900
Property operation and maintenance	52,400

--------------		-------
Insurance		15,300
Property taxes		82,100

(In this problem round all numbers to the nearest dollar.)

CASE 10

a. As a step to preparation of the 4C Company's preliminary budget for year 0002, calculate the forecast revenue based on year 0001 actual results adjusted as follows: lunch and dinner seat turnover figures will not change (see Case 6). Note that at lunch the guest count figure will increase as a result of the advertising plan discussed in Case 8. The ratio of food to beverage sales on the average checks will stay the same, but overall the average check for lunch will increase by $0.50 and for dinner by $0.95. No additional seats will be added in the restaurant and days open will remain the same. Calculate the total forecast revenue for food, and for beverages.

b. Complete the budgeted income statement for year 0002 with reference to Case 9 (for fixed and variable cost data) and the following additional information.

- Food and beverage cost percentages will remain as in year 0001 (see Case 3).

- Salaries and wages. First deduct Charles's present salary of $18,000 from the 0001 total. Add the cost of the new employee to be hired as the result of the newspaper advertising (see Case 8). Apply a general across the board 10 percent increase for all employees (except Charles) for year 0002. Then add on Charles's salary, which is to be $25,000 next year.

- Laundry percent to revenue will remain unchanged.

- Kitchen fuel. Fixed amount will increase by $400; the variable portion percent to revenue will remain unchanged.

- China, glass, etc. percent to revenue will remain unchanged.

- Contract cleaning. A $600 increase is anticipated in year 0002.

- Licenses. No change anticipated.

- Other operating expenses percent to revenue will be as before.

- Administrative and general. A 10 percent increase should be budgeted for.

- Marketing. The only increase will be the $3,000 to be spent on newspaper advertising.

- Energy costs. The fixed cost is expected to rise by $2,000, and the variable portion percent to revenue will be as before.
- Insurance. A 10 percent increase is expected.
- Rent. As agreed with the building owner (see Case 2) a 10 percent increase is contracted for.
- Interest will decrease to $19,500.
- Depreciation. Calculate on straight-line basis.
- Income tax will be 25 percent of income before tax.

c. How does your budgeted income statement for year 0002 compare with the actual result for year 0001? Explain why the net income is down despite an increase in revenue.

11 Working Capital

Chapter Highlights

In this chapter the reader is introduced to the concept and importance of working capital. Working capital is defined as current assets less current liabilities.

The purposes of the statement of source and use of working capital are listed, as are the basic transactions that create sources and uses of working capital.

The method of compiling a statement of source and use of working capital is demonstrated using opening and closing balance sheets, an income statement, a statement of retained earnings, and other necessary information.

A statement of changes in working capital, which shows how the balances in individual working capital accounts have changed over a period of time, is illustrated.

Finally, the question of how much working capital a firm should have is discussed, as is the value of calculating the current ratio (the ratio of current assets to current liabilities).

Chapter Objectives

After studying this chapter the reader should be able to:

1. Define working capital.
2. List and briefly explain some of the sources and some of the uses of working capital.
3. Prepare a statement of source and use of working capital, given appropriate information.
4. Prepare a statement of changes in working capital, given appropriate information.
5. Explain why net income and cash on hand are not necessarily synonymous.
6. Define the term "current ratio," and explain why hospitality industry enterprises can operate at a relatively low ratio.

WORKING CAPITAL

On a balance sheet, listed under the assets, is a section called current assets (including cash, accounts receivable, marketable securities, inventories, and prepaid expenses). On the other side of the balance sheet is a section for the current liabilities (including accounts payable, accrued expenses, income tax payable, deposits and credit balances, current portion of long-term mortgage, and dividends payable). The difference between total current assets and total current liabilities is known as working capital.

Current assets − Current liabilities = Working capital

STATEMENT OF SOURCE AND USE OF WORKING CAPITAL

One of the useful supporting statements that can accompany a balance sheet, an income statement, and a statement of retained earnings is a statement of source and use of working capital. Like the income statement, it covers a period of time ending on the balance sheet date. Its purposes are

Purposes of statement	1. To show how working capital was increased (sources) and how it was decreased (uses) during the period.

1. To show how working capital was increased (sources) and how it was decreased (uses) during the period.

2. To show the net change in working capital from the beginning of the period to the end.

3. To provide management with information concerning the effectiveness of the handling of working capital during the period.

4. To provide prospective lenders with some information about the risk involved in lending the hotel or restaurant some funds.

SOURCES OF WORKING CAPITAL

The following are the major sources of working capital (sometimes known as sources of funds):

Income from Operations. In general terms, income is revenue less all expenses incurred (including income tax) to generate that revenue. Since revenue is generated by cash, or on credit (accounts receivable) that eventually becomes cash, and since expenses have to be paid for, any net income on the income statement should eventually increase the organization's cash account and/or bank account, and thus increase working capital. However, the net income amount after income tax is frequently arrived at after deducting expenses that do not require an outlay of cash. Such an expense is the adjustment on the books of the value of a building and furniture and equipment. This reduction in book value is known as depreciation and is recorded each accounting period on the income statement as an expense, even though it does not require an outlay of cash. Therefore, in order to convert net income after income tax to the correct increase in working capital figure, any such depreciation expenses must be added to the net income amount. Alternatively, the net income amount may be left as is and shown as a source of working capital; the depreciation amounts may be shown on a separate line of the statement as a source of funds. Other items that are handled in the same way as depreciation are amortization of a long-term, prepaid franchise fee, or an amortization of goodwill.

Expenses not requiring cash outlay

Amortization like depreciation

Sale of Long-Term or Other Asset. The sale of a long-term or other (noncurrent) asset, either for cash or on credit, is an increase in working capital.

Increase in Long-Term Liabilities. An increase in a long-term liability by way of a loan, mortgage, bond, or debenture is a source of funds, and therefore an increase in working capital.

Issuance of Stock (Shares). Equity financing, by selling stock, increases a current asset account, and is, therefore, a source of working capital. In a proprietorship or partnership (that is, an unincorporated company), stock is not issued; however, any investment by the owner(s) is handled in the same way as stock: it is shown as a source of funds or working capital.

USES OF WORKING CAPITAL

The following are the major items that are a use of (or decrease in) working capital:

Loss from Operations. Just as net income is an increase in working capital, so a loss is a decrease in working capital. When a loss occurs, expenses have exceeded revenue, more cash is going out than is being received, therefore working capital is being reduced. Note, however, that just as net income has to be adjusted for noncash expenditures (depreciation, franchise, or goodwill, write-downs, or amortizations), so must losses be similarly adjusted for. In other words, the loss must be reduced by any such expenses shown on the income statement.

Losses reduce working capital

Purchase of a Long-Term or Other Asset. The purchase of any noncurrent asset (such as land, building, or furniture and equipment) is a reduction of working capital, or use of funds. The cost of any other assets (such as the prepayment of a long-term franchise fee) would also be a use of funds.

Payment of Long-Term Liabilities. Any payments reducing the amount owing on long-term (not current) debt are a reduction in the cash account and therefore a use of working capital.

Redemption of Stock. If any issued stock is redeemed (purchased) by the company this, too, requires a cash outlay and is therefore a use of working capital.

Payment of Dividends. Any dividends declared are an obligation by the company to its stockholders requiring an outlay of cash and are thus a use of working capital. In a nonincorporated company (partnership or proprietorship) any withdrawals (reductions of capital investment) made by the owner(s) are a use of working capital.

USEFULNESS OF STATEMENT

Statement shows causes of change

Explanations illustrating how to compile a statement of source and use of working capital will be given later in the chapter. However, to demonstrate how a statement can be useful, let us consider the following three situations in turn. The situations concern three different restaurants, each with working capital at the beginning of the year of $88,000, and at the end of the year $100,000: an increase in working capital over the year of $12,000. This information is readily visible from the balance sheets. Not so apparent, without a statement of source and use of working capital, are the causes of this change, and a banker, from whom each of the three restaurants wishes to borrow $15,000 (repayable, with interest, over three years), would be very interested in having the information showing the causes of this change.

Healthy situation

Restaurant A: Exhibit 11.1. In this case, assuming the restaurant's business is going to stay healthy over the next three years, there should be little risk in the bank lending the restaurant the money. The restaurant is generating enough working capital from operations to pay out dividends and to be able to repay $5,000 a year, plus interest, to reduce the loan.

Borderline situation

Restaurant B: Exhibit 11.2. In this case, the bank might be concerned about lending the restaurant $15,000. Starting next year the restaurant has to pay back $5,000 a year, plus interest, on the loans from stockholders. If it also has to pay $5,000 a year, plus interest, on the new bank loan—making a total of $10,000 a year plus interest—will it be able to do so? A modest decline in net income over the next few years might create difficulties and/or force the restaurant to reduce its dividends in order to meet its loan obligations. There is a risk involved.

Risky situation

Restaurant C: Exhibit 11.3. In this last case there would be a high risk for the bank to lend the company $15,000 because its current year's

Exhibit 11.1   Restaurant A: Statement of source and use of working capital for the year ending December 31, 0005.

Sources	
Net income after income tax	$20,000
Uses	
Dividends paid to stockholders	8,000
Net change in working capital	$12,000

Exhibit 11.2 Restaurant B: Statement of source and use of working capital for the year ending December 31, 0005.

Sources		
Net income after income tax	$20,000	
Loans from stockholders, repayable over 4 years with interest	20,000	$40,000
Uses		
Investment in new building	$20,000	
Dividends paid to stockholders	8,000	28,000
Net change in working capital		$12,000

Exhibit 11.3 Restaurant C: Statement of source and use of working capital for the year ending December 31, 0005.

Sources		
Net income after income tax	$ 4,000	
Loan from private investor, repayable in year 0006	16,000	$20,000
Uses		
Dividends paid to stockholders		8,000
Net change in working capital		$12,000

net income of $4,000 was not sufficient to meet the dividend payment of $8,000. If net income remains at this level, how is the restaurant going to be able to pay dividends in future years and repay the present loan of $16,000? There would be an extremely high degree of risk indeed for the bank to lend the restaurant a further $15,000.

Although this third illustration is probably extreme, it does point out the way in which information provided by the statement of source and use of working capital can be of value in decision making.

TRANSACTIONS AFFECTING CURRENT ACCOUNTS ONLY

It should be noted that all the items listed earlier under sources or uses of working capital affected a current account (either a current asset or a current liability) and a noncurrent account (a long-term asset, a long-term liability, or stockholders' equity). Since the statement of source and use of working capital show the cause of changes in net working capital and do not show detail about changes in the individual current asset or current liability accounts, any transactions affecting only such current accounts will not appear on the statement of source and use of working capital. For example, consider the following balance sheet information.

Transactions not on statement

Current Assets		Current Liabilities	
Cash	$10,000	Accounts payable	$11,000
Accounts receivable	5,000	Bank loan	4,000
Inventories	3,000		
Total	$18,000	Total	$15,000

The working capital is $3,000 ($18,000 − $15,000). If $5,000 cash were used to pay off part of the accounts payable (a transaction affecting only two current accounts), our new balance sheet would look like this

Current Assets		Current Liabilities	
Cash	$ 5,000	Accounts payable	$ 6,000
Accounts receivable	5,000	Bank loan	4,000
Inventories	3,000		
Total	$13,000	Total	$10,000

Because this transaction was between two current accounts, our working capital has not changed. It is still $3,000 ($13,000 − $10,000). Therefore, because we are not concerned with changes between individual current accounts, our statement of source and use of working capital are readily put together using only the following information.

Information required

a. A balance sheet at the close of the previous accounting period.

b. A balance sheet at the close of the current accounting period.

c. An income statement for the current period.

d. A statement of retained earnings, or information about the retained earnings on the balance sheet.

e. Any other information not fully disclosed in the above documents (for example, information about the purchase or sale of individual long-term assets, or detail about long-term liabilities or share transactions).

COMPILATION OF STATEMENT OF SOURCE AND USE OF WORKING CAPITAL

First step: calculate change

To illustrate how a statement of source and use of working capital can be readily put together, we will refer to Exhibits 11.4 (balance sheets, including information about retained earnings), 11.5 (income statement), and 11.6 (retained earnings). See Exhibit 11.4.

The first step is to calculate the change in working capital from the previous balance sheet date to the current balance sheet date.

The year ending 0001 balance sheet gives the following:

Current assets	$18,000
Current liabilities	15,000
Working capital	$ 3,000

The year ending 0002 balance sheet gives the following:

Current assets	$24,000
Current liabilities	17,000
Working capital	$ 7,000

Figures must agree

The change in working capital is therefore an increase in working capital of $4,000 ($7,000 − $3,000) from year 0001 to year 0002. This figure must agree with the change in working capital figure that appears as the difference between sources and uses on the statement of source and use of working capital.

Once we have calculated this figure, we can then ignore the current asset and current liability sections of our balance sheets. We only need information from the rest of the balance sheet, the income statement, and the statement of retained earnings.

Using working papers

Although accountants generally use a system of working papers for gathering the information that is to appear on the statement of source and use of working capital, most such statements can be compiled quite readily without working papers.

The easiest method is to take the balance sheet, the income statement and the statement of retained earnings in turn, listing the relevant items as either a source or use of working capital.

Balance Sheet Information

Ignore current items

Commence with the balance sheet (Exhibit 11.4). As has already been stated, we need concern ourselves no further with current assets and current liabilities. So first we will deal with the long-term assets.

Exhibit 11.4 Illustrative balance sheets.

Assets	Year 0001	Year 0002	Liabilities and Stockholders' Equity	Year 0001	Year 0002
Current assets			*Current liabilities*		
Cash	$ 10,000	$ 12,000	Accounts payable	$ 4,000	$ 5,000
Accounts receivable	5,000	8,000	Accrued expenses	0	4,000
Inventories	3,000	4,000	Bank loan	11,000	8,000
Total	$ 18,000	$ 24,000	Total	$ 15,000	$ 17,000
Long-term assets			*Long-term liability*		
Land	$ 30,000	$ 30,000	Mortgage	185,000	175,000
Building	250,000	250,000	*Stockholders' equity*		
Furniture and equipment	35,000	40,000	Share capital	$100,000	$105,000
Total	$315,000	$320,000	Retained earnings	18,000	20,000
Less: accumulated depreciation	(15,000)	(27,000)	Total	118,000	125,000
Total	300,000	293,000			
Total	$318,000	$317,000		$318,000	$317,000

Exhibit 11.5 Condensed income statement for the year 0002.

Revenue	$100,000
Operating expenses	(82,000)
Income before depreciation	$ 18,000
Depreciation	(12,000)
Net income	$ 6,000

There has been no change in the land account ($30,000 in both years) or in the building account ($250,000), but the furniture and equipment account has increased in year 0002 from $35,000 to $40,000. We can assume (there will be further comment about this assumption later in the chapter) that, during the year, $5,000 has been spent on new furniture and equipment. This is a use of funds.

Use: purchase of new furniture and equipment $5,000

Ignore accumulated depreciation

The next item under long-term assets is accumulated depreciation, which has increased by $12,000 over the year. However, since accumulated depreciation is simply a write-down of the value of the related assets and does not affect any working capital account, we can ignore this change.

If we now move to the long-term liability section of the balance sheet, we see that the mortgage has been reduced from year 0001 to year 0002 by $10,000. This reduction required cash.

Use: reduction of mortgage $10,000

The next item, under stockholders' equity, is the share capital account, which has increased during the year from $100,000 to $105,000. We can therefore assume that $5,000 more shares were issued for cash, which would increase our cash account.

Exhibit 11.6 Statement of retained earnings for the year 0002.

Retained earnings January 1, 0002	$18,000
Add: Net income for year	6,000
	$24,000
Less: Dividends declared and paid	(4,000)
Retained earnings Dec. 31, 0002	$20,000

Refer to details of retained earnings

The final item on the balance sheet is the retained earnings, which has changed from year 0001 to year 0002. However, for details concerning this change we need to refer to the statement of retained earnings (Exhibit 11.6), which we will do after we have looked at the income statement (Exhibit 11.5).

Income Statement Information

The income statement shows a net income of $6,000. However, as has already been explained, the recording of depreciation (and accumulated depreciation) on the books of a business does not affect the cash account, since no expenditure is required in making this entry. Therefore, we are interested only in the income excluding any depreciation, in this case $18,000. It is this amount that affects our working capital position.

Source: income from operations $18,000

Retained Earnings Information

Profit already adjusted for

The final statement (Exhibit 11.6) gives details concerning the change in retained earnings from the beginning to the end of year 0002. The first item, an increase in retained earnings as a result of making a profit during the year, has already been adjusted for (see income statement). The other item was the declaration and payment of dividends of $4,000. This would have required an outlay of funds.

Use: declaration and payment of dividends $4,000

Since no other information is provided, we can assume we have all the data required for compiling our statement of source and use of working capital. In summary it is as follows:

Use: purchase of new furniture and equipment	$ 5,000
Use: reduction of mortgage	10,000
Source: additional shares issued	5,000
Source: income from operations	18,000
Use: declaration and payment of dividends	4,000

This information can now be arranged in an orderly fashion (see Exhibit 11.7) in the form of a statement of source and use of working capital.

Exhibit 11.7 Statement of source and use of working capital for the year ending December 31, 0002.

Sources		
Income from operations	$18,000	
Additional shares issued	5,000	$23,000
Uses		
Purchase of new furniture and equipment	$ 5,000	
Reduction of mortgage	10,000	
Declaration and payment of dividends	4,000	19,000
Net change in working capital (increase)		$ 4,000

Figures to agree

Note that the net change in working capital shown on this statement, an increase of $4,000, agrees with the amount previously calculated from the current asset and current liability totals appearing on the balance sheet (Exhibit 11.4).

An alternative method for presenting this information is shown in Exhibit 11.8.

Further Information Required

Analyze certain accounts

Sometimes further information is required for completion of the statement of source and use of working capital than is shown on the balance sheet, the income statement, and the statement of retained earnings. With reference to Exhibit 11.4 and the furniture and equipment account, which had increased from year 0001 ($35,000) to year 0002 ($40,000) by $5,000, it was stated earlier that we could assume that new furniture and equipment had been purchased in that amount. However, in practice, it would be necessary to ensure (by reference to the actual account page in the general ledger and related invoices) that this was indeed the case. For example, the following situation could have occurred:

Typical situation

Furniture and equipment account December 31, 0001	$35,000
New equipment purchased during year 0002	7,000
Old furniture sold during year 0002	(2,000)
Furniture and equipment account December 31, 0002	$40,000

A $5,000 increase in the account has occurred, but the change is accounted for by two separate transactions, and these two transactions should be recorded separately on the statement of source and use of working capital.

Exhibit 11.8 Alternative statement of source and use of working capital for the year ending December 31, 0002.

Working capital December 31, 0001	$ 3,000
Sources (show details)	23,000
	$26,000
Uses (show details)	(19,000)
Working capital December 31, 0002 (an increase of $4,000).	$ 7,000

Source: furniture sold	$2,000
Use: equipment purchased	$7,000

Complete disclosure

Any other accounts where similar source and use transactions took place during the period would have to be detailed so that the source and use of working capital statement can provide complete disclosure about working capital changes during the period.

Changes in Individual Working Capital Accounts

To reiterate the statement of source and use of working capital shows only the net change in total working capital between one accounting period and the next. It does not show how the individual accounts that are part of working capital have changed. If this information is required, it is usually shown separately in a statement of changes in working capital. If we use the current asset and current liability sections of the previously used balance sheet (Exhibit 11.4), we could summarize the changes in individual working capital accounts as in Exhibit 11.9.

Analysis of individual account changes

An analysis of individual account changes can be made as a result of preparing a statement of changes in working capital. Questions could then be asked. The cash account has increased by $2,000 or 20 percent ($2,000 divided by $10,000); do we need this extra cash on hand or could it be better used to pay off some of the bank loan and thus save on interest expense and further increase net income? The accounts receivable have gone up by $3,000, or 60 percent; has our total revenue increased 60 percent, or have we changed our credit policies, or are we not following up effectively on the collection of accounts? These, and other questions, are raised by having the information that the statement of changes in working capital accounts provides.

The problem of cash management and the control of individual working capital accounts, such as inventory, accounts receivable, and accounts payable is covered in Chapter 12.

Exhibit 11.9   Summary of individual working capital account changes.

	Year 1	Year 2	Working Capital Increase	Working Capital Decrease
Current assets				
Cash	$10,000	$12,000	$2,000	
Accounts receivable	5,000	8,000	3,000	
Inventories	3,000	4,000	1,000	
Totals	$18,000	$24,000		
Current liabilities				
Accounts payable	$ 4,000	$ 5,000		$1,000
Accrued expenses	0	4,000		4,000
Bank loan	11,000	8,000	3,000	
Totals	$15,000	$17,000		
Working Capital	$ 3,000	$ 7,000		
			$9,000	$5,000
Net change in working capital				4,000
Totals			$9,000	$9,000

How Much Working Capital?

How much working capital does a hotel or restaurant need? This cannot be answered in general terms with an absolute dollar amount. For example, suppose it were a rule of thumb that an operation should have working capital of $5,000. A small restaurant might find itself with the following balance sheet items:

Current assets	$15,000
Current liabilities	10,000
Working capital	$ 5,000

Larger businesses have higher amounts   A much larger restaurant would have to have larger amounts of cash, inventories, accounts receivable, and other items that are current assets. Also, it would probably have larger amounts in its various current liability accounts. Its balance sheet might therefore look like this

Current assets	$100,000
Current liabilities	95,000
Working capital	$ 5,000

The smaller restaurant is in much better financial shape than the larger one. The former has $1.50 of current assets for each $1.00 of current liabilities, a comfortable cushion. The latter has just over $1.05 ($100,000 divided by $95,000) of current assets for each dollar of current liabilities, a not-so-comfortable cushion.

A general rule in business is that a company should preferably have at least $2.00 of current assets for each $1.00 of current liabilities. This would mean that its working capital ($2.00 minus $1.00) is equivalent to its current liabilities. However, this rule is primarily for companies that need to carry very large inventories (such as manufacturing organizations) that do not turn over very rapidly. On the other hand, restaurants have inventories of food and beverage that, partly because of their perishable nature and partly because daily purchases are possible, turn over (or are replaced) more frequently. This means that the amount of current assets (relative to current liabilities) can be less than 2:1.

Relatively low ratio

Hotels have an inventory that is primarily made up of rooms that appear under long-term assets. So, relatively speaking, hotels frequently operate with a very low ratio of current assets to current liabilities, often as low as 1:1. In other words, for each $1.00 of current assets, there is $1.00 of current liabilities. This means that the hotel has, in fact, no working capital. At certain times of the year, hotels or restaurants can even operate with negative working capital. In other words, current liabilities will be greater than current assets. This might be typical for a hotel or restaurant that was very seasonal in nature. Such an operation would have current assets vastly in excess of current liabilities during the peak season. But the reverse situation could prevail in the off season. During the preopening period of a hotel or restaurant, negative working capital (since there is no revenue being received) could also occur.

SUMMARY

One of the useful supporting documents accompanying a set of financial statements is the statement of source and use of working capital. Working capital is defined as current assets less current liabilities.

As well as showing how working capital changed in amount from one accounting period to the next, and what items caused this change, the statement of source and use of working capital also provides management with information about its effectiveness in the handling of working capital and creditors with information about the creditworthiness of the establishment.

The major sources of working capital are:

1. Income from operations, with depreciation added back.
2. Sale of long-term or other assets.

3. Additional long-term borrowings.

4. Sale of stock.

The prime uses of working capital are for the following:

1. Losses from operations.

2. Purchase of long-term or other assets.

3. Principal payments on long-term liabilities.

4. Redemption of stock.

5. Payment of dividends.

A transaction affecting only two current accounts, for example, purchase of food inventory (a current asset) on credit or an account payable (a current liability), does not change the working capital and would not appear on the statement of source and use of working capital.

In order to prepare a statement of source and use of working capital, the following are required:

1. Balance sheets for the end of the previous, and for the end of the current accounting periods.

2. An income statement for the current period.

3. Information about changes in the retained earnings account.

4. Other necessary information (for example, about changes in fixed asset or long-term liability accounts not evident on the balance sheets).

The statement of source and use of working capital only shows the change, and the causes of the change, in net working capital. It does not show changes in individual current asset or current liability accounts. If this detail is required, it must be prepared separately.

The amount of working capital (that is, current assets minus current liabilities) is not, by itself, very meaningful. What is more useful is the relationship between current assets and current liabilities expressed in the form of a ratio known as the current ratio. In the hospitality industry this ratio can vary from 1.5:1 to less than 1:1. A ratio of 1.5:1 means that there are $1.50 of current assets for each $1 of current liabilities.

DISCUSSION QUESTIONS

1. What is working capital?

2. Of what value is a statement of source and use of working capital?

3. List three major and common sources of working capital and three major and common uses of working capital.

4. Explain why depreciation can be referred to as a source of working capital.

5. If marketable securities were traded in for cash and the cash used to pay off accounts payable, would this transaction appear on the statement of source and use of working capital? Explain your answer.

6. If a long-term asset account on two successive balance sheets had increased from $70,000 to $80,000, can we automatically assume that the company has used $10,000 of working capital to buy new fixed assets? Explain your answer.

7. What is a statement of changes in working capital?

8. Explain the value of a statement of changes in working capital.

9. Why is the amount of working capital by itself not a very meaningful figure?

10. If a company has a current ratio of 1.25:1 what does this mean?

11. Why can hotels and motels, unlike manufacturing companies, continue to operate with a 1:1 current ratio or less?

PROBLEMS

11.1 A motel has the following balance sheet information for two successive years:

	Dec. 31 Year 0005	Dec. 31 Year 0006
Assets:		
Cash	$ 4,100	$ 5,200
Accounts receivable	5,900	6,200
Inventory	3,000	3,600
Marketable securities	8,000	7,000
Prepaid expenses	1,200	1,500
Land	30,000	30,000
Building, cost	150,000	150,000
Accumulated depreciation, building	(41,900)	(50,200)
Furniture and equipment, cost	22,700	25,400
Accumulated depreciation, furniture and equipment	(15,400)	(19,100)
Total	$167,600	$159,600

	Dec. 31 Year 0005	Dec. 31 Year 0006
Liabilities and stockholders' equity:		
Accounts payable	$ 6,900	$ 6,800
Accrued expenses	1,400	1,900
Income tax payable	2,000	1,500
Current portion of mortgage	11,500	10,400
Long-term mortgage payable	100,000	89,600
Common stock	23,000	23,000
Retained earnings	22,800	26,400
Total	$167,600	$159,600

From this information, prepare a statement of changes in working capital (see Exhibit 11.9).

11.2 With the balance sheet information from Problem 11.1, and with the following additional information from the income statement and statement of retained earnings, prepare the motel's statement of source and use of working capital for the year ending December 31, 0006.

Income Statement,
Year Ending December 31, 0006

Revenue	$204,900
Operating costs	173,800
Income before depreciation, interest and tax	$ 31,100
Depreciation	12,000
Income before interest and tax	$ 19,100
Interest	10,800
Income before tax	$ 8,300
Income tax	1,500
Net income	$ 6,800

Statement of Retained Earnings
Year Ending December 31, 0006

Retained earnings January 1, 0006	$22,800
Add: Net income for year	6,800
	$29,600
Deduct: Dividends paid	3,200
Retained earnings December 31, 0006	$26,400

11.3 You have the following information about a restaurant for the year ending December 31, 0002:

a. Net income for year $7,000. Annual depreciation of $1,000 was included as an expense to arrive at net income.
b. New equipment costing $4,000 was purchased.
c. Dividends of $6,000 were paid out.
d. New shares (100 at $10 each) were issued.
e. The long-term loan was increased by $2,000.
The balance sheets for years 0001 and 0002 are as follows:

	Dec. 31 Year 0001	Dec. 31 Year 0002
Assets:		
Cash	$14,800	$15,600
Accounts receivable	8,300	7,700
Food and beverage inventories	7,900	9,700
Funiture and equipment	15,500	19,500
Accumulated depreciation	(3,500)	(4,500)
Total	$43,000	$48,000
Liabilities and stockholders' equity		
Accounts payable	$ 5,600	$ 7,800
Income tax payable	1,400	200
Long-term loan	25,800	27,800
Common stock	4,200	5,200
Retained earnings	6,000	7,000
Total	$43,000	$48,000

Calculate the amount of change in working capital and prepare the restaurant's statement of source and use of working capital for the year ending December 31, 0002.

11.4 A catering company had the following balance sheets for two successive years:

	Dec. 31 Year 0003	Dec. 31 Year 0004
Assets:		
Cash	$ 8,600	$ 15,000
Accounts receivable	19,800	15,800
Inventory, food	6,100	6,300
Prepaid expenses	1,200	1,700
Building	0	150,000
Accumulated depreciation, building	0	(7,500)

	Dec. 31 Year 0003	Dec. 31 Year 0004
Equipment	31,700	33,900
Accumulated depreciation, equipment	(5,800)	(6,200)
Total	$61,600	$209,000

Liabilities and stockholders' equity:		
Accounts payable	$21,200	$ 25,400
Accrued expenses	7,500	8,800
Current portion of mortgage payable	0	7,100
Long-term mortgage payable	0	132,900
Common stock	3,000	13,000
Retained earnings	29,900	21,800
Total	$61,600	$209,000

The statement of retained earnings of the catering company for the year ending December 31, 0004, showed the following:

Retained earnings December 31, 0003	$29,900
Operating loss for year 0004	(8,100)
Retained earnings December 31, 0004	$21,800

The equipment account, and the related accumulated depreciation account indicated the following:

	Equipment	Accumulated Depreciation
Balance December 31, 0003	$31,700	$5,800
Purchased new equipment	6,300	
Disposed of fully depreciated old equipment	(4,100)	(4,100)
Depreciation expense year 0004		4,500
Balance December 31, 0004	$33,900	$6,200

Other information:

1. During 0004 the catering company purchased the building it had previously been renting. The purchase price was $150,000. The company paid $10,000 cash and assumed a mortgage (long-term) of $140,000. The building was depreciated by $7,500 during the year

0004. Note that, at the end of year 0004, $7,100 of the mortgage was shown as a current liability since it is payable in year 0005.

2. New stock was issued for cash, 200 shares at $50.00 each.

Prepare the catering company's statement of source and use of working capital for the year ending December 31, 0004.

11.5 A motel has the following balance sheets at the end of each of its most recent two years of operation:

	Dec. 31 Year 0006	Dec. 31 Year 0007
Assets:		
Cash	$ 8,800	$ 0
Accounts receivable	17,200	30,600
Inventory	2,100	5,500
Land	20,000	20,000
Building	50,600	100,600
Accumulated depreciation, building	(30,000)	(40,000)
Total	$68,700	$116,700
Liabilities and Stockholders' equity:		
Accounts payable	$ 6,700	$ 12,800
Bank loan	0	7,900
Long-term mortgage on building	0	30,000
Common stock	2,000	2,000
Retained earnings	60,000	64,000
Total	$68,700	$116,700

The income statements provide the following information:

	Dec. 31 Year 0006	Dec. 31 Year 0007
Revenue	$100,000	$110,000
Operating costs	90,000	93,200
Net income	$ 10,000	$ 16,800

The statement of retained earnings for year 0007 showed:

Retained earnings December 31, 0006	$60,000
Net income for year 0007	16,800
	$76,800

Dividends		(12,800)
Retained earnings December 31, 0007		$64,000

The owner cannot understand why, if he has $64,000 of retained earnings and if he made $16,800 of profit during the year, he has no money in the bank. Give him any explanations you can using the above information.

11.6 A small restaurant has the following statements of source and use of working capital for its first three years in business:

	Dec. 31 Year 0001	Dec. 31 Year 0002	Dec. 31 Year 0003
Sources			
Net income	$6,200	$6,700	$ 2,400
Depreciation expense	3,000	3,000	3,000
Bank loan	0	0	5,000
Total	$9,200	$9,700	$10,400
Uses			
Dividends	$5,200	$9,700	$ 9,700
Purchased car	0	0	5,000
Total	$5,200	$9,700	$14,700
Increase (decrease) in working capital	$4,000	0	($ 4,300)

An analysis of its current asset and current liability accounts on the balance sheets for opening day and each of the first three year-ends gave the following information.

	Jan. 1 Year 0001	Dec. 31 Year 0001	Dec. 31 Year 0002	Dec. 31 Year 0003
Current assets				
Cash	$3,000	$ 8,100	$ 8,600	$ 3,400
Accounts receivable	0	5,100	7,200	9,300
Food inventory	2,000	3,200	5,700	7,500
Prepaid expenses	1,100	900	1,000	2,800
Total	$6,100	$17,300	$22,500	$23,000

	Jan. 1 Year 0001	Dec. 31 Year 0001	Dec. 31 Year 0002	Dec. 31 Year 0003
Current liabilities				
Accounts payable	$4,100	$ 4,500	$ 5,100	$ 6,000
Income tax payable	0	1,600	1,700	600
Dividends payable	0	5,200	9,700	9,700
Loan payable	0	0	0	5,000
Total	$4,100	$11,300	$16,500	$21,300

The owner of the restaurant is puzzled by the fact that, at the end of year 0003 there is not enough cash in the bank to pay the dividends. She is also further puzzled by the reluctance of the bank to advance her $10,000 on a short-term loan. Explain the situation to the owner, supporting your explanations with any necessary calculations or figures.

11.7 A motel had the following successive annual balance sheets:

	Dec. 31 Year 0001	Dec. 31 Year 0002
Assets:		
Cash	$28,600	$30,300
Accounts receivable	18,100	16,800
Inventories	16,800	20,500
Furniture and equipment	30,400	38,100
Less: Accumulated depreciation	(6,200)	(8,200)
	$87,700	$97,500
Liabilities and owners' equity:		
Accounts payable	$10,800	$14,100
Income tax payable	4,200	2,900
Long-term loans	50,300	54,300
Common stock	5,000	7,000
Retained earnings	17,400	19,200
	$87,700	$97,500

Other information:

1. New furniture costing $8,700 was purchased in year 0002.
2. Fully depreciated equipment that originally cost $1,000 was disposed of (it had no scrap value), and its cost and accumulated depreciation were removed from the accounts in year 0002.

3. Furniture and equipment depreciation expense for year 0002 is $3,000.

4. The net income after depreciation in year 0002 is $12,200.

5. A long-term loan was increased by $10,000 during year 0002, and part of this amount was used to pay back a stockholder his long-term loan to the motel of $6,000.

6. Dividends of $10,400 were paid in year 0002.

Prepare a statement of changes in working capital accounts and a statement of source and use of working capital.

11.8 A hotel had the following income statement for the year ending December 31, 0011.

Revenue		$1,152,900
Cost of sales		249,000
		$ 903,900
Wages and operating costs		487,800
		$ 416,100
Other income		23,200
		$ 439,300
Administrative and general	$53,100	
Marketing	25,000	
Energy costs	30,500	
Property operation and maintenance	53,000	161,600
		$ 277,700
Property taxes	$26,800	
Insurance	11,300	
Interest	43,600	81,700
		$ 196,000
Depreciation		
building	$31,900	
equipment	30,100	62,000
		$ 134,000
Income tax		67,000
Net income		$ 67,000

The hotel's balance sheets for the years ending December 31, 0010, and 0011 are illustrated. There is the following additional information:

1. The land account has increased by $60,000; this is the result of two transactions: a sale of a parcel of land for $30,000 and the purchase of another parcel for $90,000.

2. Improvements were made to the building amounting to $39,700.
3. The furniture and equipment account increased during the year by $12,100. This was accounted for as follows:

Balance January 1, 0011	$295,900
January 15, new equipment	3,100
July 16, new furniture	7,300
September 28, equipment discarded, no scrap value, removed from account	(5,000)
December 3, new equipment	6,700
Balance December 31, 0011	$308,000

The related accumulated depreciation account for furniture and equipment recorded the following:

Balance January 1, 0011	$162,300
September 28, equipment discarded, item removed from account	(5,000)
December 31, depreciation expense for year	30,100
Balance December 31, 0011	$187,400

4. The first mortgage was reduced by $46,200 during the year.
5. The second mortgage was increased (additional borrowing to finance purchase of land) by $45,900, and reduced (by payments) by $10,800.
6. The income statement shows an interest expense deduction of $43,600, and $4,100 of this amount was deferred interest expense (see balance sheets and refer to Chapter 2 for an explanation of deferred expense).

Balance Sheets	Dec. 31 Year 0010		Dec. 31 Year 0011	
Assets				
Cash		$ 75,400		$ 71,200
Accounts recievable after allowance for bad debts		23,500		23,900
Inventories				
food	$ 6,100		$ 6,400	
beverage	5,900		7,100	
other	2,500	14,500	3,200	16,700
Prepaid expenses		3,200		4,000
Land		30,200		90,200

Balance Sheets	Dec. 31 Year 0010		Dec. 31 Year 0011	
Building	$870,600		$910,300	
Accumulated depreciation	(273,100)	597,500	(305,000)	605,300
Furniture and equipment	$295,900		$308,000	
Accumulated depreciation	(162,300)	133,600	(187,400)	120,600
Deferred interest expense		20,200		16,100
Goodwill		75,000		75,000
Total		$973,100		$1,023,000
Liabilities and stockholders' equity				
Accounts payable		$129,400		$ 82,700
Income taxes payable		24,500		67,000
Accrued wages		15,900		6,900
Current portion of mortgages		49,800		57,000
Long-term mortgages				
first		619,600		573,400
second		55,000		90,100
Common stock		30,000		30,000
Retained earnings (deficit)				
Jan. 1	($ 13,500)		$ 48,900	
Net income for year	62,400		67,000	
Retained earnings Dec. 31		48,900		115,900
Total		$973,100		$1,023,000

Required

a. A statement of changes in working capital.

b. A statement of source and use of working capital.

CASE 11

a. Given the budgeted income statement prepared in Case 10 and the following additional information, prepare the 4C Company's budgeted balance sheet as at December 31, 0002.

- Cash. As the result of carrying out a cash budget for year 0002 (this topic will be discussed in Chapter 12), the forecast cash balance at December 31, is $30,707.

- Accounts receivable. The cash to charge ratio will stay the same as in year 0001 (see Case 4), as will the percentage of accounts receivable to charge revenue at the year-end.

- Food and beverage inventories. Turnover ratios will be the same as in year 0001 (see Case 4).

- Prepaid expenses. These are estimated to be $2,400 at December 31, 0002.

- Furniture and equipment. No purchases or sales during the year 0002.

- Accounts payable. Estimated to be $9,200 at December 31, 0002.

- Accrued expenses. Estimated to be $2,510 at December 31, 0002.

- Income tax payable. Income tax for year 0002 will not be paid until year 0003.

- Current portion of loan. Estimated to be $42,741 due in year 0003.

- Common stock. $20,000 will be redeemed (bought back) by the 4C Company from Charles for cash early in year 0002.

(Note: if your balance sheet is out of balance by a dollar or two this is probably due to rounding numbers, for example, in the accounts receivable calculation.)

b. Prepare a budgeted statement of changes in working capital accounts for the year 0002. Refer to Case 2 for the December 31, 0001 balance sheet.

c. Prepare a budgeted statement of source and use of working capital for the year 0002.

12 Cash Management

Chapter Highlights

This chapter introduces the reader to the concept of cash flow, explaining how cash flows into and out of a company. The fact that net income shows on an income statement does not necessarily mean there is an equivalent amount of cash in the bank is discussed and illustrated.

The method of compiling a cash budget from cash receipts and cash disbursements is demonstrated. Negative cash flow may result at times. Various other nonrecurring transactions that could affect the preparation of a cash budget are also discussed.

The subject of cash conservation and working capital management is covered. Included are such items as cash on hand and in the bank, use of bank float, concentration banking, use of two bank accounts, accounts receivable, use of lockboxes, aging of accounts, marketable securities, inventories, and accounts payable.

Finally the topic of long-range cash flow (as opposed to short-term cash budgeting), including the use of CVP analysis (taking income tax into consideration) to convert required cash flow to a revenue figure, is discussed and illustrated.

Chapter Objectives

After studying this chapter the reader should be able to:

1. Explain why cash planning is necessary and state the two main purposes of cash budgeting.
2. Explain why net income on an income statement is not necessarily indicative of the amount of cash on hand.
3. List items that would appear under cash receipts and cash disbursements on a cash budget, and prepare a cash budget given appropriate information.
4. Define bank float and discuss the concept of concentration banking.
5. Explain some of the procedures that can be used to minimize accounts receivable outstanding at any given time, including the use of a lockbox.
6. Prepare a schedule of aging of accounts receivable.
7. Discuss the importance of marketable securities with reference to surplus cash funds.
8. Calculate inventory turnover.
9. Explain long-term cash flow budgeting, and use CVP to calculate the revenue required to provide a desired cash flow amount.

CASH MANAGEMENT

Simply stated, cash management is the management of money so that bills and debts are paid when they are due. Money does not always come into a business at the same rate as it goes out. At times there will be excess cash on hand, at other times there will be shortages of cash. Both these events need to be anticipated so that surpluses can be used to advantage and shortages can be covered. In this way the cash balance will be kept at its optimum level.

THE CYCLE OF CASH FLOW

The cycle of cash flow through an enterprise is illustrated in Exhibit 12.1. This shows that cash management is not just a problem of making sure that the balance of cash in the bank is correct and that the cashiers have the right amount of money on hand. Rather, it is management of all working capital accounts—cash, inventories, accounts receivable, plus the management of accounts payable, of loan payments—and of discretionary spending items, such as purchase of new capital assets and payment of dividends if cash is available.

Cash budgets aid in control

Control over all these various items of cash receipts and cash disbursements can be managed by preparing cash budgets. The importance of cash planning, or cash budgets, can best be explained by showing that the net income that a company has on its income statement (the excess of revenue over expenditure) is not necessarily indicative of the amount of cash the company has on hand.

Net Income Is Not Cash

Let us consider a simple illustration. An entrepreneur has an opportunity to take over a restaurant, fully equipped and furnished, for a rent of $2,000 a month. He decides that his cash savings of $10,000 should be sufficient working capital to start the business, after which the cash from revenue should keep the business going and allow him to take out a salary of $1,500 a month. Prior to opening, his balance sheet would look like this:

Assets		Liabilities and Equity	
Cash	$10,000	Owner's investment	$10,000

Cash required for inventory

However, before he can sell any food he has to use some of his cash for inventory; let us assume he needs $5,000. The balance sheet is now

Assets		Liabilities and Equity	
Cash	$ 5,000	Owner's investment	$10,000
Inventory	5,000		
	$10,000		$10,000

Accounts receivable outstanding

The owner is ready for business. During the first month he has the operating results shown in Exhibit 12.2: total revenue of $20,000, total expenses of $18,000, and a net income of $2,000.

As a result, one might expect to see the bank account increased by $2,000; but in our case this is not so. Even though revenue is $20,000, in order to achieve this level of sales the owner decided to permit some customers to sign their bills, send them invoices at the end of the month, and collect the cash in month 2. In addition, some customers used national credit cards, which he agreed to honor. As a result, at the end of the month there were $7,000 of accounts receivable and the cash income was only $13,000.

As far as expenses were concerned, the owner did not have to expend

Exhibit 12.1 Illustration of the cash flow cycle.

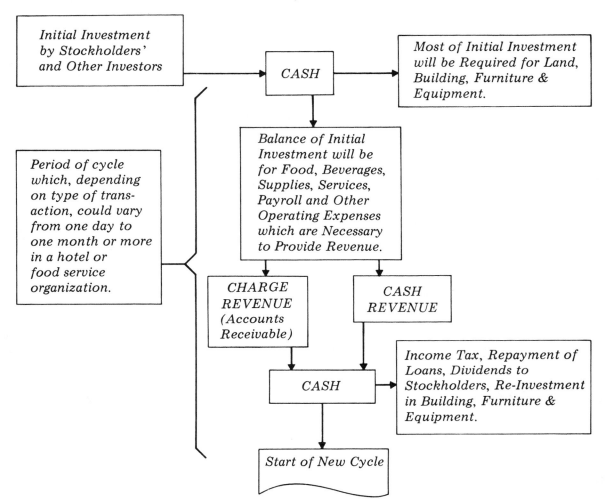

Initial Investment
by Stockholders'
and Other Investors

CASH

Most of Initial Investment
will be Required for Land,
Building, Furniture &
Equipment.

Period of cycle
which, depending
on type of trans-
action, could vary
from one day to
one month or more
in a hotel or
food service
organization.

Balance of Initial
Investment will be
for Food, Beverages,
Supplies, Services,
Payroll and Other
Operating Expenses
which are Necessary
to Provide Revenue.

CHARGE
REVENUE
(Accounts
Receivable)

CASH
REVENUE

CASH

Income Tax, Repayment of
Loans, Dividends to
Stockholders, Re-Investment
in Building, Furniture &
Equipment.

Start of New Cycle

Exhibit 12.2 Illustrative income statement.

Revenue		$20,000
Food cost		5,000
Gross profit		$15,000
Owner's salary	$1,500	
Other wages	6,500	
Supplies and other expenses	3,000	
Rent	2,000	13,000
Net income		$ 2,000

any cash for the food cost of $5,000. He simply used up the inventory, which had already been paid for.

The actual cash outlays during the first month were for owner's salary, other wages, supplies and other expenses, and rent. None of these items were obtainable on credit, so the net cash expenditures totaled $13,000. In summary:

Cash receipts	$13,000
Cash disbursements	(13,000)
Net change in bank balance	0

Replacement of inventory

However, since the food inventory has been used up, it has to be replaced, and this will require $5,000 cash. Therefore, since at the beginning of the month there was a bank balance (see earlier balance sheet) of $5,000, the month-end bank balance will be

Bank balance beginning of the month	$5,000
Change in bank balance from operations	0
Reduction in bank balance for replacement of inventory	(5,000)
Bank balance end of month	0

The month-end balance sheet will now be

Assets		Liabilities and Equity	
Cash	$ 0	Owner's investment	$10,000
Accounts receivable	7,000	Net income for month	2,000
Inventory	5,000	(Retained earnings)	
	$12,000		$12,000

The balance sheet shows us that, despite the fact there is a net income for the first month there is no cash in the bank to pay any other immediate expenses. Although this is an oversimplified illustration, it is not untypical of what happens to new businesses and indicates the danger of assuming that any net income on the income statement is going to be in the form of cash. In this case, the net income of $2,000 and the $5,000 of cash the owner started out with at the beginning of the month are now tied up in the accounts receivable of $7,000.

The same principle applies in an ongoing concern. The income statement net income is not generally synonymous with cash. The timing of the cash coming in from revenue may not parallel the timing of cash going out to pay for operating expenses. To prevent this difficulty—to see whether a business is going to have excesses or shortages of cash—a cash budget prepared in advance month by month for a year, or at least every quarter, is a useful management tool.

INCOME AND EXPENSE BUDGETS

The starting point in cash budgeting is the income statement showing the budgeted revenues and expenditures by month for as long a period as is required for cash budget preparation. In our case, a three-month period has been selected and budgeted income statements for a restaurant for the months of April, May, and June are shown in Exhibit 12.3.

In order to prepare our cash budget we need some additional information.

**Information
required for
cash budget**

1. Accounting records show that, each month, approximately 60 percent of the revenue is in the form of cash and 40 percent is charged and collected the following month. (If this were a new business, the breakdown between cash and charge revenue would have to be estimated.)

2. March revenue was $28,000. (We need this information so that we can calculate the amount of cash that is going to be collected in April from sales made in March.)

3. Purchases of food (food cost) are paid 25 percent cash and 75 percent are on credit. The 75 percent (accounts payable) is paid the month following purchase.

4. March food purchases were $11,000. (Again, we need this information so that we can calculate the amount to be paid for in cash during April.)

5. Payroll, supplies, utilities, and rent are paid 100 percent cash during each current month.

Exhibit 12.3 Illustration of budgeted income and expenses.

	April		May		June	
Revenue		$30,000		$35,000		$40,000
Food cost		12,000		14,000		16,000
Gross profit		$18,000		$21,000		$24,000
Payroll and related expense	$9,000		$10,500		$12,000	
Supplies and other expense	1,500		1,750		2,000	
Utilities	500		750		1,000	
Rent	1,000		1,000		1,000	
Advertising	500	12,500	500	14,500	500	16,500
Income before depreciation		$ 5,500		$ 6,500		$ 7,500
Depreciation		2,000		2,000		2,000
Net income		$ 3,500		$ 4,500		$ 5,500

6. Advertising has been prepaid in January ($6,000 cash) for the entire year. In order not to show the full $6,000 as an expense in January (since the benefit of the advertising is for a full year), the income statements show $500 each month for this prepaid expense.
7. The bank balance on April 1 is $10,200.

PREPARING THE CASH BUDGET

We can now use the budgeted income statements (Exhibit 12.3) and the above information to calculate the figures for our cash budget. The process is simple. Our first cash budget month is April.

Cash Receipts

Current month revenue $30,000 × 60% cash	= $18,000
Accounts receivable collections, previous month revenue $28,000 × 40% charged	= 11,200

Cash Disbursements

Current month food purchases (food costs) $12,000 × 25% paid cash	= 3,000

Accounts payable for food purchases from previous month $11,000 × 75%	=	8,250
Payroll and related expense, 100% cash	=	9,000
Supplies and other expense, 100% cash	=	1,500
Utilities, 100% cash	=	500
Rent, 100% cash	=	1,000
Advertising: already paid in January, the $6,000 would have been shown as cash disbursement for that month	=	0
Depreciation: does not require an outlay of cash, it is simply a write-down of the book value of the related assets	=	0

Our completed cash budget for the month of April would then appear as in Exhibit 12.4.

The closing bank balance each month is calculated as follows:

$$\text{Opening bank balance}$$
$$+$$
$$\text{Receipts}$$
$$-$$
$$\text{Disbursements}$$
$$=$$
$$\text{Closing bank balance}$$

Closing balance becomes opening balance

Each month the closing bank balance becomes the opening bank balance of the next month. The completed cash budget for the three-month period would be as in Exhibit 12.5. From Exhibit 12.5 it can be seen that the bank account is expected to increase from $10,200 to $30,150 over the next three months. Continuing the cash budget over the following quarter would show whether or not the bank balance is going to continue to increase or start to decline.

From Exhibit 12.5 it is obvious that in this operation there is a fairly healthy surplus of cash (as long as budget projections are reasonably accurate) that should not be left to accumulate at no or low interest in a bank account. In this particular case, management might decide to take

Use of surplus cash

$20,000 or $25,000 out of the bank and invest it in high interest, short-term (thirty-, sixty-, or ninety-day) securities. Without preparing a cash budget, it would be difficult for management to know that it was going to have surplus funds on hand which could be used to advantage to increase net income (and subsequently cash receipts). If the cash were taken out of the bank account and invested, the cash budget would have to show this (listed under disbursements); when the securities were

Exhibit 12.4 Illustration of monthly cash budget.

Opening bank balance	$10,200
Receipts	
Cash revenue	18,000
Collection on accounts receivable	11,200
Total	$39,400
Disbursements	
Cash food purchases	$ 3,000
Accounts payable	8,250
Payroll and related expense	9,000
Supplies and other expense	1,500
Utilities	500
Rent	1,000
Total	$23,250
Closing bank balance	$16,150

cashed in, the amount would be recorded on the cash budget under receipts, along with the interest earned.

As the budget period goes by, the cash budget for the remaining months in that period may need to be adjusted to reflect any changed conditions.

Negative Cash Budget

Seasonal negative cash flows

On occasion some companies, particularly seasonal operations, may find that for some months in the year their disbursements exceed receipts to the point that they have negative cash amounts. Exhibit 12.6 illustrates such a situation. As can be seen, the operation will be short of cash by an estimated $1,000 in each of months 4 and 5. However, having prepared a cash budget ahead of time, the company has anticipated the cash shortage and can plan to cover it by means of a short-term bank loan or by stockholder or owner loans.

Other Transactions Affecting Cash Budget

Other possibilities

Just as a cash investment (because of surplus cash) must be recorded on the cash budget, so must cash loans (from banks or stockholders, for example, to cover short-term requirements) be shown as receipts. Repayments of such loans are recorded as disbursements.

There are also a number of other possible transactions that could occur

Exhibit 12.5   Illustration of 3-month cash budget.

	April	May	June
Opening bank balance	$10,200	$16,150	$22,650
Receipts			
Cash revenue	18,000	21,000	24,000
Collection on accounts receivable	11,200	12,000	14,000
Total	$39,400	$49,150	$60,650
Disbursements			
Cash food purchases	$ 3,000	$ 3,500	$ 4,000
Accounts payable paid	8,250	9,000	10,500
Payroll and related expense	9,000	10,500	12,000
Supplies and other expense	1,500	1,750	2,000
Utilities	500	750	1,000
Rent	1,000	1,000	1,000
Total	$23,250	$26,500	$30,500
Closing bank balance	$16,150	$22,650	$30,150

Typical disbursements

that must be recorded on the cash budget. For example, if any new long-term loans were negotiated, the cash received during a cash budget period must be shown under receipts, as would be cash received from any new issues of stock. If any fixed assets were sold for cash, this would also affect the receipts section of the cash budget.

On the other hand, any repayments of principal amount of loans, redemption of stock for cash, or purchases of new fixed assets would require entries in the disbursements section of the cash budget.

Finally, any dividends paid would further reduce cash on hand and therefore require an entry in the disbursements section.

The cash budget, particularly if prepared for a year ahead, can not only help management in making decisions about investing excess funds and arranging to borrow funds to cover shortages, but also aids in making discretionary decisions concerning such factors as major renovations, replacement of fixed assets, and payment of dividends.

Exhibit 12.6   Illustration of negative cash flow.

	Month 1	Month 2	Month 3	Month 4	Month 5	Month 6
Opening balance	5,000	7,000	8,000	4,000	(1,000)	(1,000)
Receipts	22,000	24,000	20,000	16,000	16,000	20,000
Total	27,000	31,000	28,000	20,000	15,000	19,000
Disbursements	20,000	23,000	24,000	21,000	16,000	16,000
Closing balance	7,000	8,000	4,000	(1,000)	(1,000)	3,000

A cash budget, if carefully prepared, permits management to plan ahead to do or not do certain things, depending on cash availability. If decisions are made and plans prepared for major spending items without a cash budget having been prepared, sudden shortages of cash may develop. These shortages may not be able to be covered quickly with loans because no plans had been made to arrange for loans.

CASH CONSERVATION AND WORKING CAPITAL MANAGEMENT

Whether a company feels that a cash budget is advantageous or not is a matter for that company's management to decide. However, there are certain practices that any hospitality operator should institute as a matter of good business sense in order to conserve cash, earn interest on it (one possibility), and thus maximize net income. Some of these more common practices are discussed.

Surplus cash to earn interest

Cash on Hand. Cash on hand, as distinguished from cash in the bank, is the amount of money in circulation in an operation. This cash is used by cashiers as "floats" for change-making purposes, petty cash, or just general cash in the organization's safe. The amount of cash on hand should be sufficient for normal day-to-day operations only. Any surplus, idle cash should be deposited in the bank in savings accounts so that it can earn interest. Preferably each day's net cash receipts should be deposited in the bank as soon as possible the following day.

Cash in Bank. Cash in the bank in the current account should be sufficient to pay only current bills due or current payroll. Any excess funds should be invested in short-term securities (making sure there is a good balance between maximizing the interest rate and security and liquidity of the investment) or in savings or other special accounts that earn interest. The typical hospitality industry enterprise will probably determine an appropriate level of cash to be held after considering the following:

Considerations
- Anticipated cash flows indicated by the cash budget.
- Unanticipated events causing deviations from the cash budget.
- Ability to borrow money for emergencies above the minimal cash requirements plus any precautionary amounts.
- Desire of management to always have more than sufficient cash on hand rather than maintaining a minimum level (this minimum level may aid in increasing net income, but at the same time it will increase risk).

- Efficiency of the cash management system (the more efficient the business's system, the more surplus cash will be available for investment and increased profits).

- Historical evidence and past experience, which can be a guide to establishing satisfactory levels of cash.

Reason for difference

Use of Floats. A float is the difference between the bank balance shown on a company's records and the balance of actual cash in the bank. There is a difference because checks a company writes are deducted from its record of the bank balance at that time. However, there is a delay between that time (due to mailing and the handling of the check by the recipient and then by his bank) and the time that the check is received by the company's bank and deducted from its records. If a company can estimate the amount of this float and the period of time involved, it can then invest the amount for that period and increase its net income.

Concentration Banking. Concentration banking (also known as integrated banking) might be appropriate for chain-operated hotels or restaurants. It is a method of accelerating the flow of funds from the individual units in the chain to the company's head office bank account. The individual units will still have accounts at the bank's local branch in the city where the unit is operated, but arrangements will be made with the local bank to transfer any surplus above a predetermined level in the account to the head office's bank immediately.

Head office makes disbursements

Disbursements would be made out of the head office account on behalf of the individual units. Only sufficient cash to take care of normal day-to-day disbursements would be held in the account. Any surplus above this amount would be invested in such items as marketable securities (to be discussed later in this chapter). A concentration banking system results in more effective cash management for the entire chain. For example, there might be a temptation for a local unit manager to pay invoices before their due date to keep local suppliers happy. Also, if an individual unit requires cash, it can be provided by the head office so that the local unit manager does not have to negotiate a loan with his local banker at less favorable terms.

In concentration banking, it is important to minimize the cost of funds' transfers. In certain situations, daily transfers from the individual units to the head office account might not be the most appropriate action. To determine how frequently transfers should be made, the following equation may be used:

Transfer frequency equation

$$\text{Transfer frequency} = \frac{2 \times \text{Average bank balance}}{\text{Average daily deposit}}$$

For example, if a restaurant unit were to require an average bank balance of $10,000, and if its average daily deposit were $2,000, the transfer frequency would be

$$\frac{2 \times \$10,000}{\$2,000} = \frac{\$20,000}{\$2,000} = 10 \text{ days}$$

Elimination of transfers

This means that at the beginning of each ten-day period, the balance in the unit's bank account will be zero. At the end of ten days it will have accumulated to $20,000, at which time the full $20,000 is transferred, reducing the balance again to zero. Nine transfers are eliminated, thus minimizing transfer costs. In general, the only time that a daily transfer would be profitable for an operation would be if the average bank balance required were less than half the average daily deposit.

Two Bank Accounts. In addition to concentration banking, large chain operations can also benefit from the float effect by having one bank account on the East Coast and the other on the West Coast. Collections from the Pacific-side operations would be deposited in the West Coast bank; payments on behalf of these operations would be made from the East Coast bank. The reverse situation would exist for Atlantic-side operations.

Mail invoices promptly

Accounts Receivable. Attention to accounts receivable should be focused on two areas: ensuring that invoices are mailed out promptly and following up on delinquent accounts to have them collected. Money tied up in accounts receivable is money not earning a return. Extension of credit to customers is an acknowledged form of business transaction, but it should not be extended to the point of allowing payments to lag two or three months behind the mailing of invoices. In hotels a special situation arises. Accounts receivable in hotels are made up of city ledger accounts and house accounts. City ledger accounts include banquet and convention business, regular credit card charges for individuals using the hotel's food and beverage facilities, and the accounts of people who were staying in the hotel but who have checked out and charged their bills. Normal collection procedures prevail for collecting such accounts. The house accounts are the accounts for those registered in the hotel who have not yet checked out. In some cases such accounts can build up to large amounts in a very short time. A good policy is to establish a ceiling to which the dollar amount of an individual account may rise. Once this ceiling is reached, the night auditor can be instructed to advise the credit manager, or general manager in a smaller hotel, who must then decide whether or not any action should be taken to request payment, or partial payment, of the account, or discuss a credit arrangement with the guest.

Establish ceiling on house accounts

Where guests stay for longer periods without necessarily running up large accounts, a good policy is to give the guest a copy of the bill at least once a week. This serves two purposes. It allows the guest to confirm or question the accuracy of the account, and it suggests that payment should be made or arrangements for credit established.

One of the ways of keeping an eye on the accounts receivable is periodically (possibly once a month) to prepare a chart showing the age of the accounts outstanding. Exhibit 12.7 illustrates such a chart.

Exhibit 12.7 shows that the accounts receivable outstanding situation has not improved from March to April. In March 79.5 percent of total receivables were less than 30 days old. In April only 74.2 percent were less than 30 days outstanding. Similarly, the relative percentages in the 31- to 60-day category have worsened from March to April. By contrast, in the 61- to 90-day bracket 11.3 percent of receivables are outstanding in April, against only 3.2 percent in March. This particular aging chart shows that our accounts receivable are getting older. If this trend continued, collection procedures would need to be improved. If, after all possible collection procedures have been explored, an account is deemed to be uncollectible (a bad debt), it would then be removed from accounts receivable. The decision on its uncollectibility in a small operation should be made by the manager or owner. In a larger operation it would be made by the credit manager or comptroller.

Lockboxes. The collection of accounts receivable can also be speeded by the use of a lockbox. Lockboxes are most appropriate for chain operations. When they are used, customers are directed to mail their checks in payment of accounts to a designated post office mailbox. The hospitality establishment's bank picks up the mail and deposits the receivables' payments into the hospitality operation's bank account and subsequently notifies the establishment of the necessary detail for it to record payments in its accounts receivable. The main advantages of the lockbox system are that the individual units in the chain are freed from receiving and depositing payment checks and that the collection process is speeded by one or more days.

There is a cost attached to using a lockbox. To determine whether the

Exhibit 12.7 Analysis (aging) of accounts receivable.

Age	March 31		April 30	
0–30 days	$29,500	79.5%	$28,200	74.2%
31–60 days	5,900	15.9	4,400	11.6
61–90 days	1,200	3.2	4,300	11.3
Over 90 days	500	1.4	1,100	2.9
Totals	$37,100	100.0%	$38,000	100.0%

added efficiency is profitable, the cost should be compared with the increased income from the cash released for investment elsewhere. If income exceeds cost, the system is profitable; if the reverse is the case, it is not.

Alternatively, it may be useful to calculate the minimum level of accounts receivable payment that would make a lockbox system profitable. Suppose that the bank charges 20 cents for each payment check handled and that the opportunity cost of alternative investments is 9 percent. (The opportunity cost is the interest that the hospitality operation could earn by investing freed-up cash in, let us say, marketable securities.) By using a lockbox, the collection of accounts receivable is speeded up by two days. An equation for determining the minimum level of account receivable that would make the lockbox system profitable is

**Lockbox
equation**

$$\frac{\text{Bank charge per item}}{\text{Opportunity cost percentage per day} \times \text{Time saving in days}}$$

Using our figures, the minimum accounts receivable amount is

$$\frac{\$0.20}{(0.09/365) \times 2} = \frac{\$0.20}{0.00024666 \times 2} = \frac{\$0.20}{0.0004932} = \$405$$

Given these assumptions, this means that with a lockbox system, payments in excess of $405 on accounts receivable would be profitable and payments less than $405 would not be profitable. A decision could be made to use a lockbox if the average payment exceeded $405. Alternatively, a more profitable approach might be to handle accounts receivable according to size. For example, when the accounts are mailed out, those in excess of $405 would carry instructions to use the lockbox mailing address and those less than $405 would be handled in the regular manner.

**Making
investments**

Marketable Securities. Generally, any surplus cash not needed for immediate and precautionary purposes should be invested in some type of security. Investments could be for as short a period as one day but are usually for longer periods, although seldom more than a year. If surplus cash were available for periods of a year or more, it might then be wise to seek out long-term investments, such as building a new property or expanding an existing one, because the return on those investments over the long run could be expected to be greater than for investment in short-term securities.

Most hospitality industry enterprises, particularly those that rely for much or all of their trade on seasonal tourists, have peaks and valleys in their cash flows. Surplus cash from peak-season flows should be invested in short-term securities until it is necessary to liquidate them to take care of low, or negative, cash flows during the off season. Sometimes it is necessary to build up surplus cash amounts to take care of periodic lump sum payments, such as quarterly tax or dividend payments. These built-up amounts could well be invested in marketable securities until they were needed for payment of these liabilities.

In times of high interest rates, many companies find it profitable to invest all cash in excess of day-to-day needs in the most liquid of marketable securities: that is, those that can be converted into cash quickly if an unanticipated event requiring cash occurs. In this way, little if any precautionary cash will be carried.

Risk versus liquidity

Two important factors need to be considered when investing in marketable securities: risk and liquidity. A low risk generally goes hand in hand with a low interest rate. A more risky investment would have to offer a higher interest rate in order to attract investors. Government securities have very low risk and usually guarantee that the security can be cashed in at full face value at any time. Their interest rate, however, is also relatively low. On the other hand, investments in long-term corporate bonds, with a distant maturity date, may offer a higher interest rate. This type of security is, however, subject to economic factors that make their buy-sell price more volatile. This volatility increases the risk and can reduce the profitability of investing in them if they have to be liquidated, or converted into cash, at an inappropriate time.

Short-term, liquid marketable securities include such items as government Treasury bills, bankers' acceptances, short-term notes, bank deposit receipts, and corporate or finance company paper. Long-term, less liquid investments include corporate bonds, preferred and common stock, equipment trust certificates, and municipal securities.

Inventories. The level at which inventories should be maintained for food and beverages can be established by calculating the inventory turnover rates for each. The turnover rate for food is calculated as follows:

Inventory turnover equation

$$\frac{\text{Food cost for the month}}{\text{Average food inventory during month}}$$

The inventory turnover could be calculated annually, but it is preferable to do it monthly particularly if monthly income statements are prepared because, if the turnover rate at the end of any month is out of line, corrective action can be taken then, instead of only at the year end.

In the preceding equation, food cost is calculated as follows:

Beginning of the month inventory + Purchases during month
− End of the month inventory

Average inventory calculation

Average inventory is calculated as follows:

(Beginning of the month inventory + End of the month inventory) ÷ 2

Assuming we had the following figures:

Beginning of the month inventory	$ 7,000
End of the month inventory	8,000
Purchases during month	24,500

our calculation of the inventory turnover rate is:

$$\frac{\$7,000 + \$24,500 - \$8,000}{(\$7,000 + \$8,000) \div 2} = \frac{\$23,500}{\$7,500} = 3.1 \text{ times}$$

Trend of turnover

Traditionally, the food industry food inventory turnover ranges between two and four times a month. At this level the danger of running out of food items is minimal; on the other hand, there is not an overinvestment in inventory tying up money that could otherwise be put to use earning interest income. However, despite this range of two to four times a month, there may be exceptions. Perhaps of more importance to an organization is not what its actual turnover rate is, but whether or not there is a change in this turnover rate over time, and what the cause of the change is. For example, let us assume that the earlier figures $23,500 for food cost and $7,500 for average inventory, giving a turnover rate of 3.1, were typical of the monthly figures for this operation. If management noticed that the figure for turnover changed to two, this could mean that more money was being invested in inventory and not producing a return.

$$\frac{\$23,500}{\$11,750} = 2 \text{ times}$$

Too little in inventory

Alternatively, a change in the turnover rate to four could mean that too little was invested in inventory, and that some customers may not be able to get certain items listed on the menu.

$$\frac{\$23,500}{\$ 5,875} = 4 \text{ times}$$

In some establishments the turnover rate may be extremely low (less than two). For example, a resort property in a remote location may only be able to get deliveries once a month and is thus forced to carry a large inventory. On the other hand, a drive-in restaurant that receives daily delivery of its food items from a central commissary and carries little inventory overnight could conceivably have a turnover rate as high as thirty times a month. Each organization should establish its own standards for turnover and then watch for deviations from those standards.

Beverage inventory turnover is calculated using the same formula, but substituting beverage inventories and beverage purchases for food. (The word "beverage" here applies to alcoholic beverages only.) The normal monthly turnover rate for beverages is from one-half to one turnover a month. Again, however, there are exceptions to this rule of thumb.

Accounts Payable, Accrued Expenses, and Other Current Liabilities. The objective here, to conserve cash in the organization, is to delay payment until payment is required. However, this does not mean delaying payment until it is delinquent! A company with a reputation for delinquency may find it has difficulty obtaining food, beverages, supplies, and services on anything other than a cash basis. If a discount for prompt payments is offered, the advantages of this should be considered. For example, a common discount rate is 2 percent off the invoice total if paid within ten days, otherwise payable without discount within sixty days. On a $1,000 purchase paid within ten days, this would save $20. This may not seem a lot of money, but multiplied many times over on all similar purchases made during a year, it could amount to a large sum. However, in the example cited, the company may have to borrow the money ($980) in order to make the payment within ten days. Let us assume the money was borrowed for fifty days at an 8 percent interest rate. The interest expense on this borrowed money would be:

**Consider taking
discount**

$$\frac{\$980 \times 50 \text{ days} \times 8\%}{365 \text{ days}} = \$10.74$$

It would still be advantageous to borrow the money since the difference between the discount saving of $20.00 and the interest expense of $10.74 is still $9.26.

Other Items. There are other methods of operating with the objective of conserving cash in the business. One example is leasing, rather than purchasing, an asset in order to take advantage of a tax saving. This and other more long-range techniques are covered in Chapter 13.

LONG-RANGE CASH FLOW

The long-range cash flow budget differs somewhat from day-to-day cash budgeting. The long-range cash flow projections ignore any changes within working capital and assume that the current asset and liability amounts remain relatively constant over the long run. The long-range cash flow budget is usually prepared for yearly periods for up to five years ahead.

The starting point in preparation of a long-range cash flow budget is the annual net income figure. To this is added back the depreciation to convert the net income to a cash position, and from that amount is deducted the amount of any principal payments on long-term borrowings. A simple cash flow budget for five years appears as in Exhibit 12.8.

The long-term cash flow budget serves the following purposes:

Purposes of long-range cash budget

1. It allows the manager to see whether there will be cash available to meet long-term mortgage, bond, or other loan commitments.
2. It indicates a possible need to arrange additional long-term borrowings or the need to issue additional stock to raise cash.
3. It allows for planning replacement of or additions to long-term assets (note that if any long-term assets were bought or sold, the cash disbursed or received would be included in the cash flow projections).
4. It permits the planning of a dividend payment policy since it shows whether or not there will be surplus cash available for dividends.

Cash Flow and CVP

CVP analysis (discussed in Chapter 9) can also be applied to cash flow. It can answer the question, How much revenue is needed to produce various levels of cash flow? For example, suppose the management of the operation illustrated in Exhibit 12.8 wanted a cash flow of $38,000 in year one, rather than the $30,000 illustrated. What would this require in terms of total revenue?

Exhibit 12.8 Illustration of long-range accumulated cash flow.

	Year 1	Year 2	Year 3	Year 4	Year 5
Net income after tax	$10,000	$21,500	$30,000	$ 35,500	$ 40,000
Add back depreciation expense	80,000	72,000	65,000	59,000	55,000
	$90,000	$93,500	$95,000	$ 94,500	$ 95,000
Deduct long-term loan payments	(60,000)	(63,000)	(65,000)	(67,000)	(68,000)
Net cash flow	$30,000	$30,500	$30,000	$ 27,500	$ 27,000
Accumulated cash flow		$60,500	$90,500	$118,000	$145,000

First, the desired cash flow has to be converted to an after-tax profit figure by adding to the desired cash flow the long-term loan payments and deducting depreciation as follows:

$$\$38,000 + \$60,000 - \$80,000 = \$18,000$$

The after-tax figure then has to be converted to a before-tax amount by the following equation:

Before tax equation

$$\text{Profit before tax} = \frac{\text{After-tax profit}}{1 - \text{Tax rate}}$$

If the company's tax rate were 25 percent, this would be

$$\frac{\$18,000}{1 - 0.25} = \frac{\$18,000}{0.75} = \$24,000$$

The following CVP equation can then be used to convert the before-tax profit desired to a revenue figure:

$$\frac{\text{Fixed costs} + \text{Before-tax profit}}{\text{Contribution margin}}$$

If fixed costs (including depreciation) were $180,000 and contribution margin were 60 percent, revenue required would be:

$$\frac{\$180,000 + \$24,000}{0.6} = \frac{\$204,000}{0.6} = \$340,000$$

Proof of calculations

This is proved as follows:

Revenue		$340,000
Variable costs 40% × $340,000	$136,000	
Fixed costs	180,000	316,000
Income before tax		$ 24,000
Tax 25%		6,000
Net income		$ 18,000
Add depreciation		80,000
		$ 98,000
Deduct loan payments		60,000
Net cash flow		$ 38,000

SUMMARY

Excesses and deficiencies of cash can occur in any business. This is particularly so of the cyclical hospitality industry. Therefore, cash management becomes most important.

Net income and cash are not synonymous. An organization may have a net income but no cash available to pay bills. Alternatively, the income statement may show a loss, yet there will be cash available to pay dividends.

In order to foresee surpluses and shortages of cash, the preparation of a cash budget for up to a year can be useful. The cash budget converts the budgeted income statements to a cash position. Revenue for a particular month is not always received in cash during that month. If some sales are made on a charge basis, that cash may not be received until thirty or more days later. Similarly, expenses recorded on the income statement do not always involve an outlay of cash during that month. Payments can often be deferred. Finally, there are some items of cash revenue (the sale of a fixed asset) or cash outlay (principal payments on a loan) that do not appear on an income statement. These items can be incorporated into the cash budget so that excess funds can be foreseen (and used profitably by, for example, investing) and so that cash shortages can be forecast (and covered by arranging, in advance, for short-term financing).

Cash management involves a process of cash conservation. This simply means that the good manager will control the amount of cash on hand, and in the bank, inventory levels, accounts receivable, and accounts payable so that the most liquid cash position of the business can be maintained at all times.

Cash budgets require careful day-to-day observation of the various current asset and liability accounts in order to maximize the day-to-day cash position of the organization.

Long-range cash flow budgets differ somewhat from day-to-day cash budgets in that they ignore changes in the working capital accounts. Long-term cash flow budgets assume that the net income an enterprise makes will, over the long run, be converted into cash. Long-term cash flow budgets, prepared up to five years ahead, permit management to see whether long-term mortgage and other loan commitments can be met, or whether further mortgages and/or loans need to be arranged. They also allow management to make plans for capital asset purchases and replacements and to plan dividend payment policies.

DISCUSSION QUESTIONS

1. What is the meaning of cash management or cash planning?
2. What two main purposes are served by preparing a cash budget?
3. Why is the net income shown on an income statement not necessarily the same as cash?
4. List three items that could appear on a cash budget under the receipts section.
5. List three items that could appear on a cash budget under the disbursements section.
6. Define the term "bank float" and explain how it can be used.
7. Explain concentration banking and give the equation for funds transfer frequency when concentration banking is used.
8. What two procedures will help ensure that the total accounts receivable amount is kept to a minimum?
9. Differentiate between city ledger accounts receivable and house accounts receivable in a hotel.
10. What two procedures can be instituted in a hotel to minimize the dollar amount of house accounts?
11. Explain the procedure of aging accounts receivable.
12. Explain how a lockbox is used to minimize funds outstanding in accounts receivable.
13. Discuss the use of marketable securities with reference to temporary surplus cash.
14. What is the formula for calculating food or beverage inventory turnover?
15. Differentiate between an operating cash budget and a long-term cash flow budget.

PROBLEMS

12.1   You have the following information about a restaurant in year 0001:

Actual revenue	October	$8,400
	November	8,000
Actual purchases (cost of sales)	October	3,200
	November	3,000

Fifty percent of revenue is cash; 50 percent is credit. Of the credit revenue, half is collected in the month following the sale and the remainder in the month following that. Twenty percent of purchases are cash. The remaining 80 percent is paid in the month following purchase. The budgeted income statement for December 0001 is:

Revenue		$7,500
Cost of sales	$3,000	
Wages	2,100	
Operating expenses	1,400	
Rent	550	
Depreciation	250	7,300
Net income		$ 200

Note that the wages and operating expenses included in the income statement will be paid in December 0001. Note also that rent is prepaid in January each year for the entire year. Prepare a cash budget for the month of December 0001. Cash in the bank on December 1, 0001, amounts to $3,300.

12.2 On December 31, 0003, a motel has a bank balance of $7,100. On that same date its balance sheet showed that it had a bank loan payable of $73,900.

The motel's budgeted income statement is as follows for the year 0004:

Revenue		$403,900
Operating costs		302,300
		$101,600
Other expenses:		
Management salary	$23,000	
Building rent	18,500	
Insurance	2,400	
Interest on loan	7,600	
Furniture depreciation	9,700	61,200
		$ 40,400
Income tax		10,100
Net income		$ 30,300

Note that the motel does not accept any credit cards. All sales are on a cash basis. Similarly, it pays its expenses at the time they occur in order not to carry any accounts payable. However, the income tax amount on the year 0004 income will not be paid until March 0005.

The motel owner plans to buy new furniture in May 0004 at an estimated cost of $15,600. By December 31, 0004 the bank loan payable will have been reduced to $49,200.

Calculate the motel's bank balance at December 31, 0004.

12.3 You have the following information about a restaurant:

	Budgeted Cash Revenue	Budgeted Credit Revenue
August	$30,300	$16,000
September	29,500	14,000
October	27,900	13,000
November	25,100	12,000
December	32,400	15,800

Collections on credit revenue average 90 percent in the month following the sales, and the remaining 10 percent in the month following that.

Cost of sales (purchases) average 40 percent of total revenue. Forty percent of cost of sales is on a cash basis, and 60 percent is paid in the month following purchase.

Payroll costs (which are paid on a cash basis) are forecast to be:

October	$13,100
November	12,700
December	12,200

Other budgeted expenses according to the forecast income statements are:

	October	November	December
Rent	$2,500	$2,500	$2,500
Insurance	300	300	300
Utilities	500	450	550
Other operating costs	1,100	900	1,300
Depreciation (equipment)	4,600	4,600	4,600
Interest	400	400	400

Note that the rent, utilities, other operating costs, and interest are paid in cash each month as the expense is incurred. The insurance expense is paid in January each year in advance for the whole year ($3,600).

The restaurant financed its equipment and makes monthly payments on the balance owing (principal amount) of $1,000.

In December the restaurant plans to sell off some old equipment and estimates it will receive $1,500 from the sale. At the same time it must spend $5,400 on new equipment.

If there is sufficient cash on hand, the owner plans to pay a bonus to the staff. This bonus will amount to $3,600 and will be paid in December.

Prepare the restaurant's cash budget for each of the three months: October, November, and December. The opening bank balance on October 1 is $2,410.

12.4 You own a new restaurant that is due to open on June 1. The restaurant expects to take in $500 a day in revenue and is open seven days a week.

Revenue is estimated to be 80 percent cash and 20 percent credit. The payments on credit sales are not expected to be received until the end of the month following the sale.

Labor and food cost combined will be 70 percent of revenue. Both these expenses will be on a cash basis.

Other operating costs are estimated to be 10 percent of revenue. These costs will not have to be paid until the month following the incurrence of the cost.

Depreciation is $1,000 a month. Rent is $300 a month payable in advance on the first of each month.

Principal payments on a loan you made to get into business are $3,000 a month. The first payment is due on June 15. You have only $500 cash on hand on June 1. You will not be able to borrow any more money, and you have no income of your own other than the money generated by your new restaurant venture.

a. Produce the budgeted income statement for the restaurant for the month of June.
b. Prepare the restaurant's cash budget for the month of June.
c. Comment about the results shown by these two statements, with particular reference to any possible financial difficulties you might have.

12.5 A small hotel provided you with the following information for a three-month period showing, at each month-end, the length of time its accounts receivable were outstanding at that time:

	January	**February**	**March**
0–30 days	$21,100	$21,500	$22,100
31–60 days	4,900	7,500	8,500
61–90 days	1,000	900	1,400
over 90 days	500	400	600

During this period the revenue was approximately the same for each of the three months.

Carry out any further calculations necessary so that you can then comment about or discuss the results.

12.6 A motel chain uses a system of concentration banking. Calculate the transfer frequency for each of the following individual motels:

	Average Bank Balance	**Average Daily Deposit**
Motel A	$3,200	$1,600
Motel B	5,700	1,900
Motel C	6,500	6,500
Motel D	2,600	5,800

12.7 For each of the following alternatives, calculate the minimum account receivable payment (to the closest dollar) that would make a lockbox system profitable:

	Bank Charge per Item	Opportunity Cost	Days Saved
a.	$0.20	10%	2
b.	$0.18	8	3
c.	$0.25	8.5	4

12.8 A motel with a small dining room has prepared the following estimates for the year 0005:

Revenue
    Rooms $350,000
    Dining room   150,000
Labor cost
    Rooms   25% of rooms revenue
    Dining room   40% of dining room revenue
    Food cost   35% of dining room revenue
Other operating costs
    Rooms   5% of rooms revenue
    Dining room   10% of dining room revenue
Other income $5,500

Indirect expenses

Administrative and general	$25,600
Marketing	15,400
Property operation and maintenance	16,700
Energy costs	12,500
Land rent	28,300
Interest	11,500
Depreciation	
Building	50,200
Furniture and equipment	24,800

In July of year 0005 the owner plans to buy $30,000 of new equipment (for cash), less a $5,400 trade-in of used equipment.

During year 0005 principal payments to be made on a mortgage on the building will amount to $30,300, and principal payments to be made on a bank loan will be $25,300.

The owner, who is also the only shareholder in the company, plans to pay herself dividends of $40,000 during 0005.

a. Prepare a budgeted income statement for 0005.
b. Calculate the motel's cash flow for 0005.

12.9 From the information given below for Cato's Catering, prepare a cash budget for the six months commencing April 1.

| | Sales | | Purchases | | Other | |
	Food	Beverage	Food	Beverage	Wages	Expenses
February	$30,000	$ 9,000	$12,000	$4,400	$12,000	$10,400
March	31,000	9,600	12,200	4,800	12,400	10,400
April	34,000	10,800	13,600	5,400	13,000	10,800
May	35,600	12,600	14,000	6,400	13,800	11,200
June	46,000	13,800	14,600	6,800	15,000	11,600
July	50,000	16,200	16,600	8,200	14,800	11,400
August	45,000	14,200	14,600	7,200	13,400	10,600
September	40,800	13,000	14,200	6,400	12,200	10,200

- Assume that all sales are cash sales.
- The annual interest of $1,600 on the restaurant's marketable securities will be received in July.
- The time delay in paying suppliers for purchases is two months. For example, February purchases are paid in April.
- Wages are paid without any time delay.
- Other expenses are paid with one-month delay.
- In May, new kitchen equipment will be purchased for $10,000. Payment for this will be made in the following month.
- The restaurant's bank balance on April 1 is $30,000.

12.10 A new restaurant was incorporated on January 1, year 0001. Forty thousand shares were issued for $6.00 cash per share. The cash received from the sale of shares was used, in part, as follows:

Construction of building, estimated life 20 years	$120,000
Kitchen equipment and restaurant furniture, estimated life 10 years	90,000
China, silverware, etc., estimated life 5 years	18,000
Food and beverage inventories	6,000

The remaining cash was deposited in a bank account.

The following estimates were made about the volume of business and operating expenses for the first three months.

a. Revenue:

January	$30,200
February	60,800
March	90,400

b. Revenue will be 50 percent cash and 50 percent credit; maximum credit to be allowed is thirty days.

c. Food cost and liquor cost will average 40 percent of revenue. Half this cost each month will be cash; the balance will be paid in the month following purchase.

d. Wages and salaries: the fixed portion of wages will be $5,200 a month; the variable portion will be 30 percent of any revenue in excess of $25,000 a month. (Total wages and salaries is the sum of the fixed and variable portions.)

e. Other operating costs will be $3,800 a month to be paid in the month following incurrence of the cost.

f. Depreciation for building, equipment and furniture, china and silverware is to be calculated on a straight-line basis. The annual depreciation amount must be prorated monthly to the income statements.

Note that, because of increasing revenue, a further cash investment in food and beverage inventories of $2,000 will have to be made in February with another increase of $2,000 in March. This will increase total inventory investment to $10,000 by the end of March.

Required:

1. A cash budget for each of the first three months of year 0001.

2. A budgeted income statement for the three months ending March 31, 0001.

3. A balance sheet as of March 31, 0001.

12.11 Stew and Brew have decided to lease a new restaurant. Rent for the building will be $3,000 a month to be paid on the first day of each month. They initially invested $225,000 of their own money, which was used in part to purchase:

Furniture and equipment	$180,000
China, glass, and silverware	25,200
Food inventory	9,000

Furniture and equipment are to be depreciated straight-line over five years. China, glass, and silverware are to be fully depreciated in year one.

Sales are forecast as follows for the first three months after opening:

Month 1	$48,000
Month 2	66,000
Month 3	84,000

Sales will be 80 percent cash and 20 percent credit with the maximum credit period allowed 30 days.

Food cost is expected to average 30 percent. All purchases will be cash.

Wages and salaries will be $15,000 a month. However, in any month when sales exceed $60,000, additional staff will have to be hired and the extra wage cost is estimated to be 20 percent of any excess sales. All salaries and wages will be paid in the month during which they were earned.

Other operating costs are expected to be 10 percent of sales and will be paid in the following month.

At the end of month three, Stew and Brew plan to pay themselves back part of their initial investment. This payment will be from any cash in excess of $15,000 at that time. (In other words, they wish to leave only $15,000 in the restaurant's cash account at the end of month 3.)

Prepare

a. A forecast income statement for each of the three months.
b. A cash budget for each of the three months.
c. The balance sheet for the end of month three.

12.12 Fritz, the owner of the Ritz Cafe, needs an after-tax cash flow of $27,000 next year. Principal payments on loans are $42,000 a year, and depreciation is $21,000. Tax rate for the Ritz Cafe is 25 percent. Fixed costs (including depreciation) are $55,000, and variable costs are 30 percent of sales.

a. What level of sales will provide Fritz with his desired cash flow next year?
b. Prove your answer.

12.13 Cece Saw, a carpenter who has saved some money, has decided to build and operate, with his wife, a ten-unit highway budget motel. Cece invests $25,000 of his own money in the company ($5,000 by way of common stock and $20,000 as a long-term loan). He also obtains a long-term mortgage on the land and building for $120,000 at a 12 percent interest rate. Interest is estimated to be $1,200 per month for the first few months of the new business, and principal payments are expected to be $500 per month.

Cash was paid for land at $20,000, building construction and completion at $90,000 (estimated 30-year life), and furniture and equipment at $24,000 (estimated 10-year life). Linen was also purchased with cash for $6,000. This linen amount will be written off (depreciated) over five years. Cece's company also prepaid advertising costs of $1,200 for brochures and other items. This cost will be written off during the first year of business. The first year's insurance premium of $2,400 was also prepaid before the business started.

For the first three months of business, occupancy is forecast to be 60 percent, 65 percent, and 70 percent respectively, and, in order to build up volume, a low average room rate of $18 is to be offered. When calculating revenue, use a 30-day month for simplicity, and round monthly revenue figures to the nearest $100. All revenue will be on a cash basis. Since the motel is relatively small, Cece and his wife will run it themselves but expect to hire some casual help at a cash cost of $100 per month.

Cece and his wife will each be paid $750 a month by the company for their services. However, for each of the first six months, they will each only take $250 cash out of the business for living expenses, until they are sure the company has sufficient cash resources to pay them the balance.

Laundry and supplies are estimated to be 10 percent of monthly revenue (round this expense to the nearest $100). This will be paid in cash. Utility costs are forecast to be $200, $250, and $300 for the first three months, respectively; however, the month-one cost will not be paid until month two, and so on. Office expenses are expected to be $100 per month in cash.

For each of the first three months of the motel's operation, prepare an income statement and a cash budget. Also prepare the balance sheet for the end of month three.

CASE 12

In the preceding chapter and case, the compilation of a statement of source and use of working capital was covered. Another useful statement for purposes of cash budgeting is the statement of source and use of cash. The rules for showing an item as a source or use of cash are:

Asset accounts

- Decreases are a source
- Increases are a use

Liability and equity accounts

- Increases are a source
- Decreases are a use

With these rules, the budgeted income statement for year 0002 (Case 10), the December 31, 0001 actual balance sheet (Case 2), and the budgeted December 31, 0002 balance sheet (Case 11), prepare a budgeted statement of source and use of cash for year 0002.

13 The Investment Decision

Chapter Highlights

This chapter begins by discussing some of the problems associated with capital asset decisions, such as the long life of the assets, the initial high cost, and the unknown future costs and benefits.

Two fairly simple methods of measuring proposed investments are then illustrated and explained: the average rate of return and the payback period.

The concept of the time value of money is then discussed, and discounted cash flow is illustrated in conjunction with time value.

Discounted cash flow is then used in conjunction with two other investment measurement methods: net present value and internal rate of return. Net present value and internal rate of return are then contrasted, and capital investment control is discussed.

The chapter concludes by demonstrating how discounted cash flow can be used to help make leasing versus buying decisions.

Chapter Objectives

After studying this chapter, the reader should be able to:

1. Discuss the ways in which long-term asset management differs from day-to-day budgeting.

2. Explain how the average rate of return is calculated, use the equation, and explain the major disadvantage of this method.

3. Give the equation for the payback period, use the equation, and state the pros and cons of this method.

4. Discuss the concept of the time value of money and explain the term "discounted cash flow."

5. Use discounted cash flow tables in conjunction with the net present value method to make investment decisions.

6. Use discounted cash flow tables in conjunction with the internal rate of return method to make investment decisions.

7. Contrast the net present value and internal rate of return methods and explain how they can give conflicting rankings of investment proposals.

8. Solve problems relating to the purchase versus the rental of fixed assets.

THE INVESTMENT DECISION

Decision to invest or not

This chapter concerns methods of evaluating investments in long-term assets. It is sometimes referred to as capital budgeting. We are not so much concerned here with the budgeting process as we are with the decision about whether or not to make a specific investment, or with the decision about which of two or more investments would be best. The largest investment that a hotel or foodservice business has to make is in its land and building, which is a one-time investment for each separate property. This chapter is primarily about more frequent investment decisions for items such as equipment and furniture purchases and replacements. Investment decision making, or capital budgeting, differs from day-to-day decision making and ongoing budgeting for a number of reasons. Some of these will be discussed.

Long Life of Assets

Decision affects many years

Capital investment decisions concern assets that have a relatively long life. Day-to-day decisions concerning current assets are decisions about items (such as inventories) that are turning over frequently. A wrong decision about the purchase of a food item does not have a long-term effect. But a wrong decision about a piece of equipment (a long-term asset) can involve a time span stretching over many years. This long life of a capital asset creates another problem, that of estimating the life span of an asset to determine how far into the future the benefits of its purchase are going to be spread. Life span can be affected by both physical wear and tear on the equipment and by obsolescence, the fact that a newer, better, and possibly more profitable piece of equipment is available.

Costs of Assets

Recovery value of asset

Day-to-day purchasing decisions do not usually involve large amounts of money for any individual purchase. But the purchase of a capital asset or assets normally requires the outlay of large sums of money, and one has to be sure that the initial investment outlay can be recovered over time by the net income generated by the investment.

Future Costs and Benefits

As will be demonstrated, analysis techniques to aid in investment decision making involve future costs and benefits. The future is always uncertain; on the other hand, if we make a decision based solely on historic costs and net income, we may be no better off since they may not be representative of future costs and net income. For example, one factor to be considered is the recovery (scrap) value of the asset at the end of its economic life. If two comparable items of equipment were being evaluated and the only difference from all points of view was that one was estimated to have a higher scrap value than the other at the end of their equal economic lives, the decision would probably be made in favor of the item with the highest, future trade-in value. However, because of technological change, that decision could eventually be the wrong one five or more years hence.

Such, then, are some of the hazards of making decisions about capital investments. The hazards can seldom be eliminated, but there are techniques available that will allow the manager to reduce some of the guesswork. Although a variety of techniques are available, only four will be discussed in this chapter. They are

<table>
<tr><td>Investment
techniques</td><td>
<ul>
<li>Average rate of return</li>
<li>Payback period</li>
<li>Net present value</li>
<li>Internal rate of return</li>
</ul>
</td></tr>
</table>

To set the scene for the average rate of return and the payback period methods, consider a restaurant that is presently using a manual system of processing guest checks, with a cashier taking care of this function on a part-time basis. The part-time wages of the cashier total $4,000 a year. The restaurant is investigating the value of installing a precheck machine system that will eliminate the need for the cashier, since the servers can operate the machine and look after their own cash until the end of the shift. Two machines are being considered, and we have information about them as shown in Exhibit 13.1.

AVERAGE RATE OF RETURN

The average rate of return method compares the average annual net income (after taxes) resulting from the investment with the average investment. The formula for the average rate of return (ARR) is:

ARR equation

$$\frac{\text{Net annual saving}}{\text{Average investment}}$$

Using the information from Exhibit 13.1, the ARR for each machine is:

Machine A

Calculation of ARR

$$\frac{\$1,000}{(\$5,000 \div 2)} \times 100 = \frac{\$1,000}{\$2,500} \times 100 = \underline{40.0\%}$$

Machine B

$$\frac{\$880}{(\$4,700 \div 2)} \times 100 = \frac{\$800}{\$2,350} \times 100 = \underline{37.4\%}$$

Note that average investment is initial investment divided by 2. If a machine had a trade-in value at the end of its economic life, average investment would then be:

Average investment calculation with trade in

$$\frac{(\text{Initial investment} + \text{Trade-in value})}{2}$$

Exhibit 13.1 Data concerning two alternative machines.

	Machine A	Machine B
Cash cost, including		
installation	$5,000	$4,700
economic life	5 years	5 years
trade in value	0	0
depreciation	$\dfrac{\$5,000}{5} = \$1,000/\text{year}$	$\dfrac{\$4,700}{5} = \$940/\text{year}$
Saving wages of cashier	$4,000	$4,000
Expenses		
maintenance	$ 350	$ 300
stationery	650	1,000
depreciation	1,000	940
total	$2,000	$2,240
Net saving before tax	$2,000	$1,760
income tax 50%	1,000	880
Net annual saving	$1,000	$ 880

In the example given, the assumption was made that net annual saving is the same for each of the five years. In reality, this may not always be the case. For example, there might be expenses in year one (or in any of the other years) that are nonrecurring, for example, a training cost or a major overhaul. Alternatively, the amount of an expense may change over the period, for example, depreciation computed on a declining balance basis. (Different depreciation methods were fully discussed in Chapter 1.) One way to take care of this is to include such items in the calculations and project total savings and total costs for the entire period under review. The total savings amount less the total costs amount will give us a net saving figure for the entire period. This net saving figure for the entire period can then be divided by the number of years in the period to give an average annual net savings figure to be used in the equation.

Fluctuations in net annual saving figure

Let us illustrate this for Machine A only. Savings and expenses are as in Exhibit 13.1 except that in year three there will be a special overhaul cost of $1,000 and the sum-of-the-years digits method of depreciation (rather than straight line) will be used. Exhibit 13.2 shows the results.

Total net saving over the five-year period will be the sum of the individual years' saving. This amounts to $4,500. The average annual net saving will be $4,500 divided by 5 equals $900. Our ARR will then be:

Recalculation of ARR

$$\frac{\$ 900}{\$2,500} \times 100 = 36.0\%$$

Exhibit 13.2 Net saving for Machine A after special overhaul and declining balance depreciation.

	Machine A				
	Year 1	**Year 2**	**Year 3**	**Year 4**	**Year 5**
Wage saving	$4,000	$4,000	$4,000	$4,000	$4,000
Maintenance	350	350	350	350	350
Stationery	650	650	650	650	650
Depreciation	1,667	1,333	1,000	667	333
Overhaul			1,000		
Total	$2,667	$2,333	$3,000	$1,667	$1,333
Net saving, (before tax)	1,333	1,667	1,000	2,333	2,667
Tax 50%	666	834	500	1,166	1,334
Net saving	$ 667	$ 833	$ 500	$1,167	$1,333

The same approach should be carried out for Machine B and then a comparison can be made. Note that in Exhibit 13.2 the change to the sum-of-the-years digits method of depreciation, by itself, did not affect the change in the ARR since average depreciation is still $1,000 per year, and average tax and average net saving are the same. In this particular case, the only factor that caused our ARR to decrease from 40.0 to 36.0 percent for Machine A was the $1,000 overhaul expense.

Pros and cons of ARR

The advantage of the average rate of return method is its simplicity. It is frequently used to compare the anticipated return from a proposal with a minimum desired return. If the proposal's return is less than desired it is rejected. If greater than desired, a more in-depth analysis using other investment techniques might then be used. The major disadvantage of the average rate of return method is that it is based on net income rather than on cash flow.

PAYBACK PERIOD

The payback period method overcomes the cash flow shortcoming of the average rate of return method. The payback method measures the initial investment with the annual cash inflows. The formula is:

Payback period equation

$$\text{Payback period (years)} = \frac{\text{Initial investment}}{\text{Net annual cash saving}}$$

Since Exhibit 13.1 only gives us net annual saving and not net annual cash saving, we must first convert the figure to a cash basis. This is done by adding back the depreciation (an expense that does not require an outlay of cash). The cash saving figures are:

<table>
<tr><td></td><td>Machine A</td><td>Machine B</td></tr>
<tr><td>Net annual saving</td><td>$1,000</td><td>$ 880</td></tr>
<tr><td>Add depreciation</td><td>1,000</td><td>940</td></tr>
<tr><td>Net annual cash saving</td><td>$2,000</td><td>$1,820</td></tr>
</table>

Conversion to net annual cash saving

Therefore our payback period for each machine is:

Calculation of payback periods

Machine A	Machine B
$\dfrac{\$5,000}{\$2,000} = 2.5 \text{ years}$	$\dfrac{\$4,700}{\$1,820} = 2.58 \text{ years}$

ARR considers all benefit flows

Despite its higher initial cost, Machine A recovers its initial investment in a shorter period of time than does Machine B. This confirms the results of the average rate of return calculation made earlier. However, the ARR calculation takes into account all of the benefit flows from an investment and not just those during the payback period. For this reason, the average rate of return method could be considered more realistic.

Note that in this illustration straight-line depreciation was used and it was assumed the net annual cash saving figure was the same for each year. This may not be the case in reality. For example, the use of an accelerated method of depreciation (such as declining balance) will increase the depreciation expense in the early years. This, in turn, will reduce income taxes and increase cash flow in those years, making the calculation of the payback period a little more difficult. To illustrate, consider an initial $5,000 investment with the following annual cash flows:

Using accelerated depreciation

Year 1	$2,000
Year 2	1,500
Year 3	1,200
Year 4	900
Year 5	700

By the end of year three, $4,700 ($2,000 + $1,500 + $1,200) will have been recovered, with the remaining $300 to be recovered in year four. This remaining amount will be recovered in one-third of a year ($300 divided by $900). Total payback time will therefore be three and one-third years.

Payback method only considers speed of investment recovery

The payback period analysis method, although simple, does not really measure the merits of investments, but only the speed with which the investment might be recovered. It has a use in evaluating a number of proposals so that only those that fall within a predetermined payback period will be considered for further evaluation using other investment techniques.

Common fault

However, both the payback-period and the average rate of return methods still suffer from a common fault: they both ignore the time value of cash flows, or the concept that money now is worth more than the same amount of money at some time in the future. This concept will be discussed in the next section, after which we will explore the use of the net present value and internal rate of return methods.

DISCOUNTED CASH FLOW

The concept of discounted cash flow can probably best be understood by looking first at an example of compound interest. Exhibit 13.3 shows, year by year, what happens to $100.00 invested at a 10 percent compound interest rate. At the end of four years, the investment would be worth $146.41.

Discounted cash flow reverse of interest compounding

Discounting is simply the reverse of compounding interest. In other words, at a 10 percent interest rate, what is $146.41 four years from now worth to me today? The solution could be worked out manually, but can much more easily be solved by using a table of discounted cash flow factors. Exhibit 13.4 illustrates such a table, and, if we go to the number (called a factor) that is opposite year four and under the 10 percent column, we will see that it is 0.6830. This factor tells us that $1.00 received at the end of year four is worth only $1.00 × 0.683 = $0.683 right now. In fact, this factor tells us that any amount of money at the end of four years from now at a 10 percent interest (discount) rate is worth only 68.3 percent of that amount right now. Let us prove this by taking our $146.41 amount at the end of year 0004 from Exhibit 13.3 and discounting it back to the present.

Example of discounting

$$\$146.41 \times 0.683 = \$99.99803 \text{ or } \underline{\$100.00}$$

We know $100 is the right answer because it is the amount we started with in our illustration of compounding interest in Exhibit 13.3. To illustrate with another example, assume we have a piece of equipment that a supplier suggests to us will probably have a trade-in value of $1,200 five years from now. At a 12 percent interest rate, what is the present value of $1,200? The answer is

$$\$1,200 \times 0.5674 = \underline{\$680.88}$$

Timing of cash flow assumption

The factor (multiplier) of 0.5674 was obtained from Exhibit 13.4 on the year five line under the 12 percent column. The factors in Exhibit 13.4 are based on the assumption that the money is all received in a lump sum on the last day of the year. This is not normally the case in reality since outflows of cash expenses relating to an investment (wages, supplies, and maintenance, for example) occur continuously or periodically throughout its life and not just at the end of each year. Although continuous discounting is feasible, for most practical purposes the year-end assumption, using the factors from Exhibit 13.4, will give us solutions that are acceptable for decision making.

For a series of annual cash flows, one simply applies the related annual discount factor for that year to the cash inflow for that year. For example, a cash inflow of $1,000 a year for each of three years using a 10 percent factor will give us the following total discounted cash flow.

Calculation of series of cash flows

Year	Factor	Amount	Total
1	0.9091	$1,000	$ 909.10
2	0.8264	1,000	826.40
3	0.7513	1,000	751.30
			$2,486.80

In this illustration, the cash flows are the same each year. Alternatively, in the case of equal annual cash flows, one can total the individual discount factors (in our case, this would be 0.9091 + 0.8264 + 0.7513 = 2.4868) and multiply this total by the annual cash flow.

$$2.4868 \times \$1,000 = \underline{\$2,486.80}$$

Factors for equal annual cash flows

Special tables have been developed from which one can directly read the combined discount factor to be used in the case of equal annual cash flows, but they are not included in this chapter because Exhibit 13.4 will be sufficient for our needs.

Exhibit 13.3 Compound interest, $100 @ 10 percent.

	Jan. 1 0001	Dec. 31 0001	Dec. 31 0002	Dec. 31 0003	Dec. 31 0004
Balance forward	$100.00	$100.00	$110.00	$121.00	$133.10
Interest 10%		10.00	11.00	12.10	13.31
Investment value end of year		$110.00	$121.00	$133.10	$146.41

Exhibit 13.4 Table of discounted cash flow factors.

Period	5%	6%	7%	8%	9%	10%	11%	12%	13%	14%	15%	16%	17%	18%	19%	20%	25%	30%
1	0.9524	0.9434	0.9346	0.9259	0.9174	0.9091	0.9009	0.8929	0.8850	0.8772	0.8696	0.8621	0.8547	0.8475	0.8403	0.8333	0.8000	0.7692
2	0.9070	0.8900	0.8734	0.8573	0.8417	0.8264	0.8116	0.7972	0.7831	0.7695	0.7561	0.7432	0.7305	0.7182	0.7062	0.6944	0.6400	0.5917
3	0.8638	0.8396	0.8163	0.7938	0.7722	0.7513	0.7312	0.7118	0.6931	0.6750	0.6575	0.6407	0.6244	0.6086	0.5934	0.5787	0.5120	0.4552
4	0.8227	0.7921	0.7629	0.7350	0.7084	0.6830	0.6587	0.6355	0.6133	0.5921	0.5718	0.5523	0.5337	0.5158	0.4987	0.4823	0.4096	0.3501
5	0.7835	0.7473	0.7130	0.6806	0.6499	0.6209	0.5935	0.5674	0.5428	0.5194	0.4972	0.4761	0.4561	0.4371	0.4191	0.4019	0.3277	0.2693
6	0.7462	0.7050	0.6663	0.6302	0.5963	0.5645	0.5346	0.5066	0.4803	0.4556	0.4323	0.4104	0.3898	0.3704	0.3521	0.3349	0.2621	0.2072
7	0.7107	0.6651	0.6228	0.5835	0.5470	0.5132	0.4817	0.4524	0.4251	0.3996	0.3759	0.3538	0.3332	0.3139	0.2959	0.2791	0.2097	0.1594
8	0.6768	0.6274	0.5820	0.5403	0.5019	0.4665	0.4339	0.4039	0.3762	0.3506	0.3269	0.3050	0.2848	0.2660	0.2487	0.2326	0.1678	0.1226
9	0.6446	0.5919	0.5439	0.5003	0.4604	0.4241	0.3909	0.3606	0.3329	0.3075	0.2843	0.2630	0.2434	0.2255	0.2090	0.1938	0.1342	0.0943
10	0.6139	0.5584	0.5084	0.4632	0.4224	0.3855	0.3522	0.3220	0.2946	0.2697	0.2472	0.2267	0.2080	0.1911	0.1756	0.1615	0.1074	0.0725
11	0.5847	0.5268	0.4751	0.4289	0.3875	0.3505	0.3173	0.2875	0.2607	0.2366	0.2149	0.1954	0.1778	0.1619	0.1476	0.1346	0.0859	0.0558
12	0.5568	0.4970	0.4440	0.3971	0.3555	0.3186	0.2858	0.2567	0.2307	0.2076	0.1869	0.1685	0.1520	0.1372	0.1240	0.1122	0.0687	0.0429
13	0.5303	0.4688	0.4150	0.3677	0.3262	0.2897	0.2575	0.2292	0.2042	0.1821	0.1625	0.1452	0.1299	0.1163	0.1042	0.0935	0.0550	0.0330
14	0.5051	0.4423	0.3878	0.3405	0.2993	0.2633	0.2320	0.2046	0.1807	0.1597	0.1413	0.1252	0.1110	0.0986	0.0876	0.0779	0.0440	0.0254
15	0.4810	0.4173	0.3625	0.3152	0.2745	0.2394	0.2090	0.1827	0.1599	0.1401	0.1229	0.1079	0.0949	0.0835	0.0736	0.0649	0.0352	0.0195
16	0.4581	0.3937	0.3387	0.2919	0.2519	0.2176	0.1883	0.1631	0.1415	0.1229	0.1069	0.0930	0.0811	0.0708	0.0618	0.0541	0.0281	0.0150
17	0.4363	0.3714	0.3166	0.2703	0.2311	0.1978	0.1696	0.1456	0.1252	0.1078	0.0929	0.0802	0.0693	0.0600	0.0520	0.0451	0.0225	0.0116
18	0.4155	0.3503	0.2959	0.2503	0.2120	0.1799	0.1528	0.1300	0.1108	0.0946	0.0808	0.0691	0.0592	0.0508	0.0437	0.0376	0.0180	0.0089
19	0.3957	0.3305	0.2765	0.2317	0.1945	0.1635	0.1377	0.1161	0.0981	0.0829	0.0703	0.0596	0.0506	0.0431	0.0367	0.0313	0.0144	0.0068
20	0.3769	0.3118	0.2584	0.2146	0.1784	0.1486	0.1240	0.1037	0.0868	0.0728	0.0611	0.0514	0.0433	0.0365	0.0308	0.0261	0.0115	0.0053

NET PRESENT VALUE

Estimating future savings and costs

Discounted cash flow can be used with the net present value (NPV) method for evaluating investment proposals. For example, Exhibit 13.5 gives projections of savings and costs for two machines. Machine A has an investment cost of $5,000; Machine B an investment cost of $4,700. Estimating the future savings and costs is the most difficult part of the exercise. In our case, we are forecasting for five years. We have to assume the figures are as accurate as they can be. Obviously, the longer the period of time, the less accurate are the estimates likely to be.

Note that depreciation for each machine is calculated as follows:

Calculation of straight-line depreciation

	Machine A	Machine B
Initial cost	$5,000	$4,700
Trade-in (scrap value)	(1,000)	(200)
	$4,000	$4,500
Depreciation, straight line	$\dfrac{\$4,000}{5} = \$800/\text{yr}$	$\dfrac{\$4,500}{5} = \$900/\text{yr}$

Depreciation added back

The scrap value is a partial recovery of our initial investment and is therefore added in as a positive cash flow at the end of year five in Exhibit 13.5. Note that depreciation is deductible as an expense for the calculation of income tax, but this expense does not require an outlay of cash year by year. Therefore, in order to convert our annual additional net income (saving) from the investment to a cash situation, the depreciation is added back each year. Note also that, with Machine A there is a negative cash flow in year one.

The data we are interested in from Exhibit 13.5 are the initial investment figures and the annual net cash flow figures for each machine. These figures have been transferred to Exhibit 13.6 and, using the relevant 10 percent discount factors from Exhibit 13.4, have been converted to a net present value basis. Observe how the negative cash flow for Machine A in year one has been handled.

Positive versus negative NPV

As can be seen from Exhibit 13.6, from a purely cash point of view, Machine B is a better investment than Machine A: $1,210 net present value against $547. In this example, both net present value figures were positive. It is possible for a net present value figure to be negative if the initial investment exceeds the sum of the individual years' present value. In this case, the investment should not be undertaken since, assuming the accuracy of the figures, the investment will not produce the rate of return desired.

Finally, the discount rate actually used should be realistic. It is frequently the rate that owners and/or investors expect the company to earn, after taxes, on investments.

Exhibit 13.5 Calculation of annual net cash flows for each machine.

Machine A (Investment Cost $5,000)

	Year 1	Year 2	Year 3	Year 4	Year 5
Saving (wages)	$4,000	$4,000	$4,000	$4,000	$4,000
Expenses					
Initial training cost	$3,500				
Maintenance contract	350	$ 350	$ 350	$ 350	$ 350
Special overhaul			250		
Stationery	650	650	650	650	650
Depreciation	800	800	800	800	800
Total expenses	$5,300	$1,800	$2,050	$1,800	$1,800
Saving less expenses	($1,300)	$2,200	$1,950	$2,200	$2,200
Income tax 50%	0	1,100	975	1,100	1,100
	($1,300)	$1,100	$ 975	$1,100	$1,100
Add back depreciation	800	800	800	800	800
					$1,900
Add scrap value					1,000
Net cash flow	($ 500)	$1,900	$1,775	$1,900	$2,900

Machine B (Investment Cost $4,700)

	Year 1	Year 2	Year 3	Year 4	Year 5
Saving (wages)	$4,000	$4,000	$4,000	$4,000	$4,000
Expenses					
Initial training cost	$2,000				
Maintenance contract	300	$ 300	$ 300	$ 300	$ 300
Special overhaul			100		
Stationery	1,000	1,000	1,000	1,000	1,000
Depreciation	900	900	900	900	900
Total expenses	$4,200	$2,200	$2,300	$2,200	$2,200
Saving less expenses	($ 200)	$1,800	$1,700	$1,800	$1,800
Income tax 50%	0	900	850	900	900
	($ 200)	$ 900	$ 850	$ 900	$ 900
Add back depreciation	900	900	900	900	900
					$1,800
Add scrap value					200
Net cash flow	$ 700	$1,800	$1,750	$1,800	$2,000

Exhibit 13.6 Conversion of annual cash flows to net present values.

	Machine A			Machine B		
Year	Net Cash Flow	× Discount Factor =	Present Value	Net Cash Flow	× Discount Factor =	Present Value
1	($ 500)	0.9091	($ 455)	$ 700	0.9091	$ 636
2	1,900	0.8264	1,570	1,800	0.8264	1,488
3	1,775	0.7513	1,333	1,750	0.7513	1,315
4	1,900	0.6830	1,298	1,800	0.6830	1,229
5	2,900	0.6209	1,801	2,000	0.6209	1,242
Total present value			$5,547			$5,910
Less: Initial investment			(5,000)			(4,700)
Net present value			$ 547			$1,210

INTERNAL RATE OF RETURN

As we have seen, the NPV method uses a specific discount rate to determine if proposals result in a net present value greater than zero. Those that do not are rejected.

Discounted cash flow and IRR

The internal rate of return (IRR) method also uses the discounted cash flow concept. However, this method's approach determines the interest (discount) rate that will equate total discounted cash inflows with the initial investment.

For example, suppose a motel owner decided to investigate renting a building adjacent to his motel in order to run it as a coffee shop. His investigation showed that it would cost him $100,000 to redecorate, furnish, and equip the building with a guaranteed five-year lease. The projected cash flow (net income after tax, with depreciation added back) for each of the five years is:

Projected cash flows before discounting

Projected Annual Cash Flow

Year 1	$ 18,000
Year 2	20,000
Year 3	22,000
Year 4	25,000
Year 5	30,000
	$115,000

In addition to the total of $115,000 cash recovery over the five years, it is estimated the equipment and furnishings could be sold for $10,000 at the end of the lease period. The total cash recovery is therefore $125,000 which is $25,000 more than the initial investment required of $100,000. On the face of it, the motel owner seems to be ahead of the game. If the annual cash flows are discounted back to their net present value, a different picture emerges, as illustrated in Exhibit 13.7.

Projected cash flows after discounting

Exhibit 13.7 shows that the future stream of cash flows discounted back to today's values using a 12 percent rate is less than the initial investment by almost $14,000. Thus, we know that if the projections about the motel restaurant are correct there will not be a 12 percent cash return on the investment. The IRR method determines the rate to be earned if the investment is made. From Exhibit 13.7, we know that 12 percent is too high. By moving to a lower rate of interest, we will eventually, by trial and error, arrive at one where the net present value (the difference between total present value and initial investment) is virtually zero. This is illustrated in Exhibit 13.8 with a 7 percent interest (discount) rate.

Exhibit 13.8 tells us that the initial $100,000 investment will return the initial cash outlay except for $157 ($100,000 − $99,843) and earn 7 percent on the investment. Or, stated slightly differently, the motel operator would recover the full $100,000 but earn slightly less than 7 percent interest. If the motel owner is satisfied with a 7 percent cash return on the investment (note this is 7 percent after income tax), then he could go ahead with the project.

A mathematical technique known as interpolation could be used for determining a more exact rate of interest but, since our cash flow figures are estimates to begin with, the value of this interest rate exactness is questionable. In most practical situations, knowing the expected interest rate to the nearest whole number is probably good enough for decision-making purposes.

NET PRESENT VALUE VERSUS INTERNAL RATE OF RETURN

Mutually exclusive proposals

Despite the difference in approach used by the NPV and IRR methods, they will both always give the same accept or reject decision for any single project. However, if a number of proposals that were mutually exclusive were being evaluated and were being ranked, the rankings from NPV might differ from the rankings from IRR. A mutually exclusive alternative means that, if only one of a number is accepted, the others will be rejected. For example, if a restaurant were assessing a number of different electronic registers and only one were to be selected, it would

Exhibit 13.7 Annual cash flows converted to net present value.

Year	Annual Cash Flow	×	Discount Factor 12%	=	Present Value
1	$18,000		0.8929		$ 16,072
2	20,000		0.7972		15,944
3	22,000		0.7118		15,660
4	25,000		0.6355		15,888
5	30,000		0.5674		17,022
Sale of equipment and furniture	10,000		0.5674		5,674
Total present value					$ 86,260
Less: Initial investment					(100,000)
Net present value (negative)					$(13,740)

want to select the most profitable one and reject all others, even if the others were profitable. In this sense "profitable" could mean reduction in costs from present levels.

Capital rationing

Another situation where profitable proposals are rejected is when the company is faced with capital rationing. "Capital rationing" means that there is sufficient capital to handle only a limited number of investments for any budget period. Once the maximum amount of capital budget has been exhausted, all other proposals, even if profitable, are postponed for reconsideration during some future budget period.

Conflicting rankings with NPV versus IRR

Therefore, at times, the ranking of projects in order of potential profitability is important if a company wishes to maximize the profitability from its investment. Unfortunately the NPV and IRR results can indicate conflicting ranking of profitabilities because of differences in the

Exhibit 13.8 Discount factor arrived at by trial and error.

Year	Annual Cash Flow	×	Discount Factor 7%	=	Present Value
1	$18,000		0.9346		$16,823
2	20,000		0.8734		17,468
3	22,000		0.8163		17,959
4	25,000		0.7629		19,073
5	30,000		0.7130		21,390
Sale of equipment and furniture	10,000		0.7130		7,130
Total present value					$99,843

cost of, and/or differences in the timing of cash flows from, alternative investments.

To illustrate this refer to Exhibit 13.9, which shows two alternative investments, each with the same initial cost, but each of which has different amounts of cash flow, differences in timing of cash flow amounts, and differences in total cash flow amounts. Using the NPV method at 10 percent and the IRR method, the ranking decision is contradictory. Alternative A is preferable from an NPV point of view ($4,290 to $3,973), whereas Alternative B is preferable using IRR (31 percent to 25 percent).

Assumptions under NPV versus IRR

The reason for this is that the NPV method assumes annual cash inflows are reinvested at the rate used, in our case 10 percent, for the balance of the life of the project. The IRR method assumes that the cash inflows are reinvested at the rate resulting from IRR analysis (in our case 25 percent and 31 percent for Alternatives A and B, respectively) for the balance of the life of the project, an assumption that may not be realistic.

Exhibit 13.9 Two investments and their respective NPV and IRR ranking results.

	Alternative A			Alternative B		
Net Present Value	**Annual Cash Flow**	**Discount Factor 10%**	**Present Value**	**Annual Cash Flow**	**Discount Factor 10%**	**Present Value**
Year 1	$ 3,000	0.9091	$ 2,727	$7,000	0.9091	$ 6,364
2	3,000	0.8264	2,479	4,000	0.8264	3,306
3	3,000	0.7513	2,254	3,000	0.7513	2,254
4	10,000	0.6830	6,830	3,000	0.6830	2,049
Total present value			$14,290			$13,973
Less initial cost			10,000			10,000
Net present value			$ 4,290			$ 3,973

	Annual Cash Flow	**Discount Factor 25%**	**Present Value**	**Annual Cash Flow**	**Discount Factor 31%**	**Present Value**
Internal Rate of Return						
Year 1	$ 3,000	0.8000	$ 2,400	$7,000	0.7634	$ 5,344
2	3,000	0.6400	1,920	4,000	0.5827	2,331
3	3,000	0.5120	1,536	3,000	0.4448	1,334
4	10,000	0.4096	4,096	3,000	0.3396	1,019
Total present value			$ 9,952			$10,028
Initial cost			$10,000			$10,000

| NPV versus IRR | Theoretically, the NPV method is considered to be the better method since it uses the same discount rate for alternative proposals and that rate would normally represent the minimum rate acceptable for investments to be made by the company. On the other hand, proponents of the IRR method contend that it is easier to interpret, does not require the predetermination of a discount rate, and allows a more meaningful comparison of alternatives. |

CAPITAL INVESTMENT CONTROL

Review at end of project life

One of the major difficulties in capital investment decision making is that it is only possible to approximate the investment rate to be achieved. Investment proposals are based on estimated cash flows, and the decisions based on those cash flows can only be judged as good or otherwise after actual cash flows are known. A review of all investment proposals is thus recommended at the end of each project's life. In this way, among other benefits, the process of forecasting cash flows can be reviewed and refined so that future investment decisions can be based on potentially more accurate figures.

Investment and Uncertainty

Risk factor in investments

In this chapter, we ignored the risk factor in investments, or we assumed that the risk of alternative investments was equal and was built into the discount or investment rates used. Risk is defined as the possible deviation of actual cash flows from those forecast. Also, in the illustrations, only short periods were used: five years or less. As the time grows longer for more major investments (for example, hotel or restaurant buildings that may have an economic life of twenty-five years or more), the risk factor must play a more important role. Forecasting cash flows for periods of five years or less is difficult enough. Forecasting for periods in excess of that is increasingly more difficult, and the risks thus become much greater.

Use of probabilities

Although there are techniques, such as the use of probabilities, that can be used to deal with risk, they are quite theoretical and may be difficult to use in practice, for which reason they are not discussed in this text. However, this does not imply that the business manager should ignore risk, since it does exist. The interested reader wishing to gain more insight into techniques available to encompass risks, or uncertainty, is referred to any of the excellent textbooks available on general managerial finance.

Nonquantifiable Benefits

Consideration of intangible factors

The results obtained using investment decision techniques may not be the only information needed to make decisions. Some information is not easily quantifiable, but is still relevant to decision making. One should not ignore such factors as prestige, goodwill, reputation, employee acceptability, and the social or environmental implications. For example, if a hotel invests in a redecoration of its lobby, what are the cash benefits? They may be difficult to quantify, but, to retain customer goodwill, the lobby may need to be redecorated. Similarly, how are the relative benefits to be assessed in spending $50,000 on improvements to the staff cafeteria or using the $50,000 for Christmas bonuses? Personal judgment must then come into play in such investment decisions.

TO OWN OR LEASE?

Lease payments are tax deductible

Until this point the discussion concerning long-term, or fixed, assets has been based on purchasing and owning them. However, there may be situations where renting or leasing may be favorable from a cost point of view. For example, income tax is a consideration. Since lease payments are generally tax deductible, there can be an advantage in leasing. On the other hand, ownership permits deduction for tax purposes of both depreciation and the interest expense on any debt financing of the purchase. What may be advantageous in one situation may be disadvantageous in another. Each case must be investigated on its own merits. Let us look at a method by which a comparison between the two alternatives can be made. Assume that we are considering whether to buy or rent new furnishings for a motel.

Purchase of the furniture will require a $125,000 loan from the bank. Cost of the furniture is $125,000. The bank loan will be repayable in four equal annual installments of principal ($31,250 per year) at 8 percent interest. The furniture will be depreciated over five years at $25,000 per year. It is assumed to have no trade-in value at the end of that period. The income tax rate is 50 percent. Alternatively, the furniture can be leased for five years at a rental of $30,000 per year.

Bank repayment schedule

First, with the purchase plan, we must prepare a bank repayment schedule showing principal and interest payments for each of the four years (see Exhibit 13.10).

Next, under the purchase plan we must calculate the net cash outflow for each of the five years. This is shown in Exhibit 13.11. In Exhibit 13.11 note that since depreciation and interest expense are tax deductible and since the motel is in a 50 percent tax bracket, there is an income tax saving equal to 50 percent of these expenses. Thus, in year one, the expenses of $35,000 are offset by the $17,500 tax saving. The net cost,

Income tax saving

Exhibit 13.10 Bank repayment schedule for $125,000.

Year	Interest at 8%	Principal Amount	Balance
1	$10,000	$31,250	$93,750
2	7,500	31,250	62,500
3	5,000	31,250	31,250
4	2,500	31,250	0

after tax, is therefore only $17,500. This $17,500 has to be increased by the principal repayment of $31,250 on the bank loan, and reduced by the depreciation expense of $25,000, since depreciation does not require an outlay of cash. In year one, the net cash outflow is thus $23,750. Figures for the other years are calculated similarly. Note that in year five, since there is no interest expense and bank loan payment to be made, the cash flow is positive rather than negative.

No depreciation with rental

Exhibit 13.12 shows the calculation of annual net cash outflows under the rental plan. Note that under the rental option there is no depreciation expense (since the motel does not own the furnishings), and no interest or principal payments since no money is to be borrowed.

Exhibit 13.11 Annual net cash outflow with purchase.

	Year 1	Year 2	Year 3	Year 4	Year 5
Interest expense (from Exhibit 13.10)	$10,000	$ 7,500	$ 5,000	$ 2,500	0
Depreciation expense	25,000	25,000	25,000	25,000	$ 25,000
Total tax deductible expense	$35,000	$32,500	$30,000	$27,500	$25,000
Income tax saving 50%	(17,500)	(16,250)	(15,000)	(13,750)	(12,500)
After-tax cost	$17,500	$16,250	$15,000	$13,750	$12,500
Add: principal payments	31,250	31,250	31,250	31,250	0
Deduct: depreciation expense	(25,000)	(25,000)	(25,000)	(25,000)	(25,000)
Net annual cash outflow (inflow)	$23,750	$22,500	$21,250	$20,000	($12,500)

Exhibit 13.12 Annual net cash outflow with rental.

	Year 1	Year 2	Year 3	Year 4	Year 5
Rental expense	$30,000	$30,000	$30,000	$30,000	$30,000
Income tax saving 50%	(15,000)	(15,000)	(15,000)	(15,000)	(15,000)
Net cash outflow	$15,000	$15,000	$15,000	$15,000	$15,000

Finally, the net cash flow figures from Exhibits 13.11 and 13.12 have been transferred to Exhibit 13.13 and discounted using the appropriate discount factor from Exhibit 13.4. The discount rate used is 8 percent. This rate was selected since it is the current cost of borrowing money from the bank. Exhibit 13.13 shows that from a present value point of view it would be better to rent in this particular case, since total present value of cash outflows is lower by $4,450 ($64,339 − $59,889).

Various alternative possibilities

In any buy-or-lease situation, there could be other factors to be taken into the calculations. For example, in the purchase option, a firm might use some of its own cash as a down payment and borrow less than the full purchase amount required. In such a case, the down payment is an additional cash outflow at the beginning of the first year. Under a purchase plan, there might also be a trade-in value at the end of the period. This trade-in amount would be handled in the calculations as a cash inflow at the end of the period. In a rental plan, the annual payment might be required at the beginning of each year, rather than at the end, as was assumed in our illustration. This means that the first rental payment is at time zero, and each of the remaining annual payments is advanced by one year. Under a rental plan, there might also be a purchase option to the lessee at the end of the period. If the purchase is to be exercised, it will create an additional cash outflow.

Exhibit 13.13 Total present value (converted from figures in Exhibits 13.11 and 13.12).

	Purchase			Rental		
Year	Annual Cash Outflow (Inflow)	Discount Factor 8%	Present Value	Annual Cash Outflow	Discount Factor 8%	Present Value
1	$23,750 ×	0.9259	= $21,990	$15,000 ×	0.9259	= $13,888
2	22,500 ×	0.8573	= 19,289	15,000 ×	0.8573	= 12,860
3	21,250 ×	0.7938	= 16,868	15,000 ×	0.7938	= 11,907
4	20,000 ×	0.7350	= 14,700	15,000 ×	0.7350	= 11,025
5	(12,500) ×	0.6806	= (8,508)	15,000 ×	0.6806	= 10,209
	Total present value		$64,339	Total present value		$59,889

Changing depreciation method

Furthermore, terms on borrowed money can change from one situation to another, and different depreciation rates and methods can be used. For example, the use of an accelerated depreciation method will give higher depreciation expense in the earlier years, thus reducing income tax and increasing the cash flow in those years.

Each situation different

Because of all these and other possibilities, each buy-or-lease situation must be investigated on its own merits taking all the known variables into consideration in the calculations before a decision is made.

SUMMARY

Capital asset management concerns decision making about whether or not to make a specific investment or which alternative investments would be best. Capital assets are assets with a long life that have a relatively high cost and about which future costs and benefits are uncertain.

Four methods of analyzing capital asset investments were illustrated: average rate of return (ARR), payback period, net present value (NPV), and internal rate of return (IRR).

The equation for the ARR is:

$$\frac{\text{Net annual saving}}{\text{Average investment}}$$

The disadvantage of this method is that it is based on accounting income rather than on cash flow.

The payback period method is based on cash flow and the equation is:

$$\frac{\text{Initial investment}}{\text{Net annual cash saving}}$$

The disadvantage of the payback period method is that it ignores what happens beyond the payback period. Both the ARR and the payback period methods also share a common fault. They do not take into consideration the time value of money. Discounted cash flow tables (the reverse of compound interest tables) have been developed so that flows of future cash can be readily discounted back to today's values. The NPV and IRR methods make use of these tables.

With NPV, the initial investment is deducted from the total present value of future cash flows to obtain NPV. If the NPV is positive, the investment is favorable; if negative, the investment should not be made.

With IRR, one simply uses the tables to determine the rate of interest (rate of return) that will equate the total future discounted cash inflows with the initial investment. If the rate of return is higher than the company has established as a minimum desired return, then the investment should proceed; otherwise, not.

Both the NPV and IRR methods will always give the same accept or reject decision for any specific investment. However, if a number of alternative projects were being evaluated, the rankings may differ depending on whether NPV or IRR were being used.

Regardless of the investment method used, subsequent to each investment the results should be reviewed so that the investment process can be refined and improved.

Finally, one should not ignore the potential nonquantifiable benefits of each particular investment.

There may be situations where it is preferable to rent or lease rather than purchase long-term assets. Cash flows under both alternatives can be discounted back to their present values to make a comparison. In each situation all the known variables must be taken into consideration so that the final decision can be made on its own merits.

DISCUSSION QUESTIONS

1. Discuss the ways in which long-term asset management differs from day-to-day budgeting.

2. How is the average rate of return calculated? What is the major disadvantage of using this method?

3. What is the equation for calculating the payback period? What are the pros and cons of this method?

4. Under what conditions might a hotel consider buying an item of equipment with a rapid payback rather than one with a high average rate of return?

5. Discuss the concept that money is worth more now than that same amount of money a year from now.

6. How would you explain discounted cash flow to someone who had not heard the term before?

7. In Exhibit 13.4 in the 11 percent column opposite year five is the number 0.5935. Explain in your own words what this number or factor means.

8. If an investment requires an outlay today of $10,000 cash and, over the five-year life of the investment, total cash returns were $12,000, and the $12,000 had a present value of $9,500, would you make the investment? Explain.

9. Contrast the NPV and the IRR methods of evaluating investment proposals.

10. Under what circumstances might NPV and IRR give conflicting decisions in the ranking of proposed investments?

11. Landscaping for a resort hotel is an investment for which the benefits might be difficult to quantify. In what ways might you be able to quantify them? Even if investment analysis (for example NPV) proved negative, what other considerations might dictate that the investment be made?

12. What factors other than purely monetary ones might one want to consider in a buy-versus-rent decision?

PROBLEMS

13.1 You have the following information about three electronic sales registers that are on the market. The owner of a restaurant asks for your help in deciding which of the three machines to buy.

	Register A	**Register B**	**Register C**
Cash investment required	$6,300	$6,000	$6,700
Machine life	5 years	5 years	5 years
Trade-in value at end of life	$ 500	0	$ 300
Annual operating costs (excluding depreciation)	$ 400	$ 300	$ 300
Annual saving before deduction of costs	$2,000	$2,000	$2,000

Income tax rate is 50%. Assume straight-line depreciation.
   a. Use the ARR method to decide which of the three machines would be the best investment.
   b. If the restaurant owner wanted a return on investment of at least 10 percent, what would you advise?

13.2 Using the information provided in Problem 13.1, which would be the best investment using the payback period method? If the owner wanted her cash back in less than four years, should she invest in any of the machines?

13.3 An investor is planning to open a new fast food restaurant. He has a five-year lease on a property that would require an investment estimated at

$205,000 for redecorating and furnishing. He would use his own cash. The present cost of capital (borrowed money) is 13 percent. Use this figure as the discount rate.

Calculation of net cash flow from the restaurant for the five years of operation shows:

Year	Cash Flow
1	$37,500
2	43,800
3	46,300
4	50,000
5	60,000

At the end of the lease the furniture and equipment would have a cash value of $18,500. Should he make the investment? What IRR comes closest to giving him a complete return on his $205,000 investment?

13.4 Dinah, the operator of Dinah's Diner, wishes to choose between two alternative investments providing the following annual net cash inflows over the five-year investment period:

Year	Alternative 1	Alternative 2
1	$8,000	$ 4,200
2	8,600	5,800
3	8,800	8,500
4	8,200	11,500
5	4,100	12,100

a. Calculate the payback time for each alternative, assuming an initial investment of $33,000 under each alternative.
b. Using NPV at 12 percent, would either of them be a good investment for Dinah?

13.5 A hotel manager wishes to choose between two alternative investments giving the following annual net cash inflows over a five-year period.

Year	Alternative 1	Alternative 2
1	$ 4,200	$12,100
2	5,800	9,900
3	8,500	8,600
4	11,500	5,400
5	12,000	4,000

The amount of the investment under either alternative will be $35,000.
a. Using the payback period method, in which year, under both alternatives, will she have recovered the initial investment?

b. Using NPV at 10 percent, would either alternative be a good investment?

13.6 A motel operator wishes to choose between two alternative front office machines. Machine A will cost $9,000 and have a trade-in value at the end of its five-year life of $1,500. Machine B will cost $8,500, and at the end of its five-year life will have a value of $700. Assume straight line depreciation.

Investment in the machine will mean that a part-time night auditor will not be required, and there will be an annual wage saving of $9,600. The following will be the operating costs, excluding depreciation, for each machine, for each of the five years.

Year	Machine A					Machine B				
	1	2	3	4	5	1	2	3	4	5
Training	$800					$700				
Maintenance	750	$750	$750	$750	$750	650	$650	$650	$650	$650
Overhaul			550					400		
Supplies	300	300	300	300	300	500	500	500	500	500
Electricity	100	100	100	100	100	100	100	100	100	100

Income tax rate is 50 percent. For each machine calculate the NPV by using a 12 percent rate. Ignoring any other considerations, which machine would be the preferable investment?

13.7 Pete's Pizza is planning to purchase a new type of oven that cooks pizza much faster than the conventional oven presently used. The new oven is estimated to cost $20,000 (use straight-line depreciation) and will have a five-year life, after which it will be traded in for $4,000. Pete has calculated that the new oven will allow him to increase his sales by $30,000 a year. His food cost is 30 percent, labor cost 40 percent, and other costs 10 percent of sales. Tax rate is 40 percent. For any new investment, Pete wants a minimum 12 percent return. Use IRR to help him decide if he should purchase the new oven.

13.8 You have to make a decision either to buy or to rent the equipment for your restaurant. Purchase cost would be $30,000. Of this amount, $7,500 would be paid cash now, and the balance would be owed to the equipment supplier. She agrees to accept $4,500 a year for five years as payment toward the principal, plus interest at 10 percent. The equipment will have a five-year life, at the end of which it can be sold for $5,000. Calculate depreciation on a straight-line basis over the five years.

Alternatively, the equipment can be rented for the five years at a rental cost of $7,000 a year.

Income tax rate is 50 percent. Discount rate is 8 percent.

a. Using discounted cash flow, which would be the better investment?

b. What other factors might you want to consider that would change your decision?

13.9 A delivery service is provided by a pizza restaurant. It is considering purchasing a new compact vehicle or leasing it.

Purchase price would be $6,750 (cash), which the restaurant has. Estimated life is five years. Resale price (trade-in) is $1,250.

Under the purchase plan the additional net cash income (increased revenue less additional costs such as vehicle maintenance and driver's wages) before deducting depreciation and income tax would be

Year	Cash Revenue Less Cash Costs
1	$38,000
2	47,000
3	55,000
4	60,000
5	65,000

Depreciation will be straight-line. Income tax rate is 50 percent. Under the rental plan the cash income will be the same as under the purchase plan except that vehicle maintenance will not be required (the leasor pays for this). Therefore, the given net cash income figures will have to be increased by the following maintenance amount savings.

Year	Amount
1	$1,000
2	2,500
3	2,500
4	4,000
5	5,000

However, under the rental plan, there is a rental cost based on mileage. Estimated mileage figures are

Year	Mileage
1	30,000
2	45,000
3	50,000
4	55,000
5	60,000

Rental cost is $0.20 per mile. Income tax rate will be 50 percent.

a. On a net present value basis using a 10 percent rate, would it be better to rent or buy?

b. Would your answer change if the rental cost were $1,000 a year plus $0.20 a mile? Explain your decision.

13.10 For many years a motor hotel has been providing its room guests with room service of soft drinks and ice, using the services of a part-time bellhop to deliver to the rooms. Typically, the service has been losing money. The average figures for each of the past few years are as follows:

Revenue:	soft drinks	$12,500	
	ice	1,200	$13,700
Expenses:	cost of sales	$10,200	
	labor	5,600	15,800
Loss:			($ 2,100)

The motor hotel has an offer from a soft drink vending company to install vending machines at no cost to the motor hotel. The vending company would collect the revenue (forecast to be as above for the next several years) from the soft drink machines, paying the motor hotel a commission of 10 percent on that revenue. Customers would help themselves to both soft drinks (by inserting cash in the machine) and ice (which would be free), thus eliminating the labor cost. An ice machine would have to be purchased by the motor hotel at a cost of $5,500. It would have a five-year life and a trade-in value at the end of that time of $500. Use straight-line depreciation. Annual maintenance and operating costs of the ice machine are estimated to be $100 per year. The motor hotel is in a 50 percent tax bracket.

a. Calculate the payback period.
b. Calculate the ARR.
c. Calculate the NPV of the investment using a 12 percent discount factor and state whether or not the investment should be made.

13.11 A motel presently leases out its 1,000-square-foot coffee shop, although it continues to own the equipment. The lease is due for renewal. The motel could continue to rent the space for $4 a square foot per year for the next three years, and then $5 a square foot for the following two years.

Alternatively, the motel could cancel this lease and take over the operation of the restaurant. If this occurs, the motel's management estimates that revenue in the first year would be $130,000 and that it would increase by $10,000 per year for each of the following four years. Variable operating costs of running the restaurant (food cost, wages, supplies) would be 90 percent of revenue. The motel would also have to assume certain other costs presently paid by the lessee for such items as supervision, advertising, and utilities. These are estimated to be $8,000 in year one, increasing by $500 per year for each of the following four years, so that by year 5, these costs will be $10,000.

If the motel reassumes operation of the restaurant, it will trade in some of the old equipment, for which it will get $2,000, and buy $10,000 of new equipment (this will not happen if the lease is renewed). The new equipment will have a five-year life and would be depreciated on a straight-line basis with no scrap value.

The motel is in a 25 percent tax bracket. Use NPV to decide whether the motel should operate the coffee shop itself or continue to lease it out. Use a 10 percent discount rate.

CASE 13

a. Early in year 0002 the owner of the building made Charles an offer. The lease contract has four more years to run and, as you will recall from Case 2, the rent is to be increased by 10 percent a year each year over the preceding year. The rent is payable in equal monthly installments but, for the sake of simplicity, assume it is all paid at the year end. The building owner's offer is that a lump sum payment now (early in January 0002 before the January rent check had been prepared) of $80,000 would be considered as prepaid rent for the remaining four years of the contract. If the offer is accepted Charles would borrow $80,000 from the bank. The arrangement with the bank is that $20,000 of the principal will be repaid on December 31 of years 0002 through 0005, with interest at 12 percent on the amount owing at each year end. Use the interest rate as the discount rate. Should the offer be accepted?

b. You will note in part **a** that year-end discount tables were used, even though the annual rent was paid each month. If monthly discount tables were available to you and you recalculated the present value with those monthly tables do you think your decision would change?

c. Can you suggest a way that an annual discount table might be used to give you a slightly more correct present value in a case where you were dealing with monthly payments?

14 Feasibility Studies— An Introduction

Chapter Highlights

This chapter explains what a feasibility study is designed to do and covers the highlights of the two major parts of such a study.

Part one includes the front matter, general market characteristics, site evaluation, supply and demand information, and supply and demand analysis.

The chapter illustrates a detailed approach to supply and demand analysis for a hotel and covers the four steps involved:

1. Calculate the most recent twelve-month average occupancy rate of the most competitive hotels.
2. Calculate the composite growth rate of demand from the various sources.
3. Calculate the additional rooms required year by year.
4. Calculate the future supply of rooms required.

Part two of a feasibility study covers the financial analysis. A financial analysis generally requires four major sections:

1. Calculation of the capital investment required and tentative financing plan.
2. Preparation of pro forma statements.
3. Preparation of cash flow projections from the net income forecasts.
4. Evaluation of the projections.

Chapter Objectives

After studying this chapter the reader should be able to:

1. Discuss the value of a feasibility study and the facts that would be covered in its nonfinancial sections.
2. List and briefly discuss the four steps in hotel room supply-and-demand analysis.
3. Calculate forecast rooms required from given demand information.
4. Prepare pro forma income statements for rooms, food, and beverages, from given information.
5. Convert pro forma income statements to cash flow from given information.
6. Evaluate the financial analysis projections of a feasibility study.

FEASIBILITY STUDIES

A feasibility study is an in-depth analysis of the financial feasibility of a property development, rather than a promoter's guess that a new idea will be economically viable. A feasibility study is not designed to prove that a new venture will be profitable. An independent feasibility study that is professionally prepared by an impartial third party could result in either a positive or a negative recommendation. If it is negative, both the borrower and the lender should be happy that the proposal goes no further. However, if it is positive, this should not be taken as a guarantee of success. A feasibility study can only consider what is known at present and what may happen in the future. But, since the future is impossible to forecast accurately, and so many unforeseen factors that cannot be anticipated can come into play, there can be no guarantees. In other words, a feasibility study may reduce the risk of a particular investment but does not eliminate it.

Study may reduce risk

Some feasibility studies seek out the most appropriate location for a new property and continue with the study from there. Others take a given location without considering alternatives.

FEASIBILITY STUDY FORMAT

Although the scope of a feasibility study for a suburban restaurant differs considerably from one for a major downtown hotel complex, the basic format of any feasibility study is the same. Most feasibility studies conclude with a financial analysis of the proposal. This will be covered in more depth later in this chapter. However, the other parts of a feasibility study that precede the financial analysis will be briefly discussed here. In this discussion we will assume that the feasibility study is for a hotel with food and beverage facilities. In a feasibility study for a motel with only rooms facilities data relevant to only guest rooms would be included. In a study for a restaurant, the rooms data would be irrelevant.

A suggested format for a hotel feasibility study would generally cover each of the following.

Suggested format

Front Matter

This includes an introduction covering the reasons the study was carried out, what property is being evaluated and how this evaluation was conducted, when the study was conducted and by whom, and a summary highlighting the findings, conclusions, and recommendations.

General Market Characteristics

Include descriptive and statistical data

This section covers such items as site location and the general area's population growth trends, industrial diversification and growth, building permit activity, employment and economic trends, disposable incomes, housing, transportation, attractions, convention facilities, and special factors (for example, is the area's economy highly dependent on its local university population?). Only those items relevant to the proposed new hotel should be discussed. Both descriptive and statistical data should be included. The information should be concise and primarily related to the demand for rooms (since other services offered by a hotel are generally derived directly from rooms usage).

Site Evaluation

If an in-depth section on site location is included in the study, that section should include detailed maps of the location. Wherever possible, those maps should show important subcenters of activity related to the proposal, such as industrial areas, shopping malls, and convention and support center locations. Transportation routes, including, for example, routes to and from the airport, should be shown. If auto access methods are important (as they frequently are), these auto routes should be indicated.

Physical information

Physical information about the site should be included, such as dimensions, existing improvements (buildings) on the site, and adequacy of the site for possible future expansion.

Cost of the site, site preparation costs prior to construction, and property taxes should be covered. Finally, any other important matters, such as zoning restrictions, height restrictions, parking space requirements, future traffic flow changes, and availability of utility services should be part of this section.

Supply and Demand Information

Three possibilities

There are three possible reasons for a new hotel. One is that the present demand for rooms is greater than the present supply; another is that there is a demand from a new market that is not presently served with the existing supply; and the third is that the present supply is inferior in quality to the needs of the present demand or market. It is therefore important that the study analyze the supply/demand situation in order to identify the market for a proposed new property. This is preferably done by looking at the entire local market insofar as the current situation is concerned and then adjusting for anticipated future changes.

Certain basic information should be included.

1. Occupancy trends in the local area for the past five years. This should be broken down by class of hotel (see next item) if possible.

2. A list of hotels currently serving the local market. The list should be categorized by class of hotel. Three classes are normally listed: those that would be the most competitive properties, those that would be somewhat competitive, and those that would be less competitive. The

Highlight newest properties

list should include each hotel by name, the number of rooms it has, and its current room rates. Any hotels in this list that were built in the past five years should be highlighted with added information, such as the facilities they have other than rooms (for example, number of seats in their restaurants) and the quality of those facilities.

   In addition, the most competitive hotels should be further highlighted by including additional information (if available) about their rooms occupancy rates, food and beverage facilities usage (for example, seat turnovers and average checks), and the composition of their market for rooms, food, and beverages.

3. The principal likely sources of demand should be covered. Generally, for a city hotel, the sources of room demand are from three main types of customer: the traveling businessperson, the convention delegate, and the general tourist or vacationer. For each category relevant data should be provided that could be indicative of demand for rooms.

High correlation

For the business traveler relevant data might include growth in local airport traffic, and/or growth in local office space occupancies for the past five years, since there is frequently a high correlation between these items and demand for hotel rooms.

Data concerning the convention or business meeting delegate would include the number of conventions held each year in the area, types of conventions, their size, total number of delegates, average length of delegate stay, and average conventioner daily spending.

Data concerning vacationer arrivals would include number of tourists, average length of stay, average daily spending on hotel accommodation and meals, and any change in or extension of the tourist season over the past several years.

If there is any significant demand for hotel accommodation from any special source, this should be covered. For example, sporting events can often be a major source of demand for hotel rooms close to the sporting event location.

Sources of data

Much of the information necessary for this section of the study can be obtained from local chambers of commerce, convention and visitor bureaus, hotel and motel associations, airport authorities, government agencies, and, in the case of office space occupancies, the local office building owners' association. Each individual situation will require other possible sources of information to be contacted for relevant information.

Supply and Demand Analysis

Four steps

Once the supply and demand information has been assembled and tabulated it must then be analyzed to determine if additional hotel rooms in the area can be justified. This requires four steps.

Step 1. Calculate the most recent twelve-month average occupancy of the most competitive hotels. Let us assume there are five competitive hotels and their number of rooms and occupancies are as follows for the most recent year:

Hotel	Rooms in Hotel	Average Occupancy	Average Nightly Demand
#1	320	70%	224
#2	108	75	81
#3	246	85	209
#4	170	70	119
#5	312	85	265
Total	1,156		898

For each hotel the number of rooms has been multiplied by that hotel's average occupancy percentage to arrive at average nightly demand. Total average nightly demand of 898 rooms has then been arrived at.

Average annual occupancy

The average annual occupancy of the most competitive hotels is then calculated by dividing the total average nightly demand by the total rooms available and multiplying the result by 100:

$$\frac{898}{1,156} \times 100 = 78\%$$

Step 2. Calculate the composite growth rate of demand from the various sources. Let us assume that our demand information gave the breakdown figures in percentages for each source, as well as annual compound growth rates for that source, as follows:

Source	Source of Demand	Annual Compound Growth	Composite Growth
Business travelers	75%	8%	6.0%
Convention delegates	10	5	0.5
Vacationers	15	10	1.5
Total	100%		8.0%

Estimate from historic information

Source of demand percentages have been multiplied by the annual compound growth rate percentages in the next column to provide the composite growth rate figures in the right-hand column (for example, 75% × 8% = 6.0%). The annual compound growth rate figures can be estimated from historic growth rate figures projected into the future. The total overall composite growth rate figure is 8.0 percent as indicated above.

Step 3. Calculate future rooms demand year by year. This calculation is shown as follows:

Year	Demand	Composite Growth	Future Demand
1	898	108%	970
2	970	108	1,048
3	1,048	108	1,132
4	1,132	108	1,223
5	1,223	108	1,321

In year one the current average nightly demand for rooms figure of 898 (calculated in step 1) is multiplied by the composite growth rate figure of 108 percent (100% + 8% composite growth rate figure calculated in step 2) to arrive at the future demand figure of 970 rooms in year one. The 970 figure is carried forward into year two and is itself multiplied by 108

454   *Feasibility Studies—An Introduction*

percent. Similar calculations are made for each of the remaining three years.

Step 4. *Calculate the future supply of rooms required.*

We know from step 1 that the current occupancy rate in the competitive area is 78 percent. Let us now assume that a 70 percent occupancy of hotel rooms is "normal" for our competitive area. Normal means that, at that occupancy, a hotel should be profitable. We therefore know that the local market could support additional rooms right now, since current occupancy is averaging 78 percent. We can calculate the current need for additional rooms at a 70 percent occupancy rate by dividing current nightly demand by 70 percent:

$$\frac{898}{70\%} = 1,283$$

From this we can conclude that there is currently a "shortage" of 127 rooms (1,283 that the market could support less the 1,156 that the market presently offers). Stated another way, if a new 127-room hotel were built today, given the current demand for rooms, the new overall average occupancy rate would be 70 percent.

$$\frac{898}{127 + 1,156} \times 100 = 70\%$$

Next, the future demand for additional hotel rooms is projected for the next five years as follows:

Year	Rooms Demand	Normal Occupancy	Supply Required	Current Supply	New Rooms Required
Current	898	70%	1,283	1,156	127
1	970	70	1,386	1,156	230
2	1,048	70	1,497	1,156	341
3	1,132	70	1,617	1,156	461
4	1,223	70	1,747	1,156	591
5	1,321	70	1,887	1,156	731

In the above tabulation, the future demand figures from step three have each been divided by a 70 percent occupancy rate (as was demonstrated earlier for the current year situation) to arrive at the figures in the supply required column. From each year's supply-required figure, the current supply of rooms (1,156) has been deducted. The end result is a forecast of the number of new rooms that could be supported over each of the next five years, given all the above assumptions. We see that, at the end of five years, 731 additional rooms could be supported at an average occupancy of 70 percent. Note also that the rooms-required figures in the right-hand column are cumulative year by year.

Figures are cumulative

To reduce risk we might want to assume that a 75 percent, rather than a 70 percent, occupancy should be used. In that case the year-by-year demand figures would be divided by 75 percent, resulting in a reduced number of additional rooms per year that the market could support.

Other considerations

However, before the supply/demand analysis is finalized and a recommendation is made about the size of property to be planned, some other factors may need to be considered. For example, if any of the existing competitive facilities are planned for removal from the market (demolished or converted to some other use), the supply figures should be adjusted accordingly. Similarly, if any information is available about other proposed competitive hotels in the area, this should be adjusted for in the future supply figures. Finally, the decision about whether or not to build should not be based on numbers alone. Frequently, two adjacent, competitive hotels, motels, or restaurants will have vastly different demands for their products. There are many nonquantifiable factors that cause this to be so, such as atmosphere, quality of decor, management, and staff training, to name only a few.

Space Recommendations

Suggested themes

The feasibility study at this point could include information that the architect might require in order to prepare more detailed plans. This should include not only such items as number of rooms and the proportion of rooms of various types (singles, doubles, twins), but also the proportion of space and number of seats recommended for food, beverage, and related facilities, such as meeting rooms and public spaces (lobbies), and possibly even suggested themes for bars and restaurants. Back of the house facilities and space requirements (kitchens, storerooms, offices) should be included, as should parking space requirements. Finally, any recommendations concerning recreation facilities should be covered in this section.

FINANCIAL ANALYSIS

Subsections of analysis

A major part of any feasibility study is the financial analysis section. This section is normally broken down into a number of subsections, such as the capital investment required and a tentative financing plan, pro forma income statements, projected cash flow, and evaluation of projections.

456   *Feasibility Studies—An Introduction*

Each of these subsections will be discussed in relation to the financial feasibility of a hypothetical new 100-room motor hotel that will have a 65-seat coffee shop, 75-seat dining room, and 90-seat cocktail lounge. Any income received other than from these operating departments will be incidental.

Capital Investment Required and Tentative Financing Plan

Estimates based on professional advice from architects, contractors, and other useful sources indicate that the investment required in the proposed property will be:

Breakdown of required investment

Land	$ 300,000
Building (including all professional fees for architects, designers, and lawyers)	2,100,000
Furniture and equipment	600,000
Interest on construction financing	220,000
Preopening operating expenses	100,000
Initial working capital	50,000
Total	$3,370,000

The total estimated investment required of $3,370,000 is tentatively broken down into the following possible financing plan:

	Debt	Equity	Total
Land and building (75% debt/25% equity)	$1,800,000	$ 600,000	$2,400,000
Furniture and equipment (80% debt/20% equity)	480,000	120,000	600,000
Interest on construction financing		220,000	220,000
Preopening expenses		100,000	100,000
Initial working capital		50,000	50,000
Totals	$2,280,000	$1,090,000	$3,370,000

Assumptions and other information:

Interim financing

1. Interim, or bridge, financing will be required in the amount of $1,800,000 for partial payment of land and for construction financing. This amount, advanced by the lender month by month as required, will carry a 12 percent interest rate, or 1 percent per month. Interest will be paid monthly out of equity funds available. The full amount of the advance ($1,800,000) will be refunded, just prior to opening, out of the proceeds of a permanent first mortgage to be taken out on

the land and building. Total preopening interest cost will be $220,000.

2. The permanent first mortgage of $1,800,000 will be for a twenty-year term and will carry a 10 percent interest rate for the first five years. A schedule showing the breakdown between interest and principal for the first five years, following the hotel opening, is illustrated below.

Mortgage repayment schedule

Year	Annual Payment	Interest	Principal	Balance
				$1,800,000
1	$208,000	$180,000	$28,000	1,772,000
2	208,000	177,000	31,000	1,741,000
3	208,000	174,000	34,000	1,707,000
4	208,000	171,000	37,000	1,670,000
5	208,000	167,000	41,000	1,629,000

In the above calculations figures have been rounded to the nearest $1,000. (Note that payments on such a mortgage would normally be made monthly, and the schedule of repayments calculated on this basis. However, for the sake of simplicity, annual payments have been assumed.)

3. The financing of equipment and furniture will be by way of a chattel mortgage (the chattels being the equipment and furniture) over five years at a 12 percent interest rate. Repayment will be made with combined equal annual installments of principal and interest. A schedule showing these repayment amounts broken down into principal and interest is illustrated below. (Again, all figures are rounded to the nearest $1,000.)

Chattel mortgage schedule

Year	Annual Payment	Interest	Principal	Balance
				$480,000
1	$133,000	$58,000	$ 75,000	405,000
2	133,000	48,000	85,000	320,000
3	133,000	38,000	95,000	225,000
4	133,000	27,000	106,000	119,000
5	133,000	14,000	119,000	0

4. The total initial equity investment is forecast to be $1,090,000. It is useful to prepare a schedule showing the timing of this investment, by month, prior to opening, so that the equity investors know when they have to put up the money and what it is for. This is illustrated in Exhibit 14.1 for our proposed hotel.

5. The interest expense of $220,000 on interim financing will be recorded as an expense on the income statement in the first year of operation.

6. The preopening expenses of $100,000 (for such items as insurance, property taxes, wages and staff training, advertising, and other operating costs incurred prior to opening) will be amortized (shown as an expense) over the first two years of operation.

7. For building, as well as furniture and equipment, declining balance depreciation will be used. Building depreciation will be 3.75 percent per year, and furniture and equipment, 20 percent per year. Depreciation schedules are as follows:

Depreciation schedules

BUILDING

Year	Depreciation Expense	Balance
		$2,100,000
1	3.75% × $2,100,000 = $79,000	2,021,000
2	3.75 × 2,021,000 = 76,000	1,945,000
3	3.75 × 1,945,000 = 73,000	1,872,000
4	3.75 × 1,872,000 = 70,000	1,802,000
5	3.75 × 1,802,000 = 67,000	1,735,000

FURNITURE AND EQUIPMENT

Year	Depreciation Expense	Balance
		$600,000
1	20% × $600,000 = $120,000	480,000
2	20 × 480,000 = 96,000	384,000
3	20 × 384,000 = 77,000	307,000
4	20 × 307,000 = 61,000	246,000
5	20 × 246,000 = 49,000	197,000

Pro Forma Income Statements

The next step is the preparation of pro forma income statements by two departments (Rooms and Food and Beverage).

Rooms. Room revenue is based on the assumption that, in the first year, occupancy of the 100 rooms will be 60 percent and that the average room rate will be $52. This rate would be competitive with what other motor hotels in the area are charging. In year two, and for the remaining three years of our five-year projections, occupancy is expected to climb to 70 percent, and average room rate will be increased to $56. Year one room revenue is therefore:

Rooms revenue calculation

$$100 \text{ rooms} \times 60\% \times \$52 \times 365 \text{ nights} = \$1,138,800$$

and for each of the next four years it will be:

$$100 \text{ rooms} \times 70\% \times \$56 \times 365 \text{ nights} = \$1,430,800$$

Rooms department operating costs are estimated as follows for year one:

Payroll and related expenses	$244,000
Other direct operating costs	54,000
Total	$298,000

Estimated operating costs These estimated operating costs can generally be based on a percentage of sales, using national averages for that size and type of operation, adjusting for local conditions, if necessary. In year two and the remaining years of our forecast, these costs are increased in total by $74,000 a year

Exhibit 14.1 Equity investment schedule.

Months Before Opening	Equity Amount	Land and Building	Furniture and Equipment	Interest on Interim Financing	Prepaid Expenses	Working Capital
19	$ 216,500	$215,000		$ 1,500		
18	15,000	10,000		5,000		
17	15,500	10,000		5,500		
16	16,000	10,000		6,000		
15	32,000	25,000		7,000		
14	33,000	25,000		8,000		
13	34,000	25,000		9,000		
12	35,000	25,000		10,000		
11	36,000	25,000		11,000		
10	37,000	25,000		12,000		
9	38,000	25,000		13,000		
8	39,000	25,000		14,000		
7	40,000	25,000		15,000		
6	41,000	25,000		16,000		
5	61,500	25,000	$ 20,000	16,500		
4	82,000	20,000	20,000	17,000	$ 25,000	
3	102,500	20,000	40,000	17,500	25,000	
2	103,000	20,000	40,000	18,000	25,000	
1	113,000	20,000		18,000	25,000	$50,000
TOTALS	$1,090,000	$600,000	$120,000	$220,000	$100,000	$50,000

to take care of the increased occupancy. Our rooms department income statements would now be as follows, with figures rounded to the closest $1,000:

	Year 1	Years 2 to 5
Revenue	$1,139,000	$1,431,000
Operating costs	298,000	372,000
Net department operating income	$ 841,000	$1,059,000

Food and Beverage. Food and beverage, insofar as sales and cost of sales are concerned, should be broken down into two separate components: food and alcoholic beverages. Food sales should in turn be broken down by sales area (coffee shop and dining room) and then in turn by meal period within each sales area. Sales are then calculated by using the basic equation given in Chapter 10:

Food revenue calculation

$$\begin{matrix} \text{Number} \\ \text{of} \\ \text{seats} \end{matrix} \times \begin{matrix} \text{Seat} \\ \text{turnover} \\ \text{rate} \end{matrix} \times \begin{matrix} \text{Average} \\ \text{check} \end{matrix} \times \begin{matrix} \text{Days} \\ \text{open in} \\ \text{year} \end{matrix}$$

For example, in our 65-seat coffee shop, assuming it will be open every day of the year, breakfast sales are calculated as follows, assuming one turnover and a $5.25 average check:

$$65 \times 1 \times \$5.25 \times 365 = \text{total sales } \$124,556$$

Similar calculations would have to be made for the other meal periods, and, possibly, for coffee break periods if these were expected to generate significant enough amounts of revenue. Seat turnover figures and average check amounts normally vary enough from one meal period to another to require these separate calculations. Turnover rates and average checks can often be based on an assessment of what competitive hotel restaurant operations in the local area are doing, combined with an evaluation of the type of clientele the guest rooms will be catering to.

Derived demand

In the calculation of total food revenue, it might be necessary to take into consideration sales generated in areas such as room service. In room service the rooms occupancy figure will give an indication at an estimated average check of the number of guests per day who might require some type of food service. This would give total daily sales, which should then be multiplied by 365.

In addition, the derived demand from nonfood areas may add to total food sales. For example, if food service is offered to customers in the cocktail lounge, an estimate of the number of daily orders that could be expected multiplied by an assumed average check would give a forecast of daily sales. This daily sales figure can then be multiplied by the days in the year that the lounge will be open.

Let us assume that this work has been completed and that total annual food revenue is estimated at $1,570,000. To this food figure must be added the alcoholic beverage sales in the coffee shop and dining room, as well as in the lounge. You are referred to the relevant section in Chapter 10 for forecasting beverage sales. Assume that total annual beverage sales for the proposed hotel have been calculated and are estimated to be $1,038,000. Combined food and beverage sales will be $2,608,000.

Alcoholic beverage sales

From the combined food and beverage sales figures, the direct operating costs must be deducted. As was the case with the rooms department, these costs can be estimated on a percentage of sales basis, using national restaurant industry figures for this size and type of operation, adjusting if necessary for local conditions. The departmental income statement can now be prepared:

	Food	**Beverage**		**Total**
Revenue	$1,570,000	$1,038,000		$2,608,000
Cost of sales	628,000	261,000		889,000
Gross profit	$ 942,000	$ 777,000		$1,719,000
Payroll and related expenses			$921,000	
Other direct operating expenses			519,000	1,440,000
Net departmental operating income				$ 279,000

Deduct undistributed expenses

Once the forecast departmental income statements have been finalized, the total departmental operating income can be calculated. From this can be deducted the undistributed expenses (administrative and general, marketing, property operation and maintenance, and energy costs). These expenses are generally primarily fixed in nature and can usually be estimated with some accuracy. In this case the figure is estimated to be $480,000 annually.

The forecasted departmental operating income figures, less undistributed expenses, have been transferred to Exhibit 14.2 for each of the first five years of operation. It should be noted that these figures are constant for each of the years (except for rooms departmental income from year two on, due to the anticipated increase in occupancy percentage, room rate, and direct expenses, as explained earlier). In all other cases the possibility of increasing costs has been ignored on the assumption that any increased costs will be passed on in the form of higher room rates or food and beverage prices; thus, net operating income will not change significantly. Also, for the years two through five, no upward adjustment has been made for any additional revenue that the food and beverage areas would derive from the additional rooms occupancy. At this point the revenue figures should be kept as conservative as possible.

Increasing costs ignored

Exhibit 14.2 Pro forma income statements.

	Year 1	Year 2	Year 3	Year 4	Year 5
Departmental operating income					
rooms	$ 841,000	$1,059,000	$1,059,000	$1,059,000	$1,059,000
food and beverage	279,000	279,000	279,000	279,000	279,000
	$1,120,000	$1,338,000	$1,338,000	$1,338,000	$1,338,000
Less: undistributed expenses	480,000	480,000	480,000	480,000	480,000
preopening expenses	50,000	50,000			
interim financing interest	220,000				
Income before interest and					
depreciation	$ 370,000	$ 808,000	$ 858,000	$ 858,000	$ 858,000
interest	238,000	225,000	212,000	198,000	181,000
depreciation	199,000	172,000	150,000	131,000	116,000
Income before income tax	($ 67,000)	$ 411,000	$ 496,000	$ 529,000	$ 561,000
Income tax	0	172,000	248,000	265,000	281,000
Net income (loss)	($ 67,000)	$ 239,000	$ 248,000	$ 264,000	$ 280,000

Note in Exhibit 14.2 that in years one and two $100,000 preopening operating costs have been deducted: $50,000 in each of the years. Also, the $220,000 interest expense incurred on preopening financing has been deducted in year one.

Deduct interest and depreciation

In order to arrive at the proposed hotel's overall net income (or loss), permanent and chattel mortgage interest, as well as building, furniture, and equipment depreciation, have been deducted for each of the five years. Finally, income tax has been deducted. There is no income tax in year one because of the loss of $67,000. Also, that loss is carried forward into year two and deducted from the income before income tax ($411,000 − $67,000 = $344,000) before applying the 50 percent tax rate on the $344,000 of taxable income.

Projected Cash Flow

The next step in our financial feasibility is to convert the hotel's annual net income to an annual cash flow. This is illustrated in Exhibit 14.3.

Adjustments required

First, to net income has been added back those expenses, previously deducted to arrive at net income, that did not require an outlay of cash in that year. These include depreciation (which is simply a write-down of the book value of the related assets), interim financing interest (the cash that was paid out prior to opening and is part of the equity investment amount), and the preopening expenses for years one and two (which were also paid out prior to opening from equity investment).

Finally, the principal portions of the permanent and chattel mortgage payments have been deducted, since these require an outlay of cash that is not shown as a deduction to arrive at net income. The resulting figure for each year is the net cash flow. See Exhibit 14.3.

Note that, even though there is an operating loss in year one (due to the heavy burden of the preopening interest expense), the cash flow is still positive. This means that, with the proposed financing plan, there will be no problem in meeting both the interest and principal payments on the debt.

Evaluation of Projections

Return on investment

At this point in the analysis it might be useful to determine the return on equity investment that would be achieved with the given estimates of revenue and expenses. Over the first five years the total net income from Exhibit 14.2 is:

Year 1	($ 67,000)
Year 2	239,000
Year 3	248,000
Year 4	264,000
Year 5	280,000
Total	$964,000

Use NPV or IRR

This is an average of slightly less than $193,000 a year ($964,000 divided by 5), or an average return on the initial $1,090,000 equity investment of about 17.7 percent, which, although not high for the risk involved, could be considered reasonable after income tax. However, as seen in Chapter 13, return on investment may not be the best criterion to use in evaluating an investment proposal. The net present value (NPV) and/or internal rate of return (IRR) methods discussed and illustrated in that chapter are frequently more valid measures for project evaluation.

Exhibit 14.3   Cash flow.

	Year 1	Year 2	Year 3	Year 4	Year 5
Net income	($ 67,000)	$239,000	$248,000	$264,000	$280,000
Add: Depreciation	199,000	172,000	150,000	131,000	116,000
Preopening expenses	50,000	50,000			
Interim financing interest	220,000				
	$402,000	$461,000	$398,000	$395,000	$396,000
Deduct: Principal payments	103,000	116,000	129,000	143,000	160,000
Net cash flow	$299,000	$345,000	$269,000	$252,000	$236,000

Also, the forecasts used were based on only one level of occupancy, set of room rates, and food and beverage prices. It is normal in practice to determine estimated net income from a level of sales higher than expected (thus providing a higher return on investment), as well as a level of sales lower than expected.

Try different financing

If a satisfactory return could not be anticipated, the project might be terminated at this point. Alternatively, a different financing arrangement might be attempted, using more or less leverage and/or different terms and interest rates. To do this manually may require considerable work, but today's microcomputers can be easily programmed to handle changes in a number of variables, individually or at the same time, to produce new net income and cash flow figures based on the changes.

If a plan were to be arranged that seemed to produce net income and cash flow figures that were, in the initial years, acceptable, then the cash flow projections should be continued beyond the five-year period to extend them for the entire life of the project. Finally, the lifetime cash flow figures could then be evaluated, using the NPV or IRR investment analysis methods, before a final decision, considering all necessary facts, is made to proceed or not with the development.

Feasibility of Expanding Existing Operation

Availability of historic records

Although this chapter has discussed a financial feasibility study for a new operation, the same techniques can be applied equally as well to the feasibility of expanding an existing hotel, motel, restaurant, or similar business. In that case only the marginal or incremental revenues and expenses, as well as debt and equity financing costs associated with the expansion, would be considered in the net income and cash flow projections. In fact, these projections are much easier to make for an existing business, since it has its present operation's historic accounting data to use as a basis for forecasting.

SUMMARY

A feasibility study is an in-depth analysis of the financial feasibility of a property expansion or a new property development. A feasibiiity study cannot guarantee financial success, but it does reduce much of the guesswork and risk of a new venture.

A feasibility study for a hotel can usually be broken down into two major parts. The first part includes such items as the front matter (including conclusions and recommendations), general market characteristics (location, population and industrial growth, employment, incomes, economic trends), site evaluation (including maps, transportation routes, and physical information about the site), and supply-and-demand information (market to be served, information about competitive properties, and the likely sources of demand for the facilities to be offered). The next section in the first part of the study would be a supply-and-demand analysis for guest rooms (in a hotel situation). The four steps in this analysis are:

1. Calculate the most recent twelve-month average occupancy of the most competitive hotels.
2. Calculate the composite growth rate of demand from the various sources.
3. Calculate the additional rooms required year by year.
4. Calculate the future supply of rooms required.

Once these steps have been completed, the first part of the study can be concluded with recommendations about the number and types of rooms proposed and about other facilities proposed, such as number of seats and themes for food and beverage areas.

The second part of a feasibility study is a financial analysis of the proposal based on the facilities recommended. This part is comprised of four major sections:

1. Calculation of the capital investment required and tentative financing plan. The investment required is broken down into such items as land, building, furniture and equipment, construction loan interest, other preopening expenses, and working capital. The financing plan is then broken down into its debt and equity elements.
2. Preparation of pro forma income statements. These are usually initially prepared for a minimum five-year period. Revenue for each department is first forecast, and from this are deducted estimated direct expenses (usually based on a percentage of revenue). Next are deducted the indirect expenses, construction financing interest, and other preopening expenses. Finally, mortgage interest and depreciation are deducted, as well as income tax, where relevant, to arrive at net income.
3. Preparation of cash flow projections from the net income forecasts. Net income is adjusted for depreciation and principal payments on debt financing to arrive at cash flow.
4. Evaluation of the projections to date is made at this point. If necessary, revenue levels and/or other variables can be changed to see how this might affect the results. Finally, if the proposal appears feasible, a complete evaluation of the project's entire life, using NPV or IRR

(see Chapter 13) should be carried out before making the final decision on the investment.

DISCUSSION QUESTIONS

1. Since a feasibility study for a proposed new venture cannot guarantee that the venture will be successful, of what value is such a study?

2. In a feasibility study for a restaurant in a downtown office building, what general market characteristics do you think would be relevant?

3. In preparing a feasibility study for a motor hotel to be located in an area where there are several other motor hotels, what factors would you consider to determine which of the other operations are the most competitive?

4. A resort hotel is to be located in a mountain area near a major highway about 150 miles from the closest town or city. What sources of demand might you consider in a feasibility study for this property?

5. Briefly describe how a composite growth rate of demand for hotel rooms can be calculated.

6. Two similar, competitive restaurants have quite different levels of demand (average total number of customers per day). What factors could cause this to be so?

7. In preparing the pro forma income statement for a rooms department, how do you think the average room rate and occupancy figures could be established?

8. In estimating total revenue for a coffee shop in a proposed new hotel, why is it important to begin by estimating revenue by meal period?

9. What adjustments generally have to be made to the net income figures to convert them to a cash flow basis?

10. In what way might a change in the depreciation method used affect the projected cash flow figures in a feasibility study?

11. If the initial feasibility of a proposed new hotel does not appear good from a financial point of view, what variables might one try to change in order to improve the result?

PROBLEMS

14.1 There are five competitive motels in a resort area with the following number of rooms and current occupancy rates:

Motel	Rooms	Occupancy
A	74	82%
B	45	73
C	58	85
D	48	70
E	52	75

Demand for rooms in the area is broken down into the following sources and growth rates:

Source	Percentage	Growth Rate
Business traveler	10%	5%
Vacation traveler	80	8
Other travelers	10	1

  a. Calculate the current average occupancy of the five motels.
  b. Calculate the composite rate of growth in demand.
  c. Apply the composite growth rate to the demand figures to obtain projected demand for each of the next four years.
  d. Assume that a 70 percent average room occupancy for the motels in this resort would be profitable. Calculate the future supply of rooms that could be supported for each of the next four years.

14.2 Six competitive motor hotels have the following number of rooms and current occupancy rates:

Motor Hotel	Rooms	Occupancy
#1	140	85%
#2	160	80
#3	84	75
#4	90	70
#5	120	80
#6	144	75

Demand for rooms in the area where the motor hotels are located is broken down into the following sources and growth rates:

Source	Percentage	Growth Rate
Business traveler	50%	5%
Vacation traveler	40	6
Other travelers	10	1

a. Calculate the current average occupancy of the six motor hotels.
b. Calculate the composite rate of growth in demand.
c. Apply the composite growth rate to the demand figures to obtain projected demand for each of the next four years.
d. Assume a 75 percent average room occupancy for the motor hotels in this area would be profitable. Assume also that motor hotel three is due to be demolished in year two to make way for a new highway. Calculate the future supply of rooms that could be supported for each of the next four years.

14.3 A financial feasibility study is being carried out for a proposed new 120-seat restaurant. It will be open for both lunch and dinner from Monday through Saturday and for dinner only on Sunday. For the sake of simplicity, assume a 52-week year. Seat turnover and average food check figures are estimated as follows:

	Turnover	Average Food Check
Weekday lunch	1½	$ 5.60
Weekday dinner	1¼	10.50
Sunday dinner	1¾	13.00

In addition, the restaurant has a small banquet room, and food revenue in this area is estimated at $14,000 a month. Alcoholic beverage revenue is estimated to be 12 percent of lunch food revenue and 30 percent of dinner food revenue. In the banquet room, alcoholic beverage revenue is forecast to be 40 percent of food revenue in that area. Food cost is estimated at 40 percent of total food revenue, and beverage cost 30 percent of total beverage revenue. Wage cost for salaried personnel (manager, chef, hostess, head waitress, and cashier) is estimated at $300,000 per year. Wages for all other employees will be 15 percent of total annual restaurant revenue. Employee benefits (vacations, meals, etc.) will be 10 percent of total annual wages. Other operating costs are estimated at 12 percent of total annual revenue. Undistributed costs are forecast to be $130,000 per year.

Prepare the restaurant's pro forma income statement for the first year, rounding all figures to the nearest dollar. Ignore income tax.

14.4 A new fifty-room budget motel is being planned. Total cost will be $1,450,000, of which land will be $150,000, building $900,000, furniture and equipment, $300,000, and the balance for preopening interest and other expenses. The building will be financed 70 percent by an 8 percent mortgage. The annual payment to amortize (pay back principal and interest) this mortgage will be $63,000. The furniture and equipment will be financed 75 percent by a chattel mortgage at 11 percent, repayable in five equal installments of $61,000 principal and interest. Apart from the mortgage and chattel mortgage amounts, the balance of the total investment required will be from equity.

a. Calculate the amount of the equity investment.

b. Prepare the building mortgage repayment schedule for the first five years. Round figures to the nearest $1,000.

c. Prepare the chattel mortgage repayment schedule. Round figures to the nearest $1,000.

14.5 Given the facts in Problem 14.4, assume the building will be depreciated at 6 percent declining balance, and that furniture and equipment will be depreciated at 25 percent declining balance. Prepare depreciation schedules for the first five years. Round figures to the nearest $1,000.

14.6 Given the facts in Problems 14.4 and 14.5 and the following additional information prepare the pro forma income statements for each of the first five years:

Year	Average Room Rate	Occupancy
1	$30	70%
2	30	75
3	33	75
4	35	75
5	35	80

Rooms operating costs average 60 percent of total room revenue. Indirect expenses will be $40,000 in year one and will increase by $4,000 a year for each of the next four years. The preopening interest and other expenses total $100,000 and will be amortized equally over each of the first five years. Income tax, if any, will be 25 percent of earnings before income tax. Note, however, that, if there are any losses, they may be carried forward and deducted from earnings before income tax, before the 25 percent tax rate is applied. Round all numbers to the nearest $1,000.

14.7 Given the facts in Problems 14.4, 14.5, and 14.6, calculate the net annual cash flow figures for each of the five years. What would be your evaluation of the financial feasibility of this proposed motel?

CASE 14

Although he has only been in business for a short time, Charles is already thinking about opening a second restaurant similar to the present one (a relatively medium-priced operation catering to the local neighborhood's family and small business trade).

Assume that he has asked you to do some preliminary work on a feasibility study for this second restaurant. Select a specific geographic location in your town with which you are familiar and which you think would be suitable for this new operation.

Prepare a two- or three-page report for Charles describing this location (include a map if you think it will help), explaining why that location might be suitable, and briefly discuss the economic and demographic factors (about which you would eventually need more detailed information) that would support the need for a restaurant in this location.

15 Financial Goals and Information Systems

Chapter Highlights

This chapter has two major parts: the first part is about financial goals, and the second about information systems.

The section on financial goals discusses mission statements and the objectives and purposes of financial statements. Two financial management goals are then explored: profit maximization and maximization of return on investment, neither of which is a commonly used goal.

Some time is spent on the most commonly used goal, maximization of stockholder wealth. Subgoals are then discussed, as is management by objectives (MBO). This section of the chapter also includes comments about other goals, such as social goals, and concludes with developing an action plan to achieve goals.

The second section of the chapter covers information systems. The four levels of an information system are introduced: data production, data sorting, information production, and decision making. Most of this section concentrates on the last two of the four levels, since these are the keys for a company to establish an information system that will allow it to meet its financial goals.

This section of the chapter concludes with comments about the effectiveness of a management information system.

Chapter Objectives

After studying this chapter the reader should be able to:

1. Discuss the role of mission statements with reference to financial goals.
2. Discuss the general concept of financial management and list the types of financial and other goals that a company might have.
3. Discuss the pros and cons of wealth maximization as a financial goal.
4. Define MBO, explain how it is used to measure performance, and define the term "goal congruence."
5. Discuss social goals.
6. Discuss the role of strategies and tactics with reference to developing an action plan to achieve financial goals.
7. List the four levels in the decision-making process.
8. Explain the ways in which information is obtained in an organization, list the main criteria for information to be useful in the decision-making process, and state how an information system should be judged for quality.
9. Define management by exception.

FINANCIAL GOALS

Profit versus nonprofit organizations

Regardless of the type and size of enterprise in the hospitality industry, financial management will be an ongoing aspect of the overall management of the business. This financial management may be quite unsophisticated in a small owner-operated establishment and considerably more complex in a large multiunit organization. Despite the vast range of sizes and types of establishments in the industry, any operation can benefit from an understanding of the value and importance of financial management. Even nonprofit organizations, such as hospitals, must be able to obtain funds and then invest them to maximize benefits; stated another way, they must be able to provide the most benefits at the least possible cost. The concepts of financial management are, therefore, the same for both profit-oriented and nonprofit organizations; the only difference is how the operating or financial results are measured against the objectives.

Mission Statement

Before developing financial goals, some large hospitality corporations first prepare the organization's mission or purpose in a statement. A mission statement is sometimes referred to as a statement of business purpose. This statement should be definable and measurable and should consider customer needs. For example, a mission statement for a resort hotel might read as follows:

Sample mission statement

> The Redwood Resort will position itself as the dominant luxury hotel in its area. Its prime weekday market will be corporate meeting and conference groups who will patronize both its guest rooms and food and beverage facilities. The hotel will offer a combination of first-class meeting, guest room, food and beverage, and recreational facilities in a relaxing resort environment. The major sales strategy will be to seek out meeting planners and organizers and use a personal sales approach to obtain their business.
>
> At weekends and during holiday periods, its market will include the upper end of the social scale. To satisfy the entertainment needs of both the corporate and the society markets there will be nightly live entertainment.
>
> Its pricing strategy will be to establish high prices that reflect the quality of its facilities and that the market segments selected can afford to pay. Prices will be set to yield an average minimum year-round guest room occupancy of 75 percent and allow overnight guests free use of all the resort's recreational amenities.

Philosophy of business

As well as being the focus for developing financial goals, the mission statement establishes a sense of direction for an organization by defining what the organization is, what it does, how it does it, and for whom it is being done. In other words, a mission statement is a philosophy for doing business. Mission statements for an organization can

- Provide a brief statement of its current market position.
- Show which customer groups will be its targets for the marketing plan.
- Provide guidelines for allocation of its resources.
- Indicate where its future growth will occur.
- Give an indication of how its products differ from its competitors'.
- Focus management's attention on marketing opportunities that conform to its mission.
- Serve as a basis for internal communication.
- Provide a direction to all its employees by alerting them to a common goal.
- Provide a basis for its control and evaluation.

OBJECTIVES OF FINANCIAL MANAGEMENT

Use of funds

Any business, at any particular time, has funds available to it. These funds come from creditors who lend the company money, from owners or stockholders who invest in the company or who own shares in it, and from earnings (profits) retained in the business. These funds may be kept in the business in a very liquid form, such as cash or marketable securities. They can also be tied up in food, beverage, and other inventories or in accounts receivable, or they can be invested in long-term assets, such as land, buildings, and furniture and fixtures.

At any particular point, the balance sheet will give a picture of the business's financial position. At a later date, another balance sheet will probably indicate a different financial position, because the position is never static. Funds are constantly flowing into and out of the business. The mix between the various sources of funds and the various uses of funds is constantly changing. The mix of sources and mix of uses, according to some overall plan, are what financial management is all about.

In a large organization this plan is usually coordinated by a financial manager, who works closely with the general manager. In a smaller operation the general manager and financial manager are one and the same person.

Generally, the objectives of financial management are:

Three objectives

1. To establish certain goals, such as how large the company will be, how rapidly it will expand, and how it will measure its success in meeting these goals.

2. To decide on the sources of needed capital and to obtain the funds required by the firm to meet its goals.

3. To allocate these funds effectively to the various assets of the company, again with the company's goals in mind.

Goals in monetary terms

Only with clearly stated goals can an organization effectively manage its finances; without them, a business operates without a plan. In a small owner-operated enterprise a goal may be expressed in simple terms, such as that the owner wishes to make enough net income in the first eleven months of the year to take a vacation in the twelfth month. In a large, or chain, operation, goals would be established in a much more formal way by the board of directors. Goals are frequently expressed in monetary terms. Some of these financially measurable goals will be discussed.

Profit Maximization

Profit maximization, or making the most amount of money in the shortest possible time, is one of the commonly considered objectives or goals of a company. It is argued that the total amount of profit or net income is not a realistic measure, since one can always sell more shares and invest the proceeds in marketable securities, thus increasing total net income. Because of this, maximization of earnings per share may be a better way to measure net income. In either case, however, the time element is important because of the time value of money. Most people would agree that $100,000 net income in the first year and nothing in each of the following nine years is preferable to $10,000 per year for each of ten years. The reason is that the entire $100,000 could be invested in the first year and continue to accumulate interest until the end of the tenth year, thus maximizing net income.

Timing of profits

However, one of the problems with profit maximization as a goal is that it may ignore the possible risks of an investment. An international hotel corporation could open new, profitable hotels in countries with politically unstable governments, ignoring the threat of future government expropriation of the investment. Is the immediate potential net income worth the risk?

The profit maximization goal also ignores investment financing risks. A company might become highly levered by borrowing large amounts of debt money at high interest rates in pursuit of some extra net income. Owners of shares, perceiving the risk, might begin selling their shares, thus reducing the market value of the shares. Alternatively, the company might issue new shares to obtain the financing (considerably reducing leverage), thereby diluting the value of present stockholders' shares. In other words, profit maximization as an objective might tend to ignore the company's commitment to its stockholders and create a rift between them and the company's management.

Share value dilution through leverage

Profit can also be maximized by not paying dividends or by making dividend policy a less important goal. This, too, would probably engender a negative reaction from stockholders.

Finally, if management is being measured by profit maximization, it might tend to emphasize very profitable but short-run investments while ignoring long-run, more consistently profitable investments.

Shortsighted goal

Thus, while a business must have profits, profit maximization as a sole goal is generally shortsighted, particularly if the company has many stockholders.

Maximization of Return on Investment

The maximization of percentage return on investment is a variation of the maximization of profit goal. To meet this goal, the company's management attempts to use its funds so that each dollar invested returns the most dollars of net income, or the highest return on investment.

Obviously, no investment would be made if the return were less than the cost of financing. Frequently, a minimum return on investment will be established for the company as a whole, and no individual investment will be made unless it is expected to yield at least this minimum. The return on investment goal, although it has its place, also has many of the disadvantages of the profit maximization goal.

Maximization of Stockholder Wealth

Generally speaking, most successful larger companies try, over time, to maximize stockholder wealth because this will make stockholders happier than if the wealth were not maximized. One could ask why a company attempts to maximize stockholder wealth and not the wealth of its debt lenders, or the tax department, or employees, or the company's management? The reason is that stockholders are, legally, the owners of the company. All the other groups mentioned must be given their due before the stockholders, as residual claimants, get what is left over.

Residual claimants

Maximization of stockholder wealth has as its objective the highest combination of dividend payouts by the company and increase in the market value of the price of the company's shares. With this goal, net income is not as important as earnings per share. The time value of earnings, mentioned earlier, must be a consideration, as must the relative risks of alternative investments and alternative methods of financing those investments. In emphasizing earnings per share, dividend policy and its effect on market price per share must also be considered. Note that maximizing earnings per share may not be the same as maximizing market price per share. The market price shows how well management is doing for stockholders. Dissatisfied stockholders will sell their shares and invest their money elsewhere. If enough of them do this, the market price of the shares will drop.

Never paying dividends

A company can maximize its earnings per share by never paying dividends, but this would please neither the individual stockholder nor the market for stockholders generally. The market comprises all present and prospective stockholders, who assess the risk of ownership of shares of the company, including potential future earnings, the timing and risk of these earnings, the company's dividend policy, and other factors that are deemed important to establish the price of a share. The individual in the market buys or sells shares according to his or her perception of the firm. The market price is influenced upward by those wishing to buy shares and downward by those selling. It thus serves as a barometer of how well management is doing on behalf of the stockholders.

Management barometer

Management's policies and plans will therefore be established, under the maximization of stockholder wealth goal, to ensure that wise investments are made, that they are sensibly financed, and that an appropriate dividend policy is established.

One of the disadvantages of this goal is that the price of the company's shares on the market is sometimes influenced by factors beyond the control of the company's management, such as a general recession. Management could also be so concerned with the goal of maximizing stockholder wealth that it forgets about the business's day-to-day operations, and in the interest of its own short-run survival, management might be unwilling to take reasonable risks, even though the investments would be to the stockholders' advantage. Further, where the company is large and share ownership is separate from control of the company, management may not always operate in the best interest of stockholders, although in the long run this is unlikely to occur. Sometimes managers may attempt to maximize their own wealth at the expense of stockholders, but again, in the long run, if management does not appear to maximize stockholder wealth, it can be fired by the board. Note again, however, that the board may be less responsive if stockholders are widely dispersed, and the absence of effective stockholder representation on the board may decrease the pressure on management to maximize stockholder wealth.

Maximizing management wealth

Finally, earnings per share in the hospitality industry may not fully reflect the company's true wealth. In the hospitality industry, a company's value can increase considerably through appreciation of its real estate assets, but it may not be reflected in earnings per share. Nor is it apparent on balance sheets that typically show assets at cost less accumulated depreciation (net book value). For a successful hospitality industry enterprise that has been in business for some years, those cost or net book value figures will not be very meaningful.

Subgoals

Even though a favorite goal of many organizations is maximization of stockholder wealth, some consider this goal too broad. For that reason it is often supported with subgoals, which will help the overall organization reach its objective, that department heads can relate to. These subgoals are often translated into such objectives as achieving a certain minimum rooms occupancy or restaurant seat turnover, or aiming for a specific minimum level of sales dollars within a budget period. If these subgoals are then reached, this should ensure that the overall corporate financial goal is achieved. In some cases the subgoals are not even expressed in monetary terms. For example, a restaurant may only emphasize quality, service, cleanliness, and value for money and achieve its overall financial goal by conforming to those subgoals.

Examples of subgoals

Problem of trade-offs

One problem that subgoals create is that there may have to be a trade-off between a decision in one department and a decision in another, or a conflict between short-run and long-run earnings. An example is reducing prices to gain a larger share of the market. This may lower short-run profits. Another example is the reduction in housekeeping quality standards, which may improve short-run profits but may cause occupancies to drop over the long run. The general manager's role is to maintain a balance between short-run subgoals and the long-term financial objectives of the company.

Ranking priorities

It is important to rank objectives and subgoals in order of priority and implement only those from the top of the list that are achievable. If too many objectives and secondary objectives are established and all are tackled, both financial and other resources might be spread too thin for any of them to be achieved.

Management by Objectives

Achievement of goals in an organization has to be carried out by people. Therefore, an important aspect of subgoal setting is to have the employees involved in the whole process of setting those goals. This basic concept is known as management by objectives (MBO). MBO is based on the assumption that employees can be committed to their work and allows for maximum involvement and participation in setting subgoals, personal goals, and performance standards for judging employees' work. The term "goal congruence" is often used in this regard. Goal congruence is the alignment of organizational goals with the personal and group goals of subordinates and superiors.

Goal congruence

For example, a hotel might establish as an objective increasing total sales by 10 percent for the coming year. The rooms department manager of that hotel might then set as two of its goals increasing its average room rate by 5 percent and increasing rooms occupancy by 3 percent to help achieve the hotel's overall goal. Goal congruence provides direction so that the activities of each department are working toward achievement of the organization's overall objectives and mission.

Four characteristics

There are four important characteristics of MBO:

1. The department head, or department manager, participates in establishing the criteria by which he or she will be judged.

2. These criteria are known by the person and his or her supervisor before the period begins.

3. Criteria are established in absolute or quantitative terms (such as dollars, percentages, or other units), so that results can be measured.

4. Goals should also be expressed relative to desired results to be achieved within a specified time frame.

For example, a restaurant manager might state that her objective is to increase sales by adding a special entrée each day to the menu. This is not an objective because no results have been stated in quantitative terms and no time frame has been established. Instead, the restaurant manager has stated how she is going to achieve something. Stating how something is to be achieved is not an objective. The restaurant manager in this situation would not find it difficult to implement what she says the objective is, but there is no way to measure the results. A more comprehensive objective for this restaurant might be to increase sales by increasing customer average check by $1 by the end of a ninety-day period.

Research has shown that the more objective a performance measure is, the more likely it is that supervisors and those they supervise will work with effort. Accounting systems play a key role in this because they can provide relatively objective performance evaluations. Research further shows that unless those being measured think that their behavior can influence the performance measure, they are unlikely to invest effort to achieve goals.

Important aspect of MBO

The measurement criteria, or standards, motivate the individuals to perform according to a clear understanding of expectations. An important aspect of MBO is that the department heads are not judged on a personal basis, but rather against the mutually agreed upon standards.

If standards are not achieved, the employee is not penalized, but rather is assisted by the supervisor in locating problem areas and identifying the cause of the problem. This investigation is then used to assist the department head in future performance, or, if necessary, in reestablishing performance standards if the standards are the fault.

Other Goals

The financial goals mentioned so far have been discussed under the assumption that an individual company will decide on one or a combination of them, spell out the goal or goals very clearly, and operate toward that objective. This is probably true of very large concerns in the hospitality industry, and particularly of those whose shares are publicly traded and for whom the goal of maximizing shareholder wealth would be most appropriate.

Smaller enterprises

However, many smaller hospitality corporations do not operate with many shareholders. Indeed, they may operate with as few as two. Such companies operate under quite different circumstances. They might find it inappropriate to have as a goal maximization of stockholder wealth as indicated by market price of the shares, since the shares are not publicly traded. The majority of smaller hospitality industry companies would probably find themselves in this category. They may not even have clearly defined financial goals, and such matters as maximization of profit or stockholder wealth are not relevant in their decision making.

Internal operating decisions may be made without reference to financial objectives. For example, a hotel sales department might be convinced that sales could be considerably increased by accommodating bus tour groups. The rooms department manager might think this type of business is too disruptive to normal operations and might cause some regular customers to be denied accommodation when the hotel is full with tour groups. If this hotel had as one of its objectives the maximization of sales or revenue (and many companies do establish sales targets as goals), then management would side with the sales department. Management could also decide the issue on a compromise basis, however, agreeing to accept a limited number of tours. This would increase revenue and net income, but not necessarily maximize them, and keep regular customers —and the two departments involved—happy. Management and the stockholders (who in many cases will be one and the same) will still be satisfied with the net income. In fact, this method of operating a business is frequently known as "satisficing."

"Satisficing"

Even though companies may not have clear-cut financial goals to rely on for decision making, this should not preclude them from operating toward the other two objectives of financial management: deciding on the sources of funds required by the company and allocating those funds effectively to the various assets of the company to provide a satisfactory net income.

Social Goals

Even though the goals discussed so far have been of a financial nature, social goals cannot be ignored. Social responsibility embraces such things as protecting the consumer who buys the hotel's or restaurant's goods or services, maintaining equitable hiring practices and paying fair wages, supporting further education and training of employees, and being concerned about environmental factors.

A resort hotel that owns beachfront property would act in a socially mature way by giving access to the beach to persons other than registered hotel guests. A take-out fast-food restaurant that uses disposable paper or plastics supplies would be socially responsible if it were to hire someone to ensure that the neighboring streets were kept free of litter discarded by customers. Obviously, since they have a cost, many social goals may conflict with financial goals. On the other hand, some social goals, even with a cost attached, may improve financial results. For example, in the restaurant situation cited above, the restaurant might find that its business improves considerably as a result of its litter-cleaning decision. More customers might patronize the restaurant because they appreciate its socially responsible action or because they want to visit a restaurant that is in a clean neighborhood. To the extent that the in-

Cost of social goals

creased net income exceeds the cost of clearing litter, a benefit will accrue.

Develop an Action Plan

How to get there

After an organization has developed a suitable mission statement and established financial objectives to conform to that, it must prepare an action plan. An organization's overall mission statement and objectives define what the organization wants to achieve. The action plan shows how it is going to get there. Normally, this plan covers all functional areas of an organization, such as managerial, financial, operational, and marketing. It includes matters such as the way the premises are furnished, the theme it wishes to establish, and the types of customers it wishes to attract. At the same time, it requires an understanding of the limitations that any business has. These limitations include the physical size and condition of the property, competition, funding available, economic environment, and many similar factors.

Strategies cause changes

Strategies. An action plan first requires the establishment of strategies to achieve objectives. Objectives and strategies should not be confused. Objectives are simply generally fixed statements that, by themselves, cause no changes. Strategies are stated plans of action that will cause changes in order to meet objectives. Strategies can also be flexible, whereas objectives are often not, at least in the short run. For example, a restaurant might have as an objective to increase sales by a certain percentage over the next twelve months. Strategies to achieve this might include increasing menu prices, increasing seat turnover, selling more wine with meals, or using any combination of these and other approaches. If the chosen strategy or strategies do not work, then they can be replaced or combined in some other way.

It is also important to ensure that a strategy is not implemented while ignoring other strategic alternatives. For example, it is possible for a strategy to be based on an inappropriate or biased management style that has too narrow a focus. Note also that strategies have a life cycle, just as products and mission statements have. And even where a mission statement may still be appropriate for a particular organization, strategies that were appropriate to that mission statement in early years may no longer be practical for achieving that mission.

Short-term tactics

Tactics. Tactics to supplement strategies may need to be developed. Strategies are often long-term (a year or more) in nature, whereas tactics (of which there may be several for each strategy) are short-run because they often have to be adjusted to circumstances that are constantly changing. This does not imply that strategies do not also need to be changed in the short run. Extraordinary, unanticipated events that require both altered strategies and altered tactics may occur.

INFORMATION SYSTEMS

To achieve the objectives established for a company, it is necessary for the manager to make decisions constantly. In order to make rational decisions, it is necessary to have information and a system that provides this information.

Example of information need

For example, consider a hotel that is contemplating offering its room guests a "free" hair shampoo package as a new marketing tactic. This seems like a relatively trivial matter. What information is needed? First of all, the decision maker must have information about the type of guest that is the hotel's market: is it the vacationer or the businessperson? Predominately male or female? If the hotel is an international one, is the nationality of the guest important? Is age relevant? What about average length of stay? Obviously, guest registration cards need to be designed to provide these data, and someone must be delegated to sort through these cards to summarize the data into meaningful information.

However, the manager needs further data from suppliers concerning types of shampoo available, types of packages and their sizes, and information about costs as well as availability of any quantity purchase discounts. Finally, the manager must have information about the added costs of storage and distribution of the shampoo through the housekeeping process.

For many day-to-day decisions, much of the necessary information already exists in most hospitality enterprises. Some of it is a requirement of the law (for example, the requirement to keep accounting records for income tax filing purposes). Other information exists as a by-product of carrying out normal business transactions (such as purchasing records and sales invoices). Further information exists as a result of transactions between departments (for example, requisitions given to the storeroom for needed supplies). But quite a lot of information is available that is not even formalized (such as the chef's knowledge about the best way to tackle each day's production of food requirements).

Four Levels

The decision pyramid

Four levels can be identified in the decision-making process, and these can be viewed as a pyramid. These four are data production, data sorting, information production, and decision making.

Decision making	4
Information production	3
Data sorting	2
Data production	1

Data as a by-product

Level 1—Data Production. At the base of the pyramid is the production of data. These data are often a by-product of a regular business activity (cash register tapes, sales checks, guest registration cards). It is important to establish what is to be stored and for how long, and what is to be discarded immediately. For example, are dining room sales checks to be kept for a week, a month, a year, or for five years?

Level 2—Data Sorting. A little higher up the pyramid is the second level at which data are sorted, converted, combined, or manipulated into more useful sets of data. In other words, the data need to be classified so that specific items can be recalled or retrieved without processing the entire batch. For example, registration cards can be stored by day and then by month, but has a system been established that segregates registration cards for all VIPs so that they can be accessed without having to go through all registration cards for an entire month?

Data acquire meaning

Level 3—Information Production. These converted sets of data in turn provide the third level in the pyramid, which is the information level. Data are converted into information when they acquire meaning. For example, Exhibit 8.7 in Chapter 8 is a columnar table of two sets of data, one column showing rooms sold month by month and the second showing wage cost month by month. In Exhibit 8.9 these data have been structured in the form of a graph and have taken on a meaning, since the graph indicates information concerning the fixed wage cost.

Normally, the collection and conversion of data to provide information is a routine process that can often be done by mechanical or computerized means. It is not the manager's job to do this. The manager's task is the interpretation of the information and the actual decision making. Nevertheless, it is the manager's task to be involved in establishing the information-gathering system so that it will provide the information that he or she needs to make the kinds of decisions necessary for the company to meet its goals.

Structured information systems

As organizations grow, the information system becomes more structured. For example, in a small restaurant, the one and only cook may have the recipes stored in his head, but, in a large restaurant, recipes need to be formalized so that all cooks follow the same food preparation formulas and procedures. In other words, the most desirable system really depends on the specific organization of the business and its needs, and, as the organization changes over time, so will the information system. What is good today may not be of value in five years.

Computerized information systems also more readily allow the linking of data from different areas of an operation. For example, a room service department manager could constantly access forecasts of guest room occupancies in order to staff more adequately his department from day to day.

Value of comparisons

Some sets of data can be compared to provide information (for example, relating last year's sales to this year's, or this year's sales to a budget). At the very elementary level such comparisons are not too helpful, since they do not allow for conditions that have changed between last year and this year, or this year and budget. Also, if, for example, August last year had five Sundays, and this year only four, comparisons can be distorted. Comparisons made on the basis of indices or percentages are an improvement, as is a comparison based on a standard, such as the standard food cost system described in Chapter 7.

Further improvement in information occurs when variances between actual and standard are broken down into differences in quantity and differences in cost or price (see Chapter 10 for a discussion of variance analysis). This breakdown indicates how much of the variance is the fault of poor planning (quantity variances) and how much a failure to achieve standards (for example cost and price variances in a food cost control system). At this point the information system has reached the stage of providing a guide to solving problems and making decisions.

Information costs not considered

What prevents many managers from producing more sophisticated information, and in particular with reference to implementing a computerized system, is that costs are often considered, but no price tag is put on the benefits. In fact, some managers consider that there is, and should be, no cost for information gathering; in other words, there is no cost to having a daily food cost or for producing a manager's daily report. These are simply by-products of the accounting and/or control system, and to spend money to provide more and better information makes no sense. For many managers the concept that information is not free creates a dilemma that is difficult to resolve.

Judging information systems

An information system should be judged by how well it facilitates the achievement of a given goal or set of goals. The main criterion for judging one system against another is cost benefit. Systems cost money and benefit an organization by helping decision making. If two systems cost the same, that which provides the most desirable operating decisions is preferable. For example, this might be the decision-making factor in judging which of two computerized accounting systems to install, when they both cost approximately the same.

Level 4—Decision Making. It is the information that is provided by the system that is used to identify and help solve problems that are resolved at the top of the pyramid, or the fourth level (which is the decision-making level). The types of decisions that have to be made dictate the information that needs to be collected; the information indicates the data that are needed, and this in turn regulates the data collection system.

Any manager is constantly faced with decisions. These can be routine and simple, often requiring no action, or more complex and important. Most decisions do require the use of information and frequently the use of judgment.

Four decision-making steps

In problem solving four decision-making steps can be identified:

1. Define the problem. Without doing this, proper analysis of information and identification of alternatives cannot be carried out. If the problem is not defined, or is incorrectly defined, time and effort will be wasted.

2. List alternative solutions. Creativity is a requirement for this, but that creativity should not be subjected to the decision maker's bias or prior experience.

3. Gather all necessary information about the problem and its alternative solutions. The information gathered must be relevant, since that increases knowledge, reduces uncertainty, and minimizes the risk of making the wrong decision. It must also be presented in a format that is understood and must be received in good time to affect any decisions made. Note also that the decision-making process is often a matter of judgment based on the best information available.

Obviously, the more accurate the information available, the more value it has for planning, control, and decision making. Speed of information and the risk of incomplete information are also factors to be considered. It is sometimes better to have a rough idea of the daily food cost without taking inventory than to have a more accurate food cost twenty-four hours after taking inventory. On the other hand, in a feasibility study for expanding the business, risk is so high that the extra time involved in preparing an informative study is well spent. In any decision-making situation, the manager, given the constraints of time and data availability, must have enough important information to consider alternative decisions or solutions. Obviously, however, the more time that is spent on collecting data and information, the greater the cost.

Risk versus time

For many decisions, accounting records, forms, and reports are a major source of information. This type of information is verifiable, objective, and quantitative and can provide specific data about an activity, event, or problem. The three most important aspects of accounting information are that it is relevant and appropriate for the problem at hand, that it is current, and that it is accurate within the measurement standards imposed by the needs of the problem.

4. Actually make the decision. Even though the above three steps are followed, decision making may still be difficult, since important variables of the problem may affect one another.

In some situations the information can provide its own solution. For example, perpetual inventory cards as an aid to inventory control were described in Chapter 7. These perpetual inventory cards can show, for each storeroom item, the minimum and maximum inventory levels. If the minimum stock level for a specific product is 5, and inventory has dropped to that point, and maximum is 15, then 10 more of that item need to be ordered. However, in such a situation, no attempt is made to relate the purchase to current conditions. What if the consumption for that product is no longer as high as it used to be? Perhaps the maximum inventory of 15 should be reduced to 10 and the reorder point to 2 until conditions change again. To make such decisions from manual information might be difficult, but computerized inventory systems can be programmed to provide information concerning such matters as rate of consumption of inventory products as well as quantity discounts and inventory holding costs. In a really intelligent computerized system, the idea of fixed reorder points for any items might be completely abandoned, and the computer will consider all the relevant factors item by item and only print a list of items to be ordered and in what quantities.

**Intelligent
systems**

**Management by
exception**

One type of decision making is known as management by exception. With management by exception small deviations from normal, which do not require any management action, are not drawn to its attention. For example, the standard food cost is established at 40 percent. As long as the food cost variance is only 1 percentage point above or below 40 percent (that is, from 39 to 41 percent), it is considered acceptable. Only if food cost is below 39 percent or above 41 percent is the change drawn to management's attention.

**Opportunity
costs**

A further refinement in decision making is to examine the assumptions that were made when earlier plans were formulated and then compare not only actual and planned results, but also actual with possible results. Those possible results are opportunity costs. Earlier in this chapter the possibility of a hotel increasing its sales by accommodating bus tour groups was discussed. If bus tour groups are not accommodated, or only a limited number of them are accepted, the revenue from those not accommodated is an opportunity cost, and this opportunity cost representing lost revenue could be built into the information system for management comparison with actual results. One difficulty with building opportunity costs into the information/decision-making system in the above illustration is that some bus tour groups making requests for rooms, who were turned down, may have eventually canceled their reservations anyway, even if they had been accepted. But, if effective decisions are to be made, a well-designed information system must be able to respond to some incompleteness of information and possibly suggest where additional data might be collected to make the information more complete. Obviously, at this level of sophistication, information manipulation would be exceedingly complex without the aid of a computerized system.

The way in which an information system is designed and integrated into a hospitality enterprise is a challenge for any manager. The more appropriately it is designed to support decision making, the more effectively will the enterprise be able to compete in the marketplace and achieve its already established financial objectives.

MIS System Effectiveness

A management information system (MIS) must have stated objectives so that its effectiveness can be measured by how it meets those objectives. Management should also be concerned with whether the system is doing everything it could to be effective. There are three ways of determining this.

One way is to review the reports provided by the system to see if any employees using them have made notations or calculations on them. If any of the information had to be recalculated or redrafted in some way to make it meaningful to the user, or if information has had to be added from some other source, this could indicate that the system is not doing everything it could.

A second method is to use test observations to see whether the information system is used for decision making. If information is required for a decision before the formal MIS can provide it or if the formal MIS has to be supported by information from informal sources, then perhaps the MIS is not doing the job it was designed to do. For example, suppose a hotel has a computerized guest room system that is intended to provide housekeeping and front office personnel with information about the status of each guest room at any time. If the computer system is so slow that housekeeping and front office employees pass this information back and forth by telephone, then the formal computer information system is not performing effectively.

The third method is to have those who review system reports list or state which items on a report are relevant and which are irrelevant. If there is consensus that there is a great deal of irrelevant information that is of no use in decision making, then the system is not doing its job. A dramatic test is to temporarily stop producing a report for a period of time. If there is no protest from those who are supposed to use the report, its permanent discontinuation will simplify but not reduce the effectiveness of the information system. However, removal of a report can have unexpected repercussions. For example, department heads may presently be receiving the same report as the general manager, even though they make little direct use of it. If the report is discontinued, department heads may feel they have lost status because they are no longer deemed important enough to receive it.

System Effectiveness versus Efficiency

Terms not synonymous

Management must also be aware of the difference between MIS effectiveness and efficiency. The two terms are not synonymous. With reference to gross profit analysis (see Chapter 6) of menu items, a computerized information system might show that a different set of menu offerings will improve gross profit per guest. However, after the new menu is implemented, total gross profit declines because customers do not like the new menu. The information system was efficient but not effective because it did not consider potential customers' menu preferences.

SUMMARY

Before developing financial goals, some large hospitality operations first prepare a mission statement. Regardless of the type and size of enterprise in the hospitality industry, financial management will be an ongoing part of the business. Generally the objectives of financial management are

1. To establish certain goals, such as how large the company will be, how rapidly it will expand, and how it will measure its success in meeting these goals.
2. To decide on the sources of needed capital and to obtain the funds required by the firm to meet its goals.
3. To allocate these funds effectively to the various assets of the company, again with the company's goals in mind.

Profit maximization is one type of goal. This means making the most amount of money in the shortest possible time. Profit maximization emphasizes the short run over the long run and ignores any risks involved.

Maximization of return on investment is a goal that allows no investment that does not yield at least a minimum return on investment. The disadvantages of this goal are similar to those for the profit maximization goal.

The goal most commonly used by business is that of maximization of stockholder wealth. Under this goal management plans to ensure that wise investments are made, that they are sensibly financed, and that an appropriate dividend policy is established.

Subgoals are also often established. These could be for individual operations within a chain, and/or for individual departments within an operation. With subgoals, management by objectives (MBO) is a useful managerial technique. With MBO, managers are involved in establishing their own goals and standards against which their performance is subsequently measured. Goal congruence is an alignment of organizational goals with the personal and group goals of subordinates and superiors.

With any form of goal setting, social goals must not be ignored.

An organization's overall mission statement and objectives define what the organization wants to achieve. The action plan, through strategies and tactics, shows how it is going to get there.

To achieve its financial goals any organization must have a reliable information system that allows the best decisions to be made. Four levels can be identified in an information system: data production, data sorting, information production, and decision making. The larger the organization, the more structured is this information system.

A well-defined information system is also invaluable in problem solving. Four steps can be identified in problem solving. These are defining the problem, listing the alternative solutions, gathering all necessary relevant information, and making decisions.

Information is a resource that costs money. When comparing different information systems a cost-benefit analysis is required. An information system should be judged by how well it facilitates the achievement of a given goal or set of goals.

The way in which an information system is designed and integrated into a hospitality enterprise is a challenge for any manager. The more appropriately it is designed to support decision making, the more effectively will the enterprise be able to compete and achieve its already established financial objectives.

Finally, management also needs to be sure (and determine from time to time) that its information system is effective and also be aware that there is a difference between efficiency and effectiveness.

DISCUSSION QUESTIONS

1. Explain your understanding of a mission statement and state four purposes that it can serve.

2. Briefly describe your understanding of the meaning of financial management.

3. Explain how you think a small restaurant operation can practice good financial management.

4. What is your understanding of the term "satisficing."

5. In what way might a policy to pay no dividends affect a hotel corporation's market price of shares? If the policy were to pay out all net income in dividends, how might this affect the company's future net income? How might this affect the future share price?

6. Explain why wealth maximization, as indicated by market price of shares, may not be achieved by profit maximization.

7. Would the objective of no net income for a certain period (for example, three years) be consistent with the goal of wealth maximization? Explain.

8. What is a subgoal? Give an example of a subgoal that might be appropriate for the housekeeping department of a hotel.

9. Define MBO and explain how it is used in an organization. What is goal congruence and how does it fit in with MBO?

10. Explain why a resort hotel that is the only one in the area would or would not be likely to practice social responsibility. Do you think such a resort hotel might act differently if it were only one of a number of competitive hotels in that area? Explain.

11. Discuss the need for an action plan with reference to achieving goals, and differentiate between strategies and tactics.

12. What are the four steps in the decision-making process?

13. Discuss how you think an information system should be judged for quality.

14. What are the main criteria for information to be useful in the decision-making process?

15. Define management by exception and give an example of a circumstance where it might be used.

16. Briefly discuss two ways in which the effectiveness of a management information system can be determined.

PROBLEMS

15.1 Some hospitality enterprise entrepreneurs, even with limited education, have been successfully operating their business for many years. They have probably never heard of management by objectives (MBO). Their only goal is to work hard and make an adequate profit. In your opinion, and give examples from your own experience and/or observations where this might be helpful, why are they successful? If they are successful, why should they bother using managerial techniques such as MBO?

15.2 The following paragraph appeared in a chain motel's monthly in-house newsletter announcing the creation of a trophy that will be awarded to the motel with the most outstanding performance each year:

> The trophy will be given to the motel with the best combination of sales percentage increase and net income percentage increase. The actual calculation will be to take the sales percent increase, add the net income percentage increase, and to divide that total by 2, with equal weight given to both sales and net income growth. Only motels achieving a minimum 15 percent sales increase will be eligible.

What is your evaluation of the way performance is to be measured in this motel chain?

15.3 Following are performance objectives for three different organizations:
  a. A restaurant's manager: "To establish a position in the market by providing top-quality menu items created from the freshest locally grown produce."
  b. Year-round recreational resort hotel's marketing manager: "To establish an image for the resort as an exclusive one providing a luxurious atmosphere and environment."
  c. A hotel's nightclub manager: "To considerably increase visits to the nightclub by residents of the area living within driving distance."
  Evaluate each of these objectives. Comment about how each of them does, or does not, satisfy the criteria for a good objective. Rewrite each objective in your own words in such a way that it meets the criteria for a well stated objective.

15.4 You are the manager of the maintenance department of a hotel. You are paid a basic salary, plus a bonus. The bonus consists of another $1,000 each time your expenses are under budget plus 2 percent of the amount you are able to save. For the past six budget periods the following are the results. Note that U stands for unfavorable, or over budget, and F for favorable, or under budget.

Period	Budget	Actual	Variance
1	$80,000	$82,000	$2,000 U
2	80,000	79,000	1,000 F
3	78,000	74,000	4,000 F
4	72,000	74,000	2,000 U
5	72,000	73,000	1,000 U
6	72,500	72,000	500 F

  a. Using the above information, as a rational person, what would you do if you were the department manager running the maintenance department over again from period one?

b. If you were the hotel's general manager, what would you recommend be done, if anything, to this hotel's maintenance department's bonus system?

15.5 A small resort hotel that caters primarily to the family trade set as an objective an increase of 5 percent in its rooms occupancy over the next 12 months. Its strategy for achieving this was to convert some unused ground-floor storage space into a conference room that could seat about thirty people. It then marketed the resort property to businesses and organizations that agreed to hold two- or three-day meetings and use the guest rooms overnight. During the first conference that the hotel booked, the conference organizer complained severely about noise from children using the outdoor swimming pool and recreation facilities immediately outside the window area of the conference room. Furthermore, the conference room delegates found there was no provision for them to have an evening meal served to them in the meeting room so that they could continue their discussions in private. Conference delegates were obliged to use the resort's regular dining room, where other residents were also seated. When subsequent conference groups arrived they made the same complaints and the resort found that negative word of mouth publicity had created difficulties for them in booking further conference groups. As a result, they did not achieve the desired increase in occupancy. Discuss the resort's problem with specific reference to the strategy it used to achieve its objective.

15.6 The bellman's department of a large hotel normally has a bell captain and nine bellmen on duty during the day shift for the peak tourist months. During the past peak month, there have been far more than the normal number of guest complaints about the slow service received, creating a problem for the rooms department manager.

The following are descriptions of several situations or events pertaining to the bell service department. For each separate item, state in which of the four areas of the problem-solving process the item belongs. The four areas are defining the problem, identifying alternatives, gathering information, and making the decision.

a. Several guests have complained to the front office manager that they are experiencing a longer than usual wait for service or that they have been receiving poor service.

b. The bell service department has priorities for jobs. Guest check-out baggage is handled first. Second is guest check-in baggage. Third is delivery of other items to guest rooms. Fourth is the sale of airport limousine, bus tour, and theater tickets. Fifth is other requests for service.

c. One guest complained that his theater ticket was for the wrong night.

d. One guest suggested replacing the bell captain with a better organizer.

e. One guest complained that his request to have flowers purchased and then delivered to another guest's room was never carried out.

f. The paging system that allows the bell captain to signal to bellmen when they are away from the service area has malfunctioned three times in the last month and has taken as long as twenty-four hours to repair.

g. One of the desk clerks suggests that the sale of theater and bus tour tickets be handled by a new person who will operate strictly on a commission basis.

h. The rooms department manager will consider having a commission arrangement for next summer, since it is too late to do anything about it this year.

i. The bell captain suggests hiring one more bellman.

j. One bellman has been away sick for the past two weeks.

k. While the sick bellman was away, he was replaced by a temporary employee not familiar with the hotel and its operating procedures. His work was marginal.

l. Guests who complain are advised of the bell service desk's order of priorities.

m. During the past month, the hotel's occupancy has been 10 percentage points above normal for that month, creating extra demands by guests for service.

n. The rooms department manager has approved the hiring of one extra temporary bellman for as long as occupancy stays above normal.

o. A new paging system will be purchased with a maintenance contract guaranteeing instant service.

15.7 In late January 0026 George Jarvis, president of Restoration Resort Ltd., is concerned about how he could finance the more than $200,000 he estimates he needs to convert, improve, and expand present resort facilities. The resort has very little cash, and George and his wife have only about $20,000 in savings.

The land on which the resort is located has been in the Jarvis family for forty years. The twelve-unit motel was constructed twenty-five years ago. The motel is open year-round. Occupancy of rooms in the peak summer months (mid-June to mid-September) is 100 percent, but a lower occupancy during the shoulder and winter months reduces overall annual occupancy to 60 percent. In the winter months the rooms are rented on a monthly basis.

About twenty years ago, a swimming pool was added along with a change house, snack bar/souvenir shop, and a twenty-space trailer park. The trailer park is only open during the summer months (approximately 150 days), and, during that period, spaces are 90 percent occupied.

Although losses have occurred in earlier years, the resort is now reasonably profitable. However, the resort has not until now been considered the main business of the Jarvis family, since both George (who inherited the resort from his parents ten years ago) and his wife do work at other jobs and look at the resort as a part-time business. However, it has become increasingly apparent to them that, because of the economic times, they will have to make changes to the resort and work at it full-time if it is to remain successful.

After considerable thought and discussion, the Jarvises decided that the following changes would have to be made to bring the resort up to a standard acceptable to today's traveling public:

a. Add eight fully furnished 400-square foot cabins with a potential of thirty-two additional overnight guests.

b. Fill in the present pool, which has become badly corroded from minerals in the water. This pool has been fully depreciated.

c. Construct a new 3,300-square-foot swimming pool.

d. Renovate and modernize the combined frame change house and snack bar.

e. Add an extension to the change house that includes shower rooms for trailer park guests and houses the resort's office.

f. Expand the trailer park area from twenty to fifty stalls and provide electrical and sewer hookup to all stalls.

In addition to the Restoration Resort land, George personally owns land that includes a hill at the back of the property, which has potential for skiing. This piece of land is estimated to be worth about $50,000 at today's prices. However, George feels that the investment required to develop it for skiing would not make the project feasible at the present time, even though it might considerably improve the winter rooms occupancy.

The investment costs for the proposed changes to the present property are estimated as follows:

Construction/renovation of buildings	$128,000
Swimming pool	27,000
Furniture, equipment, and fixtures	16,000
Trailer park site improvements	21,000
Contingency	10,000
Total	$202,000

A balance sheet for the year ending December 31, 0025, follows, as are income statements for the years 0024 and 0025.

Restoration Resort balance sheet as of December 31, 0025:

Assets

Current assets		
cash	$ 8,700	
inventory	3,000	$ 11,700

Assets

Fixed assets		
land	$ 70,200	
buildings	83,800	
furniture & equipment	14,600	
swimming pool	15,400	
station wagon	5,600	
	$189,600	
Accumulated depreciation	(64,200)	125,400
		$137,100

Liabilities and Owner Equity

Current liabilities		
bank loan	$ 4,300	
accounts payable	2,100	
current mortgage	12,800	$ 19,200
Long-term liabilities		
mortgage	$ 24,600	
loan from shareholder	8,700	33,300
Owner equity		
capital—shares issued	$ 40,000	
retained earnings	44,600	84,600
		$137,100

Restoration Resort income statements:

	Year Ending Dec. 31, 0024		Year Ending Dec. 31, 0025	
Revenue				
rooms and trailer rentals	$65,100		$74,400	
snack bar/souvenir shop	23,900	$89,000	26,700	$101,100
Expenses				
salaries and wages	$36,700		$40,100	
maintenance and repairs	14,100		16,200	
supplies and other expenses	9,000		9,900	
interest	3,200		2,800	
depreciation	6,900	69,000	6,300	75,300
Income before tax		$19,100		$ 25,800
income tax		4,800		6,400
Net income		$14,300		$ 19,400

	Year Ending Dec. 31, 0024	Year Ending Dec. 31, 0025
Retained earnings beginning of year	$10,900	$ 25,200
Add: net income for year	14,300	19,400
Retained earnings, end of year	$25,200	$ 44,600

Revenue for the year 0026 is estimated to be about 5 percent above 0025, primarily as a result of a price increase, rather than an increase in occupancy. Expenses are estimated in total to be about 5 percent higher than in 0025.

a. Given the balance sheet and income statements, calculate whatever financial ratios (see Chapter 4) you feel are appropriate that will indicate the present financial health of the Restoration Resort.

b. List the information that you would like to have that is not shown on the present financial statements, but would make it easier to carry out some financial projections as a preliminary step before going ahead with a complete feasibility study (see Chapter 14) for expansion.

CASE 15

With the possibility of branching out into a second restaurant, Charles is concerned that he does not have any formal financial objectives, although he does understand that most successful companies do need to have financial, as well as other, objectives. Write a report to Charles summarizing possible financial objectives that he might wish to consider. Include an explanation of MBO and how it differs from conventional management (where the employee is judged by personal traits such as initiative and integrity) typically used by small businesses. What specific recommendations do you have for Charles? Support these recommendations with reasons.

Appendix: Computers in Hospitality Management

Throughout most of this book, manual systems of financial control have been discussed and demonstrated. Today, many hotels and foodservice operations are using computers in this area of management.

In the three decades or so since computers have been commercially produced they have become a major factor in our lives. Despite this, they have been slow to impact the hospitality industry. Initially, this was so because of their high cost and space requirements. For that reason, only chain operations or quite large independent operations used them. For example, some large hotels have been using computers in their reservation, guest history, registration, and guest accounting area for many years, as well as in back office accounting. Similarly, many restaurants

Computerized sales registers

have been using computerized sales registers to record not only sales dollars but sales per server (for labor productivity analysis) and sales of individual menu items (for menu analysis) for a decade or more. More recently, computers have been put to valuable use to remove much of the drudgery present in manual cost control systems, such as budgeting, inventory control, and recipe costing.

Today, the small and low-cost (but still very powerful) microcomputer, or personal computer, has made computers available to even the small independent hospitality entrepreneur who manages most hospitality operations. These microcomputers are so low in price that a separate computer can be used cost-effectively by a single department within a large operation. An example of this might be for maintaining storeroom inventory records.

Speed and Accuracy

The main difference between a computerized system and a manual one is the computer's speed and accuracy. Computerized systems, however, cannot do anything that cannot be done manually, and they do not relieve management from the responsibility of decision making once the information is produced.

Computers no longer have to be expensive, take up otherwise valuable space, and require a highly skilled technical person to operate them. No longer is it necessary for them to be operated by specialist computer departments, remote from day-to-day operations and decision making, which produce voluminous reports long after the need for the information they provide is past.

Change in behavior

The new, low-cost computers may dictate a change in the way that hospitality managers behave on the job. Competitive survival may require managers to learn to use computer resources and the wealth of information they can provide effectively.

TYPES OF COMPUTERS

Generally, computers can be categorized into three types.

Mainframe Computers

In the early days, computers were very large, requiring dedicated, air-conditioned rooms and specialist personnel to operate them. They were often remote from the departments that needed the information that they could provide. Sometimes the main computer could be accessed by a terminal located in an individual department or by an individual operation that was part of a chain. This type of computer is often referred to today as a mainframe computer.

Minicomputers

Timesharing

With the introduction of minicomputers this situation changed. A minicomputer was smaller and cheaper than its mainframe predecessors. A chain organization could now afford to have a minicomputer in each separate operation and still be linked to the head office mainframe. Also, a number of users could be connected through terminals to the minicomputer at the same time. This is known as computer time-sharing. As a time-share user accesses the minicomputer, the computer locates that user's information, receives instructions from the user to manipulate or add to it, and then stores it again until the user next wants it. For a computer to do this with several users, it needs to be programmed so that information from different users is not mixed up and so that each user is treated in turn if several are using the computer at the same time.

Slow response time

The result is that time-shared computers (either mainframe or minicomputer) operate at only about 50 percent efficiency. As the computer gets busier from more users' accessing it, it slows down. Its response time is also irregular, and a user may not know, if the computer does not respond promptly, whether the machine is slowed down because of heavy use or because the user has supplied information that the computer does not understand and cannot process.

A minicomputer may also need a complicated set of instructions and an expensive communication system, as well as extra levels of security with passwords and protected security levels, to link it with all its users and prevent unauthorized access to confidential information.

Finally, with a large time-shared mainframe or minicomputer, if the computer breaks down every user is out of business unless there is a backup computer linked to the first one.

Despite these shortcomings, mainframe and minicomputers have value where common information must be shared by several users. This might be the case in a hotel where guest reservation, registration, and accounting information can be accessed not only by front office personnel but also by accounting office, housekeeping, and marketing employees.

Microcomputers

Microprocessor

The heart of a microcomputer is the microprocessor. The microprocessor is sometimes referred to as a microcomputer on a chip, but it is actually only a processing and controlling subsystem on an electronic chip (a very small part of the actual microcomputer). Computer chips are so small that 20,000 of them can fit into a briefcase. When the microprocessor was introduced, it dramatically changed the accessibility of computer power and created a major reduction in the cost of this power. Today, a stand-alone microcomputer (or personal computer, as it is sometimes referred to) can cost as little as a few thousand dollars and can be easily placed on a manager's desk or small table. No specialist expertise is required to operate these computers. Indeed, it is no more necessary to know how a computer works in order to use it than it is to know how a car works in order to drive it.

Miniaturized systems

The terms "microprocessor" and "microcomputer" are sometimes used interchangeably, but they do not mean the same thing. A microprocessor is the physical design and structure engraved on the chips that make a microcomputer function. Microcomputers are known as microcomputers because their systems are miniaturized. A microcomputer could therefore be simply described as a small computer, although that can be misleading because today's microcomputers, small as they are, are as powerful as much larger computers were twenty years ago. Microcomputers are so independently versatile that it is often better (and cheaper) to buy an extra machine for a special type of job than it is to create a special mainframe or minicomputer time-sharing program that several users can access.

The major disadvantage of microcomputers is their somewhat limited storage capacity, which means that some of the more complex programs that a hospitality operator wishes to use may not run on them.

Networking

Microcomputers can be operated independently but can also be linked together to access the same common information that all their users need from time to time (such as reservation information in a hotel). This linking together of several independent computers is known as networking. As networking capability is further advanced, it may soon be possible for a hospitality operation to have its purchasing needs transmitted by its microcomputer to a network of suppliers' computers.

Also in the future may be electronic funds transfer, in which sales terminals in a hotel or restaurant are connected directly to a computer at a local bank, which, in turn, is networked to terminals at other banks. If hospitality industry customers pay their bills by bank credit card or check, the card or check can be verified by the local bank's computer, which then issues instructions that are transmitted to the customer's bank so that the funds are immediately transferred to the hospitality operation's local bank account. The advantage of this to the hospitality operator is the time saving of one or more days (and the resulting increase in interest income) that occurs and the reduction of losses from dishonored credit cards or not sufficient funds (NSF) checks.

HARDWARE VERSUS SOFTWARE

The hardware of a computer system is the physical equipment that follows a predetermined set of instructions in a self-directed fashion. Instructions are developed by programmers. Once a program (or set of instructions) is placed in the hardware, the computer can carry out those instructions without any operator intervention. Any intelligence that a computer has must be programmed into it, and any weaknesses in that intelligence are the fault of the program.

Software

A computer may be able to operate with many different programs for different jobs. Each program is copied into the computer when it is needed. When a new program is fed in (loaded), the previous program is replaced. When the machine is switched off, any program currently in the machine is lost to it. Thus, because of the temporary nature in the computer of each program, programs are known as software. Software is generally stored on tape or on disks, and when it is loaded into the machine it is not removed from the tape or disk but only copied.

Once stored on tape or disk, this storage medium can be used with any other computer of the same type. The information on the disk or tape is read by the computer scanning the magnetic surface and copying the encoded data into the computer's temporary memory (sometimes referred to as random access memory or RAM). Once the data are in the computer they can be amended, added to, or removed if they are no longer wanted before they are stored again on the disk or tape. In other words, software storage tapes or disks are the permanent record of a program.

Good hardware is not hard to find, but good software is the key to a computer system's performance. Software has to be written (contain instructions) in a language, or set of codes, that the computer understands, and it then usually has to convert these instructions into another internal language of its own before it can actually carry out the instructions. There are more than 2,000 different computer languages available to programmers today, and each of these languages may have several dialects of its own.

System Software

Sometimes the term "firmware" or "system software" is used. Firmware is a piece of software that is built right into the computer by its manufacturer. In other words, it is a piece of hardware that behaves like a piece of software. It generally comprises some circuits that load certain instructions into the computer immediately when it is switched on. For example, firmware might contain some identification codes for security purposes so that only users who properly identify themselves can use the computer or use some of its applications, depending on who they are. Firmware is also used for diagnostic purposes, such as detection of user errors (for example, using an inappropriate code that the computer does not understand).

Hardware Systems

Computer hardware systems usually comprise a number of components. Even a microcomputer cannot do much without the aid of some other hardware, or peripheral equipment. The main part of the computer where all the work or manipulation is carried out is sometimes referred to as the central processing unit (CPU). The CPU is often referred to as the brain of a hardware system because it controls all other hardware devices.

Read-only memory

The CPU has its own set of built-in instructions in its memory chips that cannot be altered by the user. These instructions are known as read-only memory (ROM) which the user can access and "read" but cannot change. These instructions are specified by the computer manufacturer by its own codes. Because different manufacturers use different codes, programs from one manufacturer often do not work on competitor computers.

In order to load user programs or instructions into the CPU another hardware device is required. For microcomputers that operate from programs on disks, that input device is known as a disk drive. With some microcomputers the disk drive (or drives, if there is more than one) may be built into the CPU.

Also needed is another input device so that the user can interact with the CPU as work is in progress. This input device is a keyboard, much like a typewriter keyboard. Again, this keyboard is sometimes built into the CPU instead of being a separate item of hardware linked to the CPU.

Monitors

Another hardware item is the monitor, also known as a screen, cathode ray tube (CRT), or video display unit (VDU). The monitor displays prompts to the user from the CPU, what is input from the keyboard by the user, and the result of the work that is being done. With some computers, the monitor may be built in and be part of the CPU. The keyboard and monitor together are sometimes referred to as input/output (I/O) devices.

Hard copy versus soft copy

Finally, for most work performed a printer is needed. The printer is invariably a separate piece of equipment attached by cable to the CPU. When work performed by the user is printed out, the printed material is often received as "hard copy" to differentiate it from "soft copy," or work that is only viewed on the monitor and might still have further work on it before a hard copy is needed. For example, when a guest is dining in a restaurant that has a computerized sales system, the server can view the soft copy of the guest's check on the monitor during the course of the meal and add items to it as the meal progresses. When the guest indicates he wishes to pay, the accuracy of the final copy of the guest check can be viewed on the monitor prior to printing out the hard copy (guest check) for presentation to the guest.

Obviously, with all these various pieces of hardware comprising a computer system there has to be a high degree of compatibility among them. In addition to compatibility of hardware, the software that is used must also have language compatibility with each item of hardware.

Canned Software

The question sometimes arises whether it is better to have software specifically written for an individual hospitality operation's needs or to buy an already written software package (known as canned software). Specifically written software is far more expensive than canned programs. Also, most hospitality operations are small businesses that do not have the resources necessary to carry out the systems analysis and program design work necessary to develop their own computer software.

Canned programs have normally been widely tested and any errors (bugs) in them generally have been detected and corrected. Demonstrations of canned software can usually be viewed before the purchase decision is made. The cost to buy, install, and train employees can also be determined in advance, and any compromises that need to be made between an operation's needs and the software's capabilities can be adjusted for.

A successful canned software package thus represents a proven product obtainable at much less cost than a custom-designed one. In addition, there are now available for the hospitality industry specialized canned software packages in such areas as food and beverage cost control.

Obviously, the benefits of using off-the-shelf software have to be considered against its disadvantages. A software package written for broad hospitality requirements may not be as easy to use, or as fast, as one that is custom designed.

Interactive Programs

Software programs can be either interactive or noninteractive. An interactive program prompts the user sequentially step by step. It is thus easier to use because it helps ensure that no information that should be entered by the user is omitted.

A noninteractive program provides no prompts. Thus the user must know exactly what information to enter in correct sequence line by line and in a predetermined format. This requires more user skill (and thus an added training cost). The advantage is that the program is a lot faster.

Integrated Software Systems

In a hospitality operation, some information is used for more than one purpose. The name of a guest registering in a hotel is an example of information that might be used for room reservation, registration, guest history, housekeeping, and accounting purposes. Similarly, the name of a food item might be used in receiving, storing, issuing, recipes, production, inventory, and sales control.

With a computer system it is feasible, sensible, and advantageous to use software that is integrated. In integrated software systems, the objective is to record an item of data only once and then to use it in every possible way to provide information for planning and control purposes. If the item of data had to be entered into the computer each time it was wanted, errors could be made. Correcting errors costs time and money.

One could consider a hospitality operation as an entire system and have a completely integrated package of computer software to control and plan every single aspect of its operation. However, a completely integrated software package to handle all this would be costly and complex, would probably incur higher training costs because of its complexity, and would create severe maintenance and data security problems. **System** Further, if one part of the system failed it would create difficulties in all **failures** departments or areas. For these reasons, a small property would find justifying a completely integrated system financially difficult.

Application-Oriented Software Systems

At the other extreme is a software system that is oriented to a single application. If software is application-oriented, it is generally designed to handle one specific type of job and does not allow much integration. An example is a payroll system that is not integrated with labor cost budgeting or a food inventory control system that is not integrated with purchasing and food costing.

Reduced costs Because of their relative simplicity, application-oriented software systems can be easily evaluated to see whether they will perform precisely the limited jobs that they are to carry out. These systems are cheaper to buy and install and can be introduced into an operation over time as finances allow. An ideal situation is to move from a piecemeal standalone set of application systems to an integrated system over time as long as each part can be made compatible with others. In this type of in-house network, each computer system is able to operate on a stand-alone basis but can integrate with all others for transmission of certain data.

Obviously, the narrower an application-oriented system is, the easier it is to develop and the lower will be its cost. It will also be more efficient and reliable because it controls fewer functions. However, the narrower an application system becomes, the less effective it may be as far as overall control is concerned. For example, if a food inventory control system has to be supported by a separate food cost control system, then two packages of software are required, two different computer hardware systems may be needed, and two sets of user/operator systems have to be learned.

Initially, most microcomputer applications in the hospitality industry were stand-alone applications. But as the power and memory capacity of microcomputers have improved, the software packages available have become less stand-alone and more integrated.

Three common application-oriented software packages are word processing, data base managers, and spreadsheets.

Word Processing

Word processing refers to software that is programmed to manipulate words (text). Any small computer can be programmed to handle word processing. Surprisingly, many people do not think that machines that are only used to do word processing are true computers. But if they can be programmed to do word processing, then they can be programmed to do other things as well.

Word processor uses

The purchase of a low-cost microcomputer to be used primarily for word processing is a good way to introduce computers into a business. Word processors can be very useful when a large amount of standard correspondence is handled, as in a hotel reservation department where a form letter is used to confirm reservations or in a catering operation where a standard banquet contract is used and only certain information (such as the number of expected guests, the menu selected, and the price of the meal) has to be inserted.

The main purpose of a word processor is to facilitate text creation and editing, and the ease with which this may be done is a major factor in selection of word processing software. One of the major advantages of using computers rather than typewriters for word processing is that documents can be printed more attractively. For example, with some computer printers a variety of typestyles can be used in the same document.

Spelling checkers

As well as allowing text editing, more sophisticated word processing software contains spelling checkers with a dictionary of as many as 30,000 words. If a word is typed that is not in the dictionary, it will be highlighted on the monitor. If it is a technical word not found in the regular dictionary, that word can be added to the dictionary so that it will not be highlighted the next time it is used.

Some word processing software also has graphics capabilities, meaning that bar or pie charts can be used to highlight certain types of information, such as departmental expense trends.

Data Base Manager

A data base manager is a collection of records such as addresses of regular customers, a food or beverage inventory listing, personnel data, or a file of recipes. These are all records that form a data base. A data base

Random access to files

manager allows quick access to and ready manipulation of the records that are in that data base. In other words, it is much like an office filing system where records (files) can be randomly accessed, used as required, and then restored in the same order or rearranged in some other order before storing.

For example, for one application a database of recipes can be stored in alphabetic sequence according to the main recipe ingredient and only recipes containing that ingredient can be printed out. For another application, all recipes could be stored alphabetically, regardless of ingredients, before printing them.

It may be useful to purchase a software package that includes both word processing and a data base. For example, it may be necessary for a hotel to send out a standard form letter to all the travel agencies it regularly does business with advising them of a change in room prices or commission rates. The computer can be programmed to take each travel agency's address in turn from the data base, type it on the hotel's letterhead, type in the letter from the word processor, then move to the next address and letter on a new page until all addresses have been used. All of this can be completed without any user intervention once the process has been started.

Use in yield management

A data base manager can be particularly useful in yield management (see Chapter 6) because it can be used to store guest history information and reservation patterns.

Spreadsheet

Spreadsheet software is basically a large electronic sheet with rows down the side and columns across the top, much like a work sheet for preparing a budget. Most managers have struggled with budgets using pencils and column pads and have become frustrated when they wish to see what happens, for example, if the food cost to sales ratio is altered over a twelve-month annual budget. The changes that have to be made to food cost, gross profit, and net profit require thirty-six alterations, considerable erasing and correcting, and a risk that one or more errors will occur.

"What if?" questions

A properly programmed electronic spreadsheet will allow a manager to answer this type of "what if?" question in seconds and print out the results. Indeed, multiple "what if" changes can be made at the same time at rapid speed.

Spreadsheets lend themselves not only to budgeting but also to forecasting. For example, a spreadsheet could have in its memory all the various menu items a restaurant offers, including how many of each are sold on average by meal period and day of the week for each specific month. The spreadsheet can then forecast for the current month, on the basis of past performance, how many portions of each menu item should be produced by the kitchen for each meal period each day of the current month. Spreadsheets also lend themselves well to the following applications:

- Scheduling employees for improved labor cost control.
- Preparing depreciation schedules.
- Calculating percentages (given the dollar amounts) for common-size financial statement analysis.
- Calculating the sales mix and gross profit figures, given menu items sold and their cost and selling prices.
- Converting budgeted income statements (given appropriate ratios) to cash flow budgets.
- Using NPV and IRR analysis for long-term investments.
- Preparing budget variance analyses.
- Using CVP analysis for various types of decisions.

Integrated Work Stations

As far as planning and control are concerned, word processing, data base manager, and spreadsheet software are closely related. A computer ought to be able to pass data from its data base manager to a spreadsheet and then in turn pass the results to a word processor for addition of text and final printing of a report, including graphics, where valuable. Indeed, for many microcomputers today, single software packages that include all three of these software systems on one disk are available. These are known as integrated work stations.

ACCOUNTING PACKAGES

Another area that lends itself well to an integrated software package is general accounting. Most businesses with a manual system of accounting use an integrated approach for their general ledger, sales, accounts receivable, purchases, accounts payable, payroll, and inventory control. Hotel front office, reservations, registration, and guest accounting can also be integrated into this system. Today, there are integrated software packages available for computerization of this work. In some situations, it may not be feasible or practical to integrate each of these subsystems on the mainframe computer. For example, it may be useful to separate food inventory control so that a specialized software package that will do many more things than a general accounting system's inventory control subsystem will do can be purchased. Some of these additional and desirable features will be discussed later in this Appendix.

Expense of payroll software

Similarly, it may not be practical for a hospitality operation to computerize its payroll. One of the reasons is that the expense of maintaining computerized payroll software is comparatively high. Each time the laws relating to employment change (such as for minimum wage rates, tax deduction rates, and unemployment insurance rates), the software must be rewritten to accommodate those changes. For this reason, many establishments contract out their payroll preparation to a computer service company that specializes in this kind of work.

ECR AND POS SYSTEMS

For locations where food and beverages are recorded, two types of systems are available: an electronic cash register (ECR) and a point of sale (POS) system. Basically, the ECR is a stand-alone electronic register, whereas a POS system links several ECRs together to a separate remote computer and the sales register is primarily a keyboard rather than a separate machine. Unfortunately, the terms "ECR" and "POS" are often used interchangeably. Technically speaking, however, a POS system is much more sophisticated than a stand-alone ECR, even though an ECR can provide a great deal more sales and cost of sales information than its predecessors (mechanical sales registers).

Electronic Cash Registers (ECRs)

ECRs have allowed cashiers to be dispensed with in most establishments because servers can act as their own cashiers and the machine records, among other things, sales by server so that each knows how much cash to turn in at the end of each shift.

Video displays

Most ECRs have some sort of video display, often just a strip window with space for a limited number of characters. Increasingly larger video displays are appearing on the equipment so that, for example, the entire bill for a group of people at a table can be seen on the monitor. More sophisticated models can have keys that light up to prompt the operator what to do next or have the monitor display messages about subsequent steps to make or to explain mistakes.

Most ECRs have automatic pricing (eliminating pricing errors), change control features (in some cases linked to automatic change dispensers to reduce losses from change making errors), and automatic tax calculation for jurisdictions where food and/or beverage sales tax applies.

Computerized ECRs can summarize sales not only by server (broken down into cash and charge subtotals) but also by categories, such as appetizers, entrées, and desserts. In chain operations, this sales information might be networked to the head office computer for further, more detailed processing.

Some ECRs can also be programmed to print out the most popular combinations of appetizer, entrée, and dessert that customers choose. This is useful information for menu and sales mix planning.

Inventory control

Some ECRs can also provide inventory control for items that can be easily quantified such as steaks. If it were to be used for complete inventory control, however, the ECR would have to be programmed to remember the recipe of each dish, and that sort of inventory control might be better left to a separate software control system (to be discussed later). Alternatively, the ECR can be linked to another computer and send sales information to this computer so that the food cost control work can be done there.

Payroll control

Some ECRs have time clocks built into them, allowing servers to clock in and out of work on the machine by using a magnetically striped employee ID card, thus providing hours-worked information for staff planning and payroll. At the end of each shift or day, summary reports of employee hours worked, by employee and in total, are available. Information can also be accumulated in the ECR for each weekly or biweekly payroll period. A built-in clock can also track patterns of sales by time of day or time of guest arrivals and departures. This could be valuable for staff scheduling, labor cost planning, and kitchen food production planning.

ECRs can also have scales attached to them for automatic calculation of the sales value of items (such as salads) sold by weight.

Sales check control

With most ECR systems it is not necessary to have sales checks preprinted with sequential numbers. Blank standard sales checks can be purchased (at a saving in cost without numbering) and the ECR will print a consecutive number on each when the check is first started. If the same check is used for a reorder, the employee must instruct the machine that a previous check number is being used. If the server does not use the previous number when adding items to an active sales check, the machine will assign it a new number since it assumes that it is a brand-new check. If the server collects the full amount of the check from the customer and turns in only the amount of money from the reorder, the first number will show up as a missing check and the dishonesty will be spotted because the register prints a report at the end of each shift or day of the "open" checks—that is, those that have not been closed off— and identifies the employee responsible.

Integrated Point of Sale (POS) Systems

Generally a point of sale (POS) system is a series of individual sales terminals (such as ECRs) linked to a remote central processing unit (CPU). Food and beverage POS systems may be used as stand-alone systems for each separate food and beverage outlet but may also be linked to other POS systems in other sales outlets. They can also be linked to other equipment such as a printer in the kitchen that tells the kitchen what has been recorded in the register and needs to be prepared in the kitchen without the server (who has rung up the item on the register) having to walk to the kitchen. The kitchen might also be able to send messages back to the system's monitor to prompt servers when it is time to pick up prepared food orders.

Electronic server pads

The most recent device is an electronic server pad (ESP). With an ESP, servers no longer have to write out orders at the customer's table and then go to a terminal to enter them there. They simply punch them on to a hand-held computer and the information is beamed to a central computer through low-frequency frequency-modulated (FM) waves. The central computer then relays the information to a printer in the kitchen and/or bar.

Hotel POS systems in food and beverage areas may also be linked to the front office accounting system so that hotel guests charging food and beverage items in the restaurant or bar can have the amounts automatically added to their front office accounts.

Increased capability

In other words, a POS system has a much greater capability than an ECR and can produce a much larger variety of management reports by sales outlet and in total. It is generally a totally programmable system that can be easily modified within the business to accommodate changes in menu prices and many other items.

It can also be linked to a chain head office where data can be analyzed by the mainframe computer, results compared from unit to unit, and data consolidated by region and for the chain as a whole. In some systems, analysis reports for each individual unit can be sent back to the unit in a process known as downloading. Downloading can also be used to provide each unit's computer with new menu pricing and recipe costing information.

POS disadvantage

The major disadvantage of a POS system is that if the CPU fails each POS terminal in the entire system fails (because terminals cannot operate independently of the CPU) unless the system is backed up with disk memory, or unless the individual terminals can be upgraded to operate in at least a limited way with some memory capability and to produce some reports independently of the CPU.

INVENTORY CONTROL

Computers can be very valuable as a tool in inventory control. Computers can

- Prepare purchase orders for suppliers. It is now also possible for the computer through networking to place orders automatically with approved suppliers who submit the best price for the items and quantities needed.

Order lists
- Prepare lists of items to be received from each supplier so that receiving employees can compare what is delivered with what should be delivered.

- Compare information, as products are received and product information is recorded in the computer from invoice information, against purchase orders and specifications for those items.

- Issue appropriate credit memoranda for goods short-shipped or returned to suppliers.

- Produce food and beverage receiving reports for products delivered.

- Maintain a record of all storeroom purchases from information entered from invoices and update the perpetual inventory of each storeroom item.

Adjusting perpetual inventory
- Record all issues from the storeroom from information entered from requisitions, use this information to adjust the perpetual inventory of that item, and calculate the total cost of all items issued each day to aid in the calculation of a daily food cost and beverage cost.

- Calculate the cost of items requisitioned by any individual department for any period of time.

- Compare requisition signatures (using a scanner) with a record of those signatures stored in the computer to ensure they are authentic.

- Compare at any time quantity information of actual inventory for any specific item with what the computer-maintained perpetual inventory record is and print out variance reports.

- Let both management and the food buyer know when quantities purchased exceed prescribed limits for storeroom stock.

- Provide each month a list of all items that were short-stocked during that period.

Dead-stock reports
- Issue monthly dead-stock reports showing items that have not moved in a stipulated period, such as thirty, sixty, or ninety days.

- List how many units of each item were purchased from any one supplier and whether that purchase was made at the best quoted price.

- List how many of each item was used during each month and compare this with what should have been used according to actual food and/or beverage sales based on standard recipes and portion sizes.
- Verify supplier month-end statements against receiving invoices and/or receiving reports, and issue checks in payment of those statements.

Adjusting to business volume

A sophisticated inventory control computer program can also adjust the volume of storeroom inventory required according to the level of business. Thus, instead of leaving it to management to establish a fixed minimum and maximum level of stock for each storeroom item, the computer can adjust the reorder point and the order quantity to the actual usage or sales (which may change over time or by season) for that item. Each day, the computer prints out a list of items to be ordered, the quantities needed, and the economic order quantity (if this is built into the system). In cases where particular suppliers are under contract to provide specific storeroom items at contracted prices, the actual purchase orders can be prepared for those suppliers.

Bar Codes

One of the recent advances in inventory control is the use of bar codes on product containers. The bar code is a series of parallel black bars of varying width on a white background. The scanners that read the code can be counter-level models (such as those found at check-out stands in supermarkets) or hand-held wands (the type most useful in hospitality industry receiving so that heavy cases do not have to be lifted to pass over the scanner).

Universal Product Code

A common bar code is the ten-digit Universal Product Code (UPC) system, in which the first five digits identify the manufacturer or processor and the second five digits provide information about the product. It is not necessary for the product to be in a sealed container such as a carton or box. Even open crates of fresh produce such as apples and lettuce can be bar coded. The bar code information read and recorded by the computer can include the product's name, package size, item quantity (from which inventory records can be adjusted), and other desired information. For example, part of the bar code can represent specifications for each product.

The UPC has also been advantageous to suppliers, who may have dozens of different qualities and container sizes of a particular product, each of which can be quickly identified by reading its bar code and matching it with the purchaser's purchase order specification.

Where bar coding is used by a hospitality operation it offers the following advantages:

- Fast ordering processing.
- Reduction in purchasing time.
- Reduction in specification misunderstandings between purchaser and seller.
- More accurate purchasing, ordering, receiving, and inventory records.
- Improved food, beverage, and supplies cost control.
- Improved supplier delivery schedules and performance.
- Simplification of receiving procedures.
- Improved inventory and issuing control (as items are issued they can again be passed over the scanner so that perpetual inventory count will be adjusted and proper cost information recorded on requisitions).

Note that bar codes do not contain price information because they are placed on products by the manufacturer, who usually does not know what the end price of the product will be after it has gone through various distribution levels. Thus, pricing information has to be entered into the hospitality operation's computer from invoices received from suppliers.

FOOD CONTROL SYSTEMS

In Chapter 7 a method of food cost control based on accurate costing of standard recipes was illustrated by using manual means. Unfortunately, because of the constant daily changes in food purchase costs, a restaurant with an extensive menu would find manually revising recipe costs a prohibitively time-consuming task. Even a limited menu restaurant may still find the job too time-consuming and not worth the effort.

Recipes as Basis for Control

Computers, however, can considerably simplify this work by using a data base software system that operates from a computerized file of standard recipes and their ingredients. As new purchases are made, the inventory (ingredient) quantity and cost information are entered into the computer from invoices. Alternatively, terminals can be equipped with a wand reader at the receiving area to read the UPC codes on containers. If items do not have the UPC codes the information has to be entered manually into the computer.

As new ingredient price information is entered, the computer automatically updates all total recipe costs (using current portion costs or a weighted average, depending on which method management chooses) for any recipes containing any of these ingredients. A report can be printed to show what recipes are affected and what the new food cost is in dollars and percentages for that recipe; the need to change the menu selling price can be also be flagged.

Food Production Control

Calculating standard cost

Each day before production is started it is only necessary to enter into the computer the name of each recipe item and the number of portions to be produced that day from forecast sales. The computer prints the standard cost for all those recipe items and the total, prints the recipes with the ingredient list for the required number of portions, and prints a requisition listing the ingredients and the quantities required from the storeroom. If more than a required quantity is needed for a particular day (for example a #10 can of an item when only half a can is required for production), the computer makes a note of this excess and takes it into account when future requisitions are prepared.

The computer also calculates a food cost for the day based on food produced according to forecast sales.

Inventory Control

As requisitions are printed, the computer also adjusts the storeroom inventory count for period-end stocktaking and can provide a value for items requisitioned but not yet used in production (for example, the half #10 can mentioned earlier). From time to time a normal storeroom inventory reconciliation must be carried out, comparing the physical count of items actually in stock with the computer listing of what should be there according to production usage.

Inventory taking simplified

If bar-coded products are used, inventory taking is further simplified. A manual count of those products is not required. A hand-held bar-code reader can be passed over the bar code to count all containers or products and compile the actual inventory (including pricing and total valuation). The computer can also issue a report showing how this actual inventory (either in total or product by product) differs from the computer's perpetual inventory record (compiled from invoices and requisitions) of what should be there.

Taking a physical, or actual, inventory is also easier with a computer even if products are not bar-coded. There are programs that print an inventory form, complete with current item costs, leaving only the count quantity to be inserted manually. After the count, count figures can be entered into the computer and a final inventory report showing extensions (item count times price) for each item and total inventory value produced.

Management Reports

Sales histories

Finally, management reports showing planning errors such as overproduction of menu items because of poor forecasting can be prepared. A completely comprehensive food cost control system would have built into it (by linking it to POS registers) the actual sales histories of various menu items in combination with other menu items and provide the kitchen with daily food production requirements to minimize such problems as overproduction planning errors.

Other management reports might show operational errors (wastage because standard recipes were not followed) and costing errors (loss of potential revenue in comparison with actual revenue because selling prices have not kept up with increasing food costs). Another report might show cost trends for major purchases to assist in forward menu price planning.

FRONT OFFICE SYSTEMS

The main objective of a front office system for a hotel or motel is maximization of revenue or sales. For this reason, most front office computer systems are revenue- (rather than cost-) control-oriented and are based on the reservation, registration, and guest accounting needs of the property. They can also be linked to food and beverage POS system terminals.

However, front office systems can provide cost control in certain areas. For example, front office computers can be linked to the telephone system to monitor and add to guest accounts charges for both local and long distance calls so that the hotel is not paying for telephone costs not recovered through charges on guest accounts.

Occupancy information

The front office system can also provide constantly updated information to other departments (such as housekeeping and food and beverage areas) relating to rooms occupancy and guest counts so that adequate staffing can be arranged and so that departments are not overstaffed.

Finally, front office computers can prepare and print rooms department operating ratios such as occupancy and double occupancy percentages, average daily rates, and the daily yield statistic. In this latter regard, front office computer systems can be immensely useful in maximizing yield by providing information to form a data base of guest history and reservation patterns by type of guest for yield management.

Security Control

More recently, front office systems have been keyed to security control. A computer can be programmed to allow certain keys to open doors during limited periods each day. This might mean that housekeeping staff can only have access to rooms during the room makeup period. The system can also issue "keys" to guests. These keys are simply plastic cards (about the size of a credit card) that have data encoded on them on magnetic strips or have a series of holes punched through them. The guest room door has on it a device that reads the card and allows the door to be opened.

Plastic keys

As they register, the computer issues new guests a "key" card with a unique code on it for each guest and for each specific room. At the same time, the computer erases the old code for that room in the device on the guest room door (so that a departed guest cannot reuse his card) and creates a new code corresponding to the arriving guest's card. Departing guests do not even have to turn in their "keys" on leaving. They can be discarded. In cases of emergency, the guest room card reader device can be overridden by a conventional key used by authorized hotel personnel. The plastic key cards can also be used as internal credit/ID cards so that guests can charge to their room accounts food or beverages consumed in the hotel's dining room/bar areas.

Use of credit cards

For small hotels and motels there is now available computerized equipment located at the front office that can be operated by an arriving guest. The computer accepts specified credit cards that automatically charge the amount for that room to the credit card, print a "paid" invoice for the guest, and issue a plastic key coded to let the guest open the door of the assigned room. No longer is an all-night employee required to register late-arriving or check out early-departing ones!

Glossary

The technical words and terms used in this text are briefly explained in this glossary. For more expanded definitions and discussions the reader should refer to the text itself.

Accelerated depreciation: a method of depreciation that gives greater amounts of depreciation expenses in the earlier years of an asset's life. See also *Depreciation*.

Account: a record in which the current status (or balance) of each type of asset, liability, owners' equity, revenue, and expense is kept.

Accounting cycle: a recurring series of steps that occurs during each accounting period.

Accounting equation: assets = liabilities + owners' equity.

Accounting period: the time period covered by the financial statements.

Accounts payable: amounts due to suppliers (creditors); a debt or a liability.

Accounts receivable: amounts due from customers or guests (debtors); an asset.

Accounts receivable aging: preparing a schedule classifying receivables in terms of time left unpaid.

Accounts receivable average collection period: the number of days the average receivable remains unpaid.

Accounts receivable turnover: annual revenue divided by average accounts receivable

Accrual accounting: as opposed to cash accounting, a method of accounting whereby transactions are recorded as they occur and not when cash is exchanged; the matching of revenue and expenses on periodic income statements regardless of when cash is received or disbursed.

Accrued expenses: expenses that have been incurred but not paid at balance sheet date; a liability.

Accumulated depreciation: the total depreciation that has been shown as an expense on the income statements since the related assets were purchased. See also *Depreciation*.

Acid test ratio: see *Quick ratio*.

Activity ratios: see *Turnover ratios*.

Adjusted trial balance: a trial balance of accounts after period-end adjustments have been made. See also *Trial balance*.

Adjustments: entries made at the end of each accounting period in journals and then in the accounts so that the accounts have correct balances under the accrual accounting method.

Allowance for bad debts: an amount established to cover the likelihood that not all accounts receivable outstanding at balance sheet date will be collected.

Amortization: a method of writing down the cost of certain intangible assets (such as franchises or goodwill) in the same way that depreciation is used to write down the cost of tangible fixed, or long-term, assets.

Asset: a property or resource owned by a business.

Asset shrinkage: the decline in value of assets during bankruptcy.

Audit: a verification of accounting procedures and records.

Audit tape: a continuous chronological record of each transaction recorded in a cash or sales register. The tape can usually only be removed at the end of each day by authorized accounting office personnel.

Average check: revenue divided by number of people served during a certain period of time. Sometimes called average cover, or average spending.

Average cover: see *Average check*.

Average rate of return (ARR): a method of measuring the value of a long-term investment. The equation is net annual saving divided by average investment.

Average room rate: room revenue divided by number of rooms used during a certain period of time.

Average spending: see *Average check*.

Bad debt: an account receivable considered or known to be uncollectible.

Bad debts allowance: see *Allowance for bad debts*.

Balance: the amount of an account at a point in time.

Balance sheet: a statement showing that assets = liabilities + owners' equity. A balance sheet shows the financial position of a company at a point in time.

Bank: see *Float*.

Bank float: the difference between the bank balance shown on a company's records and the actual balance of cash in the bank.

Bank reconciliation: a monthly or periodic procedure to ensure that the company's bank account balance amount agrees with the bank's statement figure.

Beverage cost: see *Cost of sales*.

Bond: a form of financing by a company. A bond is a debt or long-term liability to be repaid with interest over time.

Book value: initial cost of an asset or assets less related accumulated depreciation.

Break-even equation or formula: an equation useful in making business decisions concerning sales levels and fixed and variable costs.

Break-even point: the level of sales at which a company will make neither an income nor a loss.

Bridge financing: see *Interim financing*.

Budget: a business plan, usually expressed in monetary terms. See also *Incremental budgeting* and *Zero-based budgeting*.

Budget analysis: see *Variance analysis*.

Budget cycle: the sequence of events covered by a budget period from initial budget preparation through to comparison of actual results with budgeted estimates.

Business entity: the concept that a business, and business transactions, should be kept separate from personal transactions of the business's owners.

Capital asset: see *Fixed asset*.

Capital budget: a budget concerning long-term, or fixed, assets.

Capital rationing: occurs when only a limited amount of funds is available for long-term investments during a budget period, and even profitable investment proposals are deferred to future budget periods.

Capital stock: the amount of money raised by a company from issuing shares.

Capital surplus: the amount of money raised by a company in excess of any par or stated value of the shares.

Cash accounting: a method of accounting (as opposed to accrual accounting) whereby transactions are only recorded at the time cash is received or disbursed.

Cash budget: a budget concerned with cash in-flows and cash out-flows.

Cash disbursements: money paid by cash or by check for the purchase of goods or services.

Cash management: cash conservation and the management of other working capital accounts to maximize effectiveness of the company's use of cash.

Cash receipts: cash or checks received in payment for sale of merchandise or services.

Chattel mortgage: a long-term debt or mortgage secured by the chattels (for example, equipment and furniture) of the business. See also *Mortgage*.

City ledger: in a hotel, the accounts receivable for guests who have charge privileges in food and beverage areas, and the accounts of room occupants who have left and have charged their accounts.

Collateral: assets pledged by a company as security for a loan.

Collusion: two or more people working together for fraudulent purposes.

Common stock: a form of stock or shares issued by a company to raise money.

Comparative/common-size statements: two or more financial statements presented with all data in both dollar and percentage figures.

Comparative statements: financial statements for two or more periods presented so that the change in each account balance from one period to the next is shown in both dollar and percentage terms.

Concentration banking: a method of accelerating the flow of funds from individual units in a chain operation to the company's head office bank account.

Conservatism: a principle of accounting to help ensure revenue and assets are not overstated or expenses and liabilities understated.

Consistency: a principle of accounting to help ensure that financial statements are comparable from one period to the next.

Contra-account: accounts with a balance that is shown on the "wrong" side of the balance sheet as a reduction of a related account, for example, allowance for bad debts shown as a reduction of accounts receivable.

Contribution margin: the difference between revenue and variable costs or expenses.

Contribution statement: a form of income statement presentation whereby variable costs are deducted from revenue to show contribution margin, and then fixed costs are deducted from contribution margin to arrive at net income.

Contributory income: see *Departmental income*.

Controllable cost or expense: a cost that is controllable by an individual (such as a department head) in a company.

Cost: the price paid to purchase an asset or to pay for the purchase of goods or services. Also frequently used as a synonym for expense.

Cost center: a department (such as maintenance) in a hospitality operation that generates no revenue.

Cost management: an awareness of the various types of cost and the effect that the relevant ones have on individual business decisions.

Cost of sales: generally referred to simply

as food cost or beverage cost. Calculated by adding beginning of the accounting period inventory to purchase during the period, and deducting end of the period inventory, adjusting where necessary for items such as employee meals and/or interdepartmental transfers.

Cost variance: the difference between budgeted cost and actual cost.

Cost-volume-profit analysis: an analysis of fixed and variable costs in relation to sales as an aid in decision making. See also *Break-even equation.*

Credit: 1. an entry on the right-hand side of an account; 2. to extend credit or to allow a person to consume goods or services and pay at a later date.

Credit invoice: an invoice prepared by a supplier showing, for example, that goods delivered to a company have been returned as unacceptable.

Credit memorandum: a dummy credit invoice made out by a company prior to receipt of a credit invoice from the supplier.

Creditor: a person, or company, to whom a firm owes money.

Current assets: cash or other assets likely to be turned into cash within a year.

Current dollars: historic (previous periods') dollars converted to terms of today's dollars for purposes of comparison.

Current liabilities: debts that are due to be paid within one year.

Current liquidity ratios: ratios that indicate a company's ability to meet its short-term debts.

Current ratio: the ratio of current assets to current liabilities.

Day rate: the rate charged by a hotel or motel for the use of a room for a portion of the day and not overnight.

Debenture: a form of financing by a company. A debenture is a debt or long-term liability to be repaid with interest over time.

Debit: an entry in the left-hand side of an account.

Debt: money owed to a person or organization; an obligation.

Debt to equity ratio: the amount of debt (liabilities) expressed as a ratio of stockholders' equity.

Declining balance depreciation: a method of accelerated depreciation whereby higher amounts of depreciation expense are recorded in the earlier years of an asset's life.

Deferred expense: an expense that has been incurred that is going to be written off over a period of time greater than one year.

Deficit: a deficit situation exists when losses accumulated since a business began exceed accumulated net incomes.

Demand, elasticity of: see *Elasticity of demand.*

Department budget: an operating budget prepared for an individual department in a multi-department organization.

Departmental income: the income of an individual operating department after direct expenses have been deducted from revenue; sometimes referred to as a contributory income.

Dependent variable: an item that is affected by what happens to another item. For example, labor cost is affected by level of sales; labor is the dependent variable.

Depreciation: a method of allocating the cost of a fixed asset over the anticipated life of the asset, showing a portion of the cost, for each accounting period of the life, as an expense on the income statement.

Derived demand: the business that one department has as a result of business in another department, for example, cocktail lounge revenue resulting from customers having drinks while eating in the dining room.

Direct cost or expense: an expense that can be distributed directly to an operating department and generally controllable by that department.

Discount: a reduction of the amount paid on a purchase because of prompt payment.

Discounted cash flow: a method of converting future inflows and/or outflows of cash to terms of today's dollars.

Discount grid: a table that shows the additional hotel room occupancy required to compensate when rack rates are discounted at various percentages.

Discretionary cost or expense: one that could be incurred but does not have to be at the present time.

Dividend: an amount paid out of net income, after tax, to stockholders as a return on their investment in the company.

Double-entry accounting: an accounting procedure that requires equal debit and credit entries in the accounts for every business transaction. This ensures the accounting equation is kept in balance.

Double occupancy percent: the percentage of rooms occupied in a hotel or motel that are occupied by more than one person.

Drawings: see *Withdrawals.*

Earnings per share: net income for the year divided by average shares outstanding during the year.

Elasticity of demand: the effect that a change in price has on demand for a product or service.

Expenditure: payment in cash for purchase of a good or service, or incurrence of a liability for purchase of a good or service.

Expense: goods or services consumed or used in operating a business.

Feasibility study: a study prepared prior to starting a new business or expanding an existing one, to indicate whether or not the proposal seems feasible and will provide an adequate return on the investment.

Financial position: the financial condition of a business as indicated by its balance sheet.

Financial statements: a balance sheet and an income statement and, where appropriate, a statement of retained earnings, a statement of source and use of working capital, and other supporting information.

Financing: raising money by debt (liability) or equity (owners).

Financing, interim: see *Interim financing.*

Fiscal period: an annual accounting period that may not coincide with the calendar year.

Fixed asset: assets of a long-term or capital nature that will be depreciated over a number of years.

Fixed asset turnover: annual revenue divided by average fixed assets.

Fixed budget: one that is not flexible or variable; one that is not adjusted to compensate for various possible levels of sales or revenue.

Fixed charges: indirect costs such as property taxes, insurance, interest, and depreciation. Sometimes referred to as indirect costs. See also *Direct cost* and *Undistributed operating cost.*

Fixed cost or expense: a cost that does not change, in the short run, with changes in volume of business.

Flexible budget: a budget based on more than one level of possible revenue.

Float (or bank): an amount of money advanced to an employee for change-making purposes. See also *Bank float.*

Folio: the account of a guest staying in a hotel or motel. Usually kept in the front office until paid.

Food cost: see *Cost of sales.*

Franchise cost: the cost to purchase the

right to use the name and/or services of another organization.

Full disclosure: a principle of accounting whereby financial statements provide all the relevant information that a reader of them should have.

General ledger: a book of accounts holding those accounts from which the financial statements are prepared.

Goal congruence: the alignment of organizational goals with the personal and group goals of subordinates and superiors.

Going concern: an accounting assumption that a business entity is to remain in business indefinitely.

Good will: the value of an established business, based on its name or reputation, above the value of its tangible assets.

Graph: a method of illustrating accounting information in pictorial form.

Gross profit: revenue less cost of sales.

Gross return on assets: see *Return on assets*.

Guest account: see *Folio*.

Historic cost: the cost of something at the time it was paid for, not adjusted to current cost.

House accounts: the accounts of guests staying in a hotel. See also *City ledger*.

Hubbart formula: a method of calculating required average room rate so that at a particular level of occupancy all costs will be covered and a desired return on investment achieved.

Income statement: a financial statement showing money earned from sales of goods and services, less expenses incurred to earn that income, for a period of time; sometimes referred to as the profit and loss statement.

Incremental budgeting: a method of budgeting whereby an increase, generally on a percentage basis, is automatically applied to last year's budget. See also *Zero-based budgeting*.

Independent variable: an item that is not affected by what happens to another item. For example, guest rooms sales are not affected by the number of maids on duty; rooms sales are the independent variable.

Indirect cost or expense: a cost not allocated directly to an operating department. See also *Direct cost, Fixed charges* and *Undistributed operating cost*.

Integrated banking: see *Concentration banking*.

Integrated pricing: a method of reviewing prices in two or more departments to ensure products are not priced independently of each other.

Interim financing: financing that is required for a new project from the time that construction is started until the project is completed. Sometimes referred to as bridge financing.

Internal audit: an appraisal of the operating and accounting controls of an establishment to ensure that internal control and procedures are being followed and assets adequately safeguarded.

Internal control: a system of procedures and forms established in a business to safeguard its assets and help ensure the accuracy of the information provided by its accounting system.

Internal rate of return (IRR): a method of measuring the value of a long-term investment using discounted cash flow. See also *Discounted cash flow*.

Inventory: merchandise (generally food and beverages) purchased but not yet used to generate revenue. See also *Physical inventory*.

Inventory turnover: cost of sales for a period of time divided by the average inventory for that period.

Investment: money loaned to a company either by way of a debt (liability) or equity (stock).

Invoice: document prepared to record the sale of goods or services and giving details about the transaction and total value of the sale.

Invoice approval form: a form or stamp showing that all necessary control steps have been carried out to ensure that an invoice is correct and can be paid.

Jigger: a measuring device for portion control of small quantities of beverages used in cocktails. See also *Shot glass*.

Job analysis: a review, preferably annually, of each job position to determine its contribution to net income and to try to increase that contribution.

Job description: a description of what a job entails, the tasks that must be performed, and when those tasks must be performed. See also *Task procedures*.

Joint cost or expense: one that is shared by more than one department.

Journal: accounting record summarizing business transactions as they occur prior to posting the information to the individual accounts.

Journal entry: the recording of a business transaction in a journal.

Kiting: writing a check on one bank, failing to record it as a disbursement, and depositing it in another bank for fraudulent purposes.

Labor productivity standard: a predetermined level of employee productivity, such as the number of guest rooms to be cleaned during a normal shift, or guests to be served during a meal period.

Lapping: a method of fraud that can occur when an employee has complete control of accounts receivable and payments received on these accounts.

Lease: the renting of a building and/or equipment, usually in lieu of a purchase.

Leasehold improvements: architectural and interior design changes made to rented (leased) premises.

Ledger: a book of accounts in which business transactions are entered after having been recorded in journals.

Leverage: a method of financing whereby the amount of debt (liabilities) is increased in proportion to equity (owners' investment).

Liability: a debt; an obligation.

Liquidation: the closing of a business by selling its assets and paying off the liabilities.

Liquidity: the financial strength of a business in terms of its ability to pay off its short-term or current liabilities without difficulty; a healthy working capital position; a good current ratio.

Loan: an amount borrowed; a debt; a liability.

Loan principal: the repayment of the initial amount borrowed on a loan is a principal payment as distinct from interest that is in addition to principal payments.

Lockboxes: a special bank service to speed up the collection of accounts receivable.

Long-range cash flow: a cash flow budget for periods of time generally in excess of one year.

Long-term assets: see *Fixed asset*.

Long-term budget: a budget for a period of time generally in excess of one year.

Long-term liability: a debt or obligation to be paid off more than one year hence.

Long-term solvency ratio: ratios that indicate a company's ability to meet its long-term liabilities as they fall due; an example is the debt to equity ratio.

Loss: an excess of expenses over revenue.

Management by objectives (MBO): a concept based on the assumption that employees can be committed to their work, allowing for maximum involvement and participation in setting subgoals, personal goals, and performance standards for judging employees' work.

Manager's daily report: a report prepared daily, generally by the accounting office, to indicate each day's key business operating statistics such as rooms occupancy percentage and average food check by meal period.

Marginal cost or expense: see *Variable cost or expense*.

Marketable securities: investments in notes or similar securities that can be readily converted into cash.

Market segment: a type of customer (such as business travelers) with whom an operation does business.

Market value: the current value of an asset, sometimes known as replacement value.

Markup: the difference between the cost of an item and its selling price.

Master budget: the overall budget for an establishment embracing all other budgets.

Matching: a principle of accrual accounting relating expenses to the revenue earned during a period regardless of when the cash was received or the expenses paid.

Materiality: the significance of an item in relation to the total business. If an item is not significant, other accounting principles may be ignored for reasons of practicality.

Memorandum invoice: a temporary, dummy invoice prepared in the absence of a proper invoice.

Mission statement: a statement detailing the purpose of a business.

Mortgage: a long-term debt or liability generally secured by using long-term assets (such as land and/or building) as collateral. See also *Chattel mortgage*.

Mutual exclusivity: a mutually exclusive alternative requires that if only one of a number of proposals (such as a long-term investment) is accepted, all others will be rejected.

Net assets: see *Net worth*.

Net book value: see *Book value*.

Net income: total revenue from sales and other income less total expenses.

Net income to revenue ratio: net income divided by revenue and multiplied by 100.

Net present value (NPV): a method of measuring the value of a long-term investment using discounted cash flow. See also *Discounted cash flow*.

Net return on assets: net income after income taxes divided by total average assets for the period.

Net worth: total assets less total liabilities; owners' equity.

Noncontrollable cost or expense: costs or expenses that are generally fixed in nature in the short run, such as rent or interest.

Note payable: a liability documented by a written promise to pay at a specified time.

Note receivable: an asset documented by a written promise from the borrower to pay it.

Objectivity: a principle of accounting requiring all business transactions to be documented in writing.

Obligation: see *Debt*.

Occupancy percentage: the ratio of rooms occupied to rooms available expressed in percentage terms.

Operating budget: a budget concerned with revenue and/or expenses.

Operating cost: see *Expense*.

Operating department: a department concerned with a particular segment of a business such as rooms or food.

Operating leverage: the relationship between fixed and variable expenses; high fixed expenses compared to variable expenses indicate high operating leverage.

Operating ratios: key business ratios (such as restaurant seat turnover and guest room occupancy percentage) that are often calculated daily.

Opportunity cost: the cost of not doing something. If a company does not invest surplus cash, the interest income not gained by this is the opportunity cost.

Organization chart: a document showing levels of responsibility and authority, and lines of communication for an establishment.

Outstanding check: a check issued in payment of a debt that has not yet been cashed in by the payee, or has been cashed in but has not yet been deducted from the payer's bank account.

Owners' equity: total assets minus total liabilities; net worth.

Partnership: an unincorporated business owned by two or more persons.

Payback period: the time it takes to recover an investment; initial investment divided by net annual cash saving.

Periodicity: an accounting principle that states that the operating results of a business should be monitored by preparing financial statements for periods of time.

Perpetual inventory card: a form that is used to record the movement of all items in and out of storage rooms. One card is used for each item.

Petty cash: a fund of money controlled by an individual from which minor purchases of goods or services can be paid.

Physical inventory: the actual counting, recording, and pricing of assets.

Portion size: see *Standard portion*.

Posting: recording of business transactions in accounts, or from journals to accounts.

Preferred stock or shares: a form of stock or share issued by a company to raise money, generally ranking before common stock with reference to dividends.

Prepaid expense: an expense paid for and shown as an asset until it is matched up with related revenue and shown as an expense. See *Matching*.

Present value: see *Discounted cash flow*.

Price earnings ratio: for a company whose shares are publicly traded, market price per share divided by earnings per share.

Price variance: difference between budgeted price and actual price.

Product differentiation: a method of presenting a product or service in a different way from competitors, for example by creating a unique ambience or providing superior service.

Productivity standard: see *Labor productivity standard*.

Profit: see *Net income*.

Profit and loss statement: see *Income statement*.

Profit center: a department (such as the rooms department) that generates revenue.

Profit margin: see *Net income to revenue ratio*.

Profit to sales ratio: see *Net income to revenue ratio*.

Profitability: the net income of a company related to the value of its assets, to the owners' equity, and to revenue.

Profitability ratios: ratios that measure profitability such as return on assets, return on investment, and net income to revenue.

Pro forma: forecast or tentative figures; a budgeted income statement is a pro forma statement.

Proprietorship: an unincorporated business owned by a single individual.

Prorate: to allocate an amount on a logical basis; for example, to allocate overall company rent expenses to the operating departments on a basis of square footage occupied by each department.

Purchase order: a form prepared by the purchasing department authorizing a supplier to deliver needed goods and services to the establishment.

Purchase requisition: a form, usually prepared by a department head, requesting the purchasing department to buy required goods or services. See also *Requisition.*

Purchasing department: the department responsible for ensuring that supplies, equipment, and services are available to the establishment as required.

Quantity variance: the difference between budgeted and actual quantity.

Quick assets: cash and readily convertible securities and/or receivables.

Quick ratio: the ratio of quick assets to current liabilities.

Rack rate: the normal maximum rate charged for a hotel guest room.

Ratio: the relationship of one item to another. For example, $2,000 of current assets to $1,000 of current liabilities would be a 2:1 ratio.

Ratio analysis: the use of various ratios to monitor the ongoing progress of a business.

Receiving report: a form, completed daily, listing all goods received for the day.

Recipe: see *Standard recipe.*

Regression analysis: a statistical method of breaking down semifixed or semivariable expenses into their fixed and variable components.

Relevant cost or expense: one that is important and to be considered in a particular business decision.

Replacement value: see *Market value.*

Requisition: a form, completed by an authorized person, requesting that needed items be issued from the storeroom.

Resort hotel: generally one that has extensive recreational facilities.

Responsibility accounting: a method of accounting in which department heads or managers are made responsible for the departmental profit achieved.

Retained earnings: accumulated net incomes less accumulated losses less any dividends paid since the business began.

Return on assets: income before interest and income tax divided by total average assets for the period.

Return on investment: net income after income tax divided by average owners' equity for the period.

Revenue: money earned from sales and/or income received in exchange for goods or services.

Revenue mix: the ratio of revenue among various departments in a multidepartment establishment. See also *Sales mix.*

Room rate: the price charged for a guest room in a hotel or motel.

Room rate ratio: a hotel's actual average room rate for a period of time expressed as a percentage of the potential or maximum average room rate.

Sales: see *Revenue.*

Sales check: a document used in food and/or beverage operations to record the sales of goods.

Sales mix: the ratio of what people select from various menu items offered. See also *Revenue mix.*

Scrap value: see *Trade-in value.*

Seat turnover: number of seats available in a food and/or beverage operation divided into the number of seats used or occupied during a particular period.

Semifixed or semivariable cost or expense: one that has both fixed and variable elements and is neither entirely fixed nor entirely variable in relation to sales.

Share: see *Common stock* and *Preferred stock.*

Shift schedule: see *Stacked schedule*.

Short-term budget: a budget prepared for a period of time generally less than a year.

Short-term liability: see *Current liability*.

Shot glass: a measuring device for portion size control of standard bar drinks. See also *Jigger*.

Skip: a person who has consumed goods or services in an establishment and has left without paying the bill.

Social goals: goals that are generally nonfinancial in nature but that may have an effect, positive or negative, on financial results.

Solvency: the ability of a company to meet its debts as they become due.

Stacked schedule: a stacked, or shift, schedule is a staff schedule used in departments where groups of employees arrive on the job at the same time and then leave together at the end of their shift. See also *Staff schedule* and *Staggered schedule*.

Staff schedule: a schedule, usually prepared in advance week by week, showing which employees will be on duty each day, and the hours each one will be working. See also *Stacked schedule* and *Staggered schedule*.

Staffing guide: a form developed for each department showing the number of employees, by job category, that should be on duty to meet various possible levels of business volume.

Staggered schedule: a staff schedule used when individual employees in a department arrive on the job at various times and leave at various times at the end of their shift. See also *Stacked schedule* and *Staff schedule*.

Standard cost or expense: what the cost should be for a particular level of sales or revenue.

Standard portion: the quantity of a food or beverage item that is to be served to a guest to achieve a desired standard cost. See also *Standard cost*.

Standard recipe: a written formula stating the quantities of each ingredient required to produce a specific quantity and quality of a food or beverage item.

Statement of business purpose: see *Mission statement*.

Statement of changes in working capital: a statement showing in dollars the amount of change from one period to the next in each individual current asset and current liability account.

Statement of retained earnings: a statement showing previous balance sheet figure, plus net income for the period, less any dividends paid during the period, to arrive at current period-end retained earnings.

Statement of source and use of working capital: a statement showing previous period working capital balance plus funds received during the period (sources) less funds paid out during the period (uses) to arrive at current period-end working capital.

Stock: see *Common stock* and *Preferred stock*.

Stockholder: an investor who owns shares in a company by way of common and/or preferred stock.

Stockholders' equity: see *Owners' equity*.

Stock redemption: the purchase by a company of shares that it had originally sold to investors or stockholders.

Straight-line depreciation: a method of depreciation whereby equal portions of the amount paid for an asset are shown as an expense during each accounting period of the life of the asset.

Strategic budget: a long-term budget for periods of time generally in excess of one year.

Sum-of-the-years digits depreciation: a method of accelerated depreciation that allocates larger amounts of depreciation as an expense during the earlier years of the life of an asset.

Sunk cost or expense: a cost incurred that is no longer relevant and cannot affect any future decisions.

T-account: a simplified form of account in the shape of a T, with account title on top, debit on the left, and credit on the right.

Task procedures: detailed, step-by-step procedures, preferably in writing, of how a particular task is to be performed.

Trade-in value: the scrap or cash value of an asset at the time its useful life is over or when it is exchanged with cash for a new asset.

Transaction: a business event requiring an entry in the accounting records.

Trend index: in a series of periods of operating results, the result for the first (base) period is given the value of one hundred. Subsequent period results are then given a number higher or lower than one hundred to better reflect each period's change relative to the base year.

Trend results: business operating results compared for a number of sequential periods.

Trial balance: a totaling of all debit balances and credit balances in accounts to ensure that total debits equal total credits.

Turnover ratios: ratios that measure the activity of an asset during an accounting period, such as inventory turnover.

Undistributed operating cost or expense: one that is not normally controlled by or the responsibility of an operating department. See also *Direct cost* and *Fixed charges*.

Uniform system of accounts: a method of presenting financial statement information so that comparison is made easier between establishments or with hospitality industry averages.

Units of production depreciation: method of depreciation basing expense on number of units used or produced by the asset during an accounting period to total estimated units to be used or produced during the life of the asset.

Variable budget: see *Flexible budget*.

Variable cost or expense: one that increases or decreases in direct, or linear, fashion with increases or decreases in related sales or revenue.

Variance analysis: a method of comparing budgeted figures with actual results breaking differences down into quantity variance and price or cost variance.

Volume: level of sales expressed in dollars or units.

Voucher: a document supporting a business transaction.

Voucher system: a method of preparing special documents (vouchers) to support each purchase transaction to help control disbursements.

Window dressing: a method of adjusting current asset and current liability accounts to improve the current ratio.

Withdrawals: monies taken out of a business by individual owners in a proprietorship or partnership (similar to dividends in an incorporated company).

Working capital: current assets less current liabilities.

Working capital management: see *Cash management*.

Working capital turnover: revenue divided by average working capital for the period.

Working papers: informal accounting records prepared as an aid to completion of the formal accounting records.

Yield management: a method in a hotel of matching customers' rooms purchase patterns and their demand for rooms to derive more precise occupancy forecasts and develop appropriate room rates to maximize revenue.

Yield statistic: actual total room revenue for a period of time divided by potential revenue for that period and multiplied by 100.

Zero-based budgeting: a method of budgeting that starts from a zero base and requires budget managers to justify each element of the present budget as well as any requested additions to it. See also *Incremental budgeting*.

Index